New Directions in German Studies

Vol. 27

Series Editor:

IMKE MEYER

Professor of Germanic Studies, University of Illinois at Chicago

Editorial Board:

KATHERINE ARENS
Professor of Germanic Studies, University of Texas at Austin

ROSWITHA BURWICK
Distinguished Chair of Modern Foreign Languages Emerita,
Scripps College

RICHARD ELDRIDGE
Charles and Harriett Cox McDowell Professor of Philosophy,
Swarthmore College

ERIKA FISCHER-LICHTE
Professor Emerita of Theater Studies, Freie Universität Berlin

CATRIONA MACLEOD
Edmund J. and Louise W. Kahn Term Professor in the Humanities
and Professor of German, University of Pennsylvania

STEPHAN SCHINDLER
Professor of German and Chair,
University of South Florida

HEIDI SCHLIPPHACKE
Associate Professor of Germanic Studies,
University of Illinois at Chicago

ANDREW J. WEBBER
Professor of Modern German and Comparative Culture,
Cambridge University

SILKE-MARIA WEINECK
Professor of German and Comparative Literature,
University of Michigan

DAVID WELLBERY
LeRoy T. and Margaret Deffenbaugh Carlson University Professor,
University of Chicago

SABINE WILKE
Joff Hanauer Distinguished Professor for Western Civilization and
Professor of German, University of Washington

JOHN ZILCOSKY
Professor of German and Comparative Literature, University of Toronto

Volumes in the series:

Vol. 1. *Improvisation as Art: Conceptual Challenges, Historical Perspectives*
by Edgar Landgraf

Vol. 2. *The German Pícaro and Modernity: Between Underdog and Shape-Shifter*
by Bernhard Malkmus

Vol. 3. *Citation and Precedent: Conjunctions and Disjunctions of German Law and Literature*
by Thomas O. Beebee

Vol. 4. *Beyond Discontent: "Sublimation" from Goethe to Lacan*
by Eckart Goebel

Vol. 5. *From Kafka to Sebald: Modernism and Narrative Form*
edited by Sabine Wilke

Vol. 6. *Image in Outline: Reading Lou Andreas-Salomé*
by Gisela Brinker-Gabler

Vol. 7. *Out of Place: German Realism, Displacement, and Modernity*
by John B. Lyon

Vol. 8. *Thomas Mann in English: A Study in Literary Translation*
by David Horton

Vol. 9. *The Tragedy of Fatherhood: King Laius and the Politics of Paternity in the West*
by Silke-Maria Weineck

Vol. 10. *The Poet as Phenomenologist: Rilke and the* New Poems
by Luke Fischer

Vol. 11. *The Laughter of the Thracian Woman: A Protohistory of Theory*
by Hans Blumenberg, translated by Spencer Hawkins

Vol. 12. *Roma Voices in the German-Speaking World*
by Lorely French

Vol. 13. *Vienna's Dreams of Europe: Culture and Identity beyond the Nation-State*
by Katherine Arens

Vol. 14. *Thomas Mann and Shakespeare: Something Rich and Strange*
edited by Tobias Döring and Ewan Fernie

Vol. 15. *Goethe's Families of the Heart*
by Susan E. Gustafson

Vol. 16. *German Aesthetics: Fundamental Concepts from Baumgarten to Adorno*
edited by J. D. Mininger and Jason Michael Peck

Vol. 17. *Figures of Natality: Reading the Political in the Age of Goethe*
by Joseph D. O'Neil

Vol. 18. *Readings in the Anthropocene: The Environmental Humanities, German Studies, and Beyond*
edited by Sabine Wilke and Japhet Johnstone

Vol. 19. *Building Socialism: Architecture and Urbanism in East German Literature, 1955–1973*
by Curtis Swope

Vol. 20. *Ghostwriting: W. G. Sebald's Poetics of History*
by Richard T. Gray

Vol. 21. *Stereotype and Destiny in Arthur Schnitzler's Prose: Five Psycho-Sociological Readings*
by Marie Kolkenbrock

Vol. 22. *Sissi's World: The Empress Elisabeth in Memory and Myth*
edited by Maura E. Hametz and Heidi Schlipphacke

Vol. 23. *Posthumanism in the Age of Humanism: Mind, Matter, and the Life Sciences after Kant*
edited by Edgar Landgraf, Gabriel Trop, and Leif Weatherby

Vol. 24. *Staging West German Democracy: Governmental PR Films and the Democratic Imaginary, 1953–1963*
by Jan Uelzmann

Vol. 25. *The Lever as Instrument of Reason: Technological Constructions of Knowledge around 1800*
by Jocelyn Holland

Vol. 26. *The Fontane Workshop: Manufacturing Realism in the Industrial Age of Print*
by Petra S. McGillen

Vol. 27. *Gender, Collaboration, and Authorship in German Culture: Literary Joint Ventures, 1750–1850*
edited by Laura Deiulio and John B. Lyon

Gender, Collaboration, and Authorship in German Culture

Literary Joint Ventures, 1750–1850

Edited by
Laura Deiulio and John B. Lyon

BLOOMSBURY ACADEMIC
NEW YORK • LONDON • OXFORD • NEW DELHI • SYDNEY

BLOOMSBURY ACADEMIC
Bloomsbury Publishing Inc
1385 Broadway, New York, NY 10018, USA
50 Bedford Square, London, WC1B 3DP, UK
29 Earlsfort Terrace, Dublin 2, Ireland

BLOOMSBURY, BLOOMSBURY ACADEMIC and the Diana logo
are trademarks of Bloomsbury Publishing Plc

First published in the United States of America 2019
This paperback edition published in 2021

Copyright © Volume Editors' Part of the Work © Laura Deiulio and John B. Lyon, 2019
Each chapter © of Contributors

Cover design: Andrea F. Bucsi
Cover image © Caspar David Friedrich, *Auf dem Segler* (1818–20)/
The State Hermitage Museum

For legal purposes the Acknowledgments on p. xiii
constitute an extension of this copyright page.

All rights reserved. No part of this publication may be reproduced or transmitted in any form or by any means, electronic or mechanical, including photocopying, recording, or any information storage or retrieval system, without prior permission in writing from the publishers.

Bloomsbury Publishing Inc does not have any control over, or responsibility for, any third-party websites referred to or in this book. All internet addresses given in this book were correct at the time of going to press. The author and publisher regret any inconvenience caused if addresses have changed or sites have ceased to exist, but can accept no responsibility for any such changes.

Whilst every effort has been made to locate copyright holders the publishers would be grateful to hear from any person(s) not here acknowledged.

Library of Congress Cataloging-in-Publication Data
Names: Deiulio, Laura Christine, 1967- editor. | Lyon, John B., 1966- editor.
Title: Gender, collaboration, and authorship in German culture : literary joint ventures, 1750-1850 / edited by Laura Deiulio and John B. Lyon.
Description: New York, NY : Bloomsbury Academic, 2019. | Series: New directions in German studies ; vol. 27 | Includes bibliographical references and index.
Identifiers: LCCN 2019009801 (print) | LCCN 2019018905 (ebook) | ISBN 9781501351013 (ePub) | ISBN 9781501351020 (ePDF) | ISBN 9781501351006 (hardback : alk. paper)
Subjects: LCSH: German literature–18th century–History and criticism. | German literature–19th century–History and criticism. | Authorship–Collaboration–History–18th century. | Authorship–Collaboration–History–19th century. | Influence (Literary, artistic, etc.)–History–18th century. | Influence (Literary, artistic, etc.)–History–19th century. | Creation (Literary, artistic, etc.)–History–18th century. | Creation (Literary, artistic, etc.)–History–19th century. | Man-woman relationships–Germany–History–18th century. | Man-woman relationships–Germany–History–19th century.
Classification: LCC PT313 (ebook) | LCC PT313 .G46 2019 (print) | DDC 830.9–dc23
LC record available at https://lccn.loc.gov/2019009801

ISBN:	HB:	978-1-5013-5100-6
	PB:	978-1-5013-7833-1
	ePDF:	978-1-5013-5102-0
	eBook:	978-1-5013-5101-3

Series: New Directions in German Studies

Typeset by Integra Software Services Pvt. Ltd.

To find out more about our authors and books visit www.bloomsbury.com and sign up for our newsletters.

Contents

	Notes on Contributors	ix
	Acknowledgments	xiii
	Introduction *Laura Deiulio and John B. Lyon*	1
1	The Gottscheds: Conjugal Authorship as a Disjointed Venture *Margaretmary Daley*	21
2	A Dynamic Interplay: Cooperation between Sophie von La Roche, Christoph Martin Wieland, and Goethe on Their Way to Authorship *Monika Nenon*	45
3	"Collaborating with Spirits": Cagliostro, Elisa von der Recke, and the Phantoms of *Unmündigkeit* *Michelle Stott James and Rob McFarland*	75
4	A Freedom Apart: Feminine *Bildung* in Sophie Mereau's "Marie" and *Amanda und Eduard* *Tom Spencer and Jennifer Jenson*	105
5	Scenes from a Marriage: Friedrich and Dorothea Schlegel, Collaboration as Symphilosophy and After *Adrian Daub*	125
6	Holy Hermaphrodite: The Collaboration between Caroline and Friedrich de la Motte Fouqué *Eleanor ter Horst*	155
7	Concepts of Collaboration: *Märchenomas*, the Woman Writer, and the Brothers Grimm *Julie L. J. Koehler*	181

8 A Meeting of Minds? The Dialogue between Voices Female and Male in the Poems of the West–Eastern Divan
Charlotte Lee — 209

9 The Correspondence of Rahel Levin Varnhagen and Ludwig Robert: Epistolary Writing as a Space for *Symphilosophieren*
Laura Deiulio — 227

10 Reflexive Authorship in Bettina Brentano-von Arnim's *Die Günderode*: Narrative Disunity, Hölderlin, and Günderrode
Karen R. Daubert — 253

11 "Where Words Are Not Enough": Audience and Authorship in the Marriage Diaries of Robert and Clara Schumann
Brian Tucker — 273

12 Therese Robinson's *Die Auswanderer* (1852) as Goethe's Future Novel of America
Judith E. Martin — 295

Index — 320

Contributors

Margaretmary Daley has studied at Stanford University, the Freie Universität at Tübingen, and Cambridge University, and earned her PhD from Yale. She is Associate Professor at Case Western Reserve University, where she chaired the programs in Modern Languages and Literatures, and Women's and Gender Studies. Past chapters include "Faints, Fevers, and Fictions," in *Weibliche Kreativität um 1800*, edited by Linda Dietrick and Birte Giesler (2015), and "Literary Classic or Pop Fiction? Reading Julchen Grünthal," in *A Different Germany: Pop and the Negotiation of German Culture*, edited by Claude Desmaris (2014). Her research on Sophie von La Roche will be published in a forthcoming chapter in a volume on women's leadership, and she is currently writing her second monograph, provisionally titled *No Trivial Talent*, which hypothesizes an inclusive literary canon of women's novels around 1800.

Adrian Daub is Professor of German Studies and Comparative Literature at Stanford University, where he directs the Program in Feminist, Gender, and Sexuality Studies. He is the author of *Uncivil Unions: The Metaphysics of Marriage in German Idealism and Romanticism* (2012), *Tristan's Shadow: Sexuality and the Total Work of Art after Wagner* (2013), and *Four-Handed Monsters: Four-Hand Piano Playing and Nineteenth-Century Culture* (2014). His most recent articles appeared in *Deutsche Vierteljarhsschrift für Literaturwissenschaft und Geistesgeschichte*, *Merkur*, *German Quarterly*, *German Life and Letters*, *Opera Quarterly*, and *19th-Century Music*.

Karen R. Daubert, Washington University in St. Louis, holds a PhD from Princeton University. Her research and everyday practice focus on collaborative systems that counter polarizing paradigms and contribute to long-term social sustainability. A leader at Washington University Public Affairs and in the governance of the Fair Labor Association, she is also the author of "'Free-lance Modernists' at Work, Together: The

Early Textual Dialogue of Robert Graves and Laura Riding," in *The Art of Collaboration: Essays on Robert Graves and His Contemporaries*, edited by Dunstan Ward (2008).

Laura Deiulio is Associate Professor of German at Christopher Newport University and Chair of the Department of Modern and Classical Languages and Literatures. She received her PhD from Princeton University. She has published essays that examine Rahel Levin Varnhagen's correspondences with Auguste Brede and Pauline Wiesel, as well as contributions on Esther Gad and Lou Andreas-Salomé. Currently, she is working on a book-length study of Rahel Levin Varnhagen's thought.

Michelle Stott James teaches German language and literature at Brigham Young University. Through the "Sophie Project," she has worked with colleagues and students to make hard-to-access texts by early women authors available in digital format in the *Sophie Digital Library of Early German-Language Women's Work* (http://sophie.byu.edu). With Rob McFarland, she produced the edited volume *Sophie Discovers Amerika: German-Speaking Women Write the New World* (2014), and at present, she is collaborating with Lisabeth Hock and Priscilla Layne on a companion volume, *Afrika and Alemania: German-Speaking Women, Africa, and the African Diaspora*. In addition, she is currently preparing the five-volume *Critically Annotated Collected Works of Elisa von der Recke*, the first volume of which is nearing completion.

Jennifer Jenson is a PhD student in Germanic studies at the University of Chicago. She received a bachelor's degree in German studies and interdisciplinary humanities from Brigham Young University, and a master's degree in German studies with a certificate in holocaust, genocide, and memory studies from the University of Illinois at Urbana-Champaign. Her current academic interests include the interplay and representation of memory, trauma, and healing.

Julie L. J. Koehler is the Coordinator of the Basic German Language Sequence and a lecturer of German at Wayne State University. She completed her PhD at Wayne State in the fall of 2015. Her most recent publications include "The Persecuted History of Cinderella: A Case for Oral Tradition in Western Europe," in *Gramarye*, and "When the Inexhaustible Purse Runs Dry: Bettina von Arnim's 'Tale of the Lucky Purse,'" in *Marvels and Tales*. Dr. Koehler is also working on an anthology of fairy tales written by European women in the nineteenth century, together with her colleagues in French and English. The anthology is tentatively titled *Women Writing Wonder*.

Contributors   xi

Charlotte Lee is University Lecturer in Modern German Studies at Murray Edwards College, Cambridge. She earned her PhD at Cambridge in 2013, and her first book, *The Very Late Goethe: Self-Consciousness and the Art of Ageing*, was published in 2014. She has published articles with the *Modern Language Review*, *German Life and Letters*, the *Goethe Yearbook*, *Publications of the English Goethe Society*, and the *Jahrbuch des Freien Deutschen Hochstifts*. She has also co-edited a special number of *German Life and Letters*, entitled *Embodied Cognition around 1800*, which appeared in 2017.

John B. Lyon is Professor of German at the University of Pittsburgh. His research and teaching interests include German literature, philosophy, and culture of the eighteenth and nineteenth centuries. He is the author of two monographs: *Crafting Flesh, Crafting the Self: Violence and Identity in Early Nineteenth-Century German Literature* (2006), and *Out of Place: German Realism, Displacement, and Modernity* (Bloomsbury, 2013), and has published articles on Georg Büchner, Johann Caspar Lavater, Clemens Brentano, Heinrich von Kleist, Friedrich Hölderlin, Friedrich Schiller, Goethe, and German realism. He is currently working on a monograph on the nineteenth-century European adultery novel.

Judith E. Martin holds a PhD in German and comparative literature from Washington University in St. Louis. She is Professor of German at Missouri State University. Her research explores nineteenth-century German women authors in comparative contexts. She is the author of *Germaine de Staël in Germany: Gender and Literary Authority (1800–1850)* (2011), and she has published articles on the female artist novel and on race and gender in German writings on America. Her recent research focuses on comparative post-colonial studies of nineteenth-century German women's writings.

Rob McFarland is Professor of German at Brigham Young University and the co-director of *Sophie: A Digital Library of Works by German-Speaking Women* (http://sophie.byu.edu). He received his PhD from the University of California, Berkeley. Professor McFarland writes about representations of cities and architecture in German literature and film, and about the European reception of the Americas. He recently published a monograph titled *Red Vienna, White Socialism and the Blues: Ann Tizia Leitich's America* (2015). He is currently working as one of the editors of the *Red Vienna Sourcebook*, scheduled to appear in 2019.

Monika Nenon is Professor of German at the Department of World Languages and Literatures at the University of Memphis. She is the author of *Autorschaft und Frauenbildung: Das Beispiel Sophie von La Roche* (1988), and *Aus der Fülle der Herzen: Geselligkeit, Briefkultur und Literatur um Sophie von La Roche und Friedrich Heinrich Jacobi* (2005). She has published articles on Sophie von La Roche, Wieland, Goethe, Klopstock, F. Jacobi, and Lessing, and is serving as review editor of the *Lessing Yearbook*. She is currently working on the reception of Rousseau's *Julie; ou, La Nouvelle Héloïse*.

Tom Spencer is Associate Professor of German at Brigham Young University in Provo, Utah. He holds a PhD in comparative literature from the University of North Carolina at Chapel Hill. His recent published articles and chapters address metaphysical problems in Kant, *Kunstreligion* in the German *Frühromantik*, Kleist's use of the paranormal, and Herder's position on the immortal soul. Currently he is working on a book project on the occult in the German nineteenth century.

Eleanor ter Horst is Associate Professor and Chair of the Department of Modern and Classical Languages and Literature at the University of South Alabama. Her research interests include comparative literary studies, gender studies, and the reception of the classics in eighteenth- and nineteenth-century German and French literature. She is the author of *Lessing, Goethe, Kleist and the Transformation of Gender: From Hermaphrodite to Amazon*, and has published articles on Guillaume Apollinaire, Ingeborg Bachmann, Friedrich de la Motte Fouqué, Johann Wolfgang von Goethe, E. T. A. Hoffmann, Heinrich von Kleist, Rainer Maria Rilke, and Friedrich Schlegel.

Brian Tucker is Associate Professor of German at Wabash College. His research interests include German literature and culture of the eighteenth and nineteenth centuries, critical theory, and aesthetics: areas of inquiry that come together in his book *Reading Riddles: Rhetorics of Obscurity from Romanticism to Freud* (2011). He has published articles that range in topic from boredom to wordplay, from historicism to graphic novels, and that examine authors such as Celan, Fontane, Kleist, and Tieck. He is currently working on a monograph on irony and avowal in Theodor Fontane.

Acknowledgments

This volume is the product of many fortuitous collaborations: a discussion between one of the co-editors and Lynne Tatlock that nurtured the initial intellectual spark; a German Studies Association panel series that brought together five of the fifteen contributors in this volume; professional and personal connections that led ten other exceptional scholars to join this venture; and conversations and interactions with other potential contributors—Matt Erlin, Gail Hart, Kathryn McEwen, Brian McInnis, Jessica Riviere, and Michael Taylor. Although not every fruitful conversation developed into a chapter in the volume, they all gave further intellectual insight and impetus to the endeavor. Collaborations with departmental colleagues, interlibrary-loan librarians, and administrators at our home institutions likewise allowed this project to move forward. And, as we approached publishers, we benefited from excellent feedback from Jim Walker at Camden House and from Imke Meyer at Bloomsbury. The two anonymous reviewers of the manuscript—we have since learned that one was Laurie Johnson—provided invaluable feedback on the volume as a whole and on individual essays. And Haaris Naqvi, Amy Martin, and the team at Bloomsbury did an exceptional job in making our vision a reality. We are grateful to these many collaborators for their contributions. As for any errors in this volume, they are ours to own—jointly.

Introduction

Laura Deiulio and John B. Lyon

Gender and Authorship around 1800

The idea that genius is a necessary precondition for authorship emerged in the eighteenth century and has characterized judgments of literary value well into the twentieth. Genius determines which writers are considered important, and which works are worthy of continued reading and interpretation. Jochen Schmidt, in his overview of the concept of genius in German culture, points to several factors that influenced the model of authorship in the eighteenth century: changes in patronage patterns for artists, the development of a middle-class reading public, and a casting off of conventions and authority figures during the Enlightenment.[1] While social and economic factors fostered the rise of the genius model, the aesthetics of movements such as *Sturm und Drang* (Storm and Stress) and German Romanticism—bound to the development of the individual, creative self—certainly contributed to the cult of genius.

In addition, the emerging concept of copyright, under which the author anchors a marketable work, contributed to the higher social status of artists and writers. Heinrich Bosse argues that the legal concept of copyright was connected to the view of the author as a genius, because to produce a work worthy of copyright, a writer had to produce something that would be considered original.[2] At the same time, the rise of copyright laws around 1800[3] protected the economic rights of authors,

---

1 Jochen Schmidt, *Die Geschichte des Genie-Gedankens in der deutschen Literatur: Philosophie und Politik 1750–1945*, Vol. I, *Von der Aufklärung bis zum Idealismus*, 2nd rev. edn. (Darmstadt: Wissenschaftliche Buchgesellschaft, 1988 [1985]), 1–22.
2 Heinrich Bosse, *Autorschaft ist Werkherrschaft: Über die Entstehung des Urheberrechts aus dem Geist der Goethezeit*, new edn., with foreword by Wulf D. v. Lucius (Paderborn: Fink, 2014), 10.
3 While copyright laws for the entirety of Germany did not go into effect until later in the nineteenth century, the concept of regulating publishers' and authors' rights can be traced back to the Prussian Allgemeines Landrecht of 1794 (Bosse, *Autorschaft ist Werkherrschaft*, 8–9).

strengthening their position within society.⁴ Martha Woodmansee, in her book *The Author, Art, and the Market: Rereading the History of Aesthetics*, links the economic sphere to the aesthetic debates on artistic quality of the eighteenth century. Namely, she argues that writers of demanding literature used the concept of originality in order to justify copyright protection, and thus economic gain, for their works.⁵

Arguments such as Bosse's and Woodmansee's are important because they explore the economic and social conditions that contribute to our concept of the "great author." While Woodmansee briefly treats the dimension of gender in our understanding of the genius model, other scholars, such as Ina Schabert and Barbara Schaff, emphasize this element more explicitly. In the introduction to their edited collection of essays, Schabert and Schaff conclude that the concept of the single, male, genius author that arose in the eighteenth century and lasted well into the twentieth century is actually an anomaly that grew out of specific historical and social conditions.⁶ Christine Battersby would concur that in the time period around 1800 women were ineligible for genius status, for she contends that Romanticism was dominated by a "logic of exclusion" that identified works of high art as exclusively masculine.⁷ Even when women successfully became writers, they were not viewed as "authors." Corinna Heipcke, for instance, concedes the development of an "Autorinnen-Funktion" (female author function) but contends that it existed as an alternative construct that did not threaten the (male) "Autor-Funktion" (author function).⁸

Heipcke also points out that the development of a separate sphere of influence for female writers occurred at the same time that the gender polarization—described by theorists such as Karin Hausen and Thomas Laqueur—took place.⁹ Susanne Kord indirectly addresses this polarization when she indicates that aesthetic writers around 1800 often relegated women to certain genres (such as letters or novels) considered more feminine, excluding them from valued genres such as the epic and the drama. While Kord has established that women indeed

---

4   Bosse, *Autorschaft ist Werkherrschaft*, 7, 9.
5   Martha Woodmansee, *The Author, Art, and the Market: Rereading the History of Aesthetics* (New York: Columbia University Press, 1994), 39–40.
6   Ina Schabert and Barbara Schaff, eds., *Autorschaft: Genus und Genie in der Zeit um 1800*, Geschlechterdifferenz und Literatur: Publikationen des Münchner Graduiertenkollegs 1 (Berlin: Erich Schmidt, 1994), 10, 13.
7   Christine Battersby, *Gender and Genius: Towards a Feminist Aesthetics* (Bloomington, IN: Indiana University Press, 1989), 6.
8   Corinna Heipcke, *Autorrhetorik: Zur Konstruktion weiblicher Autorschaft im ausgehenden 18. Jahrhundert*, Studien zur neueren Literatur 11 (Frankfurt am Main: Peter Lang, 2002), 161.
9   Heipcke, *Autorrhetorik*, 17–18.

chose genres typically gendered masculine, she also points out that later scholarship often excluded women from canonical genres without questioning this exclusion.[10] At the same time, turning our attention to previously excluded genres and seeking to understand them without prejudice opens up new areas of study and new ways of understanding literary productivity between 1750 and 1850. Similarly, examining modes of interaction that provide an alternative to the model of the genius author in isolation permits a more complete understanding of the literary landscape during the late eighteenth and early nineteenth centuries. For these reasons, this volume focuses on collaborative ways of working.

In many ways, women authors of the time period from 1750 to 1850 were disadvantaged in comparison with their male colleagues. Lack of legal autonomy *(Mündigkeit)*, gendered social expectations for women, and unequal access to education and the professions made it more difficult for women writers to find their voice, let alone to achieve success in a competitive book market.[11] In many cases, women wrote and published without institutional support, often using a pseudonym to protect their social status and prevent public discovery of their literary ambitions.[12] Yet, the period around 1800 saw women begin to write in greater numbers. The expansion of the book market in the eighteenth century, the increased use of German instead of Latin in publications, and the expansion of the literate public in the wake of the Enlightenment all meant that, for the first time, a generation of women writers emerged who could no longer be considered anomalies.[13]

---

10 Susanne Kord, *Sich einen Namen machen: Anonymität und weibliche Autorschaft 1700–1900*, Ergebnisse der Frauenforschung 41 (Stuttgart: J. B. Metzler, 1996), 60.
11 For an overview of the conditions constraining women's writing around 1800, see the chapter "Rahmenbedingungen für Schriftstellerinnen im späten 18. und frühen 19. Jahrhundert: Problematik der 'Mündigkeit', 'Bestimmung des Weibes' und die 'Producte der weiblichen Muse,'" in Barbara Becker-Cantarino, *Schriftstellerinnen der Romantik: Epoche—Werke—Wirkung*, Arbeitsbücher zur Literaturgeschichte (Munich: C. H. Beck, 2000), 19–69.
12 Kord, *Sich einen Namen machen*; Barbara Hahn, *Unter falschem Namen: Von der schwierigen Autorschaft der Frauen* (Frankfurt am Main: Suhrkamp, 1991); Becker-Cantarino also discusses anonymity (*Schriftstellerinnen der Romantik*, 61–3).
13 Helga Gallas and Anita Runge have documented 110 women writers who produced 396 works of fiction between 1771 and 1810 (statistic quoted in Helen Fronius, "'Nur eine Frau wie ich konnte so ein Werk schreiben': Reassessing German Women Writers and the Literary Market 1770–1820," in *Frauen in der literarischen Öffentlichkeit 1780–1918*, ed. Caroline Bland and Elisa Müller-Adams [Bielefeld: Aisthesis, 2007], 32). Karin Tebben's edited volume *Beruf: Schriftstellerin. Schreibende Frauen im 18. und 19. Jahrhundert* (Göttingen: Vandenhoeck & Ruprecht, 1998), which collects essays about ten women, demonstrates that many women writers understood themselves as professionals.

Recent scholarship has begun to question the dichotomy between successful male geniuses and struggling female dilettantes. Helen Fronius's research directly challenges this divide, for she has documented women's increased participation in the book market and investigated the conditions that made this work possible.[14] In a study of correspondence between female writers and the publishers Georg Joachim Göschen and Friedrich Nicolai, she finds that in their business letters, women displayed a confident attitude and an awareness of the worth of their intellectual work that contradicted prevailing gender ideology.[15] Anne Fleig, too, notes that scholars no longer can assume that women were excluded from literary and cultural discourses in the past, arguing, among other things, for a reexamination of the concept of authorship.[16] Finally, noting that the concept of genius is a social construct, Linda Dietrick and Birte Giesler's collection of essays illustrates how women around 1800 developed alternative models of creativity.[17]

The reflections of Dietrick and Giesler point to the fact that as a part of recovering work by forgotten female writers, scholars of the period around 1800 have found that they must carefully evaluate the worth of alternative models of cultural production. While some women did choose to write and publish in more established literary genres such as the novel, the essay, or the drama, other women created unique literary forms, or left behind only fragmentary texts or personal correspondence. Bettina Brentano-von Arnim's first publications, for example, were unique montages of redacted personal letters and fiction-writing, and Rahel Levin Varnhagen chose to express her ideas primarily through epistolary writing.

In addition, many literary women around 1800, including Rahel Levin Varnhagen, distinguished themselves by creating social gatherings or salons, a form of intellectual cultural production that is difficult

---

14 Fronius, "Nur eine Frau," 31–3. Helen Fronius further develops many of her arguments in her book *Women and Literature in the Goethe Era 1770–1820: Determined Dilettantes*, Oxford Modern Languages and Literature Monographs (Oxford: Clarendon Press, 2007).
15 Helen Fronius, "Der reiche Mann und die arme Frau: German Women Writers and the Eighteenth-Century Literary Marketplace," *German Life and Letters* 56, no. 1 (2003): 1–19 (5); and Fronius, *Women and Literature*, 159–60.
16 Anne Fleig, "Forgotten Women Writers? Reflections on the Current State and Future Prospects of Gender Studies," in *German Women's Writing of the Eighteenth and Nineteenth Centuries: Future Directions in Feminist Criticism*, ed. Helen Fronius and Anna Richards (Cambridge: Legenda, 2011), 17, 21–3.
17 Linda Dietrick and Birte Giesler, eds., *Weibliche Kreativität um 1800/Women's Creativity around 1800* (Hanover: Wehrhahn, 2015), 14, 16–17.

to study because of its ephemerality. The salon as a space in which women and men could interact and share ideas has captured the scholarly imagination, for it was a quintessential space for collaboration, in which (at least in theory) aristocrats and members of the bourgeoisie, Jews and gentiles, women and men, could freely discuss their ideas with one another.[18] While it is easy to exaggerate the intellectual and social freedom of the Berlin salons, the development of intellectual ideas in conversation corresponds to the concept of *Symphilosophieren* (symphilosophizing), a central idea that emerged from the work of Friedrich Schlegel and his Romantic circle in Jena. This concept suggests that the sharing of ideas in a group represented a valued form of intellectual activity—one that was in direct contradiction to the "genius" model of authorship, which privileges a single published voice at the expense of other contributors. Stated simply, women drew on a variety of forms of cultural production, some collaborative, some competitive, and some even antagonistic. A range of these responses is represented in the current collection.

In this volume, we wish to interrogate the notion that literary production in the later eighteenth and earlier nineteenth centuries was limited to the model of the author as single (male) genius. In addition to forms of sociability represented by the salon and *Symphilosophieren*, interpersonal exchange and collaboration likewise characterized the period. By illuminating the collaborative matrix out of which many ideas emerged, we hope to add a new dimension to our understanding of the era. We are not suggesting a return to older models of scholarship, which considered women's work to be valuable only if it were associated with that of a great male companion or mentor. Nor do we wish to diminish the important work of feminist scholars who have revolutionized our understanding of women's contributions during this era. However, by examining the various ways in which female and male thinkers contributed collaboratively to cultural production, we hope to question a silo mentality that still persists in literary studies, where scholarship on male and female writers seldom overlaps. We highlight many examples of women and men working together and producing literary and creative works in order to challenge the practice of viewing men's and women's literary production separately. By examining twelve examples

---

18 Marjanne E. Goozé provides a solid overview of the topic of the literary salon in an essay in which she stresses continuities between the salons of France and those of Rahel and her circle in Berlin. See "Mimicry and Influence: The 'French' Connection and the Berlin Jewish Salon," in *Readers, Writers, Salonnières: Female Networks in Europe, 1700–1900*, ed. Hilary Brown and Gillian Dow, European Connections 31 (Bern: Peter Lang, 2011), 49–71.

of collaborative writing, this volume expands the conventional understanding of writing in the period from 1750 to 1850 and demonstrates that the borders between male and female literary production were much more fluid than has been acknowledged previously.

Authorship and Collaboration

The "joint ventures" under consideration here highlight the historically and culturally specific contexts in which they emerged: the rise of the *Geniekult* (cult of the genius) before 1800, changing models of copyright and publication at this time in German lands, and the challenge for women to publish and express themselves within a patriarchal society. Yet they also point to theoretically significant issues that, although likewise historically situated, have relevance beyond the times and locations discussed here. Most notable is the challenge to the myth of single authorship that persists in literary scholarship. During the era under discussion in this volume, that myth came to be known as the *Geniekult*, but it has persisted in various forms across time and space. This myth reinforces dominant societal values: it privileges male over female creative production; the individual over the couple or the collective; and, in many cases, those who conform to dominant classifications of ethnicity, race, gender, and sexuality over those who don't. It draws on the myth of a single, creative author to diminish or exclude all other contributions to the creative process, and thus provides a single, biographical lens through which to interpret a given creative work. It likewise guarantees that a work has cultural and financial value—lesser-quality works by well-known artists gain value simply through association with that name. An otherwise unremarkable piece of literature, music, or visual art increases in both financial value and public appreciation and is given a ready-made interpretative framework as soon as it is associated with a well-known artist.[19]

In contrast to the myth of the single, genius author, this volume explores collaborative ways of working between 1750 and 1850. Rather than suggest a single alternative to the genius model of authorship, we understand "collaboration" as a variety of activities that disrupt the notion of authorship as an individual (usually male) action. We do not aim to offer a comprehensive theory of collaboration; instead, we are attempting to capture different types of literary work and the variety of practices that destabilize the genius-author model. As the essays demonstrate, these run the gamut through cooperation, critical engagement, influence,

---

19 For a persuasive example, see Jack Stillinger's discussion of John Keats's poem "Sonnet to Sleep," in *Multiple Authorship and the Myth of Solitary Genius* (New York: Oxford University Press, 2001), 9–16.

and antagonism. The range of activities reflects both the ambition and the uncertainty that women felt regarding their craft.

This flexible approach to the idea of collaboration builds on a recent scholarly tradition that challenges the myth of single authorship. Beginning in the early 1990s, studies by Anglo-American literary scholars, followed soon by German scholars, highlighted a variety of alternatives to the single-author model. These kinds of collaborations included male homoerotic partnerships,[20] female partnerships,[21] and male–female partnerships,[22] as well as other configurations.[23] They demonstrate that cooperative work is quite common in literary and artistic production, that the modes of collaboration are as varied as the artists who practice them, and that collaborations compel us to rethink our notions of creativity and interpretation insofar as they link a creative product to a single author or a single gender. Collaboration is one of many artistic challenges to the idea of single authorship. Others include works by an anonymous author, automatic writing,[24] or works emerging from oral traditions where a story is passed on and transformed in each telling. The myth of the single author would devalue or dismiss these kinds of contributions. And so, as Bette London asserts: "To study collaboration, then, [is] to study the conditions of its erasure."[25]

Scholars of literature and culture have attacked the single-author model of creativity from multiple theoretical perspectives. Early in the twentieth century, the New Critics eschewed biographical criticism for an exclusive focus on the text, a point that Roland Barthes later gave its most extreme formulation in "The Death of the Author."[26] For

---

20 Wayne Koestenbaum, *Double Talk: The Erotics of Male Literary Collaboration* (New York: Routledge, 1989).
21 Bette London, *Writing Double: Women's Literary Partnerships* (Ithaca, NY: Cornell University Press, 1999); and Lorraine York, *Rethinking Women's Collaborative Writing: Power, Difference, Property* (Toronto: University of Toronto Press, 2002).
22 Annegret Heitmann, Sigrid Nieberle, Barbara Schaff, and Sabine Schülting, eds., *Bi-Textualität: Inszenierungen des Paares* (Berlin: Erich Schmidt, 2001); and Marjorie Stone and Judith Thompson, *Literary Couplings: Writing Couples, Collaborators, and the Construction of Authorship* (Madison: University of Wisconsin Press, 2006).
23 Lisa Ede and Andrea Lunsford, eds., *Singular Texts/Plural Authors: Perspectives on Collaborative Writing* (Carbondale, IL: Southern Illinois University, 1990); Stillinger, *Multiple Authorship*, 1991; Janis Forman, *New Visions of Collaborative Writing* (Portsmouth, NH: Boynton/Cook, 1992); and James S. Leonard, Christine E. Wharton, and Robert Murray Davis, eds., *Author-ity and Textuality: Current Views of Collaborative Writing* (West Cornwall, CT: Locust Hill, 1994).
24 London, *Writing Double*, 6.
25 London, *Writing Double*, 9.
26 Roland Barthes, "The Death of the Author," in *Image Music Text*, ed. and trans. Stephen Heath (New York: Hill and Wang, 1977), 142–8.

Barthes, not only was authorial intention unknowable, but the notion of a unique type of creativity residing in the author also yielded to the concept of the author as a "scriptor," one who produces a work but cannot explain it. The writer's text is more a product of its audience than its creator. During the mid-twentieth century, Mikhail Bakhtin argued that literary texts are not monologic, but dialogic—that is, they are in constant dialogue with other works of literature—and that, as examples of heteroglossia, they contain multiple voices and points of view.[27] And Michel Foucault, in "What Is an Author?," argues that the literary canon is constituted by "authorly" texts, that is, texts where an "author function" offers an easy means to classify and evaluate knowledge and cultural production. Texts that exist outside of this system of authorship are more difficult to codify and value within this system and thus are often marginalized. Foucault highlights how the very concept of an author reinforces a structure of power.[28]

This critical tradition exposes the weaknesses of the solitary-author model and points to other models for understanding literary production. For example, Marjorie Stone and Judith Thompson propose a model of authorship as "heterotextual"; that is, authors are "woven of varying strands of influence and agency, ascribing or incorporating different subjectivities, and speaking in multiple voices." It is a concept that acknowledges authorship to be a culturally constructed identity inextricably linked to the works an author produces.[29] Yet, as liberating as such an approach may be, it also comes at a cost, for the solitary-author model offers simpler, more accessible models of both the creative and the interpretative process than these alternative, more complex models can. Solitary authorship "evades the untidiness of a discursive exchange in which the alien intelligence/psyche injects discordant, therefore unwanted, elements—postulating instead a single, closely held understanding."[30] Stated simply, collaborative or joint ventures are messy: while unsettling the solitary-author model and exposing its

---

27 See Mikhail M. Bakhtin, *The Dialogic Imagination: Four Essays by M. M. Bakhtin*, ed. Michael Holquist, trans. Caryl Emerson and Michael Holquist (Austin, TX: University of Texas Press, 1981).
28 Michel Foucault, "What Is an Author?" in *Language, Counter-Memory, Practice: Selected Essays and Interviews*, ed. Donald F. Bouchard, trans. Donald F. Bouchard and Sherry Simon (Ithaca, NY: Cornell University Press, 1977), 113–38.
29 Marjorie Stone and Judith Thompson, "Contexts and Heterotexts: A Theoretical and Historical Introduction," in *Literary Couplings: Writing Couples, Collaborators, and the Construction of Authorship*, ed. Marjorie Stone and Judith Thompson (Madison: University of Wisconsin Press, 2006), 3–37 (19).
30 James S. Leonard and Christine E. Wharton, "Breaking the Silence: Collaboration and the Isolationist Paradigm," in *Author-ity and Textuality*, ed. Leonard *et al.*, 25–40 (27).

weaknesses, they offer a higher degree of complexity and lack the simple uniformity of the single-author model.

There is no single dominant model for creative collaborative endeavors. They are idiosyncratic, and each collaborative relationship discussed in this volume offers a different configuration of the creative process. Scholars have attempted to codify at least some of the models in general terms. Lisa Ede and Andrea Lunsford identify two predominant modes in women's collaborative writing, namely a hierarchical mode—highly structured, assigned roles for each contributor, with specific goals in mind—and a dialogic mode—loosely structured roles that are more fluid, where the process of working together may be as important as the goals themselves.[31] If we extrapolate from their exclusive focus on female–female collaborations—admitting that to extrapolate from specific historical situations and power contexts is risky—to apply their ideas to collaborations in general, we might consider these two modes as poles on a spectrum, with a variety of possible positions between the extremes of hierarchical and dialogic collaborations. But even with such a broad approach, Ede and Lunsford's model accounts primarily for intentional and deliberate collaborations, where both parties are actively involved, and where power relationships between the two collaborators are relatively balanced. There are multiple examples in this volume, however, where two parties contribute to a collaboration, but where one party is unaware of the other's contribution (e.g., Goethe's "collaboration" with Hafiz in the *West–östlicher Divan* [West–Eastern Divan] or, in turn, Therese Robinson's "virtual" collaboration with Goethe in *Die Auswanderer* [The Exiles], both discussed in later chapters). These examples challenge the distinction between collaboration and artistic influence, and resonate with earlier theoretical work by Harold Bloom in *The Anxiety of Influence* (without his explicitly patriarchal preference for "strong poets"), where poetic creation is understood not as passive influence, but as active and even agonistic engagement with a literary predecessor.[32] This blurring between influence and collaboration points to the two meanings of the word "collaboration." On the one hand, in artistic contexts, collaboration typically implies willing cooperation between two creative parties. Yet in a political context, specifically during war, the term collaboration also suggests not only

---

31 Lisa Ede and Andrea Lunsford, "Rhetoric in a New Key: Women and Collaboration," *Rhetoric Review* 8, no. 2 (1990): 234–6, cited in Holly Laird, "Preface," *Tulsa Studies in Women's Literature* 13, no. 2 (Autumn, 1994): 235–40 (236).
32 Harold Bloom, *The Anxiety of Influence: A Theory of Poetry* (New York: Oxford University Press, 1973).

cooperation, but also duplicity by at least one of the cooperative partners: a collaborator aligns with two sides in order to subvert one. This subversive element drives certain scenes of collaboration, where one party "collaborates" with the other in order to subvert the other's creations towards her or his own ends.

This definition of collaboration points to the power relationship, implicit or explicit, in collaborative endeavors. Wayne Koestenbaum analyzes historically and culturally specific instances of collaboration—male homoerotic collaborations of the late nineteenth and early twentieth centuries—and identifies power relationships inherent in these, specifically dominant and submissive and active and passive sexual roles. The act of collaboration mirrors the sexual act and the creative work is equivalent to a child from that union.[33] Attempts to extrapolate a larger model of collaboration from this specific context are highly fraught, especially when Koestenbaum derives his terms from sex acts between men and the collaborations discussed in the current volume are between men and women. Nonetheless, the power differentials that Koestenbaum identifies inhere at some level in all collaborations and are certainly evident in this volume. In Brian Tucker's essay, for example, Robert and Clara Schumann begin their marriage diary as equals, with explicit expectations as to how often each partner will contribute. Yet, as Tucker points out, they were unable to sustain this effort on an equal basis, and their journal, like their marriage, reflects this imbalance of power.

Such imbalances of power can be difficult to avoid when collaborations cross gender lines. Koestenbaum, for example, hypothesizes that collaborations between women can be more successful than those between the sexes: "When women enter the force field of male collaboration, they are subsumed as mediums and mediators; but when women collaborate, they create their own force field ... in which men have no place."[34] While the present volume overall aims to challenge Koestenbaum's assertion that women in a male–female partnership can have a voice only as mediums and mediators, our contributors certainly highlight many difficulties intrinsic to collaboration across gender lines.

Koestenbaum's assertion, moreover, perpetuates overly rigid gender binarisms. Recent years have seen significant scholarly efforts to challenge the binary, patriarchal model that prevailed around 1800 by studying alternative understandings of relationships and sexuality. Studies on homosexuality and literature in this era demonstrate that the male/female binary was not monolithic, that alternative models of

---

33 Koestenbaum, *Double Talk*, 3.
34 Koestenbaum, *Double Talk*, 173.

relationship were possible, at least in the literary imaginary.[35] Yet even these alternatives were often coded in relation to a dominant gender binary, as Catriona MacLeod asserts in her analysis of androgyny during this era: "androgyny does not simply leave gender binarisms intact … androgyny may even serve as a mythical, theoretical vehicle for the inscription of difference, acquiring iconic status as the prime cultural symbol of heterosexual union." She traces a shift in the late eighteenth century from "the (homo)erotic and genuinely polymorphous ideal of androgyny proposed by Winckelmann to a model grounded in heterosexual complementarity, drained of sexuality."[36] In other words, even those who challenged binary gender roles in this period had difficulty escaping their constraints.

In addition, in institutional and economic spheres, including in the publishing industry, a strong binarism prevailed and women were typically subordinate to men. The aim of our volume is thus not to reconceive the understanding of gender itself during this era, as important an endeavor as that may be, but to analyze how received binary gender roles shaped both the production and reception of literature, and how women and men shared ideas despite these roles. We accept the pervasiveness of binary gender models in the society of this time as a starting point from which to question such binarisms. The binary model of gender may have constrained writers in this era, but it is a testament to their resilience that they found ways to engage in a variety of writing practices. We hope that the examples in this volume will stimulate ongoing research into these practices, which have been neglected by scholars who superimpose an unnecessary gendered binary on their understanding of the period.

First, we contest the notion that the male's work will always dominate in male–female relationships. For example, in Michelle Stott James and Rob McFarland's analysis of Elisa von der Recke, we see how a woman, initially under the control of a charlatan, ultimately resists his power, asserts her own autonomy, and establishes herself in the elite intellectual circles of the European Enlightenment. Yet stories such as

---

35 See, for example, Paul Derks, *Die Schande der heiligen Päderastie: Homosexualität und Öffentlichkeit in der deutschen Literatur 1750–1850* (Berlin: Rosa Winkel, 1990); Alice Kuzniar, ed., *Outing Goethe and His Age* (Stanford: Stanford University Press, 1996); Robert Tobin, *Warm Brothers: Queer Theory and the Age of Goethe* (Philadelphia: Penn State University Press, 2000); and W. Daniel Wilson, *Goethe Männer Knaben: Ansichten zur Homosexualität* (Berlin: Insel, 2012).
36 Catriona MacLeod, "The 'Third Sex' in an Age of Difference: Androgyny and Homosexuality in Winckelmann, Friedrich Schlegel, and Kleist," in *Outing Goethe and His Age*, ed. Alice Kuzniar (Stanford: Stanford University Press, 1996), 194–214 (195).

von der Recke's often go unnoticed. Part of the challenge here is that, as London notes, we are "trained to read [women's] roles as ancillary, we lack the vocabulary to describe them otherwise."[37] In addition, as Lorraine York points out, the "persistent critical desire to find the real, strong, or gifted partner in a collaboration is born of the implicit denial of collaborative textuality."[38] In reading gender roles outside of this lens and this vocabulary, we highlight not only examples of women whose work became just as successful, if not more so, than that of their collaborators (and in some cases antagonists), but also writing projects where a genuinely discursive rather than monological creative process held sway. By attending to binary relationships, we see how writers challenged the inherent imbalances of this binary.

Second, we would challenge the very notion of creativity that inheres in Koestenbaum's statement, that mediums and mediators are somehow inferior or even different from creators. This statement frames creation as an act *ex nihilo*, where only those creators who are original merit respect. Such thinking values primary work, as if the processes of editing and revision—the dialogic nature of the work—did not exist. Yet this volume aims to redeem other artistic acts, to question the distinction between primary and secondary contributions to an artistic creation, to demonstrate that a creative work is seldom the product of a single mind and that, in many cases, without the mediums and mediators, artistic works would be diminished. We consider the work of male–female couples as both bound by and a challenge to patriarchal society, or, as Annegret Heitmann, Sigrid Nieberle, Barbara Schaff, and Sabine Schülting assert, "Writing couples thereby represent historically fixed conventions of male and female authorship and simultaneously call them into question."[39] Tracing this history of male–female collaboration is a fraught task, but nonetheless yields insights, however idiosyncratic, into how men and women negotiated the power inequities inherent in a patriarchal society dominated by a belief in a solitary author.

This volume does not attempt a taxonomy of modes of collaboration. As our survey of other scholars' work has suggested, the varieties of possible collaboration are so numerous that a consistent analytical model to explain all of them simultaneously is impracticable. Even within the demarcated field of male–female collaboration, this volume manifests the idiosyncratic nature of collaborations, how each collaborative relationship finds its own way to navigate differences in power,

---

37 London, *Writing Double*, 20.
38 York, *Rethinking Women's Collaborative Writing*, 14.
39 Heitmann, "Introduction," in Heitmann et al., *Bi-Textualität*, 11–20 (16).

talent, resources, and aspirations. Nonetheless, in offering a wide range of examples, we hope to highlight the frequency, variety, and potential of male–female collaborations and to demonstrate that the myths of the solitary creative (male) genius and the distinct separation of male and female literary spheres stand in stark contrast to actual practice during this era.

Survey of Individual Contributions

The twelve essays in this volume, arranged roughly chronologically and written by individual women and men, as well as collaborative pairs, range from the Enlightenment to the period following the March Revolution of 1848. They describe collaborations between husband and wife, brother and sister, student and teacher, charlatan and betrayed follower, and author and text. They focus on both canonical authors (Goethe, Schlegel, Hölderlin, Günderrode, Bettina Brentano-von Arnim, and the Grimms) and lesser-known authors in an effort to expand our understanding of writing around 1800. They do not assert a unified response to the economic and cultural challenges to women during this patriarchal era; instead, they offer idiosyncratic alternatives to the single-author model of production that for us, today, characterizes the time period, providing us with a richer image of this era and suggesting that the *Geniekult* model was neither monolithic nor inevitable. Nor do they uniformly valorize collaborations; in some cases the collaborative ventures ultimately became one-sided and manifested more imbalance than balance.

The roughly 100 years separating the Gottscheds from Therese Robinson saw a great deal of social and intellectual change. Arguing that any one work during this culturally diverse era could fit a single category would be overly simplistic, and yet with that caveat, it may be useful to group the contributions into fluid categories that will highlight specific emphases in this study.

The first useful category might be the uncovering of cooperation in instances where a collaboration was previously hidden or understudied. For instance, Margaretmary Daley looks at Luise Adelgunde Victorie Gottsched's intellectual cooperation with her husband, Johann Christoph Gottsched, to highlight the complexity of conjugal co-authorship. The Gottscheds' co-authorship offers a different model from collaborations between friends (such as that of Goethe and Schiller) and from a conjugal model in which a wife is a muse to a husband. This husband and wife were intellectual peers, and their marriage produced literary publications, yet they were equal neither in the public sphere nor in their private understanding of the roles of husband and wife. In the traditional view of authorship, both were authors, but he more than she. Still, Daley demonstrates that L. A. V. Gottsched was an influential intellectual and writer of literary texts. She may have seen herself as contributing to the same project as her husband (raising the standards for authors of German literature), yet she brought a different perspective to their work than he did.

In a similar vein, Eleanor ter Horst interprets three texts by Caroline and Friedrich de la Motte Fouqué around 1811–12, examining how they address the topic of gender polarity. Ter Horst finds a hermaphroditic concept of gender in these texts; the texts link creativity to the expression of both conventionally masculine and conventionally feminine qualities, as they draw on the concept of an originary, mythological femininity that encompasses both genders. She thus posits the concept of hermaphroditic collaboration, a concept that was productive for the Fouqués, but challenged both their contemporaries and later scholars of their work.

Julie Koehler explores how Jacob and Wilhelm Grimm worked with both men and women, some of them writers in their own right, to collect tales for their internationally successful collection of fairy tales, *Kinder- und Hausmärchen* (Children's and Household Tales). She points out that, for the Grimms, these female collaborators were merely passive vessels of German culture, so that collaboration was actually an appropriation of creative female work pressed into service for the male *Autor*. But Koehler also highlights how women writers leveraged this supposed partnership to subvert, resist, and replace the reductive dualisms that made true collaboration between creative women and men appear impossible. As Koehler concludes, "they resisted reductive concepts of the *Autor* and the *Märchenoma* [fairy-tale grandma]; and they replaced them with new conceptions of creative women, supportive men, female mentors, and art as collaboration."

Charlotte Lee focuses on the *Buch Suleika* (Book of Suleika) in Johann Wolfgang von Goethe's *West–östlicher Divan*, examining Goethe's imagined exchange with the Persian poet Hafiz in light of Goethe's own collaboration with Marianne von Willemer, who composed several poems in the volume. Lee asserts that this book is not only a joint venture, where two poets—in this case Goethe and Marianne—contribute to the same work, but is also a reflection on joint ventures as such. Despite Goethe's reluctance to acknowledge Marianne's contribution, the text itself conceives of men and women as equal partners in a creative endeavor.

A second grouping of contributions addresses the topic of theories of collaborative authorship characterized by both real and virtual co-operation. Rob McFarland and Michelle Stott James explore how Elisa von der Recke's reaction to the charlatan Count Cagliostro helped her develop her own authorial voice. This was less a willing collaboration and more a willful, polemic collision between two powerful minds—Recke provides her readers with a fascinating example of a woman's battle for agency in the face of a frightening and powerful male authority. This antagonistic interaction later influenced and led to interactions with some of the leading Enlightenment thinkers and political figures of Europe at the time. What began with private séances and intimate lectures came to be a powerful force in European philosophy, art, and politics, as the unlikely collaboration between Recke and Cagliostro became the catalyst that propelled the young spiritual enthusiast into the light of Enlightenment rationality, and gave her the voice to speak the truth she discovered there.

Tom Spencer and Jennifer Jenson examine a virtual collaboration by examining the ways in which Sophie Mereau, who collaborated with or was strongly influenced by thinkers such as Schiller, Fichte, Goethe, and Rousseau, responded to the contemporary ideal of *Bildung* (intellectual development). Mereau challenges male models of creativity and sociality in her writing by presenting *Bildung* narratives that are socially disconnected, but are nonetheless not marked as deviant or failed. Mereau's stories of feminine *Bildung* reflect an emerging unsociable tendency, self-absorption, and disillusionment and isolationism, due, in part, to the ugliness of society. Yet most important in this model of *Bildung* is Mereau's sexual anthropology, which sees a woman as inherently whole, leaving her no other vocation than self-awareness and self-maintenance. This vocation depends initially upon social and especially erotic relationships—it begins as a joint venture—but ultimately transcends the need for them. Collaboration is an important stage in female *Bildung*, but female autonomy is, in the end, inseparable from social detachment.

In contrast, Adrian Daub takes a concrete collaboration as his topic—the joint projects of Friedrich and Dorothea Schlegel—and traces the changing nature of their collaboration over time. Scholars have asserted that, after her novel *Florentin*, Dorothea became little more than a copyist for her narcissistic husband, yet Daub maintains that it is just as easy to overstate Dorothea's independence from Friedrich's cosmos of ideas *before* 1800 as it is to overstate her dependence on him after 1800. Instead, in an analysis that spans decades of literary production, Daub argues for a more complex understanding of this creative relationship: that the two evolved together, that between them—given their differing understanding of creation and need for publicity—a kind of tug of war obtained that lasted well beyond Friedrich's death.

In her contribution, Karen Daubert analyzes the ways in which Bettina Brentano-von Arnim created a virtual collaboration with Friedrich Hölderlin and Karoline von Günderrode. She asserts that Brentano-von Arnim created a model of authorship in which the authority of a single writer splits into an unstable relationship between multiple entities

16   Gender, Collaboration, and Authorship

that work together, which Daubert names "reflexive authorship." This is not a direct collaboration in the traditional sense, but an implicit theory of collaboration: it facilitates an indirect collaborative interaction by incorporating multiple voices and by destabilizing the authorial voice. Brentano-von Arnim's project brings together the two distinct writers Friedrich Hölderlin and Karoline von Günderrode, asserting reciprocal thought between the two through the figure of Bettine.

Judith Martin's contribution examines a virtual collaboration between Therese Robinson and Johann Wolfgang von Goethe. Rather than focus on Robinson's most successful work, a collaboration with Goethe on the *Volkslieder der Serben* (Folksongs of the Serbs), Martin analyzes one of her later novels, *Die Auswanderer* (The Exiles), and reads it as a virtual collaboration with Goethe. Its complex content and form adapt suggestions he made in an 1827 book review for combining information and plot in a new form of American narrative, yet her relationship to Goethe is far from imitative. Hybridity and polyvocality emerge in her text, allowing her to critique Goethe indirectly, even though he provided many of the structuring principles for the novel. The dialogic dimension of the novel allows us to see Robinson's subtly oppositional discourse on gender and its interconnections with her sociohistorical and theological interests.

As a third grouping, several contributors have looked at collaborations that took place outside of conventional publication venues. Monika Nenon explores emerging authorial identities as documented in personal correspondence in her study of the interactions of Sophie von La Roche with Christoph Martin Wieland and Johann Wolfgang von Goethe. Nenon demonstrates that a "dynamic interplay," mutually beneficial to the participants, characterized each of these relationships. While La Roche's emotional support and intellectual stimulation fostered Wieland's poetic development, he provided her with editorial support and encouragement. Notably, he assisted her in entering the literary market with her first novel, the highly successful *Geschichte des Fräuleins von Sternheim* (The History of Lady Sophia Sternheim). When she later encountered Goethe, La Roche was considerably older and more established, yet both writers contributed to the formation of a literary network within the "culture of sociability" created in Sophie von La Roche's home in Koblenz-Ehrenbreitstein.

Laura Deiulio also draws on initially unpublished work in her contribution, in which she examines the correspondence of the salonnière Rahel Levin Varnhagen and her brother, the playwright Ludwig Robert. Deiulio reads the siblings' letters as an example of Romantic *Symphilosophieren*, in which each partner created and negotiated an intellectual identity through conversations over the course of a lifetime. Rahel made concrete contributions to Robert's career as a writer, both by providing material for his journalistic texts and by acting as a respected reader of his plays. Furthermore, Deiulio argues that the attempts of both siblings to construct an identity as German intellectuals of Jewish heritage also represents an intellectual project. As the two writers negotiated the difficult move from the Jewish community of their birth into the larger German-speaking cultural community, they turned to cultural figures such as Goethe and Fichte as touchstones of their intellectual views.

Finally, Brian Tucker explores the diary kept jointly by the musicians Clara and Robert Schumann during the first several years of their marriage. The diary, originally intended only for personal use, served the conventional purpose of recording daily events, but it also afforded the spouses a space for dialogue when they had trouble articulating their feelings and requests orally. Tucker thus argues that the writing reflects an attempt by the spouses to negotiate the difficulties of a two-career marriage, in which Clara Schumann's concert tours required extended absences from the home, and Robert Schumann's composing necessitated peace and quiet when his wife would have preferred to practice the piano. The gaps and imbalances found in the turn-taking of their diary entries represent stresses that emerged as a result of their separate pursuits, leading Tucker to conclude that the cessation of writing after several years reflects a lessened desire to create a joint authorial voice.

Readers will certainly note that our collection of essays by no means offers an exhaustive survey of literary joint ventures around 1800. Caroline Neuber's efforts to work with Johann Christoph and Luise Adelgunde Victorie Gottsched to reform the German theater, Friedrich Schiller's interactions with female contributors to *Die Horen*, and Caroline Schlegel-Schelling's central role in early German Romanticism would all make fruitful topics for further study. However, the aim of this volume is to offer a representative sample, not an exhaustive catalogue, of alternatives to the male single-author model. Our survey of projects around 1800 highlights a wide variety of collaborative male–female literary endeavors during this era, and in doing so, offers several contributions. It explores in detail women's ways of working, demonstrating that, despite the imbalance of power between genders during this era, women nonetheless found meaningful opportunities to express and assert themselves. It also shows that male and female spheres of creation were not as distinct as may have been thought previously. By doing so, it demonstrates that the (male) single-author model that has dominated literary studies since the late eighteenth century was not inevitable and that viable alternatives to it existed. Finally, it demands that we rethink definitions of an author and a literary work in ways that account for the complex modes of creation from which they arose.

Bibliography

Bakhtin, Mikhail M. *The Dialogic Imagination: Four Essays by M. M. Bakhtin*. Ed. Michael Holquist. Trans. Caryl Emerson and Michael Holquist. Austin, TX: University of Texas Press, 1981.

Barthes, Roland. "The Death of the Author." In *Image Music Text*, ed. and trans. Stephen Heath, 142–8. New York: Hill and Wang, 1977.

Battersby, Christine. *Gender and Genius: Towards a Feminist Aesthetics*. Bloomington, IN: Indiana University Press, 1989.

Becker-Cantarino, Barbara. *Schriftstellerinnen der Romantik: Epoche—Werke—Wirkung*. Arbeitsbücher zur Literaturgeschichte. Munich: C. H. Beck, 2000.

Bloom, Harold. *The Anxiety of Influence: A Theory of Poetry*. New York: Oxford University Press, 1973.

Bosse, Heinrich. *Autorschaft ist Werkherrschaft: Über die Entstehung des Urheberrechts aus dem Geist der Goethezeit*. New edn., with foreword by Wulf D. v. Lucius. Paderborn: Fink, 2014.

Derks, Paul. *Die Schande der heiligen Päderastie: Homosexualität und Öffentlichkeit in der deutschen Literatur 1750–1850*. Berlin: Rosa Winkel, 1990.

Dietrick, Linda and Birte Giesler, eds. *Weibliche Kreativität um 1800/Women's Creativity around 1800*. Hanover: Wehrhahn, 2015.

Ede, Lisa and Andrea Lunsford, eds. *Singular Texts/Plural Authors: Perspectives on Collaborative Writing*. Carbondale, IL: Southern Illinois University Press, 1991.

Fleig, Anne. "Forgotten Women Writers? Reflections on the Current State and Future Prospects of Gender Studies." In *German Women's Writing of the Eighteenth and Nineteenth Centuries: Future Directions in Feminist Criticism*, ed. Helen Fronius and Anna Richards, 16–26. Cambridge: Legenda, 2011.

Forman, Janis. *New Visions of Collaborative Writing*. Portsmouth, NH: Boynton/Cook, 1992.

Fronius, Helen. "'Nur eine Frau wie ich konnte so ein Werk schreiben': Reassessing German Women Writers and the Literary Market 1770–1820." In *Frauen in der literarischen Öffentlichkeit 1780–1918*, ed. Caroline Bland and Elisa Müller-Adams, 29–52. Bielefeld: Aisthesis, 2007.

Fronius, Helen. "Der reiche Mann und die arme Frau: German Women Writers and the Eighteenth-Century Literary Marketplace." *German Life and Letters* 56, no. 1 (2003): 1–19.

Fronius, Helen. *Women and Literature in the Goethe Era 1770–1820: Determined Dilettantes*. Oxford Modern Languages and Literature Monographs. Oxford: Clarendon Press, 2007.

Foucault, Michel. "What Is an Author?" In *Language, Counter-Memory, Practice: Selected Essays and Interviews*, ed. Donald F. Bouchard, trans. Donald F. Bouchard and Sherry Simon, 113–38. Ithaca, NY: Cornell University Press, 1977.

Goozé, Marjanne E. "Mimicry and Influence: The 'French' Connection and the Berlin Jewish Salon." In *Readers, Writers, Salonnières: Female Networks in Europe, 1700–1900*, ed. Hilary Brown and Gillian Dow. European Connections 31, 49–71. New York: Peter Lang, 2011.

Hahn, Barbara. *Unter falschem Namen: Von der schwierigen Autorschaft der Frauen*. Frankfurt am Main: Suhrkamp, 1991.

Heipcke, Corinna. *Autorrhetorik: Zur Konstruktion weiblicher Autorschaft im ausgehenden 18. Jahrhundert*. Studien zur neueren Literatur 11. Frankfurt am Main: Peter Lang, 2002.

Heitmann, Annegret, Sigrid Nieberle, Barbara Schaff, and Sabine Schülting, eds. *Bi-Textualität: Inszenierungen des Paares*. Berlin: Erich Schmidt, 2001.
Koestenbaum, Wayne. *Double Talk: The Erotics of Male Literary Collaboration*. New York: Routledge, 1989.
Kord, Susanne. *Sich einen Namen machen: Anonymität und weibliche Autorschaft 1700–1900*. Ergebnisse der Frauenforschung 41. Stuttgart: J. B. Metzler, 1996.
Kuzniar, Alice, ed. *Outing Goethe and His Age*. Stanford: Stanford University Press, 1996.
Laird, Holly. "Preface." *Tulsa Studies in Women's Literature* 13, no. 2 (Autumn, 1994): 235–40.
Leonard, James S., Christine E. Wharton, and Robert Murray Davis, eds. *Author-ity and Textuality: Current Views of Collaborative Writing*. West Cornwall, CT: Locust Hill, 1994.
London, Bette. *Writing Double: Women's Literary Partnerships*. Ithaca, NY: Cornell University Press, 1999.
MacLeod, Catriona. "The 'Third Sex' in an Age of Difference: Androgyny and Homosexuality in Winckelmann, Friedrich Schlegel, and Kleist." In *Outing Goethe and His Age*, ed. Alice Kuzniar, 194–214. Stanford: Stanford University Press, 1996.
Schabert, Ina and Barbara Schaff, eds. *Autorschaft: Genus und Genie in der Zeit um 1800*. Geschlechterdifferenz und Literatur: Publikationen des Münchner Graduiertenkollegs 1. Berlin: Erich Schmidt, 1994.
Schmidt, Jochen. *Die Geschichte des Genie-Gedankens in der deutschen Literatur: Philosophie und Politik 1750–1945*. Vol. I, *Von der Aufklärung bis zum Idealismus*. 2nd rev. edn. Darmstadt: Wissenschaftliche Buchgesellschaft, 1988 [1985].
Stillinger, Jack. *Multiple Authorship and the Myth of Solitary Genius*. New York: Oxford University Press, 2001.
Stone, Marjorie and Judith Thompson. *Literary Couplings: Writing Couples, Collaborators, and the Construction of Authorship*. Madison: University of Wisconsin Press, 2006.
Tebben, Karin. *Beruf: Schriftstellerin. Schreibende Frauen im 18. und 19. Jahrhundert*. Göttingen: Vandenhoeck & Ruprecht, 1998.
Tobin, Robert. *Warm Brothers: Queer Theory and the Age of Goethe*. Philadelphia: Penn State University Press, 2000.
Wilson, W. Daniel. *Goethe Männer Knaben: Ansichten zur Homosexualität*. Berlin: Insel, 2012.
Woodmansee, Martha. *The Author, Art, and the Market: Rereading the History of Aesthetics*. New York: Columbia University Press, 1994.
York, Lorraine. *Rethinking Women's Collaborative Writing: Power, Difference, Property*. Toronto: University of Toronto Press, 2002.

One The Gottscheds
Conjugal Authorship as a Disjointed Venture

Margaretmary Daley

Introduction: Gottsched or Gottsched

Johann Christoph (1700–66) and Luise Adelgunde Victorie Gottsched (1713–62) were married to each other from 1735 to her death in 1762, and each contributed significantly to German-language literary arts in the eighteenth century. It is fascinating to read their individual biographies and to imagine their marriage as a joint literary biography: indeed they worked together as editors, scholars, and thinkers and they worked apart as translators, writers, and critics.[1] They have not been neglected by

---

1 See the essays in Gabriele Ball, Helga Brandes, and Katherine R. Goodman, eds., *Diskurse der Aufklärung: Luise Adelgunde Victorie und Johann Christoph Gottsched* (Wiesbaden: Harrassowitz, 2006); Gabriele Ball, *Moralische Küsse: Gottsched als Zeitschriftenherausgeber und literarischer Vermittler* (Göttingen: Wallstein, 2000); Helga Brandes, "Nachwort der Herausgeberin," in *Die vernünftigen Tadlerinnen 1725–1726*, ed. Johann Christoph Gottsched (Hildesheim: Georg Olms, 1993), 1*–30*; Hilary Brown, *Luise Gottsched the Translator* (Rochester, NY: Camden House, 2012); Susan Cocalis, "Der Vormund will Vormund sein," in *Gestaltet und Gestaltend: Frauen in der deutschen Literatur*, ed. Marianne Burkhard (Amsterdam: Rodopi, 1980), 33–55; Ruth Dawson, *The Contested Quill: Literature by Women in Germany 1770–1800* (Newark, DE: University of Delaware Press, 2002); Katherine R. Goodman, *Adieu Divine Comtesse: Luise Gottsched, Charlotte Sophie Gräfin Bentinck und Johann Christoph Gottsched in ihren Briefen* (Würzburg: Königshausen & Neumann, 2009); Magdalene Heuser, "Neuedition der Briefe von Louise Adelgunde Victorie Gottsched," in *Chloe: Beiheft zum Daphnis. Editionsdesiderate zur Frühen Neuzeit*, ed. Hans-Gert Roloff and Renate Meincke (Amsterdam: Rodopi, 1998), 319–39; Susannah Kord, *Little Detours: The Letters and Plays of Luise Gottsched* (Rochester, NY: Camden House, 2000); Susanne Niefanger, *Schreibstrategien in moralischen Wochenschriften: Formalstilistische, pragmatische und rhetorische Untersuchungen am Beispiel von Gottscheds "Vernünfftigen Tadlerinnen"* (Tübingen: Max Niemeyer, 1997); and Marie Hélène Quéval, *Les paradoxes d'Eros; ou, L'amour dans l'oeuvre de Johann Christoph Gottsched* (Bern: Peter Lang, 1999).

critical studies; on the contrary, both Gottscheds are mentioned in standard reference works, at least as far back as 1883 in Scherer's *Geschichte der deutschen Literatur* (History of German Literature), and as recently as 2004.[2] The standard view sees them as a stellar example of a great (male) author and an ideal (female) assistant married to each other; acknowledges the disparity in prestige; and notes their shared desire to see German literature in the hands of an elite, where it would be "a handmaiden for the moral edification of the uneducated populace."[3] In their *German Literature*, the Garlands (another married couple devoted to German literature) note: "Her collaboration with her husband in translating Bayle's *Dictionnaire* is particularly noteworthy for her untiring commitment to a work that appeared under her husband's name."[4] The Gottscheds strove to develop the German language as a vehicle as capable as Latin of producing sophisticated and beautifully crafted works of art. In this sense, both contributed to the notion of the author as the privileged originator (in the Romantic period, it will be termed "genius") of works of literature. Yet this notion of the author is complicated by collaboration and by creative translations, a major practice of the Gottscheds. Therefore, I explore below many of the interesting, implicit, and frequently inconsistent aspects of collaborative authorship in this example. As Gottsched and Gottsched, they were intellectual peers, yet they were equal neither in the public sphere nor in their private understanding of husband and wife. Johann Christoph Gottsched's programmatic desideratum for literature as a handmaiden to moral edification was not merely figurative.

In some respects his wife did act as a charming handmaiden—especially when compared to other literary women of the period. As one of the Gottscheds, as half of a conjoined couple, she is the more difficult spouse to understand. She and her husband did not put both of their names in the author place on a book, as did, for example, Henry and Mary Garland. But we cannot shelve her as a frustrated foremother of the unfulfilled housewives who inspired Betty Friedan to say that a woman, just as a man, could only find "self-realization in a career."[5]

---

2   Wilhelm Scherer's *Geschichte der deutschen Literatur* was first published in 1883 and became a reference work so "standard" that it had over fourteen printings. On the impact of Scherer's book, see also Peter Salm, *Three Modes of Criticism: The Literary Theories of Scherer, Walzel and Staiger* (Cleveland, OH: Press of Case Western Reserve University, 1968).
3   David E. Wellbery, ed., *A New History of German Literature* (Cambridge, MA: Harvard University Press, 2004), 352.
4   Henry Garland and Mary Garland, eds., *The Oxford Companion to German Literature*, 3rd edn. (Oxford: Oxford University Press, 1997), 299.
5   Betty Friedan, *Interviews with Betty Friedan*, ed. Janann Sherman (Jackson: University Press of Mississippi, 2002), xii, 4.

It is also difficult to define her solely on the basis of her career. On the one hand, L. A. V. Gottsched did produce her own creative writing: she composed tributary, pathos-toned poems and sarcastic comedies, and twenty-first-century scholars are raising awareness of these contributions as well as of her translations.[6] On the other hand, she did not define herself through her career. Instead, her biography reveals someone who valued domestic life and wanted to have children and be a parent. She did not have children. She did contribute to German life and letters; therefore, perhaps the least confusing summary is to see her as an influential intellectual and literary producer, though she may have seen herself as contributing to one project (that of raising the standards for authors of German literature) while simultaneously practicing in a different way. As a couple, the Gottsched-and-Gottsched partnership left posterity with a sizable group of texts. Consequently, then, we need to reevaluate the theoretical definition of "the author" in order to understand the Gottscheds' complex conjugal practice.

Defining the Theoretical Co-author Based on an Antediluvian Author

An author, in common understanding, is the person who thought up and wrote down the words of a literary work. But this is unsatisfactory when a different individual originally thought up the ideas that someone else then sets down. Who had the means to reproduce it and then to control and profit from its publication? And most importantly here, what happens when two people are filling these roles: how do they divide up the work and how do they combine their efforts to produce a joint venture? And, to put it bluntly, how do we credit a woman who contributed reluctantly or vaguely? The proliferation of questions and exceptional cases makes extracting a theoretical definition difficult. Despite the difficulty of definition, many nineteenth- and early-twentieth-century critics extolled the author to the point of an extreme. Roland Barthes attacked such deification of the "*auteur*" in an essay provocatively titled "The Death of the Author." As the phrase "the Great Author" is a circumlocution of the Judeo-Christian God dating back before the times of the Gottscheds, the heresy Barthes invokes is intentional: the author is not to be worshipped, because he is a problematic construct, a fiction that did not exist as secondary literature assumed, and therefore his biographical details are radically irrelevant.[7]

---

6 See n. 1.
7 Roland Barthes, "The Death of the Author," in *Image Music Text*, trans. Stephen Heath (London: Fontana Press, 1977), 142–8.

Michel Foucault responded to Barthes and restored the concept of an "author," yet not as a martyred human being; instead, Foucault put a pliable "author-function" in place of the both canonized and dead genius whose text had been liberated from his intent.[8] Were we, too, to craft our tool of analysis from Foucault's theories, we would have to conclude that the Gottscheds were "founders of a discursivity," like Ann Radcliffe, or Karl Marx and Sigmund Freud.[9] Accordingly the author-function represented by Gottsched and Gottsched produced a discourse using and developing quality German language about literary merit, and they chose as their primary generic tool the periodical. Seen this way, Gottsched and Gottsched are guilty of the same error Jürgen Habermas finds among structuralists and post-structuralists, namely that the style of their own critical essays is as important as the message, that their critique can "no longer discern contrasts, shadings and ambivalent tones."[10] More importantly, we have been led astray by Barthes's anachronistic death and return before the very birth of the author. By this, I mean that although each wrote fiction, the Gottscheds function in this essay as writers of non-fiction, or as literary critics even though their critical analysis predates most literary theory that serves to understand them. In fact, that prodigious preliminary work was necessary before the German language could be the vehicle for art worthy of serious critique is a constant undercurrent in the Gottscheds' oeuvre.[11] And most importantly, both Barthes and Foucault have a skewed if edenic view of the individual, named author. There is no room for an author-couple. Jürgen Habermas introduces into this abstract discussion an insightful concept that allows us to entertain the theoretical notion of co-authors and the specific case of the Gottscheds.[12] One of these concepts shows that while we can discuss "the author" and communicate reasonably about the abstract

---

8   Michel Foucault, "What Is an Author?," in *Textual Strategies: Perspective in Post-Structuralist Criticism*, ed. Josué V. Harari (Ithaca, NY: Cornell University Press, 1979), 141–60.
9   Foucault, "What Is an Author?," 155–6.
10 Jürgen Habermas, *The Habermas Reader*, ed. William Outhwaite (Cambridge: Polity Press, 1996), 342–3.
11 The periodical *Die vernünftigen Tadlerinnen* introduced a "Frauenzimmerbibliothek"; this is a list of recommended readings to develop readers' sophistication with the German language. Gabriele Ball points out that J. C. Gottsched's weekly differs from that of his competitors in Hamburg and Zürich in this respect (Ball, *Moralische Küsse*, 73).
12 Jürgen Habermas, "Arbeit und Interaktion: Bermerkungen zu Hegels Jenenser 'Philosophie des Geistes,'" in *Technik und Wissenschaft als "Ideologie"* (Frankfurt am Main: Suhrkamp, 1969), 7–47.

notion, when we try to be very precise, we find that we have been ambiguous: "Stability and absence of ambiguity are rather the exception in the communicative practice of everyday life. A more realistic picture is that ... of a diffuse, fragile, continuously revised and only momentarily successful communication in which participants rely on problematic and unclarified presuppositions and feel their way from one occasional commonality to the next."[13] In addition, employing Habermas's keen theoretical insights on the author neatly brings us back to the time around 1800: Habermas advertises that he is commenting on Hegel's ideas from his time in Jena. This is helpful for two reasons. First, the notion of the author that Barthes deconstructs was coming into use at the time of the publications of the Gottscheds, but it was not solidified. Nor was there a clear and consistent practice of legal copyright across the different German lands. This worked for and against the Gottscheds. J. C. Gottsched was able to earn substantial income from his edited publications that included many contributions from others and translations without, presumably, paying the contributors particularly well, or the translated "authors" at all: "Wenn ich von meinem Professions Salario hätte leben wollen, würde ich eine schlechte Figur gemacht haben. Mein Bücherschreiben hat mir ebensoviel, ja noch mehr eingetragen" (If I had had to live from my salary as a professor, I would have cut a poor figure. My writing of books brought in just as much, indeed more).[14] J. C. Gottsched does not claim the term "author" for himself—he uses a more modest gerund: "my writing of books." Second, Habermas maintains Hegel's dynamic approach; this allows different shadings to the term "author" to be used over time, including one in which it is a substitute for parenting: "Thus deeply immersed in this cosmopolitan environment and remaining childless, [L. A. V.] Gottsched was able to throw herself into scholarly work."[15] In its etymology, the root of the word "author" refers symbolically to fathering, and yet it is rarely noted when a male partner remains childless. As married co-authors, the Gottscheds have an inverse relationship between their biological parenting (producing no children) and symbolic parenting (producing books).

---

13 Habermas, *Reader*, 148. Cf. Jürgen Habermas, *Theorie des kommunikativen Handelns: Handlungsrationalität und gesellschaftliche Rationalisierung*, 2 vols. (Frankfurt am Main: Suhrkamp, 1981), I, 150.
14 As cited in Katherine R. Goodman, *Amazons and Apprentices: Women and the German Parnassus in the Early Enlightenment* (Rochester, NY: Camden House, 1999), 218. My translation. Unless otherwise noted, all translations are my own.
15 Brown, *Luise Gottsched*, 32.

Before marrying, J. C. Gottsched generated (or "parented") the impressive literary periodical titled *Die vernünftigen Tadlerinnen* (The Reasonable Female Tatlers). After their marriage, L. A. V. Gottsched adopted this work, thus making the periodical an interesting case on which to test authorship and co-authorship. Using the common understanding of the author, we may ask who wrote it and look inside the work's pages. In the first issue, an "I" addresses the readers and announces that the journals will be written by a group of women named Phyllis, Calliste, and Iris. That "I" sounds like an author and claims to have collaborating authors. Yet they are not the authors, for these unrealistic names drawn from an imaginary and literary realm signaled a fiction upon a fiction, or fictitious authorship.[16] In the last issue, the readers are addressed again by a first-person speaker, whom we, in our antediluvian understanding of authorial voice, may take to be J. C. Gottsched, and who reveals co-writers named M. J. May, J. G. Hamann, and L. G. (Lucas Geiger).[17] Finally, the journals were revised, expanded, and reprinted a decade later. At that time, L. A. V. Gottsched offered original prose that was included in the later publications. But to claim that *Die vernünftigen Tadlerinnen* was authored by both Gottscheds is, as suggested by Gabriele Ball, incorrect.[18] At the same time, the refutation that the Gottscheds collaborated equally on parts of *Die vernünftigen Tadlerinnen* does not cancel the discrete contribution that L. A. V. Gottsched made to the periodical. In fact, there is particular interest in her two essayistic pieces, and these are included in the reprint that is otherwise based on the earlier edition. We could say the later version was co-authored by J. C. Gottsched and others, including L. A. V. Gottsched, and possibly count the words from the various co-authors and list them in order of magnitude. This would favor quantity over concept, however, and confounds the question of what constitutes authorship.

The Gottscheds were active at a time when the prescriptive lines between author and editor were not yet drawn. Richard Steele "authored" the majority of the British periodical *The Tatler* in 1709

---

16 "Gottsched wählte nun die Fiktion einer Autorinnengemeinschaft. Daß es sich um eine Frauengruppe handelt, die ihresgleichen anspricht, ist das Neuartige daran ... Durch die Wahl dieser auch in der Schäferdichtung gebräuchlichen Namen wird—bei vehementer Beteuerung der Authentizität der weiblichen Verfasserschaft—die Fiktionalität der drei Autorinnen bereits signalisiert" (Niefanger, *Schreibstrategien*, 13). Cf. Helga Brandes, "Im Westen viel Neues: Die französische Kultur im Blickpunkt der beiden Gottscheds," in Ball et al., *Diskurse der Aufklärung*, 191–212 (194).
17 Ball, *Moralische Küsse*, 52.
18 Ball, *Moralische Küsse*, 175.

before persuading Joseph Addison and Jonathan Swift to contribute. Similarly, Sophie von La Roche's and Mariane Ehrmann's work on their respective periodicals *Pomona für Teutschlands Töchter* (Pomona for Germany's Daughters, 1783–4) and *Amaliens Erholungsstunden* (Amalie's Leisure Hours, 1790–2) falls under both editorship and authorship.[19] When trying to answer who the author of the Gottscheds' or these concomitant periodicals is, the task becomes frustrating because the definition of the "author" seems "diffuse, fragile, and constantly revised," to borrow from Habermas. This is a larger problem of communicative situations for which Habermas has a heuristic solution. In "Arbeit und Interaktion" (Work and Interaction), he makes a case for the importance of three dialectical conceptions: language, work, and interaction in his reading of Hegel's philosophy of mind. Habermas remarks that Hegel only pondered this systematic in his Jena years, a place of much male–female co-authorship.[20] As abstract a task as it is to read Habermas reading Hegel (reading Kant after Foucault reading Barthes), it gives us a new way to think about co-authorship. While "Arbeit und Interaktion" has been read primarily to understand how Habermas draws on Hegelian philosophy in constructing his theory of communicative rationality, it serves here to identify analytical rubrics needed for the construct of the "co-author" without a totalizing perspective. Habermas's rubrics are language, work, and interaction—all clearly key components of multiple people writing words together—and the introduction of the dialectic avoids the vicious circle of asking which author originated the idea. Habermas sidesteps the structuralist dilemma of whether consciousness or language comes first; he sees language as a dialectic dynamic that shapes the "I" at the same time as the "I" shapes language. For the Gottscheds, the German language was in a culturally puerile condition. It was in need of figurative parenting (moral principles in fictional works) and acquiring experience (via translations of culturally sophisticated works from other languages). Tentatively, then, co-authors are real historical people, who in the symbolic dialectical medium of language worked in an interactive way, sharing ideas with each other and then an audience. Their names do not need to appear on the front page of a publication. We will try to use this revised way of thinking about authorship and about the "original text" in what follows.

---

19 On La Roche and her journal *Pomona* as nearly single-authored, see Monika Nenon, *Aus der Fülle der Herzen: Geselligkeit, Briefkultur und Literatur um Sophie von La Roche und Friedrich Heinrich Jacobi* (Würzburg: Königshausen & Neumann, 2005), 151.
20 Habermas, "Arbeit und Interaktion," 37.

The Gottscheds: Pronouncements on Collaborative Authorship versus Practice

Within the fictional dramatic text arguably authored by L. A. V. Gottsched and titled *Die Pietisterey im Fischbein-Rocke* (Pietism in Petticoats), an oft-cited scene illustrates collaborative authorship.[21] A group of religious intellectuals decides that their ideas are so valuable they should collect them and publish them. It is also of pivotal importance to the satire that the group consists entirely of women. One says, "But our men would have to read the work first." Submitting to masculine oversight is agreeable to all the women. Yet the interesting aspect is that this scene shows that a thinking person, tasked with being a scribe on a topic of great interest, will not mechanically record the words. She or he will interfere—she or he will want her or his ideas to prevail. Collaboration fails. It fails because the co-workers cannot co-think with the same language; each finds the other's ideas to be highfalutin words without cohesive meaning. The ironic joke known to the audience is that not a single one of these women actually has any ideas worthy of publication and that the very man whom they enlist to settle their dispute is himself a pompous windbag. That joint paper, thankfully, never gets written.

J. C. Gottsched offers a similarly disgruntled digression on co-authorship in the introduction to his *Neuer Büchersaal* (New Library):

> Man kann sich zwar einen, oder mehrere Gehülfen zu solcher Arbeit wählen: allein, wie vielen Schwierigkeiten ist man dabey nicht ausgesetzt, wenn man lauter recht geschickte Leute dazu finden will? Gesetzt aber, man fände sie; wie lange wird man sie behalten? Reisen, Beförderungen, andre Arbeiten, ja gar der Tod, pflegen, ehe man sichs versieht, solche Gesellen sehr oft zu trennen: wo nicht noch vorher, der schädliche Eigennutz, die liebe Bequemlichkeit, oder oft ein bloßer Eigensinn die löblichsten Bündnisse zerreißen.[22]
>
> (Indeed one can select an assistant or several for such a project: however, how many difficulties will one not be subjected to, if one wishes to find truly qualified people? Assuming, then, that one found them, how long can one keep them? Journeys, promotions, other projects, even death, tend to detach such assistants all too soon: if these most admirable relationships have not been earlier torn asunder by deleterious self-interestedness, sweet complacency, or mere obstinacy.)

---

21 See Brown, *Luise Gottsched*, 65–6; Goodman, *Amazons*, 228–9; Kord, *Little Detours*, 143–5.

22 Johann Christoph Gottsched, *Neuer Büchersaal der schönen Wissenschaften und freyen Künste* (Leipzig: Bernhard Christoph Breitkopf, 1745), "Vorrede" (Preface), 5–6.

His use of the terms *Gehülfe* and *Gesellen*, now antiquated terms for assistants who are more qualified than apprentices and not yet masters of their trade, indicates a common practice of collaboration. He goes on to specify that contributors need to have "eine[] gründliche[] Gelehrsamkeit" (a thorough foundation in learning) combined with "ein reifes und männliches Urtheil" (a mature and masculine critical judgment).[23] Such erudition can be acquired outside the doors of the university lecture hall, a practice in which L. A. V. engaged when her husband's lecture room adjoined hers.[24] With such statements testifying to the failure of collaborative authorship, one wonders how there was any success for Gottsched and Gottsched. The absence of reliable archival material to ascertain exactly what each wrote has frustrated scholars.[25] We do have, however, two other means of viewing their collaboration. The first is his description of how they worked together on the translation of the monumental reference work by Bayle:

> Sie hat mir nicht nur die deutsche Uebersetzung des Wörterbuchs von Blatt zu Blatt laut vorgelesen, indessen daß ich in den Grundtext sah, und auf die Richtigkeit der Dollmetschung acht hatte: sondern auch mit eigener Hand die nöthigen Ausbesserungen, daran sie selbst keinen geringen Antheil hat, an den Rand geschrieben. Sie hat ferner bey der Ausbesserung des andern Abdrucks alle Bogen, die ich selbst laut verrichtete, den französischen Text vor Augen gehabt, und aufs genaueste beobachtet ... Sie hat auch außerdem alle die oftmals sehr langen Stellen aus Amiots französischem Plutarch ... in den lateinischen Uebersetzungen nachgeschlagen, und mit eigener Hand abgeschrieben, um die Lücken der deutschen Uebersetzung damit auszufüllen. Sie hat endlich nicht nur das schwere Sonnet ... in ein deutsches Sonnet aufs genaueste übersetzt; sondern auch ein ziemliches Stück ... und vornehmlich die leibnitzischen Antworten auf den Artikel von Rorarius übersetzet ... Und also hat sie denn, durch so viel neue Stück, abermals Proben ihrer Stärke in der Feder abgelegt, deren Schönheit man billig andern, sowohl der Sache kundigen als unparteyischen Lesern zu beurtheilen, und nah Werthe zu schätzen überläßt.[26]

---

23 Gottsched as cited in Ball, *Moralische Küsse*, 174.
24 Johann Christoph Gottsched, "Leben der weil. hochedelgebohrnen, nunmehr sel. Frau, Luise Adelgunde Victoria Gottschedinn, geb. Kulmus, aus Danzig," in *Ausgewählte Werke*, ed. P. M. Mitchell (Berlin: Walter de Gruyter, 1980), XI.2, 507–83 (514).
25 Goodman, *Adieu Divine Comtesse*, 201.
26 Johann Christoph Gottsched, "Vorrede zum vierten und letzten Theil des Baylischen Wörterbuchs," in *Ausgewählte Werke*, ed. P. M. Mitchell, X.1 (Berlin: Walter de Gruyter, 1980), 151–2.

(Not only did she read the German translation out loud to me page by page while I looked at the original text to pay attention to the correctness of the translation, but she also wrote herself in the margins the necessary emendations, to which her contributions were not minor. Further, when proofreading the sheets for the next printing, she held the French text before her eyes while I dictated the corrections, and she observed it most precisely ... Additionally, she looked up the often quite long passages from Amiot's French Plutarch in the original Latin, and wrote these out with her own hand, in order to fill in the lacunae from the French version in the German translation. Finally, she translated extremely accurately a very difficult sonnet into a German sonnet, and not only that, she also elegantly translated Leibnitz's responses to the entry on Rorarius ... And thus, she, with so many new pieces, once again produced a sample of the strength of her quill, whose beauty can be appreciated by others, whether with expert knowledge or unbiased readers.)

He does not name her, but calls her his "Freundinn" and "treue und unermüdete Gehülfinn" (female friend [and] loyal and indefatigable helpmate [151]) and thereby contributes to the anonymity of literary women. Nevertheless, the specific details and many positive attributes make clear that he regards their personal spousal relationship as supplemented by a professional one. Unlike the stage characters in *Pietism in Petticoats*, Gottsched and Gottsched developed a shared language, performed intellectual labor, and interacted as co-authors would.

The second glimpse into their conjugal collaboration must be inferred from factual comparison between the two editions *of Die vernünftigen Tadlerinnen*. The first printing, in 1725 and 1726, contained a series of issues with shorter pieces written by J. C. Gottsched, a handful of named male colleagues, and a few anonymous women, and all issues appeared before the Gottscheds' marriage.[27] In the second printing of 1738, the issues were not significantly changed except for a

---

27 "Im letzten Stück der 'Tadlerinnen' (VT 26, 52) gibt Gottsched Auskunft über die wirklichen Verfasser. Demnach hatte er anfangs zwei Mitautoren. Jedem war eine der 'Tadlerinnen' zugeordnet. Hinzu kam ein dritter Verfasser, der unter dem Name 'Clio' zwei Stücke verfaßt hatte (VT 25, 8; VT 25, 29). Es handelt sich um Johann Friedrich May, Johann Gottfried Hamann und Lucas Geiger. Da diese ... ausschieden, schrieb Gottsched unter Benutzung der drei Namen allein weiter. Er betont allerdings auch, daß eine Reihe von Frauen einen Beitrag zu der Wochenschrift geleistet haben. Er nennet die Schurmannin, Gertraud Möllerin, Curia, Frau von Breßler" (Niefanger, *Schreibstrategien*, 14). Also, Christiana Mariana

minor expansion. That expansion came from three new contributions written by L. A. V. Gottsched. Two of the three contributions that she wrote construct an unbalanced gender binary, yet one with which she is pleased.[28] It begins in childhood, where a boy's only teacher is his mother until he reaches six years, while a girl's teacher is her mother until ten.[29] L. A. V. Gottsched prioritizes and admires men's achievements: "Die Erfindung der Buchdruckerey, die Verbesserung der Sternkunst, der Mathematik, der Kriegeskunst, der ganzen Philosophie überhaupt, und vieler anderen Sachen" (The invention of the printing press, knowledge of the stars, mathematics, the art of war, philosophy, and many others) and then she explains that these areas of knowledge are "freylich für unser Geschlecht zu hoch" (clearly too high for our [female] gender).[30] The consolation for women is that their work is useful for the world. It consists of raising children and doing it well, as, for example, the wife of Julius Caesar did. This service is as worthy of eternal fame, perhaps worthier than the deed of an angry Alexander. Further important work assigned to women includes taking care of the house; care of the men; and doing these jobs with reason, understanding and accomplishment. Her facetious illustrations include the example of women who carry around a partially hand-knit sock for weeks in order to be able to say explicitly and give the implicit appearance

---

Ziegler was among the unnamed female contributors; see Susanne Schneider, "Christiana Maria von Ziegler (1695–1760)," in *Deutsche Frauen der Frühen Neuzeit: Dichterinnen, Malerinnen, Mäzeninnen*, ed. Kerstin Merkel and Heide Wunder (Darmstadt: Primus, 2000), 139–52.

28 Johann Christoph Gottsched, ed., *Die vernünftigen Tadlerinnen: 1725–1726. Herausgegeben von Johann Christoph Gottsched: Im Anhang einige Stücke aus der 2. und 3. Auflage 1738 und 1748*, 2 vols., ed. Helga Brandes (Hildesheim: Georg Olms, 1993). The reprint reproduces the original's lack of pagination. The two contributions by L. A. V. Gottsched are titled by Brandes: "Lob der Arbeit" and "Die Rolle der Frau als Gattin, Mutter, Hausfrau" (II, 60–9, 248–59). L. A. V. Gottsched's contribution to the subsequent 1748 printing contains an essay on virtue.

29 Luise Adelgunde Victorie Gottsched, "Die Rolle der Frau als Gattin, Mutter, Hausfrau," in J. C. Gottsched, *Die vernünftigen Tadlerinnen*, II, 248–59 (256).

30 A longer excerpt makes her viewpoint clear: "Die Erfindung der Buchdruckerey, die Verbesserung der Sternkunst, der Mathematik, der Kriegeskunst, der ganzen Philosophie überhaupt, und vieler anderen Sachen das sind die edlen Beschäfftigung solcher großen Seelen gewesen ... Sie lesen hier die Namen solcher Wissenschaften, die freylich für unser Geschlecht zu hoch sind ... Die Erziehung der Kinder ist allein ein Werk, wodurch sich manche Cornelia unsterblich gemacht, und der Welt einen größern Dienst gethan hat, als mancher wüthende Alexander. Die Besorgung des Hauswesens, und die Verpflegung der Männer, liegen uns einmal ob, und wir haben, in Wahrheit, viel Verstand und Geflissenheit nöthig, diesen unseren Pflichten eine Genüge zu thun" (Gottsched, *Die vernünftigen Tadlerinnen*, II, 61–3).

that they are thrifty homemakers when visiting other women. That, she explains, would be ridiculous and irrational. Those pretentiously non-pretentious women are more likely—so reasons the wifely author of the new contributions—to be masking their own domestic incompetence. It is in fact the inverse of the feminine mystique: she encourages women to purchase socks made more efficiently by others and to eschew the mystique of domestic arts in favor of just getting housework done. Katherine Goodman summarizes L. A. V. Gottsched's views as deriving from Lutheran tenets: "There is ample evidence that Kulmus [L. A. V. Gottsched] subscribed to and emphasized the concept of enlightened perfectibility of individuals: that learning increased virtue; and that virtue brought true happiness"; yet Goodman does not gloss over L. A. V. Gottsched's anti-feminist disapproval of Mariana von Ziegler (1695–1760).[31] Ziegler was a published poet, the primary librettist for Johann Sebastian Bach, and elected by J. C. Gottsched to the elite literary society the *Deutsche Gesellschaft*. L. A. V. Gottsched rejected public ownership of her authored material. At the same time, the inclusion of her new contributions in a journal that was a closed chapter for her husband indicates that she played a kind of conjugally modified authorial role.

Both Gottscheds ultimately subscribe to a gender binary, a philosophy of either/or that subjected female labor and creativity to male appropriation and oversight while permitting some women some exceptional moments. Subscribing to the notion that masculine and feminine are opposites does not mean, to the Gottscheds, that a real woman cannot be intellectually emancipated. Nor did it mean—again to the Gottscheds around 1800—that the independent intellectuals cannot be in a relationship of teacher to taught and simultaneously intellectual collaborators; that is, in writing "I" on a page, each constructs a rhetorical autonomous self even when that self is asking to be constructed and mentored by another. This autonomy, as Inka Kording has noted in her analysis of the courtship correspondence of the Gottscheds, is "surprising."[32] J. C. Gottsched's partner choices (not only

---

31 Goodman, *Amazons*, 204, 217.
32 "Um so überraschender erscheint es daher, dass sich ein Konzept von autonomer, zumindest in Teilen autoedukativer und selbstbewusster Individualität un-mittelbar—also im Wortsinne nicht vermittelt, verdeckt oder sonst ein anderes Mittel oder Medium zu Hilfe nehmend—ausspricht und Akzeptanz einklagt." Inka Kording, "Konstruktionen der Unmittelbarkeit—Individualität in den Brautbriefen Louise Gottscheds," in Ball, Brandes, and Goodman, *Diskurse der Aufklärung*, 65–88 (75).

in his first but also in his second marriage) confirm his desire for a loving wife and female co-author. Marie Hélène Quéval identifies love as a central concept in J. C. Gottsched's body of writing and life, primarily in his creative works.[33] While he deploys a concept of love based on the loving self's recognition of the opposite (his ode to his wife is one example), her creative works do not respond to his; there is no meta-dialogue in their publications. Instead, the Gottscheds "avoided the gendered battle for the Parnassus of the salons in favor of the national battle for the elevation of German culture."[34] The Gottscheds' conceptions of joint authorship are, from some perspectives, all too disjointed; however, they persisted both in their conjugal and literary activities and in their persistence generated in a compelling, guild-like model with remarkable results.

Translation as Collaborative Authorship: The Author and a Gottsched

The battle for the elevation of literature in German towards erudition, excellence, and propriety that was defined as the Gottscheds' joint desideratum was protracted over decades and required arduous work. The Gottscheds worked together in this venture, certainly initially. And they both agreed that the goal would be well served by introducing the German reading public to many works from other cultures via translation, "a crucial part of [the] reforms."[35] Translation today is generally construed as reproducing another's original words in a different language; however, translation at the time of the Gottscheds prioritized the ideas reaching a new readership over the translator's fidelity to the source text. This increases interest in the interaction between the Gottscheds. While the standard view demotes the

---

33 "Leur amour a sa source dans leur goût commun pour la poésie. Loin d'être exceptionnel, ce phénomène se reproduira lors des secondes noces du sexagénaire. Gottsched désire sincèrement l'émancipation intellectuelle de la femme, qui seule, rend l'amour-amitié possible. A la différence de l'amour galant, cette amitié n'a plus pour origine l'amour de soi, mais celui d'autrui." (Their love has its source in their common taste for poesy. Far from being exceptional, this phenomenon reproduced itself again in the sixty-year-old's second marriage. [J. C.] Gottsched sincerely desired woman's intellectual emancipation, which alone makes companionate-love possible. Differing from courtly love, this love has its origin not in self-love but rather in that of the other.) Quéval, *Les paradoxes d'Eros*, 108–9.
34 Goodman, *Amazons*, 254.
35 Brown, *Luise Gottsched*, 15.

translator to a mere tool, Katherine Goodman and Hilary Brown revise this view.[36] Goodman argues that the working relationship between the married Gottscheds paralleled that of senior and junior editors in a literary enterprise: rather than translate *Gehülfin* as a wifely helper, she stresses the connotation of journeyman: "the next higher rung on the professional ladder from apprentice to master in the guilds. The meaning likely also underlay Gottsched's usage (as it had Luther's)."[37] Brown makes a good case for the argument that L. A. V. Gottsched exerted her own choice of texts in the interaction with her husband, or guild supervisor: "Most of her translations appeared with her name emblazoned on the front cover, and they often included prefaces written and signed by the *Uebersetzerinn* [translator]. She developed her own profile, and her name became a selling-point."[38] Luise Gottsched put her name on published translations, yet withheld it from creative works, and, in both cases, worked with Johann Christoph Gottsched to some degree.

This interpretation acknowledges a hierarchy while granting each Gottsched autonomy. The example to support this is that L. A. V. Gottsched chose de Gomez's work *Triomphe de l'éloquence* (Triumph of Eloquence) on her own initiative and rejected her husband's suggestion (Scudéry's *Bains de Thermopyles* [The Bath of Thermopylae]).[39] Brown also refutes that L. A. V. Gottsched was enslaved like an oarsman in the galleys because of her husband forcing work, asserting rather a host of reasons, including the distance in their marriage, the attacks on the Gottsched camp from outside, exhaustion, physical health, and the Seven Years War.[40] Nevertheless, it was the facetious wordsmith L. A. V. Gottsched herself who selected the phrase "galley slave" to describe her contribution to the conjugal collaboration. Rather than be alarmed by this description of a marriage, I see here the wife's predilection for satiric genres and facetious diction. The phrase appears in a letter to her intimate friend Dorothea von Runckel, a text where L. A. V. Gottsched

---

[36] There is scholarly interest in a more nuanced understanding of translation. On translation in the decades after the Gottscheds, see Maike Oergel, ed., *(Re-)Writing the Radical: Enlightenment, Revolution and Cultural Transfer in 1790s Germany, Britain and France* (Berlin: De Gruyter, 2012), especially Barry Murnane, "Radical Translations: Dubious Anglo-German Cultural Transfer in the 1790s" (44–60); and Susan Gustafson, "The Dismissal and Elision of 'Disturbing' Love Relationships in English Translations of Goethe's *Die Geschwister* and *Stella*," *Lessing Yearbook* 44 (2017): 149–66.
[37] Goodman, *Amazons*, 216.
[38] Brown, *Luise Gottsched*, 35.
[39] Actually Part IX of Book II of Madeleine de Scudéry, *Artamène; ou, Le grand Cyrus* (Artamène; or, Cyrus the Great), 1649–53 (Geneva: Slatkine Reprints, 1972).
[40] Brown, *Luise Gottsched*, 35–7.

would have felt completely free to engage in caustic humor without having to explain to her reader that she was being ironic, as she had to the general public of the *Tadlerinnen*. While Susanne Kord sees L. A. V. Gottsched as a stymied author trapped in a master–slave relationship with her husband, Hilary Brown presents her as canonical translator in a culture that made little distinction between "original" and "translated" text, a culture where there was no hierarchy of disciplines that placed fiction at the pinnacle. Aware that our understanding of disciplinary as well as marital relationships has evolved, Brown then concludes that her "partnership with Johann Christoph enabled" her work, and sides with Goodman in likening their partnership to a guild.[41] Citing the 1971 work by Anneliese Senger, *Deutsche Übersetzungstheorie im 18. Jahrhundert (1734–1746)* (German Translation Theory in the Eighteenth Century [1734–1746]) and others, Brown explains that "a translation could look like an adaptation or even an original," and that the "new reader was more important than the source-text author."[42] Steinwehr, a contemporary of the Gottscheds, wrote in 1735 that the translation should even fool the reader into thinking she or he is reading an original, a suggestion so far from current practice as to sound unethical.[43]

Four Co-Worked Literary Interactions of Gottsched and/or Gottsched

After their marriage, the Gottscheds lived together in the same city, Leipzig, and the correspondence that has served to document the work and interaction between them ceased. Collaboration certainly continued—probably intensified. "Almost immediately [after their wedding] her husband began training her to help him with his editorial work on his journal *Critische Beyträge* [Critical Essays]."[44] Works with some degree of collaboration include the *Critische Beyträge* of 1736[45] and the aforementioned new contributions by L. A. V. Gottsched in the 1738 reissuing of his *Vernünftige Tadlerinnen*, in particular two interesting opinion pieces on women's social roles.[46] Further, L. A. V. Gottsched translated all nine volumes of the English periodical the *Spectator* into German (1739–43). In addition to the French work by Bayle, she also

---

41 Brown, *Luise Gottsched*, 37–8.
42 Brown, *Luise Gottsched*, 185.
43 Brown, *Luise Gottsched*, 197 n. 7: W. B. A. von Steinwehr, "M. Tullii Ciceronis sechs Reden," *Beyträge zur critischen Historie der deutschen Sprache, Poesie und Beredsamkeit* 13 (1735): 28.
44 Goodman, *Amazons*, 216.
45 "By his own account he soon turned to her as 'eine Gehülfinn' ... 'helpmate'; and ... the word for 'journeyman,' the next higher rung on the professional ladder from apprentice to master." Goodman, *Amazons*, 216.
46 Ball, *Moralische Küsse*, 171.

translated the two-volume British periodical the *Guardian* in 1745.[47] In fact, it is unintentionally ironic that in their courtship correspondence he compliments her by dubbing her "Sappho," and she, in her letter of reply, states that she had to look up the reference in her copy of Bayle. As periodical author, she was a consistent contributor, and he was an active editor who dealt with the publishing houses. While we cannot conclude that Gottsched and Gottsched were equal contributors to those publications, the extent of their interaction was, in Habermas's sense, too substantial to ignore, and we do not need to be pedantic in our usage of the term "author." Recent academic editions such as Johann Christoph Gottsched's letters, for which the editors in 2007 included L. A. V. Gottsched's name on their title page (see bibliography), demonstrate agreement with this interpretation.

If we take the most radical deconstruction of the "author," then soften it with Habermas's communicative compromises, we can apply the result to the writerly output of the Gottscheds. By writerly output I do not mean the work that is synonymous with a text, but rather the labor done by interacting. I find up to four titles that can be assayed as co- authored works. The first of these four is usually regarded as her translation: L. A. V. Gottsched, when she was still L. A. V. Kulmus, translated a French language text by Lambert, and J. C. Gottsched brought it to print. One of her letters makes clear that they disagreed on which European language was the more perfect.

> Ich habe nunmehro auf zwey Schreiben zu antworten, die der Papa mir in kurzer Zeit von Ew. hochedlen eingehändigt. In dem ersten nehmen sie sich der Englischen Sprache an, und wollen es ewig nicht zugestehen, daß sie unvollkommener sey, als die Französische ... [Englisch ist] ein unordentliches Mischmasch so vieler andern ... Dafern die Französische, Lateinische, Italiänische und Deutsche Sprache eine jede das Ihrige von der Englischen wiedernähmen, würden ja Ew. Hochedlen nicht so viel Wörter behalten, ein Stück Brodt zu fordern ... Wollen sie die Menge schlechter Ubersetzungen [sic] mit der Meinigen vermehren? Oder wollen sie dadurch die Frau von Lambert warnen ... die Flattermäuse entlegener Handels=Städte zu ihrer Ubersetzung einfinden? ... ich [kann] natürlicher Weise nicht in den Druck der neulichen Ubersetzung willigen.[48]

---

47 Brandes, "Nachwort," 2.
48 Johann Christoph Gottsched, *Johann Christoph Gottsched Briefwechsel: Historisch-kritische Ausgabe*, 5 vols., ed. Detlef Döring, Rüdiger Otto, and Michael Schlott (Berlin: Walter der Gruyter, 2007–11), Vol. II (2008), *Briefwechsel: Unter Einschluß des Briefwechsels von Luise Adelgunde Victorie Gottsched*, Kulmus to Gottsched, April–May 1731, 56.

(I have to respond now to two letters that Papa has given to me from you recently. In the first, you take on the English language and are not willing to admit that it is more imperfect than French ... [It is] a disorderly mish-mash of so much else ... To the extent that if the French, Latin, Italian and German languages each took their own back from the English language, your Grace would not have enough words left to request a piece of bread ... Do you wish to increase the number of poor translations by adding mine? Or do you wish to warn Mrs. von Lambert ... that lamebrains from backwater towns are trying their hands at translating her? ... I cannot of course agree to the publication of the recent translation.)

This long excerpt showcases the kind of agree-to-disagree working relationship that the Gottscheds had, certainly at the beginning and throughout the courtship correspondence. On the main points, they agree; on details, they may disagree and even enjoy their disagreement. The pleasure of divergent opinions can be seen in the playfulness of her letter.[49]

Each of the four works that can be assayed for co-authorship has a complex genesis, a long title, and a belabored editorial history. The publication's title page reads: *Der Frau Marggräfin von Lambert Neue Betrachtungen über das Frauenzimmer, aus dem Französischen übersetzt durch ein junges Frauenzimmer aus ... und herausgegeben von einem Mitgliede der Deutschen Gesellschaft in Leipzig* (To the Lady Margravine of Lambert, New Observations on the Young Woman, Translated from the French by a Young Woman from ... and edited by a Member of the German Society of Leipzig).[50] This title page buries the actual essay within the mention of three people, only one of whom is named, the Margravine Lambert. The other two who remain anonymous are Gottsched and Gottsched. Neither's name appears on this page. It appeared in 1731 (before their wedding), and consists predominantly of her translation of an expository text on fitting behavior and activities for young women (numbered pages 1–48). However, approaching it as a communicative structure allows us to interpret it cover-to-cover. This collaborative

---

49 In January of 1733, she wrote another playful letter proposing a Pomeranian marriage society for 1,000 single people, equally divided along the gender binary, who could share profit as each member married out. Because the source for this letter is Runckel, we cannot know just how cleverly and how comically L. A. V. Gottsched actually wrote.
50 Luise Adelgunde Victorie Gottsched, *Der Frau Marggräfin, von Lambert Neue Betrachtungen über das Frauenzimmer, aus dem Französischen übersetzt durch ein junges Frauenzimmer aus ... und herausgegeben von einem Mitgliede der Deutschen Gesellschaft in Leipzig*, ed. Johann Christoph Gottsched (Leipzig: Bernh. Christoph Breitkopf, 1731).

endeavor has the translation and a three-page dedication, as well as a four-page introduction (by him: "Geneigter Leser!" [To the Willing Reader]) and also a two-page preface from the author to the reader ("Vorrede der Verfasserinn an den Leser" [Preface by the Author]). As the closing bookend, there are two texts: thirty pages of poems by the translator ("Der Uebersetzerin Eigene Gedichte," [Original Poems by the Translator], 49–78) and also a two-page letter from her to the editor (78–80). The number of pages of other material nearly equals the number of pages of the translation. Once the author is a function and not an individual genius, then the work of literature must similarly be a function. The work of literature here is not merely the inset translation, performed by a single person. Instead, I argue, the work of literature is the book in its entirety, and it is co-authored by Gottsched and Gottsched. As evidence, there are over a dozen poems, which do not relate thematically to the translation of Lambert; composed for various celebratory occasions, those poems express the sentiments of the "young lady" who translates. These "and-also" texts may be dismissed as paratexts by the reader seeking Lambert, but to those understanding the collaboration, they are essential to any integrity the publication may be said to have. Let us take a closer look at the personal letter included in the volume. The letter appears strangely unedited. It starts by mentioning two prior letters, beginning in the middle of a correspondence. However, this is not a handwritten letter but a typeset text now shared with a wider public in the company of other texts. Its meaning has changed as its function has been coopted. It serves to remind the reader that it is a cooperative endeavor and yet originally an unintentional one. The letter is supposed to represent its writer, not the conjoined efforts of its writer and editor. It also makes the reader look back to the title page and determine whether it provides more information on authorship. All in all, the translation is surrounded by collaborative and original texts, embedded in a lanky body that includes individual work (poems), joint ventures (personal letter), and an exterior packaging that can persist in time. Far from being a one-off, I argue, this method of collaboration works as an iterative instance of conjugal yet disjointed authorship.

In part, their intellectual divergence is revealed because of a physical reality: she was in Danzig and he in Leipzig, and the distance precluded face-to-face meetings. Instead, the distance facilitated not an oral exchange but a written one, which in turn facilitated intellectual collaboration. While we may think of epistolary discourse as formally marked by an I–you dialectic, theirs is compounded by a linguistic system of formal address that turns personal letter intimacy into a dialectic of a writing "I" who apostrophes a "most honored Sir," through which a "you" is implied. The written identity that each invents is a hybrid

"I" that engages in personal flirtation and professional negotiation.[51] Thematically, the premarital correspondence embraces intellectual interaction; exchange of opinions on literature in German, French, and English; and their opinions on classical and coetaneous authors.

A correspondence as rich in disciplinary themes as theirs may possibly be the second Gottsched-and-Gottsched work to border on the loosely defined territory called co-authorship. However, his letters to her are now missing, though he refers later to them in his biography of her. More tenuously, the print product was edited by Dorothea von Runckel, who, as Magdalene Heuser and Susannah Kord have shown, was as heavy-handed an editor as L. A. V. Gottsched was a translator.[52] Runckel did not see L. A. V. Gottsched's original letters as an author's text, nor her task as editor to transcribe them faithfully. Rather, Runckel changed every letter, most sentences, phrases, and diction, and removed passages without signaling her changes. Thus, the book version of L. A. V. Gottsched's letters must be seen as having another level of "proliferation of meaning," to speak with Foucault, and as continuously revised, to speak with Habermas. It is arguably not a conjugal venture but instead a three-way collaboration. Finally, J. C. Gottsched had harbored the idea of publishing his and her correspondence, telling his readership that he had her historical letters in his hands, "together with his own, and that these might some day result in a not unfavorable model of an innocently intimate correspondence."[53] However, as J. C. Gottsched did not produce that conjugally authored publication, Runckel's edition must serve in its stead, but not as a work authored by L. A. V. Gottsched.

The Gottscheds' correspondence from their meeting in 1729 until their marriage in 1735 had, arguably, more potential co-authorship than the translation, yet the presence in the publication of Dorothea von Runckel and the absence of a competing edition from J. C. Gottsched means that such potential was unrealized. The second hypothetical case (the heavily embedded translation of Lambert's essay on women) yields better results. The third, arguably co-authored work again calls the integrity of the term "work" into question because it is a periodical series. From 1745 until 1750, J. C. Gottsched published a monthly magazine of reviews titled *Neuer Büchersaal*. Looking back on this series of publications, he comments on her collaboration:

---

51 In the subsection "Der Selbstentwurf von Identität," Kording examines L. A. V.'s development of the self (Kording, "Konstruktionen," 68–70).
52 Heuser, "Neueedition"; Kord, *Little Detours*, 25–32.
53 "Er hat selbige mit den seinigen noch alle in Händen, und diese würden dereinst kein übles Muster von einem unschuldig zärtlichen Briefwechsel abgeben." Johann Christoph Gottsched, "Leben," 512.

> Und auf eben diesen Schlag hat sie auch nachmals, in dem neuen Büchersaale der schönen Wissenschaften und freyen Künste, imgleichen in dem Neuesten aus der anmuthigen Gelehrsamkeit, mit einer schon geübtern Feder viele wichtigere Werke, auf eine so gründliche als angenehme Art beurtheilet und bekannt gemachet, daß die Leser allemal höchst vergnügt damit gewesen.[54]
>
> (And in just this vein she also subsequently wrote critiques of many more important works for the *New Library for Belles Lettres and the Liberal Arts*, likewise in the most recent; with graceful erudition, using her well-practiced quill, and in a manner equally rigorous as pleasant, she made these works known and brought indeed great pleasure to the readers.)

Gabriele Ball notes that he promised to collect a list of her submissions, yet never did. Nevertheless, Ball establishes that L. A. V. Gottsched is the central figure of the periodical and gave it its overall character.[55] Here, we are more interested in reintegrating the contributions. On the one hand, there were clearly more authors involved in this periodical than just the Gottscheds, and the "work" is a series. However, viewed in its entirety and in appreciation of the impact such a "work" had on German life and letters, the *Neuer Büchersaal* may be counted as a co-authored project.

The fourth and final candidate is more of a coherent, single work than the third, yet it has a title as long as the second. Its full title is *Der Frau Luise Adelgunde Victoria Gottschedinn, geb. Kulmus sämmtliche Kleinere Gedichte, nebst dem, von vielen vornehmen Standespersonen, Gönnern und Freunden beyderley Geschlechtes, Ihr gestifteten Ehrenmaale, und Ihrem Leben, herausgegeben von Ihrem hinterbliebenen Ehegatten* (Collected, Shorter Poems, as Well as Texts in Memoriam Mrs. Luise Adelgunde Victoria Gottsched, née Kulmus, from Many Elegant Noble Persons, Well-Wishers, and Friends of Both Sexes, as Edited by Her Surviving Spouse). As the title page spells out, this written and published project contains material of, from, for, and about L. A. V. Gottsched, and some of her own creative work—poetry, not drama—and many components of this work were not written by the Gottscheds. The published project includes such diverse texts as a biography (*Leben*) authored by J. C. Gottsched, and letters of sympathy written to him upon her death. It also includes musical compositions by L. A. V. Gottsched. Therefore, this literary work has much the same layering of source material,

---

54 Ball, *Moralische Küsse*, 179.
55 Ball, *Moralische Küsse*, especially the section "Luise Adelgunde Victorie Gottsched als zentrale Gestalt unter den Beiträgern des 'neuen Büchersaals,'" 171–200.

translation, adaptation, and genre variety as the first co-authoring on the basis of Lambert, and may, arguably, be seen as the final conjugal collaboration by Gottsched and Gottsched. These few examples differ from J. C. Gottsched's work with Ziegler and others in that they focus on the married pair. Perhaps this is why some critics, seeking to interpret L. A. V. Gottsched, are irritated by the co-presence of her husband.[56] Treating these examples as conjugal literature, rather than trying to make them the work of one or the other, alleviates this problem.

Collaborators, Co-workers, Co-habitors, and Conclusion

In the traditional view of the author, the one against whom Barthes polemicized and Foucault functionalized, Gottsched and Gottsched were each "authors," yet he more than she. His list of original works is longer than hers, and his position as "great author" more stable than hers. More critical studies that approach her writing without the need to mention her husband or biography are welcome as a corrective to the imbalance. However, the contribution of Gottsched and Gottsched cannot be denied, although it needs the fragile notion of conjugal co-authorship. With Goethe and Schiller and the *Xenien*, one imagines fraternal co-authoring wherein one individual wrote some lines, they perhaps revised in each other's presence, and then each did so again separately at their writing desk while exchanging letters until publication. However, with the Gottscheds, the collaboration is even more elusive because their personal relationship is more codified: not two "great authors" but co-habiting spouses. Their interaction takes place in ways not knowable to us now. We can be sure that he published writing he created under his name. We can be sure that she allowed some of her authored texts to be published anonymously. We also know that he solicited writing from her; that she delivered translations and adaptations; and that again he, as "compiler" (*Vermittler*), published her work. Based on this, we must extract some new concepts for authorship in the eighteenth century. A wife creates, generates, and lives; her husband creates, conjoins, and publishes. A husband writes and woos; she incorporates him into her letters, which are later published. Thus each translates the other's lived creativity into literary discourse. After her death, he makes a book out of her (her life, her discourse, her reflection in the

---

56 See Kord, *passim*, especially 170; and Goodman, *Amazons*. See also Gabriele Ball, who sees this not as a co-authored work but as J. C. Gottsched's attempt to construct L. A. V.'s life according to his opinion; "Die Büchersammlungen der beiden Gottscheds: Annäherung mit Blick auf die *livres philosophiques* L. A. V. Gottscheds, geb. Kulmus," in Ball, Brandes, and Goodman, *Diskurse der Aufklärung*, 213–60 (223).

discourse of others). The Gottscheds' conjugal co-authorship offers a different model from that in which a wife is a muse to a husband. Her life had a literary and consequently quasi-public component from her teen years until her death. His publications have a social and therefore personal or private dimension. As "the Gottscheds," their marital life is a potential primary source for literary publication, accessible even to themselves. Given the nineteenth- and then twentieth-century portraits of the author as lonely, struggling artist or as a privileged intermediary to the divine, the model presented by the Gottscheds as authorial constellation seems enviable. It blurs the harsh line drawn between authors of primary and secondary literature and casts a charming and chummy gloss on the real work of writing and publishing. There is no surprise that the Gottscheds' disjointed and issueless marriage, coupled with their immensely productive, conjugal co-authorship, continues to fascinate.

Bibliography

Ball, Gabriele. *Moralische Küsse: Gottsched als Zeitschriftenherausgeber und literarischer Vermittler*. Göttingen: Wallstein, 2000.

Ball, Gabriele, Helga Brandes, and Katherine R. Goodman, eds. *Diskurse der Aufklärung: Luise Adelgunde Victorie und Johann Christoph Gottsched*. Wiesbaden: Harrassowitz, 2006.

Barthes, Roland. "The Death of the Author." In *Image Music Text*, trans. Stephen Heath, 142–8. London: Fontana Press, 1977.

Bohm, Arnd. "Authority and Authorship in Luise Adelgunde Gottsched's *Das Testament*." *Lessing Yearbook* 18 (1986): 129–40.

[Bougeant, Guillaume-Hyacinth]. *La femme docteur; ou, La théologie tombée en quenouille: Comédie*. Liège: Veuve Procureur, 1730.

Brandes, Helga. "Im Westen viel Neues: Die französische Kultur im Blickpunkt der beiden Gottscheds." In *Diskurse der Aufklärung: Luise Adelgunde Victorie und Johann Christoph Gottsched*, ed. Gabriele Ball, Helga Brandes, and Katherine R. Goodman, 191–212. Wiesbaden: Harrassowitz, 2006.

Brandes, Helga. "Nachwort der Herausgeberin." In *Die vernünftigen Tadlerinnen 1725–1726*, ed. Johann Christoph Gottsched, 1*–30*. Hildesheim: Olms, 1993.

Broad, Jacqueline and Karen Green. *A History of Women's Political Thought in Europe, 1400–1700*. Cambridge: Cambridge University Press, 2009.

Brown, Hilary. *Luise Gottsched the Translator*. Rochester, NY: Camden House, 2012.

Burke, Seàn. *The Death and Return of the Author: Criticism and Subjectivity in Barthes, Foucault and Derrida*. Edinburgh: Edinburgh University Press, 1999.

Cocalis, Susan. "Der Vormund will Vormund sein." In *Gestaltet und Gestaltend: Frauen in der deutschen Literatur*, ed. Marianne Burkhard, 33–55. Amsterdam: Rodopi, 1980.

Dawson, Ruth. *The Contested Quill: Literature by Women in Germany 1770–1800*. Newark, DE: University of Delaware Press, 2002.

Foucault, Michel. "What Is an Author?" In *Textual Strategies: Perspective in Post-Structuralist Criticism*, ed. Josué V. Harari, 141–60. Ithaca, NY: Cornell University Press, 1979.

Friedan, Betty. *Interviews with Betty Friedan*. Ed. Janann Sherman. Jackson: University Press of Mississippi, 2002.

Garland, Henry and Mary Garland, eds. *The Oxford Companion to German Literature.* 3rd edn. Oxford: Oxford University Press, 1997.
Goodman, Katherine R. *Adieu Divine Comtesse: Luise Gottsched, Charlotte Sophie Gräfin Bentinck und Johann Christoph Gottsched in ihren Briefen.* Würzburg: Königshausen & Neumann, 2009.
Goodman, Katherine R. *Amazons and Apprentices: Women and the German Parnassus in the Early Enlightenment.* Rochester, NY: Camden House, 1999.
Gottsched, Johann Christoph. *Ausgewählte Werke.* 12 vols. Ed. Joachim Birke and P. M. Mitchell. Berlin: De Gruyter, 1968–87.
Gottsched, Johann Christoph. *Johann Christoph Gottsched Briefwechsel: Historisch-kritische Ausgabe.* 5 vols. Ed. Detlef Döring, Rüdiger Otto, and Michael Schlott. Berlin: Walter de Gruyter, 2007–11. Vol. II (2008), *Briefwechsel: Unter Einschluß des Briefwechsels von Luise Adelgunde Victorie Gottsched, 1731–1733.*
Gottsched, Johann Christoph. "Leben der weil. hochedelgebohrnen, nunmehr sel. Frau, Luise Adelgunde Victoria Gottschedinn, geb. Kulmus, aus Danzig." In *Ausgewählte Werke*, ed. P. M. Mitchell, XII.2, 507–83. Berlin: Walter de Gruyter, 1980.
Gottsched, Johann Christoph. *Neuer Büchersaal der schönen Wissenschaften und freyen Künste.* Leipzig: Bernhard Christoph Breitkopf, 1745.
Gottsched, Johann Christoph, ed. *Die vernünftigen Tadlerinnen: 1725–1726. Herausgegeben von Johann Christoph Gottsched: Im Anhang einige Stücke aus der 2. und 3. Auflage 1738 und 1748.* 2 vols. Ed. Helga Brandes. Hildesheim: Georg Olms, 1993.
Gottsched, Johann Christoph. "Vorrede zum vierten und letzten Theil des Baylischen Wörterbuchs." In *Ausgewählte Werke*, ed. P. M. Mitchell, X.1, 151–2. Berlin: Walter de Gruyter, 1980.
Gottsched, Luise Adelgunde Victoria. *Der Frau Marggräfin, von Lambert Neue Betrachtungen über das Frauenzimmer, aus dem Französischen übersetzt durch ein junges Frauenzimmer aus ... und herausgegeben von einem Mitgliede der Deutschen Gesellschaft in Leipzig.* Ed. Johann Christoph Gottsched. Leipzig: Bernh. Christoph Breitkopf, 1731.
Gottsched, Luise Adelgunde Victoria. *Die Pietisterey im Fischbein-Rocke.* Stuttgart: Reclam, 1986.
Gottsched, Luise Adelgunde Victoria. *Sämmtliche kleinere Gedichte.* Leipzig: Breitkopf, 1763.
Gustafson, Susan. "The Dismissal and Elision of 'Disturbing' Love Relationships in English Translations of Goethe's *Die Geschwister* and *Stella*." *Lessing Yearbook* 44 (2017): 149–66.
Habermas, Jürgen. *The Habermas Reader.* Ed. William Outhwaite. Cambridge: Polity Press, 1996.
Habermas, Jürgen. *Technik und Wissenschaft als "Ideologie."* Frankfurt am Main: Suhrkamp, 1969.
Habermas, Jürgen. *Theorie des kommunikativen Handelns: Handlungsrationalität und gesellschaftliche Rationalisierung.* 2 vols. Frankfurt am Main: Suhrkamp, 1981.
Heuser, Magdalene. "Neuedition der Briefe von Louise Adelgunde Victoria Gottsched." In *Chloe: Beiheft zum Daphnis. Editionsdesiderate zur Frühen Neuzeit*, ed. Hans-Gert Roloff and Renate Meincke, 319–39. Amsterdam: Rodopi, 1998.
Kord, Susannah. *Little Detours: The Letters and Plays of Luise Gottsched.* Rochester, NY: Camden House, 2000.
Kording, Inka. "Konstruktionen der Unmittelbarkeit—Individualität in den Brautbriefen Louise Gottscheds." In *Diskurse der Aufklärung: Luise Adelgunde*

Victorie und Johann Christoph Gottsched, ed. Gabriele Ball, Helga Brandes, and Katherine R. Goodman, 65–88. Wiesbaden: Harrassowitz, 2006.

Kording, Inka. *Louise Gottsched—"mit der Feder in der Hand." Briefe aus den Jahren 1730–1762*. Darmstadt: Wissenschaftliche Buchgesellschaft, 1999.

Molière, [Jean-Baptiste Poquelin]. *Les femmes savantes: Comédie en cinq actes*. Ed. Wilhelm Scheffler. Bielefeld: Velhagen und Kalsing, 1914.

Nenon, Monika. *Aus der Fülle der Herzen: Geselligkeit, Briefkultur und Literatur um Sophie von La Roche und Friedrich Heinrich Jacobi*. Würzburg: Königshausen & Neumann, 2005.

Niefanger, Susanne. *Schreibstrategien in moralischen Wochenschriften: Formalstilistische, pragmatische und rhetorische Untersuchungen am Beispiel von Gottscheds "Vernünfftigen Tadlerinnen."* Tübingen: Max Niemeyer, 1997.

Oergel, Maike, ed. *(Re-)Writing the Radical: Enlightenment, Revolution and Cultural Transfer in 1790s Germany, Britain and France*. Berlin: De Gruyter, 2012.

Quéval, Marie Hélène. *Les paradoxes d'Eros; ou, L'amour dans l'oeuvre de Johann Christoph Gottsched*. Bern: Peter Lang, 1999.

Salm, Peter. *Three Modes of Criticism: The Literary Theories of Scherer, Walzel and Staiger*. Cleveland, OH: Press of Case Western Reserve University, 1968.

Scherer, Wilhelm. *Geschichte der deutschen Literatur*. Berlin: Weidmann, 1883.

Schneider, Susanne. "Christiana Maria von Ziegler (1695–1760)." In *Deutsche Frauen der Frühen Neuzeit: Dichterinnen, Malerinnen, Mäzeninnen*, ed. Kerstin Merkel and Heide Wunder, 139–52. Darmstadt: Primus, 2000.

Scudéry, Madeleine de. *Artamène; ou, Le grand Cyrus*. 10 vols. Geneva: Slatkine Reprints, 1972.

Wellbery, David E., ed. *A New History of German Literature*. Cambridge, MA: Harvard University Press, 2004.

Two A Dynamic Interplay
Cooperation between Sophie von La Roche, Christoph Martin Wieland, and Goethe on Their Way to Authorship

Monika Nenon

The final third of the eighteenth century was characterized by social, political, and cultural changes: an increasing move to cities, scientific and technological progress, and an emerging consumer society in German-speaking countries gave rise to a new demand for the dissemination of knowledge and for entertainment. The percentage of the population who could read also increased steadily during this time. New media such as newspapers, journals, and letters accompanied the nascent culture of sociability, and new genres such as epistolary novels provided a space in which these new cultural demands found their expression. The literary public sphere also became more differentiated, as it was beginning to involve not only learned men who were university-educated, but also women who were coming to participate in the literary scene as authors and readers as well.[1]

One important question that can be posed against the backdrop of this changing literary landscape is how it was possible to become an author and establish oneself in the literary marketplace. Of course, the answer is complicated, since it depended on a whole range of factors and was somewhat different in each case. The following study will describe the collaboration between Sophie von La Roche and Christoph Martin Wieland and between her and Johann Wolfgang von Goethe

---

1 See, with regard to the changing literary public sphere, Helen Fronius, who states: "Not only had women entered the market in large numbers, thereby legitimizing each other's presence, but they had a large female readership, which in turn supported their writing." Helen Fronius, *Women and Literature in the Goethe Era 1770–1820: Determined Dilettantes*, Oxford Modern Languages and Literature Monographs (Oxford: Clarendon Press, 2007), 180.

as they were tracing out their respective paths to authorship. It will inquire into the ways that La Roche and Wieland and she and Goethe worked together and mutually supported each other as they cooperated to establish themselves in the literary public sphere. The primary source for this study will be the correspondence she maintained with Wieland and Goethe that documents their interactions. One thing that becomes clear, of course, is that the paths to authorship were very different for women than they were for men in light of the social and cultural conditions of the eighteenth century and the different starting points that follow from those circumstances. Access to education was without doubt one crucial prerequisite for authorship and it was primarily dependent on ancestry, estate, and gender. Moreover, under the patriarchal order of the age, gender was also a decisive factor affecting one's access to the literary market. In spite of this fact, though, there were many women who developed strategies to overcome the obstacles they faced and found their way into the literary public sphere. One of the strategies was to form cooperations with more established (male) writers and to build literary networks. Surprisingly, these relationships were by no means one-sided, but carried mutual benefits. One will find that women played a larger role in the literary public sphere and were more recognized as authors than previously thought.

This study shows that the cooperation between Sophie von La Roche and Wieland and between La Roche and Goethe is best understood as a dynamic interplay between each of these pairs whereby each move one of them makes supports the other person and brings about a new constellation in which that person is now able to reciprocate. The support is thus not only mutual but also constantly evolving.

Sophie von La Roche and Christoph Martin Wieland (1750–1771)

When Sophie von La Roche, or Sophie Gutermann von Gutershofen, and Christoph Martin Wieland met and became engaged in the late summer of 1750, neither of them had yet gained entry into the literary enterprise. Their personal circumstances were problematic and conflicted, but in different ways for each of them. As a twenty-year-old woman, Sophie Gutermann was at an eligible age for marriage and was just putting the painful dissolution of her engagement to the physician Giovanni Bianconi behind her.[2] Wieland was three years younger than Sophie Gutermann and had completed a comprehensive education but

---

2   Giovanni Lodovico Bianconi (1717–81) was personal physician to the prince-bishop of Augsburg. He supported the education of his fiancée through instruction on Italian literature, history, art history, and mathematics. Regarding the

was not sure what his career path would be. His parents wanted him to become a lawyer or a pastor, but he was attracted to the fine arts and wished to devote his life to reading and writing. When, at his parents' home, he discovered letters from his second cousin Sophie Gutermann that fascinated him, he decided to take up correspondence with her. Their relationship thus began as a written exchange, which is significant for the further course of their interactions.

In his first letter to Sophie Gutermann, dated June 1, 1750, he refers to her as a "Deesse" (goddess) whose "excellente ame" (distinguished soul) shines through in her letters and who excels in her perfection.[3] After their first meeting in August of 1750, he composes another letter, entitled "Ma bien aimée Sophie" (my very beloved Sophie), in which he presents an extensive list of the ideal feminine characteristics. These include charm, beauty, tenderness, and a fine morality, but he emphasizes: "Il s'entend, qu'elle doit être delivrée des plus grossiers prejugés des hommes ou du moins qu'elle doit avoir assez d'esprit pour admettre l'illumination de la raison, qui dissipe ces nuages, et qu'elle doit être assez curieuse pour s'informer de ce qui peut servir à la rendre plus sage et plus lumineuse" (It goes without saying, that she must be free from the most basic human prejudices or must at least have enough of a mind to be able to recognize the light of reason that disperses these clouds, and that she must be curious enough to educate herself, which can serve to make her wiser and more enlightened) (*WBr*, I, 7). It is striking that Wieland's depiction of the ideal image of a woman includes not only sensitivity and moral virtues, but also competencies and abilities such as reason, wit, freedom from prejudices, and a curiosity for learning. This feminine ideal displays traits derived from the Enlightenment and from sensibility (*Empfindsamkeit*) that also incorporate older classical and Christian notions of the "beautiful soul."[4] He also writes that

---

circumstances that led to the dissolution of the engagement and Sophie's pathway to authorship, see also Monika Nenon, *Autorschaft und Frauenbildung: Das Beispiel Sophie von La Roche* (Würzburg: Königshausen & Neumann, 1988), 27–8.

3 Christoph Martin Wieland to Sophie Gutermann, June 1, 1750, in *Wielands Briefwechsel*, ed. Hans Werner Seiffert (hereafter *WBr*), Vol. I (Berlin: Akademie, 1963), 1. All translations from French or German into English are by Thomas Nenon unless otherwise stated.

4 See Ralf Konersmann, "Seele, schöne; Seelenschönheit," in *Historisches Wörterbuch der Philosophie*, Vol. IX, ed. Joachim Ritter (Basel: Schwabe, 1995), 89–92. About the concept of the beautiful soul in the eighteenth century, cf. Marie Wokalek, *Die schöne Seele als Denkfigur: Zur Semantik von Gewissen und Geschmack bei Rousseau, Wieland, Schiller, Goethe* (Göttingen: Wallstein, 2011). Wokalek states that the "beautiful soul" becomes an important concept in the second half of the eighteenth century. She describes the changes in the concept from Plato to

Sophie perfectly personifies this ideal and that this is why she means so much to him: "Vous êtes et serez toujours la seule qui peut satisfaire à mon esprit et à mon ame" (You are and will remain the only one who can fulfill my mind and my soul) (*WBr*, I, 9). This makes possible the "harmony of souls" between the two of them. Although it is obvious that Wieland is projecting a specific ideal onto Sophie Gutermann, we should also explore why Wieland finds his notions about feminine ideals confirmed in her.

Differences in Educational Backgrounds
Sophie Gutermann[5] came from a family of scholars in Augsburg that placed high value on the acquisition of knowledge, skills, and virtues in the tradition of the middle class and lower aristocracy in the eighteenth century.[6] Her father, Georg Friedrich Gutermann, who was originally from Biberach and served as dean of the medical faculty in Augsburg, was interested in the newest results from the natural sciences, introduced many medical reforms in Augsburg, and regularly hosted a Tuesday Circle in his house that brought together a group of learned men. Sophie Gutermann's father took charge of his daughter's education, providing her access to books and helping her learn to read and develop a love of learning at the early age of three.[7] The first texts she read were typical for a pietistically oriented home: namely the Bible, and devotional works by Johann Arndt and August Hermann Francke. However, in this age of the Enlightenment she did not limit her reading to religious texts, but also read extensively on a wide range of subjects.

Wilhelm von Humboldt and points out that it was used for men and women. Whereas the beautiful soul in antiquity was connected to virtue, in Christianity God's love would be added. Plato, Socrates, the Stoics, classical rhetoric, Renaissance ethics, the Scottish moral-sense discourse, natural law, and Rousseau's social-political thought all contributed to the notion. Wieland's understanding of the beautiful soul is related to the Good and the Beautiful. The concepts of moral grace, *kalogathia*, and the virtuoso play an important role here.

5   About the family relations of Sophie Gutermann see: Gabriele von König-Warthausen, "Sophie von La Roche, geb. Gutermann," in *Lebensbilder aus Schwaben und Franken*, Vol. X, ed. Max Miller and Robert Uhland (Stuttgart: Kommission für Geschichtliche Landeskunde in Baden-Württemberg, 1966), 101–25; and Claudia Bamberg, *Sophie von La Roche* (Frankfurt am Main: Freies Deutsches Hochstift, 2007).

6   On the value system, see Michael Maurer, *Die Biographie des Bürgers: Lebensformen und Denkweisen in der formativen Phase des deutschen Bürgertums (1680–1815)* (Göttingen: Vandenhoeck & Ruprecht, 1996).

7   Sophie von La Roche published an autobiographical essay in her last work: *Melusinens Sommer-Abende*, ed. Christoph Martin Wieland (Halle: Verlage der N. Societäts=Buch=u. Kunsthandlung, 1806), IV–LVI (VI).

According to her own account, she familiarized herself with natural history, astronomy, and mathematics as well as the histories of various peoples. Her mother encouraged her to learn languages and supported her artistic talent in music, drawing, and painting. It was also typical for this time that she learned handicrafts such as needlepoint. She learned French and Italian at home. Many of her letters were written in French, which became her preferred language for writing. There is one subject area that her strict father forbade his daughter to learn: Sophie Gutermann was denied the study of classical literature and philosophy even though she fervently requested instruction in this area from him: "Mit 13 Jahren wollte der große Brucker[8] meine Erziehung und Bildung meines Geistes besorgen. Ich bat meinen Vater auf Knien um die Einwilligung, aber er wollte nicht" (When I was thirteen, the great Brucker wanted to provide for the education and development of my mind. I begged my father on my knees for his permission, but he did not want to give it).[9] Her desire for systematic instruction violates the limits of what is permitted for a girl's education at the time. Her father did not want her to be a "learned woman," but to be a woman who is educated enough to be prepared for marriage with a man of the appropriate estate.[10] The fact that Sophie Gutermann, in contrast to Wieland and Goethe, did not receive a thorough education in the classical languages and literatures will have a significant impact on her pathway to authorship.

Around 1750, the art of poetry was still understood as a rule-governed craft. Poets were generally scholars who had familiarized themselves with the works of classical poets and oriented their own verses on these models. Wieland had received a thorough education that was centered above all around the Latin language and literature, first from his father and different private tutors, and then later systematically continuing at the boarding school Klosterberge in Magdeburg. At the age of eight, he was reading works by Cornelius Nepos, and later also Horace, Virgil, and Cicero. He also read Gottsched's *Versuch einer critischen Dichtkunst vor die Deutschen* (Essay on a German Critical Poetic Theory) and poems by Barthold Heinrich Brockes. He composed his first verses at an early age, as Friedrich Sengle notes:

---

8 Jakob Brucker, pastor and historian of philosophy in Augsburg.
9 Sophie von La Roche to Johann Caspar Hirzel, November 8, 1771, in Michael Maurer, ed., *Ich bin mehr Herz als Kopf: Sophie von La Roche. Ein Lebensbild in Briefen* (Munich: Beck, 1983) (hereafter *SvLRBr*), 155.
10 Women's education at the time often depended on male mentors such as fathers, brothers, or friends. See for instance Steffen Martus, *Aufklärung: Das deutsche 18. Jahrhundert. Ein Epochenbild* (Berlin: Rowohlt, 2015), 389–90.

At the age of twelve he progressed to Latin verses and longer poems. He wrote a 600-line poem about Echo in Anacreontic style and a longer poem, "Concerning the Pygmies," that was a satire on the headmaster's wife. He undertook his first attempts at epic poetry too: when he was thirteen, he began a heroic poem on the destruction of Jerusalem. He later burned all these attempts, which his mother had preserved in whole notebooks.[11]

At Klosterberge, he also engaged intensely with Bayle's *Dictionnaire* as well as with Fontenelle, d'Argens, Voltaire, and Demokrit, along with Leibniz and Wolff. His reading of German literature included, above all, Klopstock's "Messias" and Haller's didactic poems. In addition to Latin and French, he learned Hebrew and some Greek, which he later studied at the university in Tübingen in depth. Wieland reported of himself that by the age of sixteen he had read "fast alle Autoren des goldenen und silbernen Zeitalters" (almost all the authors of the golden and silver ages).[12]

If one compares the educations of these two aspiring authors, the differences are very clear. Whereas Wieland received a comprehensive and systematic education through his father, private tutors, a boarding school, and the university, in which Latin, Greek, and Hebrew played a central role, Sophie Gutermann's education was much less systematic and was led by mentors such as her father; her first fiancé, Bianconi; and her mother. There was no regular instruction and no teaching at all in the classical languages and literatures, which her father had expressly forbidden for her. She was of course not an isolated case but, rather, typical for her time.[13] Even though both Sophie von La Roche and Wieland came from households of the educated middle class, and thus had easier access to books and were supported in acquiring skills and knowledge, gender determined several differences in their education. As a woman, Sophie Gutermann was groomed not for a professional career but for the roles assigned to women of her class in the eighteenth century as a wife, mother, and homemaker. Sophie Gutermann and Christoph Martin Wieland thus brought very different educational backgrounds with them. Nonetheless, one should also acknowledge that Sophie Gutermann's education was unusually broad for a woman in the eighteenth century and that she continued to work on extending her knowledge her entire life.

---

11 See Friedrich Sengle, *C. M. Wieland* (Stuttgart: Metzler, 1949), 18–19.
12 Sengle, *C. M. Wieland*, 22.
13 With regard to gender-specific education see Fronius, *Women and Literature*, 94–5.

Wieland as a Mentor on the Way to Authorship (1750–1753)

After their meeting in Biberach at the end of August 1750, Sophie Gutermann and Christoph Martin Wieland fell rapturously in love and became engaged soon afterwards. The lovers talked about their common interest in literature and they started exchanging letters as Wieland was beginning his studies in Tübingen. Wieland was so taken by her vivacious spirit, her intellectual curiosity, and her wish to become a writer herself that he decided to support her journey to authorship and make it his project too. A letter to Sophie Gutermann makes clear that he considers women capable of the art of poetics. It is entitled "Einige Betrachtungen über die Dichtkunst überhaupt/1. Stück" (Some reflections on the Art of Poetics in General/First Part):

> In sonderheit halte ich das schöne Geschlecht vor ungemein geschikt zur Dichtkunst, weil es uns überhaupt an natürlicher Geschiklichkeit dazu, an Zärtlichkeit des Herzens und der Empfindungen und am Geschmak weit überlegen ist. Die Exempel der vortreflichsten Dichterinnen unter den Griechen, Lateinern, Italiänern, Franzosen, Engländern u:Deutschen bestättigen diese Anmerkung.
> (In particular I consider the fair sex unusually qualified for the art of poetics because they are far superior to us in their natural abilities in terms of the tenderness of their hearts and their feelings and in terms of taste. The example of outstanding female poets and writers among the Greeks, the Romans, the Italians, French, English, and Germans confirms this observation.)
> (To Sophie Gutermann, Tübingen, between January and March 1751, *WBr*, I, 13)

He emphasizes women's suitability for poetics because of their natural talents, capabilities of sensitivity, and taste, and confirms that he is well aware of the literary history across Europe of female poets and writers. He is fully confident in Sophie's ability to become a writer and sets himself the task of actively supporting the development of her literary abilities:

> Wie erfreut bin ich nicht, Mein Engel, von Ihnen versichert zu seyn, daß Sie an edlem zärtlichen und tugendhaftem Herzen alle Dichter und Dichterinnen der ganzen Welt übertreffen, und daß in Ihrem Geiste alle die Fähigkeiten liegen, welche die göttliche Poesie erfordert. Kurz, Sie sind geschikt eine volkomne Dichterin zu werden; Sie haben mir davon Proben gegeben; und was kan mir angenehmer seyn, als zur Entwicklung und aufklärung Ihrer natürlichen ungemeinen Geschiklichkeit etwas beyzutragen.

(How glad I am, my angel, to be confident that you surpass all the male and female poets in the entire world in your nobly tender and virtuous heart, and that all the abilities are present in your soul that divine poetry requires. In short, you are capable of becoming a perfect poet; you have provided me samples of this; and what can be more pleasant than to help contribute to the development and enlightenment of your natural uncommon skills.)

(WBr, I, 14)

In order to reach this goal, Wieland gave her lessons in poetics, which according to the views of the day is a craft based on rules that the poet can learn and must master. In Wieland's view, Sophie had the necessary talent, taste, and sensitivity, but was not yet familiar with the rules of poetics because of the gaps in her education up until this point. Wieland wanted to help her eliminate that gap by recommending that she read works on poetics by Gottsched and Breitinger to help her acquire skills in the craft of writing. In the same letter, for example, Wieland describes the practice of a poet who imitates nature with words in the same way a painter does with colors, and explains to her the principles of the "poetic perspective" (WBr, I, 15). He especially emphasizes the significance of the "Beywörter" (adjectives) that the "unentberliche Eigenschaft eines Dinges anzeigen" (indicate the essential property of a thing) (WBr, I, 14). In order to make his theoretical instructions more intuitive, he quotes verses from Haller: "Bald wenn der trübe Herbst die falben Blätter pflükket, / und Sich die kühle Luft in graue Nebel hüllt" (Soon when the cloudy fall the colored leaves does pluck, / and the cool air cloaks itself in gray fog) (WBr, I, 15).

The letters bear witness to just how seriously Wieland strived to develop his fiancée's literary skills. This is important because Sophie Gutermann at that point did not possess the required familiarity with poetics in contrast to many of her male colleagues, but Wieland recognized her talent and imparted to her the knowledge necessary to develop her literary abilities. What is even more important is that he believes in her as a writer, encourages her, recognizes her, and thereby gives her the self-confidence to take up her pen and begin to compose as a writer. Wieland supports her writing in German, which at first is not easy for her since her preferred language is French. She does not have much practice in German, but she responds to Wieland's suggestions with her first literary attempt by sending some verses and a fable to which Wieland reacts with great enthusiasm, praise, and constructive criticism. In a letter to his mother, he speaks highly of Sophie Gutermann's verses (Tübingen, March 7, 1751, WBr, I, 17) and tells her that he considers the prose in her fables "unvergleichlich" (incomparable) (end of July 1751, *WBr*, I, 20). The example of the fable illustrates well how he proceeds as a mentor: "Sie gefällt mir immer besser je öfter ich sie lese. Ich habe die kleinen Fehler der schwäbischen Mundart verbessert, und sie ist nunmehr ganz fehlerfrey. Sie hat alle guten Eigenschaften einer Fabel. Sie ist sinnreich, natürlich, edel ausgedrückt und das morale fließt sehr ungezwungen. Ich danke Ihnen nochmals für dieses artige Stück" (It pleases me ever more each time I read it. I have corrected the small errors in Swabian dialect and it is now free of errors. It has all the good characteristics of a fable. It makes good sense, is natural, nobly expressed and the moral flows very freely. I thank you once again for this fine piece) (*WBr*, I, 21). He offers critiques of its language and style and makes some grammatical suggestions that he communicates to her in a charming way that is not discouraging. At the same time, he explicitly praises the composition and execution of the fable. This constructive mix of criticism and praise makes Wieland an effective mentor for Sophie Gutermann.

Wieland recognizes Sophie Gutermann as an emerging author, he takes her seriously and supports her. He recommends readings for her, expands her knowledge of poetics, and provides constructive criticism of her language and style. Especially important is his confidence in her abilities and potential as a writer: "Wie freue ich mich schon im Geiste, daß das Bildnis meiner Geliebten einst das Portrait einer Chatelet, Bassi, Gottschedin etc. so sehr überstrahlen wird" (How much I already look forward in my mind to the image of how my beloved will one day surpass that of a Chatelet, Bassi, Luise Gottsched, etc.) (*WBr*, I, 19–20). His prognosis would one day turn out to be true, even if it took several years before Sophie von La Roche introduced herself to a literary public. We should now ask the opposite question: namely what role Sophie Gutermann played for Wieland in his ambitions as an author during these years.

Sophie Gutermann as Friend and Muse

Looking back later, Wieland wrote to Sophie von La Roche about the effects of their relationship on him: "Nichts ist wohl gewisser, als daß ich, wofern uns das Schicksal nicht im Jahre 1750 zusammengebracht hätte, kein Dichter geworden wäre" (Nothing is more certain than the fact that, if fate had not brought us together in the year 1750, I would not have become a poet) (December 20, 1805, *WBr*, XVI.1, 515). This passage is striking because it might seem that he was pre-programmed to become a writer based on his talents and education. However, in the first half of the eighteenth century, there were very few who succeeded in making their living from their writing. Most authors earned their living other ways and pursued writing in their free time. Wieland's father envisaged a career in law for his son and expected him to begin studying law at the University of Tübingen in the fall of 1750. Wieland later wrote to Johann Jakob Bodmer about this period: "Ich kam hierauf hieher ... Jura zu lernen. Ich fand aber keinen Geschmak daran ... Ich schrieb im Februar, Merz, April des 1751 J. das Lehrgedicht" (I came here ... to study law, but I did not find any taste for it ... In February, March, April of 1750, I wrote the didactic poem) (March 6, 1752, *WBr*, I, 51). The *Lehrgedicht* refers to Wieland's first major literary work, *Die Natur der Dinge* (The Nature of Things), in which he lays out philosophically and poetically the relationships among God, human beings, and nature: a work that Leif Ludwig Albertsen has characterized as "das größte deutsche Wehrgedicht gegen Materialismus und Deismus" (the greatest German poetic rebuttal of materialism and deism).[14] Wieland describes the origin of the poem as follows in his preface to the third edition in 1770:

> Das System dieses Lehrgedichts hat einen Ursprung, wodurch es sich vielleicht von allen andern Systemen unterscheidet, die seit Erschaffung der Welt zur Auflösung der unauflösbarsten aller Aufgaben ausgebrütet worden sind. Es war die Frucht eines enthusiastischen Spaziergangs eines noch sehr jungen und sehr platonischen Liebhabers mit seiner Geliebten, an einem sehr heißen Sommertag des Jahres 1750, nach Anhörung einer etwas kalten Predigt über den Text: Gott ist die Liebe; und wenn die Musen die poetische Darstellung so gewiss eingegeben hätten, als die Liebe das System, so würde es die Nachsicht, womit es im Jahre 1751 aufgenommen wurde, wenigstens von einer Seite gerechtfertigt haben.[15]

> (The system in this didactic poem has an origin that perhaps distinguishes it from all other systems. It was the fruit of an enthusiastic walk by a still very young and very platonic lover with his beloved on a very hot summer day in the year 1750 after hearing a somewhat cold sermon on the text 'God is love'; and if the muses have undoubtedly inspired this poetic presentation just as love inspired the system, then the charity with which it was received in 1751 was justified from at least one perspective.)

---

14 Leif Ludwig Albertsen, *Das Lehrgedicht: Eine Geschichte der antikisierenden Sachepik in der neueren deutschen Literatur* (Aarhus: Akademisk Boghandel, 1967), 317, quoted in Jutta Heinz, ed., *Wieland Handbuch: Leben-Werk-Wirkung* (Stuttgart: Metzler, 2008), 153.

15 Christoph Martin Wieland, "Vorbericht zur dritten Ausgabe von 1770, *Die Natur der Dinge*," in C. M. Wieland, *Sämmtliche Werke XIII*, ed. Hamburger Stiftung zur Förderung von Wissenschaft und Kultur in collaboration with Wieland-Archiv and Dr. Hans Radspieler (Nördlingen: C. H. Beck, 1984), 5–6.

In response to the wishes of Sophie Gutermann, Wieland worked out his worldview in *Die Natur der Dinge*, which was soon published and which he sent to Bodmer in Zürich in December of 1751, requesting his support and help. Dieter Martin has identified three other texts that were composed around the time of *Die Natur der Dinge* and emphasizes the influence that Sophie Gutermann had on them too:

> Just how much the young Wieland was fixated on his slightly older girl friend Sophie Gutermann, how much he at the same time strove to exchange the role of the student for that of the private and public teacher and thereby has written himself into a broad spectrum of literary forms of expression, can be seen in the three texts, each in a different genre, that stem from the same time as the composition of the *Natur der Dinge*. All three are accompanied by a personal correspondence, but one can recognize how he is trying to make them independent works.[16]

He then lists the texts (a letter, a poem, an essay in letter form), two of which have already been mentioned in relationship to their significance for Sophie Gutermann: (1) *La portrait de ma charmante Sophie* (The Portrait of my Charming Sophie), (2) *Tugend! O wie reizend schön bist du!* (Virtue! How Charmingly Beautiful You Are!) (*WBr.* I, 11–13), (3) *Einige Betrachtungen über die Dichtkunst überhaupt: 1 Stük* (Some Reflections on Poetry in General: Part I) (*WBr*, I, 13–16). Shortly afterwards Wieland composed the *Lobgesang auf die Liebe* (Song of Praise for Love), which was accepted by the publisher Hemmerde in Halle and appeared even before the didactic poem. In relation to this song of praise, Wieland stresses the significance of Sophie Gutermann (Diotima) as the muse for his poetry: "Das Lob welches dem 'Lobgesang auf die Liebe' darinn beygelegt worden, gehört eigentlich der vortreflichen Diotima, die den Dichter eine so erhabene Art zu lieben gelehrt hat. Ohne dieses würde er vielleicht nur ein tibullisches Lied gesungen haben" (The praise that is contained in the "Song of Praise for Love" belongs to the splendid Diotima who has taught the poet to love in such a sublime way. Without her he would have perhaps sung just a Tibullian elegy) (Tübingen, January 19, 1752, *WBr*, I, 32–3). In another letter to Klopstock from April 22, 1753, he writes that Sophie Gutermann "seiner Phantasie Schwung gäbe" (gets his imagination going) (*WBr*, I, 160).

---

16 Dieter Martin, "Frühwerk," in Heinz, *Wieland Handbuch*, 150–69 (157).

Bodmer, the literary critic and "father of the young men" whose attention Wieland sought in several letters describing himself, was so impressed with Wieland's works that he invited the fledgling poet to visit and live with him in Zürich. Wieland, who wishes for no other profession than literature, sees in Bodmer the possibility of continuing a life devoted to literature. He arrives in Zürich in the fall of 1752, following in the footsteps of Klopstock, who already had enjoyed Bodmer's support, even though his sometimes excessive lifestyle did not always please his mentor. Klopstock incants his love to his "girl" Maria Sophia Schmidt among other places in his "Oden an Fanny" (Odes to Fanny): *Die künftige Geliebte* (The Future Beloved), and *An Fanny, Selmar und Selma*. Wieland is familiar with this relationship and tries to stylize himself and his girlfriend according to this model: "Ich bin gewiß, dass der Herr Klopstock liebt, und ich glaube, daß seine Geliebte Ihnen sehr ähnlich, aber doch unvollkommener als Sie ist. So ist es bei uns vieren gerade umgekehrt. Ich weiche unstreitig dem Herrn Klopstock an vortrefflichen Eigenschaften, und seine Geliebte weicht Ihnen" (I know for certain that Herr Klopstock is in love and I believe that his beloved is very like you, but less perfect than you are. So things among the four of us are exactly the opposite. I must defer without a doubt to Herr Klopstock's superior qualities, and she must defer to you) (Tübingen, end of July 1751, *WBr*, I, 20). Just as Klopstock says that his "beloved" serves as the inspiration for his works, Wieland sees Sophie Gutermann as the muse for his poetry, as his "Doris" or "Diotima." He composes an "Ode to Doris" and sends it to Pastor Schinz in Zürich, who also has a girlfriend, Barbara Meyer. He says that Sophie Gutermann would like to correspond with her and seeks Schinz's approval for her to do that. The correspondence would give both of them the opportunity to practice writing in German and should be conducted under the names of "Doris" and "Daphne." Sophie Gutermann and Barbara Meyer do begin writing to each other. Sophie asks, for example, about Barbara's assessment of the letters by Mme. Lambert and Elisabeth Rowe-Singer, whose example they should follow. In other passages, she describes the daily routine in Wieland's parents' household, where she spends her morning "reading and writing" and then spends the afternoon in the social company of relatives and friends.[17]

Wieland even asks his muse to transpose herself imaginatively into the figure of Asenat from Bodmer's epos *Jacob and Joseph,* and to write down her thoughts and feelings in that role for Bodmer, a request that

---

17 See Sophie Gutermann to Barbara Meyer, Biberach, December 19, 1752, in *SvLRBr*, 49.

she grants.[18] Sophie Gutermann plays the game, but her impatience grows as Wieland makes no effort to find a position and some financial stability, which would be a requirement for their marriage. Faced with pressure from her family, Sophie Gutermann ended the engagement and married Georg Michael Frank La Roche towards the end of 1753 to put an end to her insecure position. With the permission of her husband, her correspondence with Wieland continued nonetheless.

We have seen how Wieland's relationship with Sophie Gutermann, their conversations and correspondence led to his first literary works and pedagogical reflections, some of which were published and attracted the attention of the literary public. These made it possible for him to go to Zürich and begin his career as an author. Sophie Gutermann provided emotional support and encouragement for Wieland to pursue his dreams as an author as he provided the same for her. In addition, she, as his only intellectual conversation partner in Biberach, also served as the source of inspiration for his literary and pedagogical endeavors. His relationship with her played an essential role in his development and the realization of his aspirations to make literature his profession. Wieland, on the other hand, played a decisive role as mentor and editor to Sophie von La Roche.

Sophie von La Roche's Pathway into the Literary Scene (1760–1772)

Wieland and Sophie von La Roche did not see each other for the next eight years. Wieland spent his time in Zürich and Bern, where he earned his living as a private tutor and continued writing his poetry and other literary works. Sophie von La Roche lived in Warthausen by Biberach and then later at the court in Mainz (1754–61), where her husband, Georg Michael Frank von La Roche, served as counselor and private secretary to the Mainz elector, Friedrich Graf von Stadion, who as the Grand Court Master in Mainz had one of the most important administrative positions in the empire.[19] The correspondence continued

---

18 Sophie Gutermann to Johann Jakob Bodmer, Biberach, January 30, 1753, in *SvLRBr*, 50–1. Cf. Monika Nenon, "The Genius and His Muse: Women as Objects of Imagination for Klopstock and Wieland," *Lessing Yearbook/Jahrbuch* 28 (1996): 199–231; Brigitte Schnegg, "Die Fahrt auf dem Zürichsee: Eine geschlechtergeschichtliche Deutung des Zerwürfnisses zwischen Bodmer und Klopstock im Jahre 1750," in *Ordnung, Politik und Geselligkeit der Geschlechter im 18. Jahrhundert*, ed. Ulrike Weckel *et al.* (Göttingen: Wallstein, 1998), 119–43.
19 Michael Embach, "Georg Michael Frank von La Roche (1720–1788)," in *Meine liebe grüne Stube: Die Schriftstellerin Sophie von La Roche in ihrer Speyrer Zeit (1780–1786)*, ed. Klaus Haag and Jürgen Vordestemann (Speyer: Marsilius, 2005), 45–64.

actively during this period nonetheless,[20] because their friendship based on a common love of literature still remained, just as Wieland had predicted after the dissolution of their engagement in 1753: "Sollte ihre neue Verbindung die zärtliche Zuneigung unserer Seelen, die sich auf die wahre Liebe des Guten und Schönen gründet, hinweg nehmen? Nein! das halte ich für unmöglich!" (Should your new connection detract from the tender attraction of our souls that is based on true love of the good and the beautiful? No! I consider that impossible!) (Wieland to Sophie Gutermann, Zürich, December 22, 1753, *WBr*, I, 188). Wieland returned in May 1760 to Biberach, where he was employed as the city scribe. After Sophie von La Roche informed Wieland in June of 1760 that she and her family were soon going to be coming back to Warthausen, Wieland wrote how elated he was that he would now have his trusted friend close to him again: "Vous etes la seule personne qui me comprend parfaitement ... Vous serés mon amie, ma confidente, la dépositaire des secrets de mon ame ... vous serés ma seur, je serai votre frere, et le digne et heureux la Roche sera le troisieme dans notre amitié" (You are the only person who understands me perfectly ... You will be my friend, my confidante, the depository of the secrets of my soul ... you will be my sister, I will be your brother, and the dignified and fortunate La Roche will be the third person in our friendship) (Wieland to Sophie La Roche, Biberach, June 14, 1760, *WBr*, III, 3–4). For the next few years, Sophie von La Roche would faithfully fulfill this role as friend, trustee of his soul, and "sister." She helped Wieland when he had financial or romantic problems, and played a mediating role when conflicts arose between Warthausen and Biberach. For two years, Wieland served as teacher to her son Fritz. As far as his authorship was concerned, since at least the publication of his *Geschichte des Agathon* (History of Agathon) (1766–7), Wieland had been a well-known author. La Roche provided her support with recognition and praise, and then later in Ehrenbreitstein with help marketing *Agathon* by soliciting subscriptions to it. The refined rococo culture in Warthausen offered distractions and entertainment. The current events in the city of Biberach provided material for the *Geschichte der Abderiten* (History of the Abderites).

Wieland for his part now increasingly serves as a mentor to her in her journey to authorship. Looking back later, she writes about him: "In Wieland, meinem Verwandten, sah ich Schöne Wissenschaft"

---

20 See *WBr*, Vol. III. *Briefe der Biberacher Amtsjahre (6. Juni 1760–20. Mai 1769)* (Berlin: Akademie, 1975). There are more than 100 letters from Wieland to Sophie von La Roche, whereas there are only a few from Sophie von La Roche to Wieland.

(In Wieland, my relative, I saw arts and literature).[21] Sophie von La Roche had returned to Warthausen in July of 1761, where Graf Stadion chose to live in his retirement. He assembled a court in the French rococo style, with Georg Michael Frank von La Roche as his secretary and Sophie von La Roche as the lady of the court. One of her tasks in this role was to entertain the count with interesting conversation. To keep herself informed in a whole range of areas, she made rich use of the count's extensive library, which contained the most recent literature and philosophy from France and England. Later she wrote about this time in somewhat idealized terms:

> schönere Tage sah ich nie ... als die in Warthausen von 1761 bis 1768 waren. Denken Sie an die tägliche Gesellschaft—Graf Stadion—seine zwey Töchter, die Frau Gräfinn von Schall, und Gräfinn Max, jetzige Fürstinn von Buchau—La Roche—Wieland—eine auserlesene sehr zahlreiche Bibliothek—eine grosse Sammlung physicalischer und mathematischer Instrumente aller Art—eine schöne weitverbreitete Gegend—ein edles grosses Schloß auf einem freundlichen Berg—ein Garten, in dessen Alleen man in der Kutsche herumfuhr—Feldbau—Sennerey in der größten Vollkommenheit.[22]

(better days I never saw ... than those in Warthausen between 1761 and 1768. Think of the daily society—Graf Stadion—his two daughters, the Frau Gräfinn von Schall, the Gräfin Max, now the Fürstin von Buchau—La Roche—Wieland—an exquisite and extensive library—a great collection of physical and mathematical instruments—a noble grand chateau on a friendly mountain—a garden in which one drove around in carriages—agriculture—stock-breeding in the most perfect way.)

She learned English; read various journals each day in order to expand what she knew; and, at the suggestion of her husband, engaged in a correspondence in French with the Abbé La Choux in Paris. The public functions as a lady of the court allowed her to extend the boundaries of her education through access to the extensive library, the acquisition of additional language skills, and the participation in the social life of the court. Her frequent interactions with Wieland were important

---

21 Sophie von La Roche, *Pomona für Teutschlands Töchter* (Speier: [n.p.], 1783/4), 428.
22 Sophie von La Roche, *Briefe über Mannheim* (Zürich: Orell, Geßner, Füßli, 1791), 354–5.

too. Wieland sent Sophie von La Roche and her husband his newest works, for example his Shakespeare translations, the *Geschichte des Agathon*, and the poems "Musarion" and "Idris und Zenide." Sophie von La Roche apparently responded in writing with both praise and criticism (Wieland to Sophie La Roche, Biberach, November 17, 1767 *WBr*, III, 480–2). Wieland's letters from the period also testify to La Roche's increasing activity as a writer herself. He receives a "Silesian anecdote" that he strongly praises "von einigen grammatischen Fehlern abgesehen" (with the exception of a few grammatical mistakes) (Wieland to Sophie La Roche, May 2, 1767, *WBr*, III, 452–4). She sends him some "contes moraux" (moral tales) (Wieland to Sophie La Roche, May 16–17, 1767, *WBr*, III, 457–9); later, some "Lettres à C." (Letters to C.) (Wieland to Sophie La Roche, Biberach, November 17, 1767, *WBr*, III, 481) are mentioned, and a "petit roman françois-Anglois" (a small English–French novel) (Wieland to Sophie La Roche, Erfurt, October 19, 1769, *WBr*, IV, 50–1). In this period, Wieland functions once again as a mentor who strives to improve her expression and style more through praise than criticism, and thereby actively supports her literary efforts. "Sie wollen wissen, was ich von Ihrem Deutsch halte.—Ohne alle Complimente, viel, viel Gutes. Ihre Schreibart ist überhaupt sehr gut und schön, in welcher von beyden Sprachen Sie auch schreiben. Aber man merkt, daß Ihnen die Uebung fehlt, und daß Sie noch nicht viel besondere Aufmerksamkeit auf die Sprache gewandt haben" (You want to know what I think of your German.—Without any compliments, [it is] very, very good. Your writing style in general is very good and beautiful, no matter in which of the two languages you write. But one notices that you lack practice and that you have not yet paid special attention to the language) (Wieland to Sophie La Roche, Biberach, between November 5 and 17, 1767, *WBr*, III, 477).

In February of 1768, Sophie von La Roche had now begun the composition of the novel *Geschichte des Fräuleins von Sternheim* (The History of Lady Sophia Sternheim), and Wieland received the first letters that would be part of the novel. He finds them "tres interessantes" (very interesting) (Wieland to Sophie La Roche, Biberach, February or March, 1768, *WBr*, III, 507). Sophie von La Roche expressly requests that he read the letters carefully and provide constructive criticism: "seit den drey Briefen (aus Frl. von Sternheim), die Sie geleßen, sind noch viere fertig geworden ... bitte Sie um unserer Freundschaft willen, einige minuten zu seiner DurchLeßung zu verwenden, und Ihre gedanken hie u. da neben hin zu schreiben" (since the three letters that you read, four more have been finished ... I ask you for the sake of our friendship to take a few minutes to read through them and to write out your thoughts about them here and there) (Sophie La Roche to Wieland, Warthausen, February 25, 1770, *WBr*, IV, 97). Wieland accepted this role as mentor and editor, and provided constructive criticism throughout the entire time the novel was being composed. He praised its style, the way it expresses feeling, and its organization, and he offered some suggestions for improvement: "Parlons ... des lettres de Votre Bösewicht ... Je les ai lues deux ou trois fois avec bien plus d'attention que les critiques ordinaires ... et j'en ai été tout à fait content ... Vous avez menagé le tout avec un art, qui ne paroît pas appartenir à une Dame, qui assurément n'a jamais étudié la théorie de l'art de composer" (Let's talk about the letters by your villain ... I have read them two or three times with much more attention than the ordinary critics ... and I was completely happy. You managed the whole thing with a skill that does not appear to belong to a lady who certainly has never studied the theory of the art of composing) (Wieland to Sophie La Roche, Erfurt, December 16, 1769, *WBr*, IV, 71). Wieland has no doubts that this work should be published and he decides that he should actively help Sophie von La Roche to find a publisher: "Allerdings, beste Freundin, verdient Ihre *Sternheim* gedruckt zu werden; und sie verdient es nicht nur; nach meiner vollen Überzeugung erweisen Sie Ihrem Geschlecht einen wirklichen Dienst dadurch. Sie soll und muß gedruckt werden und ich werde Ihr Pflegevater seyn. Reich soll sie in einer nicht üppig gezierten, aber simpel schönen Ausgabe verlegen" (Certainly, my best friend, your *Sternheim* deserves to be published; and it not only deserves to be; I am fully convinced that you are providing a genuine service to your sex by doing so. It should and must be published and I will serve as the foster-father who cares for it. Reich should publish it, not in a luxuriously decorated edition, but in a nice, simple one).[23] Wieland also took care of the copy-editing, made some suggestions about the title, and encouraged her to continue the novel in a sequel. Both parts were to appear together so that they would sell better. It appears that it was through Wieland's connections that the *Geschichte des Fräuleins von Sternheim* was published in Leipzig by the publisher Weidmanns Erben und Reich in 1771. Wieland offered his encouragement and a positive assessment of the work's literary quality. He negotiated an honorarium of 20 ducats for the second volume, which is modest in comparison to the honorarium he normally received for his own works.[24]

---

23 Christoph Martin Wieland to Sophie La Roche, Erfurt, end of April 1770, in *SvLRBr*, 104.
24 See Barbara Becker-Cantarino, "Autorschaft: Zum Briefwechsel von Sophie von La Roche und Christoph Martin Wieland," in *Vom Verkehr mit Dichtern und Gespenstern: Figuren der Autorschaft in der Briefkultur*, ed. Jochen Strobel (Heidelberg: Winter, 2006), 61–78 (68).

However, what cannot be denied is that Wieland constructively and continuously supported an author who was completely unknown in literary circles and played a key role in the composition and publication of her first novel. Some of his criticisms in the introduction[25] to the novel may appear too harsh, but his positive role in supporting this project from the very outset through to its completion should also be recognized. Sophie von La Roche's novel *Geschichte des Fräuleins von Sternheim* is a continuation of the French and English tradition of epistolary novels popularized by Samuel Richardson and Jean-Jacques Rousseau that had proven very successful in the preceding decades. She published a novel in German that certainly compared well to those of her predecessors and was immediately translated into other languages. In choosing this form she took up a contemporary genre that played an important part in the development of a literary culture and is a specifically modern development, as Gisbert Ter-Nedden and Robert Vellusig have recently reminded us: "The maxim of the 'new' novel is: do not inform the audience about things that one can know through past events, but create an awareness of participating in how things have been, of experiencing a past presence in the open horizon of its unfolding."[26] Previously the novel had occupied the "lowest position in the hierarchy of genres, but it would become the 'central genre' of the modern age."[27] The epistolary novel is especially suited to allowing the readers to participate actively in the events, an effect that Ter-Nedden has called the "cinematic effect of the epistolary novel," which is why it has the effect of being an important step on the way to late developments in media technology such as photography, film, television, and the internet. Ter-Nedden views the epistolary novel as an important step in three epoch-making transformations of the media: the rise of newspapers, journals, and the novel.[28] Occurring at the same time in the eighteenth century is the increasing literacy of the population,

---

25 See in this regard Guy Stern, "Wieland als Herausgeber der *Sternheim*," in *Christoph Martin Wieland: Nordamerikanische Forschungsbeiträge zur 250. Wiederkehr seines Geburtstags. 1983*, ed. Hansjörg Schelle (Tübingen: Niemeyer, 1984, 197–207).
26 Robert Vellusig, "Anthropologie und Mediengeschichte des Erzählens," in *Das Erlebnis und die Dichtung: Studien zur Anthropologie und Mediengeschichte des Erzählens* (Göttingen: Wallstein, 2013), 33–50 (24).
27 Robert Vellusig, "Verschriftlichung des Erzählens," in *Das Erlebnis und die Dichtung*, 73–125 (73).
28 Gisbert Ter-Nedden, "Der Kino-Effekt des Briefromans," in *Poetik des Briefromans: Wissens-und Mediengeschichtliche Studien*, ed. Gideon Stiening and Robert Vellusig (Berlin: De Gruyter, 2012), 84–127 (93).

including women, who added greatly to the size of the reading public. Under Wieland's guidance, Sophie von La Roche makes skillful use of this new contemporary genre. She develops the English and French traditions of epistolary novels, and writes a novel in German that is one of the first novels written from multiple perspectives, a work that will remain one of the most important novels written by a woman in the eighteenth century. She entered the literary scene with this work, which was warmly received by an expanding literary audience and soon brought her international recognition. As we have seen, and in contrast to other influential accounts of their relationship, Christoph Martin Wieland played an important and positive role in helping her achieve this success.[29]

Sophie von La Roche and Goethe: Partners in a Literary Network (1772–1775)

Roles were reversed in the case of Sophie von La Roche and Johann Wolfgang von Goethe. When Goethe visited Sophie von La Roche in Koblenz-Ehrenbreitstein on September 14, 1772, she had already introduced herself into the literary scene with her novel *Geschichte des Fräuleins von Sternheim*. She was forty-two years old; her husband had a prominent position as a state counselor, and later as the chancellor to the archbishop of Trier; and she had five children and lived with her family in a house of their own above the Rhine. Goethe was twenty-three years old, had just left Wetzlar and Charlotte Buff, and

---

29 In this regard my assessment is different from that of Barbara Becker-Cantarino, who notes: "Wieland helps give birth to the women's novel. He thereby invents the title for a form of literary expression, and helps support women writers at the time but simultaneously limits them to the women's corner within the general literary realm." Becker-Cantarino's judgment is based on letters, an interpretation of Wieland's preface to the *Geschichte des Fräuleins von Sternheim*, and his annotations to the novel. It is true that in the preface of the novel Wieland identifies women especially as the perceived audience of the novel, and claims that Sophie von La Roche did not want to create a piece of art but a piece of nature; however, this work by Sophie von La Roche was not read as "women's literature" per se, but instead was widely recognized—nationally and internationally—as an important and remarkable new novel. Sophie von La Roche decided to address predominantly women in her future works, mainly because she wanted to make a contribution to women's education. Becker-Cantarino's claim that Wieland put her in the women's corner, and that because of that her works stayed there, overlooks these important details. Becker-Cantarino, "Autorschaft," 62. Also Barbara Becker-Cantarino, "Muse und Kunstrichter: Sophie La Roche und Wieland," *MLN* 99 (1984): 571–88; Gudrun Loster-Schneider, *Sophie La Roche: Paradoxien weiblichen Schreibens im 18. Jahrhundert* (Tübingen: Narr, 1995).

had written little other than a few poems, reviews, and satires. At the start, then, this was the meeting of a rather unequal pair, but Goethe was well aware of the similarities: "Mit der Mutter verband mich mein belletristisches und sentimentales Streben" (To the mother [Sophie von La Roche] I was recommended by my literary and emotional tendencies), he wrote in *Dichtung und Wahrheit* (Poetry and Truth).[30] I will try to show how Sophie von La Roche and Goethe collaborated between 1772 and 1775 on establishing a common network of writers of sensibility, and mutually supported each other in this endeavor. Themes such as sociability, the culture of letter writing, and Johann Georg Jacobi's journal *Iris* will illustrate their common projects in this new communicative society. Let us look at the culture of sociability that La Roche cultivated in Koblenz-Ehrenbreitstein.

Even before Sophie von La Roche had moved from Bönnigheim to Ehrenbreitstein in 1771, she had established contacts to the leading representatives of the new literary movement of sensibility in Germany. One of them was Johann Georg Jacobi, the poet and author of the novels *Winterreise* (Winter Journey) and *Sommerreise* (Summer Journey), which soon led to an active exchange of correspondence between them. Sophie von La Roche thus developed a literary network of her own that went beyond her connections through Wieland and helped her in the publication of her works.[31] When she moved closer to the Jacobi brothers, she invited them to her new house on the Rhine. Soon afterwards, on May 13, 1771, Johann Georg Jacobi and his brother Friedrich Heinrich arrived at her home along with the prince's private tutor from Darmstadt, Franz Michael Leuchsenring, and Christoph Martin Wieland. Goethe was not present for this meeting, but later describes the house: "Das Haus, ganz am Ende des Tals, wenig erhöht über dem Fluss gelegen, hatte die freie Aussicht den Strom hinabwärts. Die Zimmer waren hoch und geräumig, und die Wände galerieartig mit aneinanderstoßenden Gemälden behangen. Jedes

---

30 Johann Wolfgang von Goethe, *Autobiographische Schriften I: Dichtung und Wahrheit. Werke*, Vol. IX, ed. Erich Trunz (Munich: DTV, 1998), 557. Translation: Johann Wolfgang von Goethe, *Poetry and Truth from My Own Life*, trans. Minna Steele Smith (London: G. Bells & Sons, 1908), 101.
31 In my book, I describe in more detail how Sophie von La Roche through her own efforts established contact with the leading representatives of this new literary movement of sensibility, developed an important literary network around herself, and was recognized in this circle. Monika Nenon, *Aus der Fülle der Herzen: Geselligkeit, Briefkultur und Literatur um Sophie von La Roche und Friedrich Heinrich Jacobi* (Würzburg: Königshausen & Neumann, 2005).

Fenster, nach allen Seiten hin, machte den Rahmen zu einem natürlichen Bilde" (The house, at the extreme end of the valley, and raised a little above the river, commanded an open view down the stream. The rooms were high and spacious, and the walls were hung with pictures, hanging side by side as in a gallery. Every window on each side was a frame to a natural picture).[32] Over the next few years, these rooms full of pictures surrounded by the beautiful landscape of the Rhine would become a cultural space located between the private and public spheres that provided opportunities for people to meet, converse, and enjoy the pleasures of nature and culture. At Goethe's first visit in September 1772, he was joined by Franz Michael Leuchsenring who, Goethe reports, brought along several "despatch-boxes" of letters that contained "many treasures."[33] At this first meeting, they read aloud letters from Julie Bondeli, who was in communication with Rousseau and was therefore held in high esteem by them. They heard and discussed poems from Johann Georg Jacobi, just as they would later read and discuss together passages from Goethe's novel *Die Leiden des jungen Werthers* (The Sufferings of Young Werther). Goethe visited the La Roche family again in August 1774 along with the well-known pedagogical writer Johann Jacob Basedow, and the Jacobi brothers were frequent visitors in the La Roche home. In this "open house," as Ulrike Weckel has called it,[34] there arose a kind of social culture similar to what would later become the salon: a culture in which friendship between persons with similar ways of thinking and feeling was cultivated and in which literary works and letters were read and discussed. Just as Goethe had done in the Darmstadt circle gathered around the Grand Countess Karoline von Hessen-Darmstadt, he participated actively in the culture of friendship and sensibility that was emerging at that time, as for instance Nicholas Boyle has emphasized.[35] These personal contacts were then continued in a series of written correspondences among friends.

---

32 Goethe, *Autobiographische Schriften I*, 557. Translation: Goethe, *Poetry and Truth*, 101.
33 Goethe, *Autobiographische Schriften I*, 559. Translation: Goethe, *Poetry and Truth*, 102.
34 Ulrike Weckel, "Frauen und Geselligkeit im späten 18. Jahrhundert: Das offene Haus der Sophie La Roche in Ehrenbreitstein," *Koblenzer Beiträge zur Geschichte und Kultur* 4 (1994): 41–60 (58). Monika Nenon, "Sophie von La Roches literarische Salongeselligkeit in Koblenz-Ehrenbreitstein 1771–1780," *German Quarterly* 75, no. 3 (2002): 282–97.
35 See Nicholas Boyle, *Goethe: The Poet and the Age*, Vol. I, *The Poetry of Desire* (Oxford: Clarendon Press, 1992), 128.

Exchanging Letters

In the years that followed their first meetings, Goethe and Sophie von La Roche maintained an active exchange of letters, of which twenty-four have been preserved from him to her and three from her to him. What were these letters like, and what function did they fulfill? According to Christian Fürchtegott Gellert and, after him, Jacobi, letters are "Gespräche mit Abwesenden" (conversations with absent people) and therefore should also take on the "Ton der Gesellschaft" (tone of polite society).[36] In a departure from the style of communication at the royal courts or in scholarly letters, a more natural style starts to become predominant in the 1750s, one that is characteristic of the letters exchanged between Goethe and La Roche. According to Reinhard Nickisch, letters serve three primary communicative functions, namely "the basic functions of conveying information, appealing to the audience, and self-expression,"[37] all three of which can be found in Goethe's correspondence with Sophie von La Roche as well. Let us begin with the last two elements, self-expression and appeals to the other. Sophie von La Roche refers to Goethe in one letter as "my friend,"[38] whereas Goethe addresses her as "Mama," presumably inspired by Rousseau's way of addressing Madame de Warens. In Goethe's letter of November 20, 1772, he writes:

> Seit den ersten unschätzbaaren Augenblicken, die mich zu Ihnen brachten, seit ienen Scenen der innigsten Empfindung, wie offt ist meine ganze Seele bey Ihnen gewesen ... Sie klagen über Einsamkeit! Ach dass das Schicksal der edelsten Seelen ist, nach einem Spiegel ihres selbst vergebens zu seufzen ... Hundertmal freuen wir uns im Geiste nach über die Augenblicke die wir in Gegenwart der schönsten Natur in dem seeligsten Zirkel genossen.[39]
>
> (Since those first inestimable moments that brought me to you, since those scenes of the most intimate feelings, how often has my whole soul been with you ... You bemoan your loneliness! Oh, that this is the fate of the most noble souls, to sigh in vain for

---

36 Johann Georg Jacobi, "Vom Briefschreiben," *Iris* 3, no. 3 (1775): 193–202 (194).
37 Reinhard M. G. Nickisch, *Brief* (Stuttgart: Metzler, 1991), 13.
38 Sophie von La Roche to Goethe, Koblenz, August 17, 1774, in Karl Robert Mandelkow, ed., *Briefe an Goethe*, Vol. I, *Briefe der Jahre 1764–1808* (Munich: Beck, 1982), 37.
39 Goethe to Sophie von La Roche, Darmstadt, November 20, 1772, in *Goethes Briefe*, ed. Robert Mandelkow (Munich: Beck, 1986), Vol. I, 136–7.

a mirror of themselves. One hundred times do we rejoice in our spirits over those moments in which we are in the presence of the most beautiful nature in the blissful circle of our fellows.)

To Auguste Countess of Stolberg, he writes on February 2, 1775: "Man weiss erst dass man ist wenn man sich in andern wiederfindet" (One only knows that one exists when one finds oneself in others).[40] Here we find an expression of the desire for an alter ego in which one can find one's reflection and obtain recognition. In the sentimental correspondence of the time, one often finds phrases such as "the concordance of souls" or "a harmony between souls"—a concept that Rousseau employs when he describes Clarens's community in his epistolary novel *Julie; ou, La nouvelle Heloïse* (Julie; or, The New Heloïse), which had exercised such a decisive influence on German discursive communities in the age of sensibility. Goethe, who sent Sophie von La Roche one of the three first copies of his *Werther*, asks her for: "ein Wort vom Herzen. Sie werden sehn, wie Sie meinem Rad Schwung geben wenn Sie meinen Werther lesen, den fing ich an als sie weg waren den andern Tag, und an einem fort! fertig ist er" (a word from the heart. You will see how you give impetus to my wheel when you read my Werther, which I started when you were away the other day, and then continued right on! It is finished).[41] Goethe is expressly seeking the friendship, recognition, and esteem that will help foster the creative process for him.

The content of the letters extends beyond just appeals and self-expression, however. They also address very concrete business matters. Since the literary market at this stage was still predominantly self-organized, it was important for authors to have access to a professional literary network that they could use to promote their publications and the distribution of their works. Both Sophie von La Roche and Goethe were in the process of expanding their networks, as the letters they exchange illustrate. Goethe sends her his newest works, for example *Götz von Berlichingen, The Sufferings of Young Werther, Clavigo,* and *Stella*. He thanks her for her "Teilnehmung an meinem Götz" (help with my *Götz*) and sends her twenty-four copies that she should help market to her literary network: "Mercken würden Sie einen Gefallen thun, denn er ist auch hier Verleger, wenn Sie beykommende Exemplare, sind 24 vor 48 Kreuzer das Stück absezzen liessen" (You would do Merck a favor, since he is also a publisher here, if you would sell the twenty-four

---

40 Goethe to Auguste Gräfin zu Stolberg, Frankfurt, February 2, 1775, in *Goethes Briefe*, 177.
41 Goethe to Sophie von La Roche, Frankfurt, early June 1774, in *Briefe Goethes*, ed. Gustav von Loeper (Berlin: Wilhelm Hertz, 1879), 42.

copies sent here for 48 Kreuzer each).[42] He also asks her to help market Merck's *Frankfurter gelehrten Anzeigen* and Merck's edition of *Ossian*: "Ich schreibe Ihnen diesmal nur in Handlungs Speditions Sachen, Merck und Comp. Hier sind zwölf Exempl. Ossian. Das eine der gehefteten bittet er Sie anzunehmen" (I am writing you this time just about some shipping matters, Merck and Comp. Here are twelve copies of Ossian. He asks you to accept one of the volumes).[43] How important this support is for the author in financial terms becomes clear in a letter of December 22, 1774, when Goethe writes: "Mir hat meine Autorschafft die Suppen noch nicht fett gemacht, u. wirds und solls auch nicht thun. Zu einer Zeit da sich so ein großes Publikum mit Berlichingen beschäfftigte, und ich soviel Lob und Zufriedenheit von allen Enden einnahm, sah ich mich genötigt Geld zu borgen, um das Papier zu bezahlen, worauf ich ihn hatte drucken lassen" (My authorship has never really put butter on my bread, and it will not and should not. At a time when such a large audience was interested in *Berlichingen*, and I received so much praise and satisfaction from all sides, I was still forced to borrow money in order to pay for the paper that I used to have it printed).[44] Goethe in turn also serves as a mentor to Sophie von La Roche as she is composing the "Freundschaftliche Frauenzimmer=Briefe" (Friendly Women's Letters) that first appear in the journal *Iris* (2, no. 2–8, no. 1) and were later published separately as *Rosaliens Briefe an ihre Freundin Mariane von St*** (Rosalie's Letters to Her Friend Mariane von St**) (1779–81). Sophie von La Roche sends him the "Briefe" and Goethe provides her with his recommendations about their style and organization.[45] His remarks include positive acknowledgment of the strengths of her work: "Hier liebe Mama die Briefe zurück die ich fürtrefflich finde. Den 29. wegen seines glücklichen Tons, womit er eine so ernsthaffte Materie vorträgt, den 38. weil er dem ganzen Ihrer Briefe eine Rundung Wendung und Weisung giebt" (Here, dear Mama, are the letters back that I found so outstanding. The twenty-ninth on account of the felicitous tone, with which it presents such serious matters, the thirty-eighth because it rounds out the entirety of your letters and gives them a nice turn and direction).[46] The theme of the twenty-ninth letter he refers to is self-love, which had been a central theme in Rousseau's *Second Discourse*, and the

---

42 Goethe to Sophie von La Roche, July 7, 1773, in *Briefe Goethes*, 15. The first edition of Goethe's *Götz von Berlichingen* appeared in 1773 with Johann Heinrich Merck's publishing house and was printed by Johann Georg Wittich in Darmstadt.
43 Goethe to Sophie von La Roche, May 12, 1773, in *Goethes Briefe*, 148.
44 Goethe to Sophie von La Roche, December 22, 1774 in *Briefe Goethes*, 92.
45 See Goethe to Sophie von La Roche, mid-February 1774, in *Briefe Goethes*, 34.
46 Goethe to Sophie von La Roche, January 3, 1775, in *Briefe Goethes*, 95.

thirty-eighth concerns a reference to Mme. Guden's independent thinking. As mentioned earlier, Sophie von La Roche's forty-one "Frauenzimmer=Briefe" were published by Johann Georg Jacobi in the journal *Iris*, which I consider a common project undertaken by the authors who made up this network, as we shall see in the next section.

The Journal *Iris* as a Group Project

At first, Goethe was not fond of the Jacobi brothers, whom he called the "Jackerls," and whom he mocked in the farce "Das Unglück der Jacobis" (The Misery of the Jacobis) (1772), which he later destroyed. In February of 1774, he still writes to Sophie von La Roche "Nach Düsseldorf kann und mag ich nicht, Sie wissen, dass mirs mit gewissen Bekanndtschafften geht wie mit gewissen Ländern, ich könnte hundertjahre Reisender seyn ohne Beruf dahin zu fühlen" (I cannot and do not want to go to Düsseldorf—you know that I feel the same way about certain acquaintances as I do about certain countries; I could travel 100 years without feeling any inclination to go there).[47] But through the efforts of Sophie von La Roche, in the summer of 1774 Betty Jacobi and Johanna Fahlmer, who was a relative of the Jacobis, became somewhat closer and arranged a first meeting between Goethe and Friedrich Heinrich Jacobi on July 23 in Düsseldorf, a meeting that would have far-reaching consequences and lead to a years-long but not always smooth friendship between them. Sophie von La Roche was friends with both, corresponded with each of them regularly, and belonged to the cultural and professional network with whose help Johann Georg Jacobi published their common project, the journal *Iris*. As mentioned earlier, the number of literate people was increasing and a newly developing consumer society involving a wider range of persons was demanding new sources of knowledge and entertainment. This now included women, who were a new audience and who were carving out freshly expanded roles for themselves in the newly oriented society. Johann Georg Jacobi describes this process of increasing civilization in his essay "Erziehung der Töchter" (On Educating Daughters) in *Iris*: "Je mehr aber Haus und Hof sich erweitern, mit Geräth und Gesinde sich anfüllen, und die Bequemlichkeiten des Lebens zunahmen, desto mehr Klugheit, Kenntnisse, Tugenden gebühren derjenigen, welche darüber walten soll" (The more we expand the house and the grounds, filling them with equipment and workhands, and the more the comforts of our life improve, all the more prudence, knowledge, and skills are required from the person who is supposed to govern it all).[48] He is referring of course to women, whose

---

47 Goethe an Sophie von La Roche, Frankfurt, mid-February 1774, in *Briefe Goethes*, 35.
48 Johann Georg Jacobi, "Erziehung der Töchter", *Iris* 1, no. 3 (1774): 11.

place has been defined as "Haus und Hof" (house and grounds), but argues now that educated women should operate there. That is why the journal *Iris* is conceived of as a journal for a female audience and aims at educating women—of course, within the framework of a patriarchal order.

Iris had between 800 and 1,000 subscribers, and appeared from 1774 through 1777. It contained excerpts from epistolary novels, lyrics, musical plays, translations of literary works, essays, anecdotes, letters, studies in history and politics, short biographies, literary recommendations, and reviews. Besides literature, it also featured articles on aesthetics, history, politics, education, and mythology. Who composed them? It is striking that the main contributors to *Iris* were recruited from the literary network we have been discussing. Johann Georg Jacobi published poems and essays; his brother Friedrich Heinrich published the first part of his literary debut work, the epistolary novel *Eduard Allwill's Papiere* (Eduard Allwill's Papers); Sophie von La Roche contributed forty-one "Frauenzimmer=Briefe" that discussed how women should lead their lives and that would be incorporated into the much larger novel *Rosaliens Briefe an ihre Freundin Mariane von St***. What about Goethe? He published some of what were to become his most famous poems there, namely the *Sesenheimer Lieder* (Sesenheim Songs), which included "Kleine Blumen, kleine Blätter" (Little Flowers, Little Leaves),[49] "Das Mayfest" (May Song),[50] "Willkommen und Abschied" (Welcome and Farewell),[51] and "Neue Liebe, Neues Leben" (New Love, New Life).[52] He also published the popular Singspiel *Erwin und Elmire*,[53] including the musical score by the famous composer, Johann André. *Iris* also featured a big advertisement for his newest epistolary novel, which would become a best-seller across Europe, his *Leiden des jungen Werther*.

How should we assess the relationship between Sophie von La Roche and Goethe during this period? We have seen how both participated in a literary and social culture of sensibility that served as a literary network for each of them. Their personal acquaintance continued as a correspondence in which they not only expressed their friendship for each other but also pursued concrete business matters. Both authors were attempting to establish and extend their positions in the literary marketplace. Sophie von La Roche had already established

---

49 Anon., *Iris* 2, no. 1 (1775): 73–4.
50 Anon., *Iris* 2, no. 1, 75–7.
51 Anon., *Iris* 2, no. 3 (1775): 244–5.
52 Anon., *Iris* 2, no. 3, 242–3.
53 Anon., *Iris* 2, no. 3, 161–224.

herself and was a fully recognized member of this circle. Goethe was still an ambitious young author at an early stage in his career who was open to a range of influences and personal contacts as he was trying to establish himself and use these new contacts to his advantage. The network of sensibility that Sophie von La Roche and the Jacobi brothers had assembled was very helpful to him in this regard. The relationship between Sophie von La Roche and Goethe at that time cannot simply be described as him as mentor and her as student. It is indeed true that he provided advice to her about the "Frauenzimmer=Briefe," but overall the letters we interpreted show that their relationship was based on a mutual recognition of each other both as people and as authors. They also collaborated in literary enterprises and assisted the publication of each other's works. Both of them benefited from this relationship, in which they each offered mutual assistance and thereby helped promote each other. As far as her status as a female author is concerned, we can see how Sophie von La Roche takes advantage of her communication skills very effectively in establishing herself in the literary market, and skillfully employs the new media. Both authors achieve their goals in this period but go their separate ways after 1775. Goethe takes a position in Weimar and develops completely different aesthetics; Sophie von La Roche stays faithful to her own aesthetic style, becomes one of the best-known female authors in the German-speaking countries during her lifetime, and attains recognition in other European countries as well. The subsequent marginalization of her achievements and those of many others in her circle in the standard histories of literature did not occur until later, and Goethe did indeed have a hand in that process.[54]

In both of the constellations we have described—Sophie von La Roche's relationship to Wieland and her relationship to Goethe—it becomes apparent that they were partners in a dynamic process of interactions and communications that was mutually profitable. Wieland and Goethe acted as mentors to Sophie von La Roche, and actively supported her work as an author. Wieland opened up the literary marketplace for her, where she had great success with her epistolary novel *Geschichte des Fräuleins von Sternheim*. For her part, she served as his

---

54 See Barbara Becker-Cantarino, "Von der *Sternheim* und vom *Werther* zur *Reise von Offenbach nach Schönebeck* und zu *Dichtung und Wahrheit*: Sophie von La Roche und Johann Wolfgang von Goethe," in *Ach, wie wünschte ich mir Geld genug, um eine Professur zu stiften: Sophie von La Roche im kulturpolitischen Feld von Aufklärung und Empfindsamkeit*, ed. Gudrun Loster-Schneider and Barbara Becker-Cantarino with contributions by Bettina Wild (Tübingen: Francke, 2010), 82–106 (85–6).

friend and muse, and offered him recognition, praise, and encouragement at a crucial point in his early career. In Goethe's case, her contribution was even greater in the way she helped market his works and provided him with opportunities to publish in *Iris* through the acquaintance with the Jacobi brothers that she helped establish. It was there that he published his *Sesenheimer Lieder* and the Singspiel *Erwin und Elmire*. We have seen how in both cases the interactions between the men and the woman involved in helping each other break into the literary scene are best viewed as a dynamic, complex process that is difficult to capture in simple categories or one-sided terms.[55]

Bibliography

Albertsen, Leif Ludwig. *Das Lehrgedicht: Eine Geschichte der antikisierenden Sachepik in der neueren deutschen Literatur*. Aarhus: Akademisk Boghandel, 1967.

Bamberg, Claudia. *Sophie von La Roche*. Frankfurt am Main: Freies Deutsches Hochstift, 2007.

Becker-Cantarino, Barbara. "Autorschaft: Zum Briefwechsel von Sophie von La Roche und Christoph Martin Wieland." In *Vom Verkehr mit Dichtern und Gespenstern: Figuren der Autorschaft in der Briefkultur*, ed. Jochen Strobel, 61–78. Heidelberg: Winter, 2006.

Becker-Cantarino, Barbara. "Muse und Kunstrichter: Sophie La Roche und Wieland." *MLN* 99 (1984): 571–88.

Becker-Cantarino, Barbara. "Von der *Sternheim* und vom *Werther* zur *Reise von Offenbach nach Schönebeck* und zu *Dichtung und Wahrheit*: Sophie von La Roche und Johann Wolfgang von Goethe." In *Ach, wie wünschte ich mir Geld genug, um eine Professur zu stiften: Sophie von La Roche im kulturpolitischen Feld von Aufklärung und Empfindsamkeit*, ed. Gudrun Loster-Schneider and Barbara Becker-Cantarino with contributions by Bettina Wild, 82–105. Tübingen: Francke, 2010.

Boyle, Nicholas. *Goethe: The Poet and the Age*. Vol. I, *The Poetry of Desire*. Oxford: Clarendon Press, 1992.

Embach, Michael, "Georg Michael Frank von La Roche (1720–1788)." In *Meine liebe grüne Stube: Die Schriftstellerin Sophie von La Roche in ihrer Speyrer Zeit (1780–1786)*, ed. Klaus Haag and Jürgen Vordestemann, 45–64. Speyer: Marsilius, 2005.

Fronius, Helen. *Women and Literature in the Goethe Era 1770–1820: Determined Dilettantes*. Oxford Modern Languages and Literature Monographs. Oxford: Clarendon Press, 2007.

Goethe, Johann Wolfgang von. *Autobiographische Schriften I: Dichtung und Wahrheit. Werke*. Vol. IX. Ed. Erich Trunz. Munich: DTV, 1998.

Goethe, Johann Wolfgang. *Briefe Goethes*. Ed. Gustav von Loeper. Berlin: Wilhelm Hertz, 1879.

---

55 I would like to thank Thomas Nenon for the translation of this chapter from German into English.

Goethe, Johann Wolfgang von. *Goethes Briefe*. Ed. Robert Mandelkow. Munich: Beck, 1986.
Goethe, Johann Wolfgang von. *Poetry and Truth from My Own Life*. Trans. Minna Steele Smith. London: G. Bells & Sons, 1908.
Heinz, Jutta, ed. *Wieland Handbuch: Leben-Werk-Wirkung*. Stuttgart: Metzler, 2008.
Jacobi, Johann Georg. "Vom Briefschreiben." *Iris* 3, no. 3 (1775): 193–202.
Konersmann, Ralf. "Seele, schöne; Seelenschönheit." In *Historisches Wörterbuch der Philosophie*. Vol. IX. Ed. Joachim Ritter, 89–92. Basel: Schwabe, 1995.
König-Warthausen, Gabriele von. "Sophie von La Roche, geb. Gutermann." In *Lebensbilder aus Schwaben und Franken*. Vol. X. Ed. Max Miller and Robert Uhland, 101–25. Stuttgart: Kommission für Geschichtliche Landeskunde in Baden-Württemberg, 1966.
La Roche, Sophie von. *Briefe über Mannheim*. Zürich: Orell, Geßner, Füßli, 1791.
La Roche, Sophie von. *Melusinens Sommer-Abende*. Ed. Christoph Martin Wieland. Halle: Verlage der N. Societäts=Buch=u. Kunsthandlung, 1806.
La Roche, Sophie von. *Pomona für Teutschlands Töchter*. Speier: [n.p.], 1783/4.
Loster-Schneider, Gudrun. *Sophie La Roche: Paradoxien weiblichen Schreibens im 18. Jahrhundert*. Tübingen: Narr, 1995.
Mandelkow, Karl Robert, ed. *Briefe an Goethe*. Vol. I, *Briefe der Jahre 1764–1808*. Munich: Beck, 1982.
Martin, Dieter. "Frühwerk." In *Wieland Handbuch: Leben-Werk-Wirkung*, ed. Jutta Heinz, 150–69. Stuttgart: Metzler, 2008.
Martus, Steffen. *Aufklärung: Das deutsche 18. Jahrhundert. Ein Epochenbild*. Berlin: Rowohlt, 2015.
Maurer, Michael. *Die Biographie des Bürgers: Lebensformen und Denkweisen in der formativen Phase des deutschen Bürgertums (1680–1815)*. Göttingen: Vandenhoeck & Ruprecht, 1996.
Maurer, Michael, ed. *Ich bin mehr Herz als Kopf: Sophie von La Roche. Ein Lebensbild in Briefen*. Munich: Beck, 1983.
Nenon, Monika. *Aus der Fülle der Herzen: Geselligkeit, Briefkultur und Literatur um Sophie von La Roche und Friedrich Heinrich Jacobi*. Würzburg: Königshausen & Neumann, 2005.
Nenon, Monika. *Autorschaft und Frauenbildung: Das Beispiel Sophie von La Roche*. Würzburg: Königshausen & Neumann, 1988.
Nenon, Monika. "The Genius and His Muse: Women as Objects of Imagination for Klopstock and Wieland." *Lessing Yearbook/Jahrbuch* 28 (1996): 199–213.
Nenon, Monika. "Sophie von La Roches literarische Salongeselligkeit in Koblenz-Ehrenbreitstein 1771–1780." *German Quarterly* 75, no. 3 (2002): 282–97.
Nickisch, Reinhard M. G. *Brief*. Stuttgart: Metzler, 1991.
Schnegg, Brigitte. "Die Fahrt auf dem Zürichsee: Eine geschlechtergeschichtliche Deutung des Zerwürfnisses zwischen Bodmer und Klopstock im Jahre 1750." In *Ordnung, Politik und Geselligkeit der Geschlechter im 18. Jahrhundert*, ed. Ulrike Weckel, Claudia Opitz, Olivia Hochstrasser, and Brigitte Tolkemitt, 119–43. Göttingen: Wallstein, 1998.
Sengle, Friedrich. *C. M. Wieland*. Stuttgart: Metzler, 1949.
Stern, Guy. "Wieland als Herausgeber der *Sternheim*." In *Christoph Martin Wieland: Nordamerikanische Forschungsbeiträge zur 250. Wiederkehr seines Geburtstags. 1983*, ed. Hansjörg Schelle, 197–207. Tübingen: Niemeyer, 1984.
Ter-Nedden, Gisbert. "Der Kino-Effekt des Briefromans." In *Poetik des Briefromans: Wissens-und Mediengeschichtliche Studien*, ed. Gideon Stiening and Robert Vellusig, 85–127. Berlin: De Gruyter, 2012.

Vellusig, Robert. "Anthropologie und Mediengeschichte des Erzählens." In *Das Erlebnis und die Dichtung: Studien zur Anthropologie und Mediengeschichte des Erzählens*, 33–50. Göttingen: Wallstein, 2013.
Vellusig, Robert. "Verschriftlichung des Erzählens." In *Das Erlebnis und die Dichtung: Studien zur Anthropologie und Mediengeschichte des Erzählens*, 73–125. Göttingen: Wallstein, 2013.
Weckel, Ulrike. "Frauen und Geselligkeit im späten 18. Jahrhundert: Das offene Haus der Sophie La Roche in Ehrenbreitstein." *Koblenzer Beiträge zur Geschichte und Kultur* 4 (1994): 41–60.
Wieland, Christoph Martin. "Vorbericht zur dritten Ausgabe von 1770, *Die Natur der Dinge*." In C. M. Wieland. *Sämmtliche Werke XIII*. Ed. Hamburger Stiftung zur Förderung von Wissenschaft und Kultur in collaboration Wieland-Archiv and Dr. Hans Radspieler, 5–6. Nördlingen: C. H. Beck, 1984.
Wieland, Christoph Martin. *Wielands Briefwechsel*. Ed. Hans Werner Seiffert. Vol. I, *Briefe der Bildungsjahre (1. Juni 1750–2. Juni 1760)*. Berlin: Akademie, 1963.
Wieland, Christoph Martin. *Wielands Briefwechsel*. Ed. Hans Werner Seiffert. Vol. III, *Briefe der Biberacher Amtsjahre (6. Juni 1760–20. Mai 1769)*. Berlin: Akademie, 1975.
Wieland, Christoph Martin. *Wielands Briefwechsel*. Vol. IV, *Briefe der Erfurter Dozentenjahre (25. Mai 1769–17. September 1772)*. Berlin: Akademie, 1979.
Wieland, Christoph Martin. *Wielands Briefwechsel*. Vol. XVI.1, *Juli 1802–Dezember 1806*. Ed. Siegfried Scheibe. Berlin: Akademie, 1997.
Wokalek, Marie. *Die schöne Seele als Denkfigur: Zur Semantik von Gewissen und Geschmack bei Rousseau, Wieland, Schiller, Goethe*. Göttingen: Wallstein, 2011.

Three "Collaborating with Spirits"
Cagliostro, Elisa von der Recke, and the Phantoms of *Unmündigkeit*

Michelle Stott James and Rob McFarland

The evening, as Elisa von der Recke remembered it, was fairly typical for a group of aspiring spiritualists. In the ornate rococo chambers of a grand house in the Baltic Courland, a small boy rubbed his eyes and looked up into the darkness beyond the candlelight.[1] A small circle of chairs held a collection of noblemen and noblewomen, hardly breathing so as not to drown out the boy's whispering voice. "He is here. I see him," the little boy said. A well-dressed man with a thick accent addressed the boy. "Describe him, what does he look like?" "I will tell you, Count Cagliostro," whispered the boy, and the onlookers' eyes widened. As the boy spoke, the listeners focused their eyes on Cagliostro, wondering what his invisible ghostly leaders would allow him to divulge. The location of treasure? The secrets of the ancients? Recke remembers her own hope as she listened to the boy and Cagliostro: she wanted more than anything to contact the spirits of her departed mother and brother. Recke wondered: could she, barely more than a teenager, use the spirit realm to foster truth, love, and spiritual growth among the fallen people of the earth?[2] That was the promise that Cagliostro had made to her: the "Umgang mit Geistern" (interaction with

---

1 Courland (German *Kurland*) is a small area on the Baltic Coast in modern Latvia surrounding the city of Riga. German knights settled the area in the thirteenth century. At the time of Recke and Cagliostro, the area was under Polish rule, soon to be returned to Russia. The ethnic German nobility retained their lands and local power until the early twentieth century.
2 For the exact transcript of this anecdote in Recke's own words, see Elisa von der Recke, *Nachricht von des berüchtigten Cagliostro Aufenthalte in Mitau im Jahre 1779 und von dessen dortigen magischen Operationen* (Berlin: Friedrich Nicolai, 1787), 72 (hereafter *Nachricht*).

spirits)³ would, he had assured her, allow her to contact departed human spirits who could help her to develop herself into a powerful source of righteousness.⁴

Years later, as a more mature Elisa von der Recke read back over her account of the evening in her diary, she noticed that—even on this awe-inspiring evening—her younger self had harbored nagging doubts about Count Cagliostro. As impressed as she had been with the panache and the self-confidence of the visitor to her home in Courland, she could not help but notice his coarse manner; his fascination with money, jewels, and treasure; and the way that he could turn vindictively upon anyone who questioned him or his methods. She had also noticed inconsistencies in his performed rituals: Why could some people enter and leave the magic circle at will, while others had to stay within its boundaries?⁵ The older Recke pondered the hesitancy of her younger self who had written in the journal. She had started as Cagliostro's ingénue and as his passionate defender. When had she first started to sense that the spiritualist was a monstrous fraud, and how had she gained the courage and self-assurance to step out of his imposing shadow and overcome her own *Unmündigkeit*, gaining the power to speak for herself without deferring to a higher authority?⁶

In this chapter we will explore the way that Elisa von der Recke's interactions with the self-fashioned "Count Cagliostro" helped her to develop her own authorial voice, hesitant at the beginning but increasingly resistant and sovereign. This voice developed over time in letters, newspaper articles, and finally in her carefully crafted exposé of Cagliostro's charlatanism. As her writings follow her changing interactions with Cagliostro—less a willing collaboration and more a willful, polemic collision between two powerful minds—Recke provides her readers with a fascinating example of a woman's battle for agency in the face of a frightening and powerful male authority. The success of her Cagliostro project, we will argue, had far-reaching implications not only for women's writings in the eighteenth century, but also for the development of Enlightenment thought and practice across the European continent. Recke's account of the way she grappled with Cagliostro's fraudulent spiritualism captured the fascination of the

---

3   *Nachricht*, 101. All translations in this chapter are our own unless otherwise noted.
4   Heinrich Funck, "Lavater und Cagliostro," *Nord und Süd: Eine deutsche Monatsschrift*, 83 (October 1897): 41–63 (44).
5   *Nachricht*, 96, 98.
6   As it is used in the context of this chapter, *Unmündigkeit* denotes legal minority, dependence on the guidance of others.

greatest and most powerful writers and philosophers of her era. Her Cagliostro writings served as the inspiration for canonical works by Johann Wolfgang von Goethe, Friedrich Schiller, and E. T. A. Hoffmann. As her notoriety grew, Recke corresponded and met with the greatest minds of her time, including philosophers such as Immanuel Kant and Johann Christian Lavater. Her writings even resonated in some of the most powerful circles in Europe, becoming entwined in the royal court intrigues surrounding Marie Antoinette of France and serving as an inspiration for satirical dramas written by Catherine the Great of Russia.

This volume is a collection of chapters about fruitful interaction between creative and imaginative men and women. Why would we approach the relationship between Cagliostro and Elisa von der Recke as an artistic collaboration? Their interactions, as they are reported in Recke's letters and her exposé, are far from the imagined ideal of literary or intellectual collaboration. Neither of the two intended to consult together on the production of any kind of text, other than perhaps letters or speeches meant to persuade other people to listen to Cagliostro's teachings. Their interactions were not a meeting of great minds in pursuit of a common goal. Any attempt to cast their relationship as a mentoring effort between a master and a novice is immediately undermined by Cagliostro's blatant charlatanism and his shameless exploitation of Recke's naïveté. How can we claim positive productivity in the interaction between a con artist and a victim? And yet there are compelling reasons to view the interactions between Cagliostro and Recke as a collaborative relationship. As Jill R. Ehnenn has argued, women's writing collaborations are always shaped by power dynamics that enforce the definitions of gender, authorship, and subjectivity.[7] The power of the male's historical position often allowed him to dominate the relationship, while the female was often the passive recipient of the male author's genius and his respected position in the artistic and creative world. Certainly Cagliostro's sheer audacity and wide success make him an easy character to map onto the figure of the lone, male, authorial genius.[8] But to cast Recke as the hapless victim of Cagliostro's fraud is to underestimate the creative potential that arose from her interactions with the mountebank spiritualist.

---

[7] Jill R. Ehnenn, *Women's Literary Collaboration, Queerness, and Late Victorian Culture* (Burlington, VT: Ashgate, 2008), 1–26.

[8] See Jack Stillinger, *Multiple Authorship and the Myth of Solitary Genius* (Oxford: Oxford University Press, 1991), 183–6. For a discussion of the male nature of this solitary writing figure, see Ehnenn, *Women's Literary Collaboration*, 25–8.

One measure of a powerful collaboration is, of course, the literary product of the interaction. In her own words, Recke sought Cagliostro's help in obtaining *"Umgang mit Verstorbenen und mit höhern Geistern"* (interaction with the departed and with higher spirits).[9] While Cagliostro initially preyed on Recke and tried to manipulate her to fulfill his own aims, Recke herself was anything but a passive accomplice. From the very beginning of her interactions with Cagliostro, Recke shaped their relationship into a written polemic. First in her own diary and later in letters, meetings, and finally her famous published exposé, Recke carefully crafted a written critique of Cagliostro's ideas, rhetorical devices, and personal behavior. Even in her moments of greatest enthusiasm for the teachings of the spiritualist, Recke gently cultivated a rational, detached counter-voice that constantly relativized and undercut the ideas of her spiritual mentor. After all, collaboration is not always a supportive endorsement of a partner's work. Enlightenment-era writers from Voltaire on, as John R. Iverson has illustrated, considered polemics to be a productive mode of collaboration.[10] Even though Cagliostro did not himself participate in the writing of his polemical interchange with Recke, she was careful to incorporate quotes, documents and eyewitness accounts of his teachings into her works. When it was published, this written account of their collaboration was a unique document that took Europe by storm and unleashed a broad discussion among the Enlightenment era's greatest minds.

Although Recke's name is relatively unknown today, during her lifetime as an author, benefactress, traveler, social critic, and salonnière, Elisa von der Recke (1756 [1754]–1833) held a position of prominence among the intellectual and social elite of Europe.[11] She was born in the Duchy of Courland to one of the oldest and most powerful German-speaking noble families in the area. As Carrie Cox has noted:

---

9 Elisa von der Recke, "Elisa an Preißler," Berlin: *Berlinische Monatsschrift*, 5 (May 1786): 385–98 (396). Italics in the original.

10 John R. Iverson, "Le dîner de philosophes: Conviviality and Collaboration in the French Enlightenment," in *Models of Collaboration in Nineteenth-Century French Literature*, ed. Seth Whidden (New York: Routledge, 2009), 25–36 (30).

11 Scholarship remains unclear on whether Recke was born in 1754 or 1756. Paul Rachel, perhaps the most thorough and accurate Recke historian, insists that Recke's actual birth year was 1754, even though this date conflicts with her own statements throughout her lifetime. Since Rachel provides no positive documentation to support his claim, we assert that 1756 is the most likely year of Recke's birth. This corresponds to her own statements and the biography of Recke published in 1818 by her long-time companion, Christoph August Tiedge.

[Recke] was positioned between the conflicting intellectual discourses of religion and rational Enlightenment; between intellect and sentiment; between the noble class, to which she belonged, and the bourgeoisie, which she preferred; between her German cultural heritage and the political heritage of Courland, linked as it was to Poland and then Russia; between traditional views of a woman's role and her own endless intellectual striving.[12]

Because of her prominent position in the political and cultural life of her time, Recke's writings constitute a treasure trove of personal observations and insights about the people, culture, literature, philosophy, religion, and historical events of her time and place. The fact that she observed and analyzed these many facets of her life through the eyes of a woman adds a unique underlying current of gendered experience to the digest of her times, which she presents in her memoirs, letters, travel journals, poetry, essays, and polemic writings. It can safely be asserted that Recke was acquainted to some degree with everyone who was anyone in central Europe during her time, from Catherine the Great to Casanova, from the Danish sculptor Bertel Thorvaldsen to Ludwig van Beethoven. The Swiss theologian Johann Kaspar Lavater[13] and the German authors J. W. Goethe and Friedrich Schiller were among her correspondents, while the Prussian authors and publishers Friedrich Nicolai[14] and Johann Wilhelm Gleim starred as her closest friends and mentors.

In spite of her far-reaching influence during her lifetime, Elisa von der Recke and her writings have unfortunately become obscure, and her works are often buried deeply in the dust of libraries and archives.[15] One notable exception is her controversial 1787 exposé of Cagliostro, titled *Nachricht von des berüchtigten Cagliostro Aufenthalte in Mitau im Jahre 1779 und von dessen dortigen magischen Operationen* (Report on

---

12 Carrie Cox, "Pushing the Scented Envelope: Elisa von der Recke at the Cultural Crossroads" (M.A. thesis, Brigham Young University, 2012), ii.
13 It was Lavater who encouraged Recke's early attempts at writing poetry. See Erich Donnert, *Schwärmerei und Aufklärung: Die kurländische Freifrau Elisa von der Recke (1754–1833) in den Geisteskämpfen ihrer Zeit* (Frankfurt am Main: Peter Lang, 2010), 11.
14 For a discussion of Recke's relationship to Nicolai, see Pamela E. Selwyn, *Everyday Life in the German Book Trade: Friedrich Nicolai as Bookseller and Publisher in the Age of Enlightenment 1750–1810* (University Park, PA: Pennsylvania State University Press, 2000).
15 A digital five-volume *Critically Annotated Collected Works of Elisa von der Recke* is currently nearing completion, edited and annotated by Michelle Stott James.

the Infamous Cagliostro's Visit to Mitau in the Year 1779 and on His Magical Operations There). While most of her oeuvre consists of travel journals, letters, and poetry, her exposé of Cagliostro is a carefully constructed argument written in clear, rational, Enlightenment-era German. Although her prose in the *Nachricht* is scientific, it also conveys a highly subjective account of both Recke's personal search for connection to the spirits of the dead and the guidance that she received from the spiritualist Cagliostro.

In her own time, Recke's *Nachricht* met with a greatly divided reception. The historian Ludwig August Schlözer praised Recke as "one of the most enlightened women of our time," who with "most delightful open-heartedness" illustrated how even a refined and educated mind could fall prey to Cagliostro's tricks.[16] Her contemporary Ludwig Ernst Borowski praised Recke, but felt that her warnings about Cagliostro had not been properly heeded, and called for the *Nachricht* to be more widely read,[17] but Recke's publication was also criticized as an attention-grabbing literary stunt, written by a woman with a workable sense of hearing and sight but no capacity for judgment.[18] She earned the scorn of public figures such as Goethe's brother-in-law, the author Johann Georg Schlosser, and the theologian Johann August Starck.[19]

In recent scholarship, Recke's exposé of Cagliostro is often cited as a source about Cagliostro, but scholars seldom focus on Recke's text itself. Walter Müller-Seidel, for example, goes so far as to call Recke's *Nachricht* an "epoch-making publication," but only mentions it in his writings about Goethe and Cagliostro.[20] John A. McCarthy sees Recke's *Nachricht* as establishing her as "one of the most celebrated women authors of the era," and he specifically positions her exposé as the starting point for her development as a ground-breaking German-language proponent of the essay form.[21] His focus, however, is on Recke's later essays, and the exposé is only briefly mentioned. Erich Donnert relies heavily on the text of the *Nachricht* in his exploration of Recke's

---

16 Donnert, *Schwärmerei*, 23–4.
17 Ludwig Ernst Borowski, "Cagliostro, einer der merkwürdigsten Abenteuerer unseres Jahrhunderts: Seine Geschichte nebst Raisonnement über ihn und den schwärmerischen Unfug unserer Zeit überhaupt," in *Cagliostro: Dokumente zu Aufklärung und Okkultismus*, ed. Klaus H. Kiefer (Munich: Beck, 1991 [1790]), 332–445 (415).
18 Borowski, "Cagliostro," 334.
19 Donnert, *Schwärmerei*, 36–41.
20 See Walter Müller-Seidel, "Cagliostro und die Vorgeschichte der deutschen Klassik," in *Literaturwissenschaft und Geistesgeschichte: Festschrift für Richard Brinkmann*, ed. Jürgen Brummack (Tübingen: Max Niemeyer, 1981), 137–8.
21 John A. McCarthy, *Crossing Boundaries: A Theory and History of Essay Writing in German, 1680–1815* (Philadelphia: University of Pennsylvania Press, 1989), 292–8.

intellectual correspondence associated with Cagliostro, and he carefully investigates the reception of her exposé. He does not, however, discuss the form or construction of the text itself.[22] Wilhelm Kühlmann focuses more closely on the "important media event" that was Recke's *Nachricht*. He takes the time to explain carefully the form of the exposé, finding—in spite of "its polemic tone"—a work that contains "some documentation value in the 'knowledge' presented by Cagliostro, both for hermeneutic purposes and for understanding its connection to day-to-day life."[23] While providing a carefully annotated list of topics, structures, and motives—he rightly illustrates that "Recke arranges her report in such a way that important literary figures of the epoch appear in a clear appraisal as alternative opposites" for example[24]—he does not focus on Recke's rhetorical demonstration of Cagliostro's role in the development of her own authorial voice. It is this collaborative authorial development—from the voice of a naïve spiritualist acolyte to a sovereign, critical voice of reason and enlightenment—that is the focus of our chapter.

In order to understand Recke's obsession with spiritualism, it is important to place her in the context of her family relationships and the expectations placed upon a young noblewoman in Courland at this time.[25] Her grandfather, Starost[26] Nicolaus von Korff (1682–1755), was a descendant of one of the original Teutonic knights who conquered the area and claimed it for Germany. He amassed a fortune, which he passed on to Recke's grandmother, Constanzia von der Wahlen (1698–1790), known by her title, Starostin von Korff. At the death of her mother, the two-year-old Elisa was given into the hands of this lavish, stern, opinionated grandmother. Recke's daily activity consisted predominantly in being preened and dressed for public exhibition, and then spending hours standing motionless at her grandmother's side while the starostin held court. Education for a woman, beyond basic skills of reading and writing, was scorned by the starostin and her family. In order to

---

22 Donnert, *Schwärmerei*, 12–39.
23 Wilhelm Kühlmann, "Cagliostro in Mitau, Elisa von der Recke und Friedrich Nicolai—Motive und Kontexte einer rationalistischen 'Selbstaufklärung,'" in *Aufklärer im Baltikum: Europäischer Kontext und regionale Besonderheiten*, ed. Ulrich Kronauer (Heidelberg: Universitätsverlag Winter, 2011), 115–32 (125).
24 Kühlmann, "Cagliostro," 131.
25 Unless otherwise noted, we have condensed all the biographical information on Recke in this chapter from two sources: *Nachricht*, and Paul Rachel, ed., *Elisa von der Recke: Aufzeichnungen und Briefe aus ihren Jugendtagen* (Leipzig: Dieterich'sche Verlags-Buchhandlung, 1900).
26 Polish *starost*—the holder of a fief bestowed by the king, a district administrator (German *Landrat*).

secure their own inheritance, Recke's cousins and aunt made it their personal task to prove to the grandmother that little Elisa was "stockdumm" (utterly stupid). They convinced the gullible young girl that if she made any effort to learn, she would become mentally incapacitated like her cousin, who was born with mental disabilities. Driven by her isolation and the mistreatment she received from her extended family, Recke gradually withdrew from emotional connection with the people around her and longed for a relationship with the spirits of the deceased. In her loneliness, she turned frequently to the Latvian serf who served as her maid. This servant told Recke many stories about her mother's childhood, building her into a saintly, angelic figure in the young girl's mind. Recke often secretly visited the portrait of her mother, attempting in her childlike way to gain some sort of spiritual connection with the parent whom she hardly remembered.

Recke's tendency towards spiritualism was intensified by her experiences after she left her grandmother's house. When she was eleven years old, Recke was returned to her father's estate, where she renewed her acquaintance with her brother Fritz, who in time became her closest companion and the source of her most preferred intellectual exchange and stimulation. Under the tutelage of her stepmother, Recke quickly gained confidence in herself and her intellectual abilities, and made rapid progress in achieving the education that was never allowed her in her grandmother's house. Recke's formal education was cut short, however, when she was manipulated into marriage with Georg Magnus von der Recke (1739–95), who was a nephew of her stepmother's previous husband. Georg was a coarse, unlearned man, a former army officer who was the overseer of a large estate. Unfortunately, the fifteen-year-old Elisa had no experience of anything other than the elegance and refinement of courtly life. Terrified of her husband's emotional brutality and his constant complaints about her "airs" and ineptness, Recke refused to bear children with him. Instead, she fled into the solace of books, letters, and intellectual pondering. She was particularly drawn to the writings of prominent religious mystics of the day: Christoph Martin Wieland, Edward Young, Lavater, and others. It was only when her grandmother ordered all her books removed, and forbade Recke to read at all until she produced a child, that she bowed to her husband's demands. Although she bore her daughter Friederike in 1774, Georg and Elisa soon separated and later divorced.[27] With the small pension available to her, and with little support from her family, Recke moved into rented rooms in Courland's capital city of Mitau (now Jelgava, Latvia) where she started to build a new life for herself and her

---

27 For a chronological explanation of these events, see Donnert, *Schwärmerei*, 9–12.

daughter. Unfortunately, Friederike died in 1777, and Recke's brother Fritz's death followed shortly thereafter, in 1778. Bereft and distraught, Recke entered into serious study of the mystical writings of authors such as Lavater, Emanuel Swedenborg, and Charles Bonnet. She frequently spent the night wandering in the cemetery, longing for contact with her departed loved ones.

It was at this critical juncture in Recke's life, in the early months of 1779, that the spiritualist Giuseppe Balsamo (1743–95) arrived in Mitau with his wife in tow, announcing himself as Count Cagliostro, a leading Freemason with personal access to "higher spirits" and magical powers.[28] He claimed to have been sent by his mysterious "Obern" (superiors)—Recke later suspected Jesuit connections—to establish a new Masonic lodge, which would include women among its initiates.[29] According to Cagliostro, this lodge would be a means of educating his acolytes in communicating with and commanding higher spirits in order to bring about good in the world. He claimed to have been trained in Egypt and Medina, and to have constant instruction from his superiors, who communicated with him through spirits. Cagliostro's claims soon caught the attention of many of Mitau's most prestigious men, including Recke's father and uncles. These men were already well acquainted with questions of alchemy and mysticism, since they were fascinated with the occult arts in their youth. Recke's father invited Cagliostro and his wife to take up residence in his home. Very quickly a group of enthralled friends joined the discussions, lectures, and spiritual "experiments"—that is, seances, or the conjuring of spirits—that Cagliostro regularly conducted there. Once the group was established, Cagliostro commanded that the membership be sealed, so that no new acolytes could be admitted.

Among the devoted followers that Cagliostro found in Mitau, none caught the attention of the spiritualist more than Elisa von der Recke. In a very short time, it became clear to Cagliostro that Recke was especially susceptible to his teachings and claims, since she so intensely desired them to be true. Over the course of Cagliostro's months in Mitau, Recke became his special protégée and his intermediary to the others in the group. Through a mixture of suggestion, double-talk, and intimidation, Cagliostro convinced Recke that she had the ability to develop to the highest level of communication with spirits, which would allow her not only to improve the lot of humanity, but to become a protector of the earth itself. Working closely with her master, Recke recruited new followers to the cause and served as his chief apologist to questioning

---

28 *Nachricht*, 12.
29 *Nachricht*, 6.

outsiders. As Cagliostro's chief collaborator, Recke worked under his tutelage to prepare herself to commune with the higher spirits that would teach her the mysteries and higher orders of magic and Freemasonry. Although the inhabitants of Mitau could not know this at the time, Cagliostro had specific reasons for coming to Mitau. As Recke later recognized, "Bey seinem hiesigen Aufenthalte, suchte er sich Anhänger zu schaffen, deren größeren Theil er auf verschiedene Art hinzuhalten wußte, um durch diese mit desto mehrerem Glanze in St. Petersburg auftreten zu können" (During his stay here, he tried to collect disciples, and he understood how to lead the larger part of these along through various means, so that through them, he would be able to appear in St. Petersburg with all the more glory).[30] Cagliostro had much to gain from a collaboration with Recke, since he hoped to groom her for service to him in St. Petersburg. As a member of the high aristocracy in Courland, she provided a potential connection through which he hoped he could gain access to the court of Catherine the Great.

On her part, Recke believed that she had much to gain from her new spiritual mentor. From the start, three principles seem to have governed the young adult Recke's intellectual interests: first, coming into contact with the spirits of beloved family members who had died; second, actively doing good works in the world; and third, maintaining strong, correct ties with God and religion, as she understood them on the basis of Bible teachings. Her strong tendency to religious enthusiasm and mysticism tended to blend these areas together in her mind. As she notes, "ich wollte immer vollkommner in der Religion werden, und so entstand der Gedanke nach und nach in mir: daß auch ich, wenn ich nach völliger Reinheit der Seele strebte, in die Gemeinschaft höherer Geister aufgenommen werden könnte" (I wanted to become ever more perfect in religion, and thus the thought gradually evolved in me, that even I, if I strove for full purity of soul, might be accepted into communion with higher spirits).[31] As a keen observer of human nature, Cagliostro sensed Recke's openness to certain aspects of the spiritualism that he was peddling.[32] Although he frequently alienated or offended his Mitau disciples through the coarseness of his manners and inconsistencies in his claims, Cagliostro seems to have discerned Recke's guiding principles fairly quickly.[33] She was not interested in his "red powder," which allegedly had the capability of turning base metal to gold,[34] nor did

---

30 *Nachricht*, 25.
31 *Nachricht*, 6.
32 *Nachricht*, 63.
33 *Nachricht*, 8.
34 *Nachricht*, 57.

she particularly care about finding buried treasure or gathering ancient occult knowledge.[35] Noting her interest in religion, Cagliostro quoted freely from the Bible and frequently used passages from scripture to support or illustrate his magical claims, a tactic that initially disarmed Recke and made her more accepting of his teachings.[36]

In the first weeks in Mitau, Cagliostro and Recke worked closely together to build up a community of believers and supporters. She quickly convinced her aunt and her cousins to join the new Masonic lodge, and then, as she reports, she led the others in efforts to proselytize: "Wir wurden bald nicht nur seine gläubigen Jüngerinnen, sondern führten ihm noch mehr Anhänger zu" (Soon we not only became his faithful disciples, but also procured more followers for him).[37] In the meetings at her father's house she acted as the hostess for Cagliostro's lectures, seances, and lodge meetings, and she appointed herself lodge historian and kept written records of the spiritualist's interaction with the group. She accompanied Cagliostro on a quest for hidden treasure to her uncle's estate at Wilzen.[38] She also worked hard to convert naysayers in Mitau, including her friend and confidant Hofrat Sigismund Georg Schwander (1727–84), a local official who had joined the lodge in order to observe the proceedings and protect her from Cagliostro's influence. As a defender of her master's reputation, Recke criticizes Schwander's insistence on the preeminence of reason: "Denn er glaubte nichts, was mit seiner Vernunft in Widerspruch stand; und ich hatte den vollen Glauben an noch immer fortdaurende Wunderkraft des Gebets frommer Christen, und wünschte einen so verehrungswürdigen Mann allmälig zu diesem Glauben zu bekehren. Durch Cagliostro hoffte ich meinem Ziele näher zu kommen" (For he believed nothing that stood in opposition to his reason, and I believed completely in the everlasting miraculous power of the prayers of pious Christians, and I desired gradually to convert such a respectable man to this belief. Through Cagliostro, I hoped to get nearer to my goal).[39] Together, Recke and Cagliostro endeavored to convert Schwander and others from enlightened skepticism to their own brand of Freemasonry.

In private, Cagliostro instructed Recke, introduced her to the subtle arts of his spiritualism, and encouraged her strong desires to collaborate

---

35 *Nachricht*, 36, 38, 40–1.
36 It was Cagliostro's knowledge and ready use of scripture that later made Recke suspect that he was a Catholic priest (*Nachricht*, xvii–xviii), and that he was probably being used by Jesuits for their own aims (*Nachricht*, xxiv–xxv).
37 *Nachricht*, 7.
38 Funck, "Lavater und Cagliostro," 46.
39 *Nachricht*, 31.

with the higher spirits. In her writings, Recke remembers the effect that Cagliostro's private instructions had upon her young mind as she gave herself over to his "große und hohe magische bildliche Lehren ... die meine Einbildungskraft erhitzten, in meiner Seele allerley Systeme über Magie erweckten, und mich aufs neue in dem Vorsatz stärkten, nach überirrdischen Kräften zu streben" (great and lofty magical pictorial doctrines ... that inflamed my imagination and awakened many different systems of magic in my soul, and strengthened anew my resolve to strive for supernatural powers).[40] In fact, Cagliostro expertly intertwined all of Recke's natural inclinations into the overarching promise that he made to his enthralled young devotee:

> daß ich, wenn ich mich unermüdet der Magie weihete, bald so weit kommen würde, nicht nur des belehrenden Umganges der Verstorbenen zu genießen, sondern auch von *meinen Obern zu geistigen Reisen in die Planeten* gebraucht, und nachgehends zu einer *der Beschützerinnen unsers Erdballs* erhöhet zu werden, bis ich als eine bewährte Schülerinn der Magie, zu noch höhern Regionen empor gehoben würde.[41]
>
> (that I, if I tirelessly dedicated myself to magic, would soon progress so far that I would not only enjoy instructive interaction with the dead, but would also be used by my superiors for spiritual voyages to the planets, and afterwards I would be exalted to be a protector of our earthy sphere, until I, as a tried and tested magical apprentice, could be exalted to even higher regions.)

Through this collaboration, both Cagliostro and Recke believed that they were reaching their longed-for ultimate goals: Cagliostro believed that she was becoming a pliable instrument in his hands, and Recke believed that she was making tangible progress towards her dream of consorting with spirits. The spiritualist thought that he had found a protégée much more reliable than Goethe's sorcerer's apprentice: There was no real magic to interfere with his plans.

Recke's initial relationship with Cagliostro was characterized by naïve trust in his teachings and her strong will to believe that what she was hearing was truth. In spite of this self-chosen blind belief, however, Recke's sharp mind and quick ability to analyze continually exploded the aura of truth that she willed to see around her master. From the first, she carefully recorded in her diary the discrepancies and contradictions

---

40 *Nachricht*, 139.
41 *Nachricht*, 101. Italics in original.

that she noticed in his lectures and private lessons. However, she only discussed these doubts in private with Cagliostro himself.[42] Recke's first open discussion of her doubts about Cagliostro can be found in her correspondence with Lavater and others after the spiritualist's departure from Mitau. In these early letters, she still believes in spiritualism, but worries that Cagliostro has crossed over to black magic.[43] In 1786, after she had become convinced that he was indeed a charlatan, she published a short denunciation of Cagliostro in the *Berlinische Monatsschrift*. This article triggered an immediate polemic debate in the newspapers about the possibility of mortal interaction with spirits. As Recke's letters and articles about Cagliostro drew increasing attention from the public, she began to organize her writings into a larger didactic project: a careful and critical account of the count's visit to Mitau, written as a detailed exposé of his teachings and methods. As she produced her manuscript, Recke consulted with the publisher and author Friedrich Nicolai. She also sent her developing ideas out for review by a broader group of intellectuals that Nicolai refers to as "Männer ... von Einsicht und geprüfter Redlichkeit" (men of discernment and proven honesty).[44] After obtaining permission from all of the parties involved in the experiences in Mitau, and in spite of the warnings of friends who worried for her safety and her reputation, Recke moved ahead and prepared the manuscript for publication.[45] The treatise was published by Nicolai's publishing house in 1787; Nicolai himself wrote the preface, celebrating "die edeldenkende freymüthige wahrheitsliebende Verfasserinn" (the noble-minded, candid, truth-loving author) and encouraging her readers to contemplate her words "mit Einsicht und Unpartheylichkeit" (with judiciousness and impartiality).[46]

The resulting book, *Nachricht von des berüchtigten Cagliostro Aufenthalte in Mitau im Jahre 1779 und von dessen dortigen magischen Operationen*, is a fascinating treatise that stands as one of the Enlightenment era's great argumentative tracts.[47] Recke specifically connects her book to the project of enlightenment. In her prologue to the *Nachricht*, written to her friends and supporters,[48] Recke considers the positive effects of

---

42 Many of these private discussions were reported by Recke in *Nachricht*.
43 Funck, "Lavater und Cagliostro," 52–3.
44 Friedrich Nicolai, "Vorrede des Herausgebers," in *Nachricht*, ix.
45 Recke, "An meine Freunde und Freundinnen in Kurland und in Deutschland," in *Nachricht*, xxi–xxxii.
46 *Nachricht*, xix–xx.
47 Wilhelm Kühlmann sees Recke's *Nachricht* as a manifestation of an "aggressiven Berliner Rationalismus" ("Cagliostro," 117). See also Müller-Seidel, "Cagliostro," 137–8.
48 Recke, "An meine Freunde und Freundinnen."

her time spent with Cagliostro while she was in the throes of her own *Schwärmerey*,[49] in that she believes the encounter to have been an important step in her education: "Mit desto froherem Danke gegen Gott würd' ich dann auch selbst auf diese Zeit zurücksehen, weil sie mir *Erziehung* ward, mittelst welcher ich sichrer meinen Gang durch die Welt und zur Ewigkeit gehen gelernt habe" (With even more joyous thanksgiving to God I would look back even at this time period, because it became an education for me, by means of which I have learned to follow my course more confidently through the world and towards eternity).[50] As someone who now has attained a strong and steady foothold, Recke feels it is her duty to provide instruction and support to others who are still caught up in a mystical approach to life. She portrays herself as part of a great struggle to free people from superstition, the great enlightening movement that started with Luther:[51] "Manche Freundinn, mancher Freund wird mich nun mit stillem Bedauern, aus dem Platze den ich in ihrem Herzen hatte, verweisen, weil ich es hier aus eigner Erfahrung frey bekenne, daß alle diese Lehren dahin abzwecken, uns in den *Schlamm* des Aberglaubens hinein zu führen, aus welchem der große Luther uns zu befreyen anfing"[52] (With silent regret, some friends will now expel me from the place that I had in their hearts, because here, from my own experience, I freely confess that all of these doctrines serve one purpose: to drag us into the mire of superstition, from which the great Luther began to free us). The movement that she

---

49 The German word *Schwärmerey* (modern German *Schwärmerei*) is difficult to render precisely in English. For the purposes of this chapter, *Schwärmerey* will hereafter be translated as "enthusiasm." In its eighteenth-century usage, as it appears here, it conveys the sense of exaggerated sentiment or enthusiasm, often with a touch of religious fanaticism. The term was usually used in relation to religious, mystical, or occult beliefs. This is the way that we will use the term in this chapter. For a deeper discussion of the term *Schwärmerey* in the Enlightenment period, see Donnert, *Schwärmerei*.
50 *Nachricht*, xxii. Italics in original.
51 At the time of Recke's writing, "The Enlightenment" as we understand it had not yet emerged as an identifiable philosophical and historical period. Rather, the ideas of rational thought were still being developed and asserted in the face of previously existing ways of looking at the world, some of which were still heavily influenced by the medieval worldview. Thus Recke is discussing "enlightenment" rather than "The Enlightenment" in the modern sense. When Recke talks of "enlightenment," she is referring to a way of looking at life that emphasizes reason, questioning, and knowledge in the face of blind belief and superstition. This is why her understanding of the term can include Socrates and Luther.
52 *Nachricht*, xxxi–xxxii. Italics in original.

mentions refers not only to Luther's reformation, but also to a broader push towards the active use of reason that spans history. Recke claims that she does not fear retribution or death in retaliation for her exposé of Cagliostro, because she sees herself as contributing to this great cause of enlightening the human mind; in her words, "Kein Uebel kann [der Tod] dem seyn, der seine Pflichten mit Treue erfüllt; denn auch *Sokrates, Mendelssohn,* und *Friedrich der Einzige* starben" ([Death] cannot be evil for those who fulfill their duty with loyalty: for even Socrates, Mendelssohn, and Frederick the Great died).[53] Recke shows no hesitation in exposing herself to the same potential violence that threatened Socrates and her contemporaries in the Prussian Enlightenment, such as Moses Mendelssohn and Frederick the Second of Prussia.[54] Enlightenment, in other words, is a cause for which she is willing to risk all.

It is not only the book's content with its passionate campaign against superstition that earns it a place among the great works of the Enlightenment, but also the form of the text. Recke arranged her book in a particularly provocative format: on the even-numbered pages, she presented the account of Cagliostro's activities and teachings that she had written during his stay in Mitau in 1779. She had kept this running written account, she explains, as a historical document that was to remain in the archive of the newly minted "Loge d'Adoption" that Cagliostro had gathered around himself. On the odd pages, lined up with the paragraphs of her earlier account, Recke printed a commentary that she wrote in 1787, an annotation that she refers to as "meine jetzige Ueberzeugung nebst den in dieser Sache gemachten Entdeckungen ... auf daß man Cagliostros Plan, und den Gang seiner Betrügereyen um so eher übersehen könne" (my present convictions along with the discoveries that I made in this matter ... so that Cagliostro's plan and the course of his deceptions might be more easily surveyed).[55] Recke begs her reader to compare the two texts and to notice how

---

53 *Nachricht*, xxvii–xxviii. Italics in original.
54 Moses Mendelssohn was in constant jeopardy because he was Jewish and an outspoken defender of Judaism. His frank critiques of religion and forceful defense of Enlightenment ideas won him numerous enemies. Although Frederick II is viewed by history as a great, enlightened ruler, he was a conqueror and an empire-builder. As such, he drew a high level of enmity to many of his actions and policies. This is particularly true in relation to his treatment of the Polish inhabitants of the areas he acquired through the first Polish Partition. As a radical reformer of his realm, from the lowest peasantry to the highest bureaucracy, he forced changes through regardless of all resistance. Thus, what we now view as positive progress was not necessarily seen in the same light in his time.
55 *Nachricht*, 22–3.

easily someone like her young self, a distressed young woman with a "Hang zum Wunderglauben" (propensity for belief in miracles) can be deceived and led astray.[56] Recke's formatting is a rhetorical tour de force, juxtaposing two versions of her own voice: the first the notes of a trusting learner beginning a spiritual journey, and the other a rational, critical perspective that not only exposes the tricks and flaws of Count Cagliostro, but also criticizes the author's own gullibility and lack of critical resistance.

It comes as no surprise that Recke eventually made a complete break with Cagliostro. She was far too astute as an observer of people and their behavior to remain in unquestioning thrall to the "Wundermann" (wonder worker) for very long.[57] Her years of voracious reading and intellectual dialogue with her brother Fritz and others in her closest circle of friends had trained her too well. From the time that she began her collaboration with Cagliostro in earnest, Recke allowed a voice of skepticism to enter into her account of the things that she heard and saw. Even in her confused state, Recke's desire for truth drove her to question Cagliostro openly, particularly about actions that contradicted what he claimed to be the guiding principles of their Masonic lodge—that is, that magical power and interaction with higher spirits were to be used to serve humankind. For example, Recke records two separate occasions on which Cagliostro, using Recke's young cousin as a medium, performs one of his experiments, or conjurations of spirits, in order to cause pain, and thus exercise revenge on someone who has annoyed him.[58] This misuse of spiritual power so shocks Recke that she openly confronts the spiritualist, and he responds to her with equal annoyance. As she writes to Lavater:

> Ich erschrak über den Rachegeist bey einer kleinen Beleidigung und sagte ihm draußen, es mißfiele mir sehr, daß er seine Wissenschaft so herabwürdigte und statt gutes zu würken schädlich würke. Er hieß mich vorwitzig, gab mir einen Ausputzer ... und sagte: "Auch Strafen sind Wohlthaten." Ich antwortete: "Ja, wenn sie bessern oder zur allgemeinen Sicherheit nützen, aber hier wäre der Fall gar nicht." Hierauf sagte er, der Jünger

---

56 *Nachricht*, 23.
57 *Nachricht*, xi.
58 One of these, carried out against Hr. v. N. N., appears in *Nachricht*, 66, 68, 70. The second, performed against the duke of Courland, is described in Funck, "Lavater und Cagliostro," 51–2.

sollte sich nicht weiser dünken als sein Meister, und wir könnten gewiß seyn, daß er noch seine geheimen Bewegungsgründe zu diesem Experiment gehabt hätte, welches zum Nutzen vieler nothwendig gewesen wäre.[59]

(I was appalled at his vengeful spirit with such a small offense, and said to him outside that it displeased me greatly that he would vulgarize his science to such a degree that, instead of doing good, he did harm. He called me cheeky, rebuked me sharply, and said: "Punishments are also good deeds." I answered: "Yes, if they improve someone or benefit the general security, but this was definitely not such a case." At this, he said that the disciple shouldn't consider herself wiser than her master, and we could be certain that he had had his secret motives for this experiment, which was necessary for the benefit of many.)

Although Cagliostro manufactures explanations in answer to Recke's questions, it is clear from his responses that she has disconcerted him, for example, in the exchange above, or on another occasion when he exclaims, "Das Ey will immer klüger seyn als das Huhn" (The egg always wants to be thought smarter than the hen).[60] Later in their relationship, Cagliostro impatiently deflects her questioning with this warning:

Ists leichtsinniger Spott der aus Ihnen spricht, so sind Sie keiner Antwort würdig. Ists aber die spitzfindige Grüblerinn, die mir diese Frage vorlegt, so muß ich Ihnen sagen: Hüten Sie sich, wenn ich nicht mehr an Ihrer Seite bin, immer das *pourquoi du pourquoi* erforschen zu wollen ... Eva, die durch den Apfelbiß fiel, und das ganze Menschengeschlecht zum Falle brachte, ist nichts als eine magische Parabel, daß Neugier, Eitelkeit und Herrschsucht bis ins tausend und tausendste Glied Unglück bringen können ... Wenn nicht bloß Wunsch, Gutes zu würken, Sie der Mystik zuführt, so gehn Sie ja nicht weiter, sonst wird zeitliches und ewiges Elend Ihr Theil werden.[61]

(If you are speaking frivolous scorn, then you don't deserve an answer. But if it is the pedantic brooder who is asking this question, then I must tell you: When I am no longer at your side, beware of always wanting to delve into the "why behind the

---

59 Funck, "Lavater und Cagliostro," 52.
60 Funck, "Lavater und Cagliostro," 46.
61 *Nachricht*, 46–8.

why" ... Eve, who fell by eating the apple, and made the entire human race fall, is nothing but a magical parable, teaching that curiosity, vanity, and a domineering nature can bring misfortune to the thousandth-upon-thousandth generation ... If anything besides just the wish to do good leads you to mysticism, go no further. Otherwise your portion will be temporal and eternal misery.)

In the diary portion of her exposé, written on the even pages, the young Recke not only records her own nagging doubts about Cagliostro's teachings and behavior, but also includes his sharp rebukes and shows that she capitulated again and again to his wishes. The calm, well-reasoned language of Recke's journal indicates that she accepted Cagliostro's rebukes and committed herself anew to following him blindly; the self-contradictory nature of her entries betrays the internal struggle that she was experiencing. It is the constant juxtaposition of her assertions of complete acceptance of Cagliostro's words with her accounts of dismay, anger, incredulity, or disgust at his inconsistencies that gives voice to the internal dissonance that she was experiencing.

Recke's growing disenchantment with Cagliostro appears in her increasingly frequent suspicions that the spiritualist had fallen from the ideals of truth and service to humanity that he claimed were foundational to his Masonic lodge. It becomes clear from the entries in her journal that Recke's self-confidence and willingness to assert her own ideals in the face of her master's demands increased proportionately as she uncovered evidence of Cagliostro's "fallen" state. During the spiritualist's final days in Mitau, Recke boldly confronted him with her concerns, as she resisted his efforts to persuade her to go to St. Petersburg with him. She writes:

> Ich beschwor ihn um des Heils seiner Seele willen: ja wachsam auf sich zu seyn und sich der Nekromantie nicht zu nähern; sagte ihm zugleich ernsthaft und sehr determinirt: Daß ich ihm und seiner Gattinn nicht nach Petersburg folgen könnte, weil er mir es doch eben selbst gesagt habe, daß er nun von bösen Geistern versucht würde, und vom guten Prinzipium abfallen könne. Ich wolle mich also nicht in die Gefahr begeben, in einem fremden Lande im beständigen Umgange eines Magikers zu leben, der von den Dämonen überwunden werden könnte.[62]

---

62 *Nachricht*, 139–40.

(I adjured him for the salvation of his soul to watch himself vigilantly, and not to draw close to necromancy; I also said to him both earnestly and with determination that I could not accompany him and his wife to Petersburg, because he had recently told me himself that he was now being tempted by evil spirits, and could depart from good foundational principles. Therefore I did not wish to put myself in the danger of living in a foreign land in the continual company of a magician who could be overcome by demons.)

It was precisely Cagliostro's deceits and indiscretions that honed Recke's predilection to critical observation of those around her, an ability that had lain dormant under her long excursion into religious enthusiasm and mysticism. Now, faced with actions and claims that jarred her inborn sense of truth, Recke began to utilize her critical abilities with increasing force and confidence. While Recke's diary entries on the even pages show the early development of her voice as she grew in her resistance to Cagliostro, her commentary on the odd pages serves not only as an explanation of her earlier thoughts, but as the chronicle of her intellectual evolution as she joined the ranks of other enlightened voices.

The final steps in Recke's progression from intellectual dependency to full acceptance of the Enlightenment ideal of reason came through another kind of unexpected collaboration, this time with a printed text. In 1779 the German Enlightenment thinker Gotthold Ephraim Lessing published his great philosophical drama *Nathan der Weise* (Nathan the Wise). The book made its way to Courland during the critical period of Recke's increasing disillusionment with Cagliostro, and her dawning understanding of the way in which he performed his deceits and trickery. Recke's friend and intellectual mentor, Hofrat Schwander, had been attempting for several years, even before Cagliostro's appearance in Mitau, to lead Recke away from her *Schwärmerey* and her belief in the ability of mortals to communicate with spirits, but Recke reports that his efforts only served to make her cling more stubbornly to her beliefs.

When *Nathan der Weise* came into Schwander's hands, he read the drama aloud to Recke with great emphasis and enthusiasm. The moment was right, and Nathan's words to his daughter Recha cut through Recke's confusion and superstition in a way that nothing else had been able to do. It is in fact Nathan's effort to convince Recha to think rationally about the one who rescued her from the fire that penetrates Recke's own blind belief in Cagliostro. Through Nathan's words, Recke comes to understand that religious enthusiasm and superstition can be used as an excuse to avoid doing the good that she herself supports as one of her foundational principles. Nathan's statement in the play is quite straightforward:

> —Begreifst du aber,
> Wie viel andächtig schwärmen leichter, als
> Gut handeln ist? wie gern der schlaffste Mensch
> Andächtig schwärmt, um nur,—ist er zu Zeiten
> Sich schon der Absicht deutlich nicht bewußt—
> Um nur gut handeln nicht zu dürfen?[63]

> (—But see how far
> It's easier to swoon in pious dreams
> Than do good actions? See how sluggish men
> Are fond of dreaming piously, because—
> Although at times of their intent not quite
> Aware—they'd shun the need of doing good?)[64]

As Recke read and reread Nathan's words to Recha, she suddenly understood that, like Nathan's daughter, she herself had been willfully clinging to her self-chosen *Unmündigkeit* and *Schwärmerey*. Time and again she had repressed the doubts and confusion that erupted into her efforts at obedient discipleship, creating excuses to cover the dissonance that her master's behaviors and teachings caused in her mind. But now, in her encounter with Lessing's text, the issue of Recke's existence as a blind disciple to a superior master was suddenly wrenched into a totally new plane. Initially, as a firm devotee of spiritualism and mystical enthusiasm, Recke had grappled with growing doubts as to her master's connection with wholesome, helpful spirits. But Nathan's words completely shredded the cloud of spiritualism that Recke had allowed to envelop her mind for so long. In forceful prose, Recke describes the intellectual transformation that the collaboration with Lessing's text awakened in her:

> Mein Herz schlug heftiger, ich las den Nathan wieder; und obgleich ich damals immer noch den Gedanken hegte, daß es viele verborgene Kräfte der Natur gäbe, und daher den Glauben hatte, daß Magie möglich sey: so erschien mir nun doch bey

---

[63] Gotthold Ephraim Lessing, *Nathan der Weise*, Act I, Scene 2, quoted in *Nachricht*, 154.
[64] Gotthold Ephraim Lessing, *Nathan the Wise*, trans. Bayard Quincy Morgan (New York: Frederick Ungar, 1980), 14.

fortgesetztem reifern Nachdenken das ganze System magischer Philosophie endlich als ein ganz schimärisches Ding, durch welches man ausser aller wahren Thätigkeit für die Welt gesetzt, und ein Spiel intriganter Gaukler wird.[65]

(My heart beat more powerfully, I read *Nathan* again; and although at the time I still cherished the idea that there were many hidden powers in nature, and therefore had the belief that magic was possible, after ongoing, more mature deliberation, now the entire system of magical philosophy appeared to me at last to be a completely chimeric thing, through which one's ability to be truly active in the world is abrogated, and one becomes a toy for scheming imposters.)

With a jolt that shook her intellectual foundations like a bolt of lightning, Recke was blasted from the shadowy world of spirits into the full light of Enlightenment rationality. Through Recha's eyes, Recke recognized how totally self-chosen her intellectual and spiritual dependence on Cagliostro had been. Lessing's text gave her the power to relinquish the phantoms of the past—the spirits of her dead loved ones—which had bound her native capabilities into a static limbo. Now she saw clearly how easily people can be manipulated and used in accordance with the agendas of others if they refuse to use their own reason to understand the events of their lives. With this, her own transformation into an *actor* was complete. The irony is that it was through Recke's interactions with Cagliostro, as she lived the experience of spiritualism with a master of deception, that her own structure of superstitious beliefs was gradually undermined. Cagliostro's trickery and deceits accomplished what Schwander had never been able to do through all his lectures on reason. In a very real way, it was Recke's willing acceptance of *Unmündigkeit* or intellectual dependence on a deceiver that proved to be the only force powerful enough to catapult her to a position where she could use her reason and intellectual maturity to stand on her own, rather than relying on the persuasion of others.

Recke's juxtaposition of her own contrasting voices resonates deeply with some of the core ideals of Enlightenment thought. It is, after all, the subjective voice and the articulation of that voice that later comes to stand as a shorthand for the whole Enlightenment project. In his 1784 essay "Beantwortung der Frage: Was ist Aufklärung?"[66] (An Answer to the Question: What Is Enlightenment?) Immanuel Kant

---

65 *Nachricht*, 155.
66 Immanuel Kant, "Beantwortung der Frage: Was ist Aufklärung?," *Berlinische Monatsschrift* 2, no. 12 (December 1784): 481–94.

describes enlightenment as the development of a subjective voice, an achievement that he calls "Mündigkeit"[67] (age of majority, maturity). In the well-known first sentence of the essay, Kant explains that *"Aufklärung ist der Ausgang des Menschen aus seiner selbstverschuldeten Unmündigkeit"*[68] (*Enlightenment is the human being's emergence from his self-incurred minority*).[69] The term *mündig* does, of course, have many different connotations, not all of them having to do with a voice. A person who is *mündig* has many different powers besides the powers of speech. But at its core, *mündig* is still etymologically a vocal image. It is the voice that represents subjective authority: *Unmündigkeit*, as Kant describes it, is "das Unvermögen, sich seines Verstandes ohne die Leitung eines andern zu bedienen"[70] (inability to make use of one's own understanding without direction from another).[71] Someone who is *unmündig* stands in need of a *Vormund*, a mouth that can, above all else, speak on behalf of someone who cannot speak. That speech may be expressed in different ways—as action, as authority, and so forth—but the foundational metaphor is based upon the act of speaking and the capacity of a voice.

Elisa von der Recke's exposé of Cagliostro stands as an extended illustration of Kant's vocal metaphor of the Enlightenment. By including the entire text of her "Aufsatz vom Jahre 1779," unedited, uninterrupted, and in its original context, Recke provides the reader with an intact and authentic voice that wonders, cries out in amazement, and also struggles to describe and understand the things that she sees. It is a sympathetic and familiar voice that readers can empathize with, a voice that sits firmly in Kant's realm of *Unmündigkeit*. Recke describes her choice to leave the voice intact with its whole account, allowing the reader to understand the scope of her own *Unmündigkeit*:

> Ich lasse diesen Aufsatz, so wie er geschrieben war; weil ich glaube, daß es dem Freunde der Wahrheit und dem Menschenkenner interessant seyn wird, das treue Gemälde einer Seele zu sehen,— die Irrthum für Wahrheit hielt, ein eignes System auf diesen Irrthum bauete, und dadurch von einem intriganten Gaukler so hingehalten ward, daß Wahrheit, und die Rechte der Vernunft, sich für sie in undurchdringliche Nebel hüllten.[72]

---

67 Kant, "Beantwortung," 482.
68 Kant, "Beantwortung," 481. Italics in original.
69 Immanuel Kant, *Practical Philosophy*, ed. and trans. Mary J. Gregor (Cambridge: Cambridge University Press, 1999), 17. Italics in original.
70 Kant, "Beantwortung," 481.
71 Kant, *Practical Philosophy*, 17.
72 *Nachricht*, 22.

(I am leaving this essay just as it was written, because I believe that it will be of interest to the friend of truth and to the expert in human nature to see the faithful portrait of a soul—who held error to be truth, built her own system on this error, and through this was so led on by a scheming imposter, that truth, and the privileges of reason, were cloaked for her in an impenetrable fog.)

Recke was certainly overpowered by her supposed mentor, led away from her own powers of rational thinking and into the misty distractions of his tricks. Her portrayal of her own *Unmündigkeit*, however, is far more than a cautionary tale or a bad example of youthful gullibility. For Recke, *Unmündigkeit* is not a permanent state; it holds within itself the potential for understanding, truth, and reason. The relationship between her two side-by-side voices is not a simple case of before-and-after enlightenment, but a kind of female *Bildungsroman* that sees the beginnings of reason stirring in the immature voice itself, and traces the slow development of the more mature, critical view that finally emerges in the 1787 annotations.

Although others had produced critiques of Cagliostro's actions prior to Recke's publication of the *Nachricht* in 1787, none of these writings seems to have reached a level of general public interest or concern.[73] It is because Recke positioned her experience with Cagliostro as a case

---

73 Prior to Recke's publication of her *Nachricht*, Cagliostro's reputation, both positive and negative, seems to have been communicated predominantly from lodge to lodge among Freemasons in the different countries he visited. A small number of texts discussing Cagliostro began to appear in the 1780s. Chief among these were Johann Joachim Christoph Bode's anonymously published tract entitled *Ein paar Tröpflein aus dem Brunnen der Wahrheit: Ausgegossen vor dem neuen Thaumaturgen Caljostros* ([Frankfurt am Main]: Am Vorgebürge, 1781); Jean-Pierre-Louis de Luchet's anonymously published pamphlet entitled *Mémoires authentiques pour servir à l'histoire du comte de Cagliostro*, 2nd edn. (Hamburg: Chez F. Fauche, 1785); and *Cagliostro in Warschau; oder, Nachricht und Tagebuch über desselben magische und alchymische Operationen in Warschau im Jahre 1780, geführet von einem Augenzeugen. Aus dem französichen Manuscripte übersetzt, und mit Anmerkungen erläutert* ([Strasburg], 1786), written by the Polish Count August Moszyński, and translated into German by Friedrich Justin Bertuch. All of these texts leveled criticism and charges of charlatanry against Cagliostro, and they seem to have been quite widely circulated—for example, Recke and other Cagliostro followers in Mitau had access to them. However, none of these accounts triggered significant public discussion or debate. After Cagliostro's condemnation by the Inquisition on charges of being a Freemason, several translations of the files kept during his trial were published, including *The Life of Joseph Balsamo, Commonly Called Count Cagliostro* (London: C. and G. Kearsley, 1791), and *Leben und Thaten des Joseph Balsamo* (Zürich: Orell, Geßner, Füßli, 1791), both of which appeared anonymously. Cagliostro himself neither wrote nor published anything relating to his

of rational awakening versus superstition and mysticism that such a powerful public debate ensued. The issue did not concern Cagliostro as such, but was rather centered upon the value of a rational worldview as opposed to the entrenched belief in spiritualism, alchemy, the occult, and mysticism. This is why Recke's *Nachricht* drew the attention of opponents of the stature of Prince Eugen von Württemberg and Pastor Starck, as well as the support of Catherine the Great. Though Cagliostro had hoped to use Elisa von der Recke to insinuate himself into Catherine's court, it was actually Recke's exposé of Cagliostro that captured the rapt attention of the empress. In a letter written to Recke in 1788 from Czarskoje-Selo, Catherine applauds Recke's attacks on the irrational forces that exist even in a time of enlightenment:

> Die zweite von Ihnen erhaltene Schrift hat mir eben so viel Vergnügen, wie die erste, gemacht. Beide tragen das Gepräge eines für die Wahrheit tief fühlenden Herzens, und zugleich eines aufgeklärten und viel umfassenden Geistes, an sich. Es ist freilich zu beklagen, daß am Ende des achtzehnten Jahrhunderts sich neuerdings Meinungen ausbreiten, die schon seit Jahrtausenden als falsch und vernunftwidrig anerkannt ... verworfen und verachtet worden sind ... so ist dennoch zu hoffen, daß allen diesen Anhängern der Isis-Tempelei, ihrem Aberglauben, und allen damit verbundenen Träumereien eben der Verfall bevorstehe ... absonderlich, wenn so gute Federn, wie die Ihrige, den Schleier des Unsinns, worein sich diese geheimen Gaukeleien einhüllen, von denselben abzunehmen, und den Weltbürgern so kräftige Gegengründe dawider darzureichen fortfahren werden.[74]

(The second document that I received from you afforded me just as much pleasure as the first one. Both bear the imprint of a heart that feels deeply about the truth, and at the same time, of an

---

Freemasonry and magical efforts. When in 1910 W. R. H. Trowbridge published his book *Cagliostro: The Splendour and Misery of a Master of Magic* (New York: E. P. Dutton), he reported that his purpose in writing the first actual biography of Cagliostro to date was to cut through the myths and popular misconceptions so as to give the "truth" about the count. In his view, "the unfavourable opinion the Countess von der Recke ... formed of Cagliostro ... has, on account of her deservedly high reputation, been largely responsible for the hostility with which history has regarded him" (141). In spite of Trowbridge's efforts, however, even at present most views of Cagliostro have been colored by Recke's presentation of the events in Mitau, and/or the opinions of the Inquisition.

74 Catherine II, empress of Russia, "Schreiben der Kaiserinn von Rußland an Frau von der Recke," in *Berlinische Monatsschrift* 2, no. 7 (1788): 129–31 (130–1).

enlightened spirit that encompasses much. It is indeed deplorable that, at the end of the eighteenth century, recently opinions have been spreading that for millennia have been recognized … condemned, and despised as false and irrational … nevertheless it is to be hoped that downfall lies in store for all of these disciples of the temples of Isis, their superstitions, and all of the flights of fancy associated with them … particularly if such fine quills as yours will continue to remove the veil of folly in which this clandestine trickery is enshrouded, and to provide the citizens of the world with such powerful counterarguments against it.)

It is not only Recke's "enlightened spirit" that Catherine lauds in her letter, but also her "fine quill," which will inspire other writers to tear through the veil of foolishness and superstition that still persists at the end of the eighteenth century. Catherine praises Recke not as a passive thinker of enlightened thoughts, but as the active writer of a foundational Enlightenment text that will serve as the inspiration for other European thinkers.

Indeed, the account of Recke's interactions with Cagliostro made a deep impact upon the cultural imagination in Europe and far beyond. For example, Catherine the Great's fascination with Recke's exposé extended much further than mere intellectual admiration. The Russian empress went on to write a comedic drama based upon Recke's description of Cagliostro.[75] But it was not only Recke's royal admirer who jumped onto the Cagliostro bandwagon in the years following her exposé, but also some of the greatest German writers of the next decades. Johann Wolfgang von Goethe's 1791 comedy *Der Groß-Coptha* (The Great Coptha) resonates with reports of Cagliostro's antics that Goethe received "von Mitau her" (from Mitau),[76] and Friedrich Schiller memorialized Cagliostro in his unfinished novel *Der Geisterseher* (The Ghost Seer).[77] The Prussian artist and caricaturist Daniel Chodowiecki depicted Cagliostro in one of his famous engravings,[78] which was later referenced in E. T. A. Hoffmann's story "Der Sandmann" (The Sandman). Indeed, Michael Rohrwasser points to passages in Hoffmann's text that closely parallel descriptions from Recke's *Nachricht*, including a sorcerer who threatens to tear an eavesdropping child into pieces.[79] This

---

75 Müller-Seidel, "Cagliostro," 143.
76 Müller-Seidel, "Cagliostro," 137.
77 Donnert, *Schwärmerei*, 27–8.
78 See Kiefer, *Cagliostro*, 259.
79 Compare with *Nachricht*, 47.

passage, as well as shared friends, connects Recke's writings to those of Hoffmann.[80] The figures from Hoffmann's "Der Sandmann" served in turn as the foundation of Sigmund Freud's essay "Das Unheimliche" (The Uncanny). In the nineteenth century, the figure of Cagliostro makes appearances in many different works of literature, art, and music, even beyond the borders of German-speaking Europe. Alexandre Dumas includes Cagliostro in several of his novels,[81] as does George Sand,[82] and Johann Strauss wrote an operetta titled *Cagliostro in Vienna*.[83] The Cagliostro figure lived on in the twentieth century in a wide variety of different incarnations, from French film pioneer Georges Méliès' film *The Mirror of Cagliostro*,[84] to Umberto Eco's novel *Foucault's Pendulum*,[85] to Todd McFarlane's graphic novel series *Spawn* and the television adaptation that the series inspired.[86] Twenty-first-century references to Cagliostro can be found in Japanese video games,[87] a viola chamber piece,[88] and the recent Marvel Comics film *Dr. Strange*, in which Benedict Cumberbatch's eponymous character searches Cagliostro's magic diary looking for spells that might save the world as we know it.[89]

---

80 Michael Rohrwasser, *Coppelius, Cagliostro und Napoleon: Der verborgene politische Blick E. T. A. Hoffmanns. Ein Essay* (Basel: Stroemfeld/Roter Stern, 1991), 36–42.
81 See, for example, the period series by Alexandre Dumas, which begins with *Joseph Balsamo* (The Marie Antoinette Romances, Book I, Part I: *The Works of Alexandre Dumas: Joseph Balsamo* [New York: P. F. Collier, 1893]), and *Memoirs of a Physician* (The Marie Antoinette Romances, Book I, Part II: *The Works of Alexandre Dumas: The Memoirs of a Physician* [New York: Peter Fenelon Collier, 1893]), both detailing the life and actions of Cagliostro.
82 George Sand, *The Countess of Rudolstadt: A Sequel to "Consuelo"* (New York: A. L. Burt, 1894), https://play.google.com/books/reader?id=2LYaAAAAYAA-J&hl=en&pg=GBS.PP7.
83 Richard Traubner, *Operetta: A Theatrical History* (New York: Routledge, 2003), 102.
84 See André Gaudreault, "From Primitive Cinema to Kine-Attractography," in *The Cinema of Attractions Reloaded*, ed. Wanda Strauven (Amsterdam: Amsterdam University Press, 2006), 85–104 (91).
85 Umberto Eco, *Foucault's Pendulum*, trans. William Weaver (New York: Harcourt, 1989), 417.
86 See "Spawn," in *Encyclopedia of Comic Books and Graphic Novels*, ed. M. Keith Brooker (Oxford: Greenwood, 2010), 583.
87 Isaak V. Kerlow, *The Art of 3D Computer Animation and Effects* (Hoboken, NJ: Wiley and Sons, 2004), 36.
88 In 2015, American composer John Zorn composed a piece for solo viola entitled *Cagliostro*.
89 See Jacob Johnson, *Marvel's "Doctor Strange": The Art of the Movie* (New York: Marvel, 2016).

As these many artistic reflections show, the repercussions of Elisa von der Recke's unplanned collaboration with Count Cagliostro spread far beyond the small circles in the Courland where she first encountered the spiritualist. The *Nachricht* is more than the mere unmasking of a fraudulent trickster. The unique structure of the text, which juxtaposes the voice of the young devotee with that of her mature critical self, affords enlightenment on several levels. At base, it reveals the process through which the critical, rational powers of a young mystical enthusiast are awakened, sharpened, and developed through constant collision with the inconsistent, rationally offensive behaviors and teachings of the one she had accepted as a trustworthy master.

On another level, we follow a woman's struggle to find and assert her own voice in the face of an intimidating, domineering male authority figure, and then, after finding that voice, to verbalize her understanding publicly. In a superficial discussion of the *Nachricht*, it is easy to lose sight of the fact that, at Recke's time, the expectation was that a "good" woman remain at home in the private sphere, and be neither seen nor heard in the male-dominated public world. And yet Recke, a noblewoman, had the temerity to publish a self-revealing document in her own name (no pseudonymous disguise here)—not only to publish, but to jump fearlessly and unashamedly into the male forum of newspaper debates, in which she was able to hold her own in the face of all criticism and negative judgment. Through this action, Recke provided a powerful example for other women as they, too, stretched towards a place in the world of publication.

And not least, the *Nachricht* reveals the process through which a human mind develops from *Unmündigkeit* to *Mündigkeit*, relinquishing its self-chosen dependency through the will to think clearly and act freely as an independent agent. It is at this level that Recke's document found its explosive way into mainstream Enlightenment thought, and excited the imagination of thinkers, authors, and artists across Europe and through the centuries. What began with private séances and intimate lectures in Mitau came to be a powerful force in European philosophy, art, and politics, as the unlikely collaboration between Recke and Cagliostro became the catalyst that propelled the young spiritual enthusiast into the light of Enlightenment rationality, and gave her the voice to speak the truth she discovered there.

Bibliography

Anon. [Johann Joachim Christoph Bode]. *Ein paar Tröpflein aus dem Brunnen Wahrheit: Ausgegossen vor dem neuen Thaumaturgen Caljostros*. [Frankfurt am Main]: Am Vorgebürge, 1781. https://play.google.com/books/reader?id=djBZAAAAcAAJ&hl=en_US&pg=GBS.PA1 (accessed September 21, 2018).

Anon. *Leben und Thaten des Joseph Balsamo*. Zürich: bey Orell, Geßner, Füßli, 1791. https://archive.org/details/lebenundthatende01marc (accessed September 21, 2018).

Anon. *The Life of Joseph Balsamo, Commonly Called Count Cagliostro*. London: C. and G. Kearsley, 1791. https://play.google.com/books/reader?id=AEsDAAAAYAAJ&printsec=frontcover&pg=GBS.PR1 (accessed September 21, 2018).

Anon. [Jean-Pierre-Louis de Luchet]. *Memoires authentiques pour servir à l'histoire du comte de Cagliostro*. 2nd edn. Hamburg: Chez F. Fauche, 1785. https://play.google.com/store/books/details?id=sSRAAAAAcAAJ (accessed September 21, 2018).

Borowski, Ludwig Ernst. "Cagliostro, einer der merkwürdigsten Abenteuerer unseres Jahrhunderts: Seine Geschichte nebst Raisonnement über ihn und den schwärmerischen Unfug unserer Zeit überhaupt." In *Cagliostro: Dokumente zu Aufklärung und Okkultismus*, ed. Klaus H. Kiefer, 332–455. Munich: Beck, 1991 [1790].

Catherine II, empress of Russia. "Schreiben der Kaiserinn von Rußland an Frau von der Recke." *Berlinische Monatsschrift* 2, no. 7 (1788): 129–31.

Cox, Carrie. "Pushing the Scented Envelope: Elisa von der Recke at the Cultural Crossroads." MA thesis. Brigham Young University, 2012.

Donnert, Erich. *Schwärmerei und Aufklärung: Die kurländische Freifrau Elisa von der Recke (1754–1833) in den Geisteskämpfen ihrer Zeit*. Frankfurt am Main: Peter Lang, 2010.

Dumas, Alexandre. *The Works of Alexandre Dumas: Joseph Balsamo*. New York: P. F. Collier, 1893. *The Internet Archive*. https://archive.org/details/worksofalexand06duma/page/76 (accessed October 16, 2018).

Dumas, Alexandre. *The Works of Alexandre Dumas: The Memoirs of a Physician*. New York: Peter Fenelon Collier, 1893. *The Internet Archive*. https://ia802606.us.archive.org/20/items/worksalexdumas07dumauoft/worksalexdumas07dumauoft.pdf. (accessed October 16, 2018).

Eco, Umberto. *Foucault's Pendulum*. Trans. William Weaver. New York: Harcourt, 1989.

Ehnenn, Jill R. *Women's Literary Collaboration, Queerness, and Late Victorian Culture*. Burlington, VT: Ashgate, 2008.

Funck, Heinrich. "Lavater und Cagliostro." *Nord und Süd: Eine deutsche Monatsschrift*, 83 (October 1897): 41–63.

Gaudreault, André. "From Primitive Cinema to Kine-Attractography." In *The Cinema of Attractions Reloaded*, ed. Wanda Strauven, 85–104. Amsterdam: Amsterdam University Press, 2006. http://www.millertheatre.com/about/press-releases/composer-portraits-begin-with-an-evening-of-premieres-from-john-zorn (accessed March 2, 2017).

Iverson, John R. "Le dîner de philosophes: Conviviality and Collaboration in the French Enlightenment." In *Models of Collaboration in Nineteenth-Century French Literature*, ed. Seth Whidden, 25–36. New York: Routledge, 2009.

Johnson, Jacob. *Marvel's "Doctor Strange": The Art of the Movie*. New York: Marvel, 2016.

Kant, Immanuel. "Beantwortung der Frage: Was ist Aufklärung?" *Berlinische Monatsschrift* 2, no. 12 (December 1784): 481–94. http://ds.ub.uni-bielefeld.de/viewer/image/2239816_004/513/ (accessed September 21, 2018).

Kant, Immanuel. *Practical Philosophy*. Ed. and trans. Mary J. Gregor. Cambridge: Cambridge University Press, 1999.

Kerlow, Isaak V. *The Art of 3D Computer Animation and Effects.* Hoboken, NJ: Wiley and Sons, 2004.

Kiefer, Klaus H., ed. *Cagliostro: Dokumente zu Aufklärung und Okkultismus.* Munich: Beck, 1991.

Kühlmann, Wilhelm. "Cagliostro in Mitau, Elisa von der Recke und Friedrich Nicolai—Motive und Kontexte einer Rationalistischen 'Selbstaufklärung.'" In *Aufklärer im Baltikum: Europäischer Kontext und regionale Besonderheiten,* ed. Ulrich Kronauer, 115–32. Heidelberg: Universitätsverlag Winter, 2011.

Lessing, Gotthold Ephraim. *Nathan the Wise.* Trans. Bayard Quincy Morgan. New York: Frederick Ungar, 1980.

McCarthy, John A. *Crossing Boundaries: A Theory and History of Essay Writing in German, 1680–1815.* Philadelphia: University of Pennsylvania Press, 1989.

Moszyński, Count August. *Cagliostro in Warschau; oder, Nachricht und Tagebuch über desselben magische und alchymische Operationen in Warschau im Jahre 1780, geführet von einem Augenzeugen. Aus dem französichen Manuscripte übersetzt, und mit Anmerkungen erläutert.* Trans. Friedrich Justin Bertuch. [Strasburg], 1786.

Müller-Seidel, Walter. "Cagliostro und die Vorgeschichte der deutschen Klassik." In *Literaturwissenschaft und Geistesgeschichte: Festschrift für Richard Brinkmann,* ed. Jürgen Brummack, 137–8. Tübingen: Max Niemeyer, 1981.

Rachel, Paul, ed. *Elisa von der Recke: Aufzeichnungen und Briefe aus ihren Jugendtagen.* Leipzig: Dieterich'sche Verlags-Buchhandlung, 1900.

Recke, Elisa von der. "Elisa an Preißler." *Berlinische Monatsschrift,* 5 (May 1786): 385–98. http://ds.ub.uni-bielefeld.de/viewer/image/2239816_007/413/ (accessed September 21, 2018).

Recke, Elisa von der. *Nachricht von des berüchtigten Cagliostro Aufenthalte in Mitau im Jahre 1779 und von dessen dortigen magischen Operationen.* Berlin: Friedrich Nicolai, 1787.

Rohrwasser, Michael. *Coppelius, Cagliostro und Napoleon: Der verborgene politische Blick E. T. A. Hoffmanns. Ein Essay.* Basel: Stroemfeld/Roter Stern, 1991.

Sand, George. *The Countess of Rudolstadt: A Sequel to "Consuelo."* New York: A. L. Burt, 1894. https://play.google.com/books/reader?id=2LYaAAAAYAAJ&hl=en&pg=GBS.PP7 (accessed September 21, 2018).

Selwyn, Pamela E. *Everyday Life in the German Book Trade: Friedrich Nicolai as Bookseller and Publisher in the Age of Enlightenment 1750–1810.* University Park, PA: Pennsylvania State University Press, 2000.

"Spawn." In *Encyclopedia of Comic Books and Graphic Novels,* ed. M. Keith Brooker. Oxford: Greenwood, 2010.

Stillinger, Jack. *Multiple Authorship and the Myth of Solitary Genius.* Oxford: Oxford University Press, 1991.

Traubner, Richard. *Operetta: A Theatrical History.* New York: Routledge, 2003.

Trowbridge, W. R. H. *Cagliostro: The Splendour and Misery of a Master of Magic.* New York: E. P. Dutton, 1910.

Four A Freedom Apart
Feminine *Bildung* in Sophie Mereau's "Marie" and *Amanda und Eduard*

Tom Spencer and Jennifer Jenson

To the German reading public of the late eighteenth century, the concept of *Bildung*—the developmental or formational process leading to maturity—was ever present. It constitutes the "vocation of man" presented in J. J. Spalding's much reprinted *Die Bestimmung des Menschen* (The Vocation of Man, 1748), and structures Lessing's equally influential *Die Erziehung des Menschengeschlechts* (The Education of the Human Race, 1780). In 1784 Kant famously declared "enlightenment" to be a process of intellectual and moral *mündig werden* (growing up), and like Spalding he considered belief in the immortal soul warranted by humanity's capacity for endless progress. Then, in the 1790s, the idea of *Bildung* underwent explosive development. Fichte's inaugural lectures at the University of Jena in 1794/5 present us with a "self-positing" rational subject engaged in an endless quest to overcome nature's resistance to the subject's self-identity. One year later Schiller's *Ästhetische Briefe* (Aesthetic Letters) reinterpret this Fichtean quest as a struggle to reharmonize our rational and sensuous faculties through the help of art. Published in 1795/6, Goethe's *Wilhelm Meisters Lehrjahre* (Wilhelm Meister's Years of Apprenticeship) demonstrates how the modern education is not only rational and aesthetic, but also sexual; Wilhelm sets out to become a great poet, to form and be formed through art, but his diverse erotic experiences with the youthful Marianne, the seductive Philine, the half-child Mignon, the nameless baroness, the actress Aurelie, the noble Therese, and the "Amazon" Natalie best mark his path of personal and social development leading to the *Turmgesellschaft* (Tower Society).

It is against the backdrop of this rich discourse on *Bildung* as a rational, aesthetic, and erotic enterprise that Sophie Mereau—in Jena/Weimar alongside Fichte, Schiller, Goethe, and the early German

Romantics—begins to write her narratives of female *Bildung*. Already an aspiring poet, Mereau came to Jena in 1793 as the young bride of the law professor Friedrich Ernst Carl Mereau, and had the distinction of being the sole female auditor of Fichte's lectures on the newly minted *Wissenschaftslehre* (Science of Knowledge). She was taken under the mentoring wing of Schiller, who admired her "spirit of contemplation" and "symbolizing" imagination.[1] He facilitated the publication of much of her poetry in his *Musenalmanach* (Muses' Almanac) and *Die Horen* (The Horae), and for several years provided her with criticism, encouragement, and career advice. Despite the significant roles that these men and others (Goethe and Rousseau most notably) played in her emergence as a writer, she put her own spin on central themes of the period.[2] For instance, most of her models understand *Bildung* as a socializing process that integrates the individual into a broader network of actors. The *Bildung* of Mereau's female protagonists, in contrast, initially depends upon social relationships, yet later reverses this direction and drifts in various ways towards greater social *dis*connection. The most important subset of these passing relationships is the erotic one between a man and a woman. Specifically, it is the joint venture of love that allows the woman to discover herself, but this very discovery subsequently disempowers the erotic and liberates the female protagonist. The man is not necessarily rejected as an obstacle or antagonist, but their relationship is no longer characterized by an emotional or metaphysical necessity. If the male–female relationship persists, it is presented as a warm friendship, and may or may not be sexual. The joint venture between the man and the woman becomes serene, egalitarian, and voluntaristic.[3] Consequently, it may also be dispensable.

---

1 "Schiller an Sophie Mereau, 18. Juni 1795," *Friedrich Schiller Archiv*, http://www.friedrich-schiller-archiv.de/briefe-schillers/an-sophie-mereau/schiller-an-sophie-mereau-18-juni-1795/. All translations in this chapter are our own.

2 Goethean influence is rife, for instance, throughout "Marie," which recounts the erotic *Bildung* of a young woman who ends up an actress, a female inversion of Wilhelm Meister. Also, the pietistic feminine ideal embodied by Goethe's "schöne Seele" is easily recognizable in the protagonist of "Elise." Rousseau's influence is unmistakable when, in *Blüthenalter der Empfindung* and "Marie," a "natural," idyllic education is plainly contrasted with the corrupting influence of civilized society. The idealization of America as a semi-primitive paradise in "Elise" is also deeply Rousseauian. A consideration of Mereau's poetry would reveal further instances of influence.

3 That Mereau would pursue such themes in print and be supported by someone like Schiller reinforces Helen Fronius's argument that around 1800 there were in fact a "variety of definitions of femininity" ranging across the conservative–liberal spectrum. These less-recognized interpretations of the woman's role in

Of course, Mereau's are not the only works in this period to present unsociable *Bildung* trajectories. For example, at the end of Hölderlin's epistolary novel *Hyperion* the eponymous hero withdraws into profound, pessimistic isolation, and Goethe's "schöne Seele" (beautiful soul) in *Wilhelm Meister* finds the endpoint of her personal development in a Pietist version of the cloistered life. Thus there is a tension in this period between the *Bildung* narrative tending towards greater socialization and alternative developmental paths leading to social withdrawal. Important for our purposes is that these alternative paths are usually marked as inferior or undesirable in some way. Hyperion's isolation is the result of catastrophic disappointment, while Goethe's "beautiful soul" is presented as having gone subtly awry. Hyperion's beloved, Diotima, is another socially withdrawn figure, but she is already perfect and undergoes no development at all. Mereau's distinctive contribution is to present socially disconnecting *Bildung* narratives that are not marked as deviant or failed, and it is not coincidence, as we shall see, that the protagonists of such narratives are women. To understand why this is the case, we must look more closely at the three forces of unsociability at work in Mereau's fiction.

The first of these forces is the unattractiveness of society itself, which can lead otherwise socially minded individuals to turn away from greater social and political engagement. Katharina von Hammerstein observes that Mereau usually presents the city, the symbol of social life, "as corrupt and misanthropic," and then contrasts it with "a pastoral idyll lauded as being harmonious with nature and romantic."[4] Clearly inspired by Rousseau, Mereau repeatedly presents us with young, innocent protagonists unspoiled by social contact. When they finally make that contact, they encounter injustice, conventionality, and triviality, which in one of Mereau's stories, *Das Blüthenalter der Empfindung* (The Spring of Feeling, 1794), results in a flight to the primitivist utopia of colonial America. While the Rousseauian sensibility is not always this pronounced, it is present to some degree in almost all of her work.

---

    this period "are more than exceptions: they indicate that fundamentally, gender roles were not stable, but the subject of continual discussion." Helen Fronius, *Women and Literature in the Goethe Era, 1770–1820: Determined Dilettantes* (Oxford: Oxford University Press, 2007), 35.

4 "Als korrupt und menschenfeindlich" and "einer als naturnah und romantisch gepriesenen ländlichen Idylle." Katherina von Hammerstein, *Sophie Mereau-Brentano: Freiheit–Liebe–Weiblichkeit. Trikolore sozialer und individueller Selbstbestimmung um 1800* (Heidelberg: Winter, 1994), 52.

The second socially isolating force is Mereau's sexual anthropology, which is largely typical of early German Romanticism/Idealism. According to this anthropology, feminine *Bildung* does not require a very large or complex social arena, and the natural outcome of that *Bildung* is a woman's diminished social dependency. Mereau's views are not always consistent on this topic, but the following unpublished fragment sounds the keynotes of her theory of the sexes.

> Die Weiber sind von Natur gut und wie sie sein sollen. Die Männer streben die ruhige Harmonie zu erreichen, die ihnen in der Natur des Weibes als Muster aufgestellt ist. Das heißt sie werden Künstler, denn Kunst ist nur ein mit Bewußtsein Nachahmen der Natur. Was sollen nun aber die Weiber? Denn etwas müßen sie an sich thun, das ... wird daraus klar, weil so [einige/wenige?] das sind was sie sein sollen.—Sie sollen sich erkennen und sich erhalten—das ist ihr einziges Geschäft—sie sind Philosophen. Deswegen können die Weiber nie künstlerisch sein, denn sie haben keine höhere Aufgabe, als das was sie sind.[5]

> (Women are naturally good and the way they should be. Men strive to reach the peaceful harmony found naturally patterned in women. In other words, men become artists, for art is a conscious imitation of nature. But what now should women do? For they must do something about themselves. That becomes clear, for only [some/few?] are what they should be.—They should know and maintain themselves—that is their sole occupation—they are philosophers. For this reason women cannot be artistic, for they have no higher duty than to be what they are.)

Although the main idea here is not original, Mereau brings new urgency to it with the question: "Was sollen nun aber die Weiber? Denn etwas müßen sie an sich thun" (But what now should women do? For they must do something about themselves). It is easy to write stories about men, because by nature they have something to do in the world: create externally the harmony they lack internally. Their perfection and the perfection of culture are one and the same. Women, by contrast, bear that harmony within themselves, at least potentially, and thus serve as a model of the goal of male creativity. Consequently, they do not have a worldly vocation of their own. Hölderlin's Hyperion and Diotima provide a perfect illustration of this sexual typology at work. Mereau

---

5 Sophie Mereau-Brentano, *"Wie sehn' ich mich hinaus in die freie Welt": Tagebuch, vermischte Prosa und philosophische Betrachtungen*, ed. Katharina von Hammerstein (Munich: Deutscher Taschenbuch, 1997), 124–5.

would find Diotima a useless *practical* model, however, because the latter has already attained feminine perfection, whereas real women know they have not. But if this deficit is not made up through creativity, as it is for men, then what is a woman to do?

Mereau's answer is that a woman is not to *do* anything in particular, but rather to *know* and *maintain* herself ("sich erkennen und sich erhalten") in her true character. This feminine vocation can be seen as a kind of *Bildung*, but it does not require the social canvas that the creative male vocation does. Or to be more precise, female socialization is a process of negative learning, in which the woman comes to know and maintain herself by recognizing her *loss* of integrity amid the temptations and deceptions of society. This, in turn, leads to a withdrawal from social entanglements, or at least a certain detachment (while still amenable to good works) within the social environment.

The third and final antisocial force, ironically, is love. In Mereau's hands the erotic relationship has a double function as both the on- and off-ramp of social integration. It can draw the innocent and sheltered protagonist into the broader world, but it can also preoccupy her so totally that she is prevented from integrating herself into that world. It can further function as the last stop—perhaps a disillusioning one—in the protagonist's retreat from social life. In any case, Mereau places so much narrative and anthropological emphasis on *eros* that relatively little room remains to develop the public and especially political dimensions of her characters, be they male or female.

The predominance of the erotic is evident everywhere in Mereau's work. In her personal notes, for instance, we find the following:

> Liebe und allenthalben Liebe, ich begreife nicht wie ohne sie nur etwas intreßant sein kann. Ist sie nicht die wichtigste Angelegenheit des Lebens?—War sie nicht der höchste Reiz des innigsten geistigsten Lebens, so bedurfte es der süßen Harmonie, die aus Mann und Weib erst Ein Wesen, den Menschen bildete, nicht, so war es der Natur genug, ein dumpfes hermaphroditisches Geschöpf hervorzubringen, das nie zum wahrem [sic] Leben erwacht.[6]

> (Love and everywhere love, I cannot comprehend how anything could be interesting without it. Is it not the most important aspect of life?—Were it not the greatest delight of our most interior spiritual life, then there would have been no need for the sweet harmony that created one being, a human, from man and woman. It would be enough for nature to bring forth a dull hermaphroditic creature that would never awake to real life.)

---

6 Mereau, "*Wie sehn' ich mich*," 110.

This passage clearly demonstrates the central and irreplaceable role that love between a man and a woman plays not only for the woman seeking autonomy (*Selbstthätigkeit*), "life," and a "freer existence," but also for the man who, like the woman, would lack the "höchsten Reiz des innigsten geistigsten Lebens" (highest allure of the most interior, spiritual life) without it. Divorced from the animating force of sexual love, humanity would only be a shadow of itself.

This point is reinforced in another unpublished fragment, "Die Leiden der Liebe" (The Sufferings of Love), which is an abbreviated arcadian myth of origins. It opens with the description of mankind's primitive, utopian condition.

> In den ersten Frühlingsjahren der neugeborenen Erde wandelten unter ihren unschuldigen Bewohnern viele Kinder des Himmels umher, die ihnen wohlthätig den Hauch ihres Wesens mittheilten. Holde Gefälligkeit, gütige Sanftmuth, zärtliche Freundschaft, theilnehmendes Mitleiden, [süße?] Geselligkeit, die alle mischten sich in ihre Gesellschaft—aber Liebe war nicht unter ihnen.[7]
>
> (In the springtime of the newborn earth, many children of heaven lived among its innocent inhabitants and benevolently shared with them the divine breath. Graceful courtesy, gentle goodness, tender friendship, heart-felt compassion, and [sweet?] sociality: all these blended together in their society—but love was not among them.)

If not for that final tag, this would seem to be the evocation of a golden age, but the concluding observation renders this a version of Eden; no matter how idyllic it seems, it is without passion and therefore seriously incomplete. We are told what is missing: "Das Auge des Jünglings stralte nicht feuriger beim Anblick *eines* Mädchens. Und das Roth der Mädchen glühte nicht höher beim Gedanken an *Einen*" (The eye of the young man burned no brighter when looking at a *certain* girl. And the girl's color glowed no brighter when thinking of a *certain* boy).[8] The text then introduces a young couple, Amanda and Licias, whom the gods have chosen as the vessels that will introduce love into the world. After it pours into them, they experience divine, or even super-divine, pleasure.

> Ein Augenblick lehrte sie den wahren Genus des Lebens, den süßen Werth ihres Daseins ... Der Jüngling dünckte sich kein Erdensohn mehr. Liebe hatte ihn zum Gott erhoben—und

---

7 Mereau, "*Wie sehn' ich mich*," 197.
8 Mereau, "*Wie sehn' ich mich*," 197. Italics in original.

das Mädchen hätte um des Geliebten Kus selbst den Himmel verschmäht.—Die Unsichtbaren laßen in ihren Seelen, und fanden daß ihre Seeligkeit den dem Menschen bestimmten Grad von Glückseeligkeit überstieg. Sie fühlten, daß selbst ihre Unsterblichkeit [diese?] Entzückungen nicht überwog.[9]

(One moment taught them the true pleasure of life, the sweet worth of their existence ... the young man deemed himself earth's son no longer. Love had elevated him to a god—and the girl would have spurned heaven itself for her beloved's kiss.—The Unseen read their souls and discovered that their bliss surpassed the degree of happiness allotted to man. The gods felt that even their immortality could not outweigh [these?] raptures.)

The Christian blessings of heaven and immortality cannot compete with the erotic bliss that is a god unto itself. In this sense there is a Gnostic potential in the erotic, which can enliven our social existence, but can also, by virtue of its purity and intensity, draw us out of the world. In "Die Leiden der Liebe," we are not explicitly told what happens to Amanda and Licias, but it is clear that they were destroyed in some way by the magnitude of their passion. Zeus proclaims pure love too intense for humanity, and he therefore spreads it out "unter tausendfache Gestalten" (among thousand-fold forms), particularly among the non-sexual forms of affection that facilitate social life. Love's "sanfter Stral" (gentle ray) now shines "bald aus dem Lächeln der zärtlichen Mutter, aus der stillen Träne des Mitleids, und aus dem heitern Auge des Menschenfreundes" (at times from a mother's tender smile, from the quiet tear of compassion, and from the cheerful eye of a friend).[10] This second casting of love—what Freud calls aim-inhibited love—draws attention to the ambivalent nature of its first, erotic casting.[11] In its raw, erotic form, love both animates society and renders the overwhelmed subject useless to society.

Two supplementary points about the erotic in Mereau are even more important for our purposes. First, although the engrossing interest of the erotic as presented above is gender-blind, there are also gendered reasons for it. In the case of women, the erotic compensates for other pleasures (*Genuss, Vergnügen*) that their social position tends to foreclose.

---

9 Mereau, "*Wie sehn' ich mich*," 198.
10 Mereau, "*Wie sehn' ich mich*," 198.
11 Sigmund Freud, "Massenpsychologie und Ich-Analyse," in *Fragen der Gesellschaft: Ursprünge der Religion*, Vol. IX of *Studienausgabe*, corrected edn. (Frankfurt am Main: Fischer, 2009), 61–134 (104).

Nur selten gelangt das Weib zu einem freien lebendigen Genuße ihrer Existenz. Verwiesen in die enge Gränze des Gefallens, verliert es beinah allen Reitz des Vergnügens, denn das ist das Wesentliche des Vergnügens, das es frei ist, keinen bestimmten nothwendigen Zweck, blos um seiner selbst willen da ist. Nur Liebe bringt Selbstthätigkeit und Leben in den dumpfen Kreis ihrer Ideen. Hier und hier allein ist es ihr vergönnt, ein freieres Dasein zu genießen und mit dem Mann die Rechte des Lebens zu theilen.[12]

(Only rarely is a woman able to achieve a free and living enjoyment of her existence. Relegated to the sphere of pleasing, she loses almost all the allure of pleasure, for the heart of pleasure is its independence, that it serves no necessary purpose, and that it is simply there for its own sake. Love alone brings autonomy and life into the dull circle of her ideas. Here and here alone it is granted unto her to enjoy a freer existence and to share with man the rights of life.)

Typical of Mereau's work, this passage has both a proto-feminist and seemingly unfeminist ring to it. She clearly finds it unjust that women should be so burdened with pleasing (*Gefallen*) that enjoyment (*Genuss*) passes them by, but there is little reformist fervor here given Mereau's solution. *Liebe*—the primary, erotic, and all-sufficient kind—requires a man anyway. Indeed, it is a romantic relationship that permits her to "enjoy a freer existence" and "the rights of life," and is consequently a necessary aspect of her development, despite the fact that she will eventually outgrow her erotic dependency on male figures. The path to freedom goes through this dependency, making feminine *Bildung* a joint male–female venture, albeit ironically.

This leads to the second supplementary point about Mereau's handling of *eros*: she is clearly reluctant to let romantic love triumph in the end, despite its centrality during the protagonists' development. In part this can be explained through the sexual-anthropological issues discussed above. Tension necessarily arises between a woman's inborn "ruhige Harmonie" (quiet harmony) and the intense feelings of lack and dependence that emerge in the erotic. No matter how fulfilling the love of man and woman may be, it does in a sense betray the self-contained harmony of feminine nature. This is why Mereau repeatedly dodges or complicates the marriage that would normally tie up all loose ends in contemporary narratives of the same general type. Instead, Mereau's protagonists might settle for friendship, or marry without passion, or

---

12 Mereau, *"Wie sehn' ich mich,"* 108.

choose God over an earthly lover. Only by derailing the erotic narrative arc in these ways can the author reestablish the *ruhige Harmonie* at the core of her protagonists' feminine nature.[13]

Having identified these three antisocial impulses in Mereau's narrative imaginary—her social pessimism, her gender typology, and her prioritization of the erotic—we must note that the overall tone of her works is not misanthropic or excessively narcissistic. These are *Bildungsgeschichten* (narratives of development), and her protagonists attain maturity by weaning themselves from social dependencies rather than rejecting social ties altogether. Their developmental path leads through these very dependencies rather than around them, making feminine *Bildung* a joint venture between a woman and society—and especially a joint erotic venture between a man and a woman—that culminates in the obsolescence of that same venture. At the very least the venture is transformed so that dependency is overcome, leaving the protagonist in a relatively isolated, yet dignified position. This dynamic plays out in many of Mereau's texts, but in this essay we will illustrate it by focusing on just two: the short narrative "Marie" (1798) and the epistolary novel *Amanda und Eduard* (1803).

"Marie"

"Marie" traces the life of the eponymous protagonist from her initial transition into society, which is facilitated by erotic relationships, to her eventual retreat into a novel form of isolation within the confines of society. Marie's life begins in seclusion. Her quiet upbringing in the rural town in which her father, Anton, raises her has few distractions, a result of his belief that happiness comes from removing oneself from the stimulation and temptation of society. Although an accomplished musician, he hides his lute in order not to upset his daughter's emotional equilibrium. While outwardly content with her circumstances, Marie begins to regret her isolation. She has no outlet for "jene Zartheit des Gefühls" (that tenderness of feeling) that nature has awoken in her, and that "sich gern und leicht zu einer höhern Bildung emporhebt" (gladly

---

13 Mereau's reliance on these tactics seems to validate Adrian Daub's claim that a tension exists between the egalitarian metaphysical conception of love embraced by Mereau and the early German Romantics, and the "gender categories that covertly subtend and support the imaginary of the metaphysical ... subject" in this period. Adrian Daub, *Uncivil Unions: The Metaphysics of Marriage in German Idealism and Romanticism* (Chicago: University of Chicago Press, 2012), 233. In other words, romantic love (in this historically specific sense) and gender roles are ultimately incompatible. We contend that given this choice, Mereau is more loyal as an author to her conception of feminine nature and its particular brand of freedom than she is to an egalitarian metaphysics.

and easily elevates itself to a further development).[14] Her discovery of her father's lute, which she learns to play in secret, does not make matters better. A chance encounter with the urban socialite Antonie and her musician companion Brandem, whose coach breaks down in front of Anton's cottage, first affords Marie's budding emotions a worthy object and provides her new developmental opportunities. The text singles out Antonie as "das erste gebildete Wesen" (the first educated being) ever encountered by Marie, who is awed by the "Kenntnisse, welche Antonie im Gespräch zeigte, die Gemälde aus der Welt, womit sie sie unterhielt, die Sicherheit, mit der sie von vielem sprach, was sie selbst kaum verworren zu denken wagte" ([the] knowledge Antonie displayed in conversation, the worldly scenes she entertained her with, and the confidence with which she spoke of many things that Marie hardly dared have muddled thoughts about).[15] With time Marie will perceive the superficiality of Antonie's attainments, which do not reflect Schillerian grace, but in the first encounter the naïve country girl falls into ecstasy at the sight of her elite counterpart: "Ihre Erscheinung versetzte Marien ganz außer sich selbst; sie konnte sich an Antonien nicht satt sehen, ihre Gestalt, ihr Ton, ihr Betragen erweckten ganz neue Bilder in ihr" (Her presence left Marie ecstatic; she couldn't look at Antonie enough. Her figure, tone, and demeanor awakened entirely new images in [Marie]).[16]

As a result of this chance meeting, Marie is invited to the city to visit Antonie, who pairs her up with Seeberg, Antonie's own fiancé, at a masked ball. In his presence Marie experiences "eine nie gefühlte unendlich süße Rührung" (a never-before felt and unendingly sweet emotion) and the two immediately fall in love. Seized by "Neuheit, Lust und der Gewalt der jungen Neigung" (newness, desire, and the power of young affection), Marie kisses him, despite having known him for only a few hours.[17] While at first concerned that this forwardness on Marie's part evidences a moral looseness, Seeberg notices her confusion and understands that her faux pas was fueled by erotic innocence. He therefore indulges his feelings for her, and Marie learns to do the same. Ironically, it is from Antonie, who has lost interest in Seeberg, that she receives morally dubious encouragement in this romantic pursuit.

---

14 Sophie Mereau-Brentano, "Marie," in *Ein Glück, das keine Wirklichkeit umspannt*, ed. Katharina von Hammerstein (Munich: Deutscher Taschenbuch, 1997), 49–83 (51).
15 Mereau, "Marie," 52.
16 Mereau, "Marie," 52.
17 Mereau, "Marie," 63.

Antonie ... hatte ihr gesagt: was sie fühle, sei nur ein sehr gerechtes Wohlwollen; und es stünde überhaupt nicht in unserer Macht, unsern Empfindungen zu gebieten. Marie beruhigte sich immer mehr. "Soll ich mein Auge und mein Gefühl den göttlichen Eindrücken des Schönen und Vorzüglichen verschließen?" dachte sie. "Da ich nichts wünsche, als ihn zu sehen, ihn uneigennützig zu lieben, was kann Antoniens Verhältnis dabei leiden?"— Regten sie hierüber ja noch Zweifel, so wußte sie die Liebe, die wie wir wissen, ihre eigene Philosophie hat, alle befriedigend aufzulösen.[18]

(Antonie ... had told her: what she felt was only a very proper feeling of good will; and that it does not lie within our power to command our feelings. Marie calmed down even more. "Should I close my eyes and feelings to the godly impressions of the beautiful and the exquisite?" she thought. "Since all I desire is to see him, selflessly to love him, how could that harm Antonie's relationship?—Should further doubts on the matter trouble her, she knew that love, which has, as we all know, its own philosophy, would satisfactorily resolve them.)

Encouraged by Antonie's false counsel and her own self-deception, Marie and Seeberg flee the city and begin a life together in idyllic, rural isolation.

Here we see multiple forces of unsociability emerging in tandem. Marie's desire for Antonie followed by her love for Seeberg brings her into society, but almost as quickly *eros* draws her back into the empty countryside. As we indicated before, this is simply the way of desire according to Mereau, which does not easily abide the restrictions of social convention. Since the engagement of Seeberg and Antonie is too far along—"beide Häuser, und mit ihnen der ganze Kreis ihrer Bekanntschaft hielten sie für entschieden" (both households, and with them their entire circle of acquaintances, considered it decided)—simply to cancel on account of emotional disinterest, *eros* opts for flight.[19] In the spirit of exonerating *eros* from the charge of irresponsibility, we might lay all the blame on convention. In the present case, if the conventions governing public engagements were more attuned to human desires and the diversity of situations, then they would not put people in desperate straits. But the text does not let *eros* off so easily. Antonie and even the Emile-like Marie indulge in specious justifications of their

---

18 Mereau, "Marie," 68.
19 Mereau, "Marie," 72.

actions without even mentioning the burden of convention, yet to act as if love "has its own philosophy" does not pass muster in an age of Kantian ethics. Eros is, at least in this story, complicit in the moral disorder that makes otherwise sociable people flee society.

But *eros* and conventionality are not the only unsociable forces in play, and Marie's story does not end in her false Eden with Seeberg. Their arcadian idyll is eventually disrupted by a visit from Antonie, who with deceitful magnanimity declares that she will relinquish her claim on her fiancé. The fickleness of desire manifests itself as "Antoniens Bild gewann in [Seebergs] Herzen bald seine vorigen Rechte wieder" (Antonie's image again obtained its earlier rights in [Seeberg's] heart).[20] As his heart returns to Antonie, he also recalls the social circles he left behind, "und ihre Meinungen, ihre Urteile machten noch tiefen Eindruck auf ihn" (and their opinions, their judgments still held sway for him).[21] Taking stock of the altered situation, Marie decides to leave Seeberg, not, however, because of (disappointed) love, but rather because of an emerging sense of feminine self-sufficiency. In her farewell letter to Seeberg, she affectionately admonishes him to care less in the future about the opinion of others. She then disappears, causing the one clearly noble character in the story—the musician Brandem, who always loved Marie from a respectful distance—to search after her. He finally discovers her making a living as an actress, and although their reunion is marked by romantic excesses of feeling, the text studiously avoids any suggestion of a sexual dimension to the relationship. Brandem is thus the anti-Seeberg; he does not compromise her independence (*Selbstständigkeit*) through erotic expectations, but rather settles for "ein dauerndes Band von Achtung, Vertrauen und Freundschaft" (an enduring bond of respect, trust, and friendship).[22]

The concluding half of the narrative thus traces a path beyond *eros* to the self-contained wholeness proper to women in Mereau's sexual anthropology. To be sure, it took the detour of her erotic venture with Seeberg to uncover her "Selbstvertrauen" and "Selbstgefühl" (self-confidence and sense of self).[23] In fact, all her past experiences constituted a *Bildung* leading to this condition of self-knowing completion.

> Der einfache Gang ihres frühern Lebens hatte ihr Zeit gelassen, über sich selbst nachzudenken, und ihre Wünsche an etwas Bestimmtes zu fesseln. Ihr natürlich heller Verstand war durch

---

20 Mereau, "Marie," 75.
21 Mereau, "Marie," 75.
22 Mereau, "Marie," 83.
23 Mereau, "Marie," 77, 79.

den Umgang mit der Welt erleuchtet, aber nicht geblendet, ihre Phantasie war beschäftigt, aber nicht verwirrt, ihr Gefühl verfeinert, aber nicht vernichtet worden. In der darauf erfolgten Einsamkeit hatte sie über vieles reiflicher nachdenken, vieles vergleichen, sich von vielem unabhängig erhalten lernen, und einen, für ihr Alter seltenen Grad von Tätigkeit und praktischer Weisheit erworben. Sie war jetzt das ganz, was sie sein wollte.[24]

(The simple course of her earlier life had given her time to reflect on herself and focus her desires on something specific. Her naturally clear intellect was enlightened by her interaction with the world, but not blinded. Her imagination was occupied, but not confused. Her feelings refined, but not extinguished. In her subsequent isolation she learned to reflect carefully on many things, to compare many things, to keep her distance from many things, and she achieved a degree of activity and practical wisdom uncommon for someone her age. She was now entirely what she wanted to be.)

Narratively, this powerful image of completed self-development ("Sie war jetzt das ganz, was sie sein wollte" [She was now entirely what she wanted to be]) emerges after Marie has relocated to an urban setting, but it is important to note that amid the hustle of city life, Marie is without significant social attachments. At least we do not hear of any apart from the one between her and Brandem, who arrives after she has already established herself. While it is true, as Daniel Purdy points out, that Marie "does not abandon society after her affair with Seeberg" and "recovers from her error in public and finds a new profession," it is questionable whether she does so "in the manner of Wilhelm Meister."[25] The counterpart to Wilhelm's dense network of relationships and ever unfolding social purpose is lacking at the end of Mereau's narrative. One might fault the extremely rapid narrative pace of the story's conclusion for this lacuna, but one must consider that this pace and lacuna are formal features that perfectly capture Marie's self-sufficiency. There is in fact no story to tell about her new life, because she is not tied up in

---

24 Mereau, "Marie," 80.
25 Daniel Purdy, "Abstraction and Sensuality in Sophie Mereau's 'Bildungsgeschichte,'" in *Sophie Mereau: Verbindungslinien in Zeit und Raum*, ed. Katharina von Hammerstein and Katrin Horn (Heidelberg: Winter, 2008), 145–61 (155). If anything, Purdy's own psychosexual interpretation of Marie's *Bildungsgeschichte* as incestuous and masturbatory itself calls into question the success of Marie's socialization and her resemblance to Wilhelm Meister. See also Hammerstein's description of Marie as "quasi ... Wilhelmine Meisterin" (Hammerstein, *Freiheit–Liebe–Weiblichkeit*, 74).

those social dependencies that generate narrative. This state of affairs is represented symbolically by Marie's choice of career. Just as an actor distinguishes himself from his roles and is not bound by them, so Marie—the newly minted actress—is not bound by the social narratives she now only play-acts on stage. An erotic relationship with Brandem would compromise this thespian liberty.

And she has reason to be cautious of such dependence, since the men in her life all in one way or another have exhibited a tendency to make her in their own image. Her father, whose good instincts urged him to keep her "Körper- und Geisteskräfte im Gleichgewicht" (physical and mental powers in balance), nonetheless attempted to impose a prolonged innocence on her. Brandem also indulged in controlling fantasies initially.[26] "Ihre Jugend, ihre Anmut, ihre gänzliche Unbefangenheit erquickten ihn, wie der Anblick eines schönen, ganz rein gestimmten Instruments, worauf der Künstler die süßesten Harmonien seiner eigenen Seele verschönert wieder zu vernehemen hofft" (Her youth, her grace, her total artlessness enlivened him, like the look of a beautiful, perfectly tuned instrument, upon which the artist hoped to hear a beautified version of the sweet harmonies of his own beautiful soul).[27] As for Seeberg, he can see Marie with nothing but the eyes of his own fantasy. "Von Jugend, Freude und Musik gespannt, gewann Mariens liebliche Gestalt vor seinen Augen immer mehr an stiller Glorie und schmückte sich mit allen den Reizen, die er sich oft, vereint, als sein Ideal weiblicher Liebenswürdigkeit geträumt hatte" (Excited by youth, joy, and music, Marie's charming form grew in Seeberg's eyes in quiet glory and adorned itself with all the charms that he had often combined as he dreamed of his ideal woman).[28] Later, after their first kiss, he exclaims, "Führt die Liebe mir jetzt das Ideal entgegen, wonach mein Herz längst mit unendlicher Sehnsucht verlangte?" (Does love now bring me the ideal, which my heart has so long and with such unending desire yearned for?).[29] She disappears beneath his idealization of her, something that Marie later recognizes. In her farewell letter to him, she argues "ich bin noch, die ich war, aber deine treulose Phantasie hat dich verlassen" (I remain who I was, but your faithless fantasy has left you).[30] In leaving Seeberg, Marie frees herself from the ideal he has constructed for her. As joint venturers in feminine *Bildung*, the man projects ideals, and the woman works

---

26 Mereau, "Marie," 50.
27 Mereau, "Marie," 53.
28 Mereau, "Marie," 63.
29 Mereau, "Marie," 64.
30 Mereau, "Marie," 77.

through and past these ideals. Such projections are part of what love means, whether paternal or sexual. In this regard, "Marie" resembles what Sigrid Weigel calls "Frauenliteratur" (women's literature): "its contents and narrative forms can be described not straightforwardly as original female forms of expression, but rather as attempts at movement within a male culture and as steps of liberation from it."[31] The only caveat would be that in "Marie," men and their ideal projections are an integral part of the emancipatory process. They are not simply "barriers" for self-emancipating women to "overcome," as one reader of Mereau suggests.[32]

The path to feminine *Bildung* in the text "Marie" thus leads into and out of social life, into and out of *eros*, and into (but not out of) a self-contained feminine *Selbstvertrauen*. While Marie eventually eschews dependence on the erotic, her personal development is instigated and advanced by it. In this sense, her *Bildung* is necessarily a man–woman collaboration, even if its realization may dissolve the collaboration. It is also a social collaboration in a more general sense, as the female protagonist must encounter society in order to develop the kind of strength that can do without its stimulations and consolations. It is thus the circular arc of the social and erotic narratives—beginning in isolation, becoming socialized, and then withdrawing libidinal investment in social bonds—that carves out the field of female autonomy.

Amanda und Eduard

The epistolary novel *Amanda und Eduard* also highlights the feminine journey towards a socially withdrawn autonomy. Amanda is a young married woman who is already socially integrated at the beginning of the novel when she meets another man, Eduard, and the two fall in love. Shortly thereafter, Eduard is called home to his father and he and Amanda are separated for years. As a result of a promise she makes to her dying husband and Eduard's belief that she no longer loves him, their communication with each other ceases and they carry on their separate lives. Years later, they are finally reunited and marry, but their union ends almost immediately with Amanda's death.

---

31 "[I]hre Inhalte und Erzählformen sind nicht umstandslos als originäre weibliche Ausdrucksformen zu beschreiben, sondern als Bewegungsversuche innerhalb der männlichen Kultur und als Befreiungsschritte daraus." Sigrid Weigel, "Der schielende Blick," in *Die verborgene Frau: Sechs Beiträge zu einer feministischen Literaturwissenschaft*, ed. Inge Stephan and Sigrid Weigel (Hamburg: Argument, 1988), 83–137 (87).
32 Lucia Sabova, *Problematik der weiblichen Identität in den Erzählungen von Sophie Mereau* (Berlin: Logos, 2011), 57.

Amanda feels that the love she has for Eduard allows her to understand herself—*sich erkennen*. In a letter to her friend, she claims, "Aber, Julie, so lange wir noch nicht geliebt haben, dürfen wir nicht hoffen, uns selbst recht zu kennen" (But Julie, we cannot hope to know ourselves if we have not yet loved).[33] Only when Eduard enters Amanda's life does something within her bloom and enable her fully to know herself, which for Mereau is a properly feminine goal. Yet Mereau's vision of a woman's purpose is not merely to know herself, but also to maintain herself—*sich erhalten*. While the erotic relationship allows Amanda to achieve this first half of her purpose, she later recognizes that the second half—achieving and maintaining her inner harmony—can only be realized as she distances herself from any relationship that would tie her down.

> Die Ungebundenheit meines Lebens; die Klarheit, mit der ich die Welt um mich erblicke; die stille Wirksamkeit die ich übe, macht mich zufrieden, und wenn ichs recht bedenke; so ist mein jetziger Zustand das Ideal einer Lage, welche ich mir oft jugendlich träumte. Mein stilles Leben faßt weit mehr in sich, und gewährt mir ein mannigfaltigeres Dasein, als meine vormalige lebendigste Lage.—Ein schöner, freier Kreis, das fühle ich lebhaft in heitern Stunden, liegt vor mir da; und indes mir in meiner Sphäre nichts entgeht, nichts zu gering ist, ergreift meine Phantasie alle ferne schönen Beziehungen des Lebens.[34]
>
> (The freedom of my life; the clarity with which I behold the surrounding world; the quiet activity that I practice makes me content, and when I fully consider it, I realize that my present situation is the ideal condition that I often dreamed of in my youth. My quiet life comprises much more and provides me a more diversified existence than my former lively condition.—In cheerful hours I can feel that a beautiful, freer horizon lies before me; and while nothing escapes my sphere, nothing is too small, my imagination grasps all distant and beautiful relationships of life.)

Quietude opens up the "ferne" (distant) relations of life instead of the close relations of social existence. To be sure, Amanda is still surrounded by friends and acquaintances at this point in the novel, but she

---

33 Sophie Mereau-Brentano, *Amanda und Eduard*, in *Das Blütenalter der Empfindung; Amanda und Eduard: Romane*, ed. Katharina von Hammerstein (Munich: Deutscher Taschenbuch, 1997), 59–224 (112).
34 Mereau, *Amanda*, 172.

is not intimate with them. Thus the detached life of self-knowing and self-maintaining need not require physical isolation, but it does require a certain emotional distance.

A small but telling example of this inner isolation is found in her relationship with Wilhelm, the son her late husband fathered with another woman before meeting Amanda. After he leaves to pursue his education, he writes to her, "Du, liebe Mutter, bist das einzige Wesen, dem ich angehören kann ... ich ehre und liebe die Natur, die ein Geschöpf, wie Dich hervorbringen, die eine solche Schöpferin schaffen konnte" (You, dear mother, are the one being to whom I can belong ... I honor and love the nature that could bring you forth, that could create such a creator).[35] To him, their relationship is the most defining element in his life, yet somehow Amanda has remained surprisingly unaware of the extent to which he cares for her. In response to Wilhelm's declaration of love and devotion, she writes to Julie, "So wert mir Wilhelm immer war; so wenig hab' ich doch, wie mir nun klar wird, auf das, was in ihm vorging, geachtet" (As much as I have always valued Wilhelm, it now becomes clear to me how little I considered what was going on inside him).[36] While she enjoys his company and is moved to tears by his words, Amanda has not developed the same depth of love for him. Indeed, this is the last time Wilhelm is mentioned in the text, as if he were a merely incidental figure in her life. She is complete without him.

What sets *Amanda und Eduard* apart from Mereau's other texts is its suggestion that the "ungebundenes" (unattached) life has the paradoxical effect of strengthening one's sense of unity with the world and ultimately with the transcendent source of the world. At one point Amanda writes to her friend: "wenn es süß ist, *ein* verwandtes Herz zu verstehen, und sich von ihm verstanden zu fühlen; so ist es heilig, sich ganz den Empfindungen hinzugeben, wo *aller* Menschen Herzen, nah oder fern in ihren reinsten Momenten zusammentreffen!" (if it is sweet to understand and feel understood by *one* sympathetic heart, then it is holy to give oneself up entirely to the feelings in which *all* people's hearts, near or far, meet in their purest moments).[37] Here we see the erotic being replaced by a desire for the mystical, and the individual by the universal. For Amanda, this is most fully achieved at the end of the novel as the beloved is replaced by God, who penetrates more intimately and completely than any human lover: "Eine fremde, höhere Macht ... reicht bis in das Heiligtum unserer Gedanken und wir *freuen* uns noch ihrer Allgewalt" (A foreign, higher power ... reaches

---

35 Mereau, *Amanda*, 212.
36 Mereau, *Amanda*, 213.
37 Mereau, *Amanda*, 171.

into the sanctuary of our thoughts and we *rejoice* in its omnipotence).[38] Historically, ecstatic religious devotion frequently coincides with the secluded life, so it is fitting that at the end of the novel Amanda finds herself at a hermitage deep in the forest, where she tells her host: "Ich selbst habe die Stimme Gottes, öfters laut in meiner Seele vernommen, ein unwiderstehlicher, seliger Drang, hat mich hinaufgezogen in den blauen, endlosen Äther, wo eine Stimme mir zurief: 'Hier bin ich! Hier ist Wahrheit!'" (I have personally heard God's voice in my soul, and an irresistible, blessed urge has pulled me up into the blue, endless ether, where a voice called to me: "Here I am! Here is truth!").[39] Mereau employs imagery derived from Goethe's "Ganymed" here to indicate how fully the erotic has been swallowed up in the religious, and it is no surprise that her long-awaited marriage to Eduard is reduced to a passing figure of the real union, through death, between Amanda and God at the narrative's close. This religious *Liebestod* (erotic death) can be seen as the natural consequence of feminine equanimity, which resembles the religious temperament. As the hermit explains, "Diejenigen, welche mit den Augen ruhiger Weisheit wahrnehmen, daß Körper und Geist also unterschieden sind, und daß es für den Menschen eine endliche Trennung von der animalischen Natur gibt, die gehen in das höchste Wesen über" (Those who discern with the eye of calm wisdom the distinction between body and spirit and the final separation from our animal nature are they who will become one with the highest being).[40] Death, or the separation of body and spirit, follows naturally from a certain stage of "ruhige[] Weisheit," which is precisely the quality achieved by a *sich-kennende, sich-erhaltende* (self-knowing, self-maintaining) woman. Appropriately, then, the novel concludes with the final flight of Amanda's soul to God through death.

While the particulars of her story are quite different from Marie's, Amanda's journey is also one of desocialization. She comes to know herself as a result of erotic love, and then removes herself from it in order to maintain her inner harmony and autonomy. Finally, this self-knowledge and self-maintenance lead to the ultimate withdrawal from society in order to become one with the divine. She thus follows the pattern set out by the hermit: "Folge deinen Neigungen, wenn sie wahr und natürlich sind, aber verehre in deiner Seele, unermüdet, das Göttliche, was du in dir fühlst, und laß dein Gemüt, nicht von den irdischen Sorgen und Freuden mit Unruh erfüllt, und herniedergezogen werden" (Follow your inclinations, when they are true and natural, but honor

---

38 Mereau, *Amanda*, 112. Italics in original.
39 Mereau, *Amanda*, 216.
40 Mereau, *Amanda*, 216.

the divine in your soul, what you feel inside you. Don't allow your mind to be filled and dragged down by worldly sorrows and joys).[41] What the hermit does not perceive is that the path of feminine *Bildung* naturally leads from a sensuous education ("folge deinen Neigungen"/ follow your inclinations) to a spiritual one ("verehre in deiner Seele, unermüdet, das Göttliche, was du in dir fühlst"/honor the divine in your soul, what you feel inside you). He need not use a contrastive conjunction to correlate these imperatives. Since sensory and emotional stimulation leads to self-knowledge, and the feminine self is, according to Mereau's sexual anthropology, innately balanced and complete, the inward turn follows on logically from worldly experience. Moreover, the inner life, the "was du in dir fühlst," was familiar stomping ground for mystics and Pietists by the end of the eighteenth century, making the path from a woman's sensuous education to her religious education a natural one.

One can also point out that the harmonious unity of parts that characterizes a woman's nature is, from a theological perspective, a natural emblem of the inner unity of creation found in God. The woman participates in, yet transcends, her environment in a way parallel to God's relationship to creation, and through Amanda's death this parallelism converges into identity.[42] Mereau does not pursue this theological angle explicitly, but it suggests itself given the religious turn in the narrative. One could argue that in a certain sense Amanda's death-into-God does not transcend the collaborative venture of *Bildung* as much as venture a collaboration in *Bildung* with the transcendent.

In summary, Mereau's *Bildung* narratives resemble those of her influential male contemporaries in many respects. The protagonist's developing faculties awaken in her a desire for self-realization, and this leads her to an aesthetic, social, and erotic education. Unlike most *Bildung* narratives, however, Mereau's stories of feminine *Bildung* are characterized by an emerging unsociable tendency. The self-absorption and disillusionment attending the erotic education are one factor contributing to this isolationism, and the ugliness of society is another. The most basic factor, however, seems to be Mereau's sexual anthropology, which sees a woman as whole by nature, leaving her no other vocation

---

41 Mereau, *Amanda*, 217.
42 This religious interpretation of Amanda's death takes the text more at face value than, say, Katharina von Hammerstein's, which sees only the veiled death-wish of Mereau, the unhappy woman. "Die Todessehnsucht, die der Furcht oder der Gewißheit entsprungen sein mag, daß unter den gegebenen gesellschaftlichen und psychologischen Bedingungen ein Glück der Frau nicht auf Dauer möglich zu sein scheint, nimmt [Mereau] in *Amanda und Eduard* voraus." Hammerstein, *Freiheit–Liebe–Weiblichkeit*, 98.

than self-awareness and self-maintenance. This vocation depends initially upon social and especially erotic relationships—it begins as a joint venture—but ultimately transcends the need for them. For Mereau, feminine autonomy is inseparable from some kind of social detachment, and those attachments that remain are purified of emotional or metaphysical dependency. In "Marie" this path leads through the life of the socialite and the lover to the life of the professional and the friend. In *Amanda* it leads by various stages through the erotic life to the religio-mystical death, which is the most dramatic form of emancipated detachment to be found in Mereau's oeuvre.

Bibliography

Daub, Adrian. *Uncivil Unions: The Metaphysics of Marriage in German Idealism and Romanticism*. Chicago: University of Chicago Press, 2012.

Freud, Sigmund. "Massenpsychologie und Ich-Analyse." In *Fragen der Gesellschaft: Ursprünge der Religion*. Vol. IX of *Studienausgabe*, 61–134. Corrected edn. Frankfurt am Main: Fischer, 2009.

Friedrich Schiller Archiv. http://www.friedrich-schiller-archiv.de/ (accessed July 22, 2017).

Fronius, Helen. *Women and Literature in the Goethe Era, 1770–1820: Determined Dilettantes*. Oxford: Oxford University Press, 2007.

Hammerstein, Katherina von. *Sophie Mereau-Brentano: Freiheit–Liebe–Weiblichkeit. Trikolore sozialer und individueller Selbstbestimmung um 1800*. Heidelberg: Winter, 1994.

Mereau-Brentano, Sophie. *Das Blütenalter der Empfindung; Amanda und Eduard: Romane*. Ed. Katharina von Hammerstein. Munich: Deutscher Taschenbuch, 1997.

Mereau-Brentano, Sophie. "Marie." In *Ein Glück, das keine Wirklichkeit umspannt*, ed. Katharina von Hammerstein, 49–83. Munich: Deutscher Taschenbuch, 1997.

Mereau-Brentano, Sophie. *"Wie sehn' ich mich hinaus in die freie Welt": Tagebuch, vermischte Prosa und philosophische Betrachtungen*. Ed. Katharina von Hammerstein. Munich: Deutscher Taschenbuch, 1997.

Purdy, Daniel. "Abstraction and Sensuality in Sophie Mereau's 'Bildungsgeschichte.'" In *Sophie Mereau: Verbindungslinien in Zeit und Raum*, ed. Katharina von Hammerstein and Katrin Horn, 145–61. Heidelberg: Winter, 2008.

Sabova, Lucia. *Problematik der weiblichen Identität in den Erzählungen von Sophie Mereau*. Berlin: Logos, 2011.

Weigel, Sigrid. "Der schielende Blick." In *Die verborgene Frau: Sechs Beiträge zu einer feministischen Literaturwissenschaft*, ed. Inge Stephan and Sigrid Weigel, 83–137. Hamburg: Argument, 1988.

Five Scenes from a Marriage
Friedrich and Dorothea Schlegel, Collaboration as Symphilosophy and After

Adrian Daub

The turn of the nineteenth century was the golden age of Romantic collaboration. Tieck and Wackenroder collaborated in Berlin. In Frankfurt, Hölderlin and Isaak von Sinclair gathered a "Bund der Geister" (Community of Spirits) around themselves. Achim von Arnim, Clemens Brentano, Bettina Brentano-von Arnim and Karoline von Günderrode began their various collaborations. The "Oldest System Program of German Idealism" meanwhile emerged from a close collaboration of roommates, so close in fact that it is still debated just whose text it is. Across the German-speaking world, genius loved company.

More and more, and above all in Romanticism's heady early phase, such collaborations occurred across gender lines. There had been plenty of famous collaborative couples and mixed-sex creative friendships throughout the eighteenth century, of course. Johann Wilhelm Ludwig Gleim and Anna Louisa Karsch, Johann Christoph and Luise Adelgunde Victorie Gottsched, had each pioneered modes of collaboration that the Romantic generation would draw on. But here, too, the last decade of the eighteenth century and the first decades of the nineteenth century saw an intensification—an intensification that, somewhat paradoxically, involved relationships that (a) transcended traditional definition and (b) elicited increasingly sophisticated attempts at definition.

As both the broader politics and the gender politics of the different Romantic circles became more conservative, the modes of collaboration characteristic of the Romantics shifted in turn. At the same time—and this will be my starting point in this chapter—collaboration did not cease simply because the protagonists began to espouse more and more doctrinaire positions on the relationship of the sexes. Collaboration did, however, undergo marked shifts. Bettina Brentano-von Arnim's cross-gender collaborations in *Goethes Briefwechsel mit einem*

Kinde (Goethe's Correspondence with a Child, 1835) and *Clemens Brentanos Frühlingskranz* (Clemens Brentano's Spring Wreath, 1844) were carefully framed and almost camouflaged—lacking the openness with which, say, *Florentin* and *Lucinde* had invited their readers to understand them as cross-gender collaborations.

If Friedrich and Dorothea Schlegel (née Brendel Mendelssohn) are the most famous Romantic collaborative couple, it is in the first place because they, unlike their eighteenth-century forebears, were not content to let the inner workings of their collaboration remain hidden and private. In the second place, however, they loom so large in the story of Romantic collaboration because their colloquy persisted for so long. They collaborated continuously over three decades, and they continuously reflected on the terms of their collaboration.

Starting in the *Athenäum* (1798–1800), Friedrich created the defining theory of collaboration of German Romanticism, in dialogue with his brother August Wilhelm, Friedrich Schleiermacher, and others. In *Lucinde* (1799) and the *Ideen* (Ideas, published in the *Athenäum* in 1800) he presented a version of it that moved from implicitly homosocial collaboration to heterosocial versions. Over the same period Friedrich engaged in a very different kind of collaboration with his lover Dorothea. Their collaborations shaped the novel *Lucinde*; he published her novel *Florentin* as "editor."

Dorothea's understanding of their collaboration proceeded from remarkably different premises, and it is my contention in this chapter that her premises, rather than his, ultimately prevailed. His is encapsulated in *Lucinde*'s "Charakteristik der Kleinen Wilhelmine" (Characteristic of Little Wilhelmine), an allegory of the generativity of chaos, the salubrious power of shocking the world out of its cognitive rut. Dorothea's is encapsulated in her references to her "guten Sohn Florentin" (good son *Florentin*). And it is a son that she at times regrets having brought into the world at all: "Der arme Mann muß sich doch auch wieder viel gefallen lassen, von dem ihm nichts träumte, so lange er noch als Idee spukte" (This poor man has to put up with so much, none of which he dreamed of when he was still just an idea haunting me).[1] Dorothea throughout her life with Friedrich (and beyond it) retains a keen sense of the cost at which things private are carried into the public.

This sense shaped the reception of Dorothea's work, for it led her to retreat from the kind of public response that *Lucinde*, and to a lesser extent *Florentin*, had brought her. Most accounts of Dorothea's and

---

1 Ernst Wieneke, ed., *Briefwechsel von Caroline und Dorothea Schlegel* (Weimar: Kiepenheuer, 1914), 334. All translations, unless otherwise indicated, are my own.

Friedrich's "bi-textuality" end with these culminating novelistic accomplishments—that is to say, almost thirty years before Friedrich's death ended their life together. Barbara Becker-Cantarino's characterization is typical: she sees Friedrich and Dorothea in genuine dialogue for the precious few years straddling the turn of the nineteenth century. But once *Florentin* is in print, once the couple's dynamic relationship ossifies into a fairly traditional marriage and their dizzying philosophy ossifies into doctrinal religiosity, she sees Dorothea as demoted to a mere copyist and sounding board for her narcissistic husband.[2]

This view is not wrong. Becker-Cantarino is correct to read *Florentin* as a rather pointed rebuke to some of Friedrich Schlegel's positions. And even though Dorothea wrote, edited, and published after *Florentin*, she would never quite attain that level of independence again. However, it is equally true that the couple continued to collaborate until (and in fact beyond) Friedrich's death. It is as easy to overstate Dorothea's independence from Friedrich's cosmos of ideas *before* 1800 as it is to overstate her dependence on him after 1800. This chapter proposes to emphasize that the two evolved together, that between them obtained a kind of tug of war that lasted well beyond Friedrich's death.

Symphilosophie

Tracing Dorothea and Friedrich Schlegel's collaboration beyond the heady days of early Romanticism requires distinguishing among three interrelated modes of collaboration in Friedrich's life. My contention is that these modes at times align, at others coincide, and at yet others drift apart. The first among them is arguably the one Schlegel is most famous for: the shared mode of philosophizing and authorship he christened *Symphilosophie*. While the term is usually associated with the early Romantic circles, with his brother August Wilhelm, with Novalis, and with Friedrich Schleiermacher, Schlegel practiced versions of this mode of collaboration throughout his life. Most versions were homosocial. Where Dorothea fit into them was not always clear.

At the same time Dorothea's and Friedrich's relationship was from the first also a collaborative one—and this presented a second, not altogether separate, mode of collaboration. If the early fragments on *Symphilosophie* tended to frame it as an implicitly homosocial pursuit, by the period that gave rise to the fragments collected as the *Ideen* (roughly 1799–1800), Schlegel clearly believed that there is room for

---

2 Barbara Becker-Cantarino, "Friedrich Schlegels *Lucinde* und Dorothea Schlegels *Florentin*," in *Bi-Textualität: Zur Inszenierung des Paares*, ed. Annegret Heitmann, Sigrid Nieberle, Barbara Schaff, and Sabine Schülting (Berlin: Erich Schmidt, 2001), 131–41 (140).

sexual difference in this kind of collective philosophizing and poeticizing, and that indeed the practice may vary depending on whether a man engages with another man, or with a woman. Friedrich tended to conceive of this relationship one way, but, at least when it came to collective creativity, Dorothea conceived of it in quite another. In his novel *Lucinde* and her reactions to the controversy the work generated, in her novel *Florentin* and the way he sought to frame it as its "editor," we find a dramatically different construal of authorship and its relationship to a public. She emphasized themes of responsibility, hesitation, and regret; he tended to valorize a kind of irresponsible putting-out-there.

But there is a third mode of collaboration that dominates Friedrich's life, one that concerns his relationships with women other than Dorothea. Throughout his life with Dorothea, Friedrich seemed to return to a particular pattern: he maintained a quasi-monogamous relationship with Dorothea, but pursued other women as partners. Whether this went so far as a sexual relationship in the cases of Sophie Mereau, Rahel Levin Varnhagen, and Karoline Paulus has been debated;[3] certainly the associations of his later life were framed along spiritual lines and were almost certainly chaste. But in each case the emphatic collaboration with Dorothea found its complement in a very different, and in its own way far more traditional, exchange with these other women: they were dedicatees of his poems; recipients of ardent letters; muses for new undertakings; or, later, keys to unlocking spiritual mysteries.

Schlegel introduced *Symphilosophie* as a matter of knowledge, an overcoming of the limitations of the particularized individual, that is to say in terms clearly analogous to the merging of individualities in love that Schlegel would describe in *Lucinde*. And yet it took him some time to say so: It is unclear whether Friedrich initially sought to distinguish the kind of collaboration subsumed under the moniker of *Symphilosophie* from the kind of sexual relationship described in *Lucinde*, or whether he simply drew on a philosophical vocabulary that tended to pull the two apart. But the sequence in which he published his various proposals around the idea of *Symphilosophie* had the effect of making erotic and sexual difference a somewhat later addition to the discourse, and to render his earliest characterizations of systematic *Symphilosophie* implicitly homosocial.

When, for instance, Schlegel likens it to an "eternal peace" of philosophy, or treats symphilosophical discourse as a prefiguration, or a sort of symbol of, "republican speech," *Symphilosophie* seems to reside in the

---

3   See for instance Hermann Patsch in Friedrich Schlegel, *Kritische Friedrich Schlegel Ausgabe*, ed. Ernst Behler, Jean Jacques Anstett, and Hans Eichner (Munich: Schöningh, 1958–), XXV, iii (henceforth *KFSA*).

polis, not the *oikos*.[4] While in this phase of his writing Schlegel often sought to relativize the clear distinction between public and private, between domestic emotions and public reasoning, it is nevertheless noticeable that *Symphilosophie* surfaces emphatically towards the public side of the spectrum. And given that *Symphilosophie* usually appears in the *Athenäum*-fragments together with its twin, *Sympoesie*, these two allegedly complementary activities carry a whiff of sexual difference almost by necessity: public-focused homosociality seems to represent only one side of the coin.

Where in *Symphilosophie* two men can share and exchange ideas, co-creating poetry means sharing one's very self with another. Schlegel claims in the "Gespräch über die Poesie" (Dialogue on Poetry), a text that presents itself as a cross-gender dialogue, that "die Vernunft ist nur eine und in allen dieselbe: wie aber jeder Mensch seine eigne Natur hat und seine eigne Liebe, so trägt auch jeder seine eigne Poesie in sich" (there is only one Reason and it is the same in everyone: but just as every person has their own nature and their own love, so every person carries their own Poetry inside themselves).[5] Reason is the medium through which exchange occurs, it is intrinsically open to others, can be in principle infinitely extended—this indeed is the concept of Republicanism. Sympathetic relationships instead have as their medium precisely something that cannot be shared, have as their *tertium comparationis* something that cannot be compared. As the "Dithyrambische Fantasie über die Schönste Situation" (Dithyrambic Fantasy about the Loveliest Situation in the World) in *Lucinde* states: "und darum liebst du mich auch ganz und überläßt keinen Teil von mir etwa dem Staate, der Nachwelt oder den männlichen Freunden"[6] (this is why you love me completely and don't relinquish any part of me to the state, to posterity, or to my friends).[7]

Public expression and private feeling enter into a complicated pas-de-deux in passages such as this one: *Lucinde* made the private public, but nevertheless insisted that there was something here that escaped public description. And the outside figured not just as society, but also as audience. *Lucinde* claimed to discount the kind of publicity by means of which poetry endures across time, but courted it in the same breath. This would emerge as the central irony that Dorothea either could not stomach or could not downplay with as much ease as Friedrich.

---

4 Gerald Izenberg, *Impossible Individuality: Romanticism, Revolution and the Origins of Modern Selfhood* (Princeton, NJ: Princeton University Press, 1992), 67.
5 *KFSA*, II, 284.
6 *KFSA*, V, 11.
7 Friedrich Schlegel, *Friedrich Schlegel's "Lucinde" and the Fragments*, trans. Peter Firchow (Minneapolis: University of Minnesota Press, 1971), 47.

Yet Schlegel clearly embarked on both male-to-male co-authorships and a co-habitation and collaboration with his later wife, the physical side of which he took pains to emphasize publicly. And he embarked on them during roughly the same period of time: his most effective moments of *Symphilosophie* may have predated the relationship with Dorothea, but his rapturous public celebrations of the same, in the *Athenäum* and elsewhere, coincided with it. How did Schlegel's immense theoretical oeuvre account for his relationship with his wife, its erotic and its collaborative aspects? And how did his practice correspond to the theory?

In the famous fragment §125 of the *Athenäum*, Friedrich Schlegel makes his case for a *Symphilosophie*. He is careful to make this new community about both "knowledge" or "science" (*Wissenschaft*), and about the arts; he speaks of *Symphilosophie* and *Sympoesie* in one breath: "Vielleicht würde eine ganz neue Epoche der Wissenschaften und Künste beginnen, wenn die Symphilosophie und Sympoesie so allgemein und so innig würde, daß es nichts Seltnes mehr wäre, wenn mehrere sich gegenseitig ergänzende Naturen gemeinschaftliche Werke bildeten"[8] (Perhaps there would be a birth of a whole new era of the sciences and arts if symphilosophy and sympoetry became so universal and heartfelt that it would no longer be anything extraordinary for several complementary minds to create communal works of art).[9] Likewise, §125 seems rather straightforwardly to liken the meeting of souls in *Symphilosophie* to Platonic *eros*. Schlegel explicitly invokes Aristophanes' famous allegory of the origin of desire in the *Symposium*: "Oft kann man sich des Gedankens nicht erwehren, zwei Geister möchten eigentlich zusammengehören, wie getrennte Hälften, und nur verbunden alles sein, was sie könnten"[10] (One is often struck by the idea that two minds really belong together, like divided halves that can realize their full potential only when joined).[11] In the *Symposium*, we read: "Each of us when separated, having one side only, like a flat fish, is but the tally-half of a man, and he is always looking for his other half."[12] *Symphilosophie*, like Platonic *eros*, brings together what should not have been separate in the first place.

Schlegel thus tethers his description of *Symphilosophie* to what is arguably the most gender-neutral part of the Platonic corpus. Whatever else

---

8 *KFSA*, II, 172.
9 Schlegel, *"Lucinde" and the Fragments*, 178.
10 *KFSA*, II, 185.
11 Schlegel, *"Lucinde" and the Fragments*, 178.
12 Plato, *The Dialogues of Plato*, trans. Benjamin Jowett (Oxford: Clarendon Press, 1953), 523.

Aristophanes' image of the half-beings commits him to, it would seem to commit Schlegel to assigning men and women exactly analogous (rather than complementary) roles in symphilosophizing. After all, in Aristophanes *either* sex could serve as the lost other half—which negated *ab initio* the kind of gender complementarity on which Rousseau's *Emile* had relied, and that Johann Gottlieb Fichte had promulgated in the appendix to his book on natural law.[13] There is complementarity in Schlegel's account, but that complementarity seems to obtain between individuals rather than sexes:

> Gäbe es eine Kunst, Individuen zu verschmelzen, oder könnte die wünschende Kritik etwas mehr als wünschen, wozu sie überall so viel Veranlassung findet, so möchte ich Jean Paul und Peter Leberecht kombiniert sehen. Grade alles, was jenem fehlt, hat dieser. Jean Pauls groteskes Talent und Peter Leberechts fantastische Bildung vereinigt, würden einen vortrefflichen romantischen Dichter hervorbringen.[14]
>
> (If there were an art of amalgamating individuals, or if a wishful criticism could do more than merely wish—and for that there are reasons enough—then I would like to see Jean Paul and Peter Leberecht [i.e., Ludwig Tieck] combined. The latter has precisely what the former lacks. Jean Paul's grotesque talent and Peter Leberecht's fantastic turn of mind would, once united, yield a first-rate romantic poet.)[15]

What, then, is the role of the erotic in this manner of combination? The traces of Platonic *eros* are clear. At the same time, feeling is naturally only one aspect of the symphilosophic relationship: In §112, Schlegel writes: "Die Philosophen welche nicht gegeneinander sind, verbindet gewöhnlich nur Sympathie, nicht Symphilosophie"[16] (Philosophers who aren't opposed to each other are joined only by sympathy, not by symphilosophy).[17] The exchange of ideas in *Symphilosophie* is founded in feeling, but transcends it. What is more, Schlegel's characterization of *Symphilosophie* contrasts rather clearly with the descriptions of physical *eros* in the "Dithyrambic Fantasy" in *Lucinde*. He writes of a situation "Wenn wir die Rollen vertauschen und mit kindischer Lust wetteifern,

---

13 See Adrian Daub, *Uncivil Unions: The Metaphysics of Marriage in German Idealism and Romanticism* (Chicago: University of Chicago Press, 2012).
14 *KFSA*, II, 185.
15 Schlegel, *"Lucinde" and the Fragments*, 178.
16 *KFSA*, II, 180.
17 Schlegel, *"Lucinde" and the Fragments*, 174.

wer den andern täuschender nachäffen kann, ob dir die schonende Heftigkeit des Mannes besser gelingt, oder mir die anziehende Hingebung des Weibes"[18] (When we exchange roles and in childish high spirits compete to see who can mimic the other more convincingly, whether you are better at imitating the protective intensity of the man, or I the appealing devotion of the woman).[19] It is worth drawing out the differences in detail: (1) The passage relies on mimesis as much as on difference; "nachäffen" (aping) isn't what is required of the different poets in *Athenäum*, §125. (2) It speaks of "roles" rather than identities —either sexual identity, or the kind of "Talent" and "Bildung" that characterize Jean Paul and Peter Leberecht (i.e., Ludwig Tieck) in the *Athenäum*-fragment. (3) While the "Dithyrambic Fantasy" too traffics in the language of complementarity, the notion of taking on one another's "roles" comes from a different semantic field altogether—the idea that one particular can exchange its character with another particular and thus blur the boundaries between them is what Schlegel calls "Chaos." (4) Rather than each particular adding its own specific contribution to the emerging whole, the whole seems to constitute itself by obscuring the specificity of any one contribution.

But perhaps most centrally, (5) there is no sense of a product here. Schlegel's *Athenäum*-fragments speak of outcomes: about the situation "wenn mehrere sich gegenseitig ergänzende Naturen gemeinschaftliche Werke bildeten" (when several complementary minds create communal works of art), about the "vortrefflichen romantischen Dichter" (excellent romantic poets) that Paul and Leberecht would "hervorbringen" (produce), were they to be combined in some way. The "schönste Situation" (loveliest situation) does seem to lead by some strange textual logic to the child Wilhelmine, but it would go too far to say that she constitutes the point of the many role reversals and imitations the "Dithyrambic Fantasy" describes. Of course, there is an admission "daß dieses süße Spiel für mich noch ganz andre Reize hat als seine eignen" (that this sweet game still has quite other attractions for me than its own). "Es ist auch nicht bloß die Wollust der Ermattung oder das Vorgefühl der Rache. Ich sehe hier eine wunderbare sinnreich bedeutende Allegorie auf die Vollendung des Männlichen und Weiblichen zur vollen ganzen Menschheit. Es liegt viel darin, und was darin liegt, steht gewiß nicht so schnell auf wie ich, wenn ich dir unterliege"[20] (And not simply the voluptuousness of exhaustion or the anticipation of revenge? I see here a wonderful, deeply meaningful allegory of the

---

18 *KFSA*, V, 13.
19 Schlegel, *"Lucinde" and the Fragments*, 49.
20 *KFSA*, V, 13.

development of man and woman to full and complete humanity. There is much in it—and what is in it certainly doesn't rise up as quickly as I do when I am overcome by you).[21]

The passage offers a rather frank defense of sexual role play for its own sake, but by that very token manages to turn it into an allegory for greater spiritual unification with another. By not having a product, it is productive. Indeed it would seem that this act of allegorizing is the ultimate *telos* of the sexual act in *Lucinde*. Erotic love points to a kind of productive confusion, to an overcoming of the boundaries of individuation. It may not be as much work, but it shares important homologies with Schlegel's vision of homosocial collaboration.

Nevertheless, as Philippe Lacoue-Labarthe and Jean-Luc Nancy have pointed out, by the time Schlegel publishes the *Ideen* in the third issue of the *Athenäum* in April 1800, the presumed homosociality of philosophical collaboration has given way to a rather insistent thematization of the role of the feminine.[22] Some of this new emphasis is certainly due to the experience of writing *Lucinde*, but it cannot be coincidence that the *Ideen* also constitute Schlegel's polite, effusive, but frequently pointed, critique of his erstwhile symphilosopher Schleiermacher.[23]

And indeed, it is only in the *Ideen* that femininity seems to begin playing an explicit role in *Symphilosophie*. In §128 of the *Ideen*, Schlegel claims that "Mysterien sind weiblich; sie verhüllen sich gern, aber sie wollen doch gesehen und erraten sein"[24] (Mysteries are female; they like to veil themselves but still want to be seen and discovered).[25] There is a pronounced sense of asymmetry, of complementarity to these fragments—instead of the "republican" model of exchange, one side provides what the other constitutively cannot. Schlegel begins to think about collaboration in explicitly familial terms, begins to emphasize love and femininity as the structuring medium for exchange: "Nur um eine liebende Frau her kann sich eine Familie bilden"[26] (A family can only be formed around a loving woman).[27]

In so doing, he begins to sound a lot like his then-lover and future wife. In certain formulations, the *Ideen* echo the kind of familial sociability we find celebrated in Dorothea's own contribution to the literature

---

21 Schlegel, *"Lucinde" and the Fragments*, 49.
22 Philippe Lacoue-Labarte and Jean-Luc Nancy, *The Literary Absolute* (Albany, NY: SUNY Press, 1988), 71.
23 Robert J. Richards, *The Romantic Conception of Life* (Chicago: Chicago University Press, 2010), 103.
24 *KFSA*, II, 232.
25 Schlegel, *"Lucinde" and the Fragments*, 253.
26 *KFSA*, II, 232.
27 Schlegel, *"Lucinde" and the Fragments*, 253.

of early Romanticism. Her novel *Florentin* persistently plays off the Schwarzenberg family's idyllic togetherness against the title character's rootlessness and loneliness. And while no one collaborates in *Florentin*, the descriptions can sound an awful lot like the early Romantic *Wohngemeinschaft*: "Keiner verleugnete sich selbst, um dem andern zu gefallen, es bestand alles vollkommen gut nebeneinander" (No one was forced to repudiate themselves in order to please anyone else; everything existed perfectly fine side by side).[28] "Ebenso stimmte alles Äußere zusammen. Allenthalben blickte durch die glänzende etwas antike Pracht die Bequemlichkeit und Eleganz anmutig durch: gleichsam der ernste Wille des Herrn, durch die gefälligere Neigung der Hausfrau gemildert. Ein allgemeines Wohlsein war ringsum verbreitet, eine gewisse Reichlichkeit und unbesorgte Ordnung" (Thus also everything external was in harmony. Everywhere behind the antique splendor a graceful coziness and elegance shone through: in this manner the seriousness of the lord's will was gentled by the more solicitous inclinations of the lady of the manor. A universal wellness was all around, a certain abundance and unconcerned order).[29] *Florentin* offers an encomium of the family as a self-governing, self-sufficient emotional and, yes, intellectual entity. At the same time, at least in the part of the plot Dorothea actually got around to writing, Florentin himself does not find a home in this entity. In a funny way, the novel both reflects the heterosocial version of *Symphilosophie* of Schlegel's *Ideen*, but presents it again and again from the perspective of an outsider looking in. "Reichlichkeit und unbesorgte Ordnung" (certain abundance and unconcerned order) are nice, but they aren't, from Florentin's perspective, ultimately enough. Whether we credit the idea that Florentin is Dorothea's self-portrait, whether we believe he is a kind of "feminized" hero, *Florentin* manages to celebrate a social formation intended to allegorize *Symphilosophie*, and to place a giant asterisk behind its celebration. Of course there is a place for Florentin in so capacious and generous a system of cohabitation as the Schwarzenberg family. Except Florentin is never quite sure. This was, it seems, Dorothea's sense of her partner's all-engulfing creativity as well.

How did the literary exchange between the two partners function during this their most mutually productive time together? There does seem to be a switching of "positions" analogous to what *Lucinde* says about the "loveliest situation": she was his critic and copy-editor, he functioned as hers. Yet even so, the letters hint at rather pronounced asymmetries. For one thing, the "Faulheit" (idleness) that he extols in

---

28 Dorothea Schlegel, *Florentin: Ein Roman* (Berlin: Ullstein, 1987), 10.
29 Schlegel, *Florentin*, 10.

Lucinde appears to be a one-way street: "Der Florentin ist beynah ganz abgeschrieben," Dorothea reports in an 1800 letter to Schleiermacher, but "der faule Mensch der Friedrich korrigirt mir immer die Fehler nicht aus den lezten Bogen" (*Florentin* is almost entirely copied, [but] that lazy man Friedrich won't edit the final mistakes from the manuscript).[30] She meanwhile serves as his faithful copyist and editor.[31]

Her letters to him are suffused with a kind of reflexive self-deprecation. Dorothea was clearly aware of her intellectual gifts and her gifts as a writer, but she couches that awareness in a kind of modesty that perhaps bespeaks the autodidact, the outsider. Given that, as Friedrich notes in *Athenäum*, §264, "man soll nicht mit allen symphilosophieren wollen, sondern nur mit denen die *à la hauteur* sind"[32] (you shouldn't try to symphilosophize with everyone, but only with those that are *à l'hauteur*),[33] the question of inferiority was a fraught, potentially highly corrosive one for romantic collaboration: was love enough to motivate and sustain a symphilosophic relationship? If not, the question of ability was always a concern. In a letter to Friedrich in 1806 Dorothea mentions that she received poems by John Freiherr Sinclair (Schlegel would include them under the *nom de plume* Crisalin). She copied and edited the poems, and doesn't appear to have much liked them: "Du wirst sie ein andersmal lesen. Obgleich, wie Du behauptest, ich den Dativ und Accusativ nicht zu unterscheiden weiss, wie einer Berlinerin wohl ansteht, so getraue ich mir doch zu behaupten, dass ich etwas geschickter mit der Sprache umzugehen weiss, als dieser Herr Gemeinderath Sinclair" (You'll read them another time. Even though, as you claim, I can never distinguish the dative and accusative, as is quite customary for a Berliner, I daresay that I have a bit more of a way with words than Mr. *Gemeinderat* Sinclair).[34] Dorothea's assessment teeters between self-assertion and self-effacement. She clearly knows she could do better, but she cannot speak to a man about another man's work without making herself look smaller—although one has to wonder if she picked her inability to distinguish accusative and dative on purpose, given that being able to distinguish these does not exactly make one a great poet. At the same time, the very fact that she functions as a first line of defense against bad writing (which often enough made it into

---

30 Friedrich Schleiermacher, *Briefwechsel 1800* (Berlin: De Gruyter, 1994), 64.
31 Barbara Becker-Cantarino, *Schriftstellerinnen der Romantik*, Arbeitsbücher zur Literaturegeschichte (Munich: Beck, 2000), 133.
32 *KFSA*, II, 210, A 264.
33 Schlegel, *"Lucinde" and the Fragments*, 200.
34 Dorothea Schlegel, *Dorothea Schlegel Briefwechsel*, ed. J. M. Raich (Mainz: Kirchheim, 1881), 178.

Friedrich's collections anyway) as a sort of glorified editorial assistant suggests that Friedrich credited her self-effacement to some extent. As Barbara Becker-Cantarino has pointed out, Friedrich "never reflected on the discrepancy" between his high-flying rhetoric on gender "and the gender differences he practiced."[35]

At the same time, Schlegel saw his job as her "Herausgeber" (editor) as both inspiring and guiding literary production—and in introducing *Florentin* he emphasizes the editor's role in coaxing out the manuscript in the first place. His job was not to guide the writing, but to make sure the writing went public. The identity of *Florentin*'s author didn't remain a mystery for long. Schlegel's opening poems probably did more to make Dorothea's authorship explicit than any other factor: dedicating a book with two sonnets to its author is a rather potent poetological signal flare. This is probably by design: while the novel *Florentin* itself takes a far less sanguine view of the public sphere, Schlegel's framing poem "An die Dichterin" structures female authorship as a kind of hiding in plain sight; to be a "Dichterin" is to withdraw from the world, but also makes that withdrawal visible:

> Die Wünsche, die dich hin zur Dichtkunst ziehen,
> Der frohe Ernst, in den du da versankest,
> Das sei dein eigen still verborgnes Leben.[36]
>
> (May the wish that drew you on to poetry,
> May the joyful seriousness it betides
> Be your own, quietly hidden, life.)

The idea that women might lead a "still verborgnes Leben" isn't exactly a new one; but it's a strange topos to surface in a dedicatory poem that reveals that a novel's author is a woman. What kind of hiddenness are we dealing with here, if it serves to frame a rather massive and still rather unprecedented incursion into the public sphere? Friedrich suggests that such retreat "auf zu des Scherzes heitern Regionen" (into the cheerful realm of wit) is natural and goes hand in hand with a "Verhüllung" (concealment) "in heiligste Gefühle" (in most holy feelings).[37] Ensconcing oneself in poetry and ensconcing oneself in a kind of domestic femininity here sound like quite the same thing—much as in the *Ideen* (§127), where Schlegel writes that "Die Poesie der Dichter bedürfen die Frauen weniger, weil ihr eigenstes Wesen Poesie

---

35 Becker-Cantarino, "*Lucinde* und *Florentin*," 140.
36 Schlegel, *Florentin*, 3.
37 Schlegel, *Florentin*, 3.

ist"[38] (Women have less need for the poetry of poets because their very essence is poetry).[39] And yet in the *Ideen*, Schlegel also claims that feminine mysteries "wollen doch gesehen und erraten sein" (still want to be seen and discovered): withdrawal is tantamount to an invitation to interpretative effort.

This explains why Friedrich calls Dorothea's "Verhüllung" from the world "heilig." Schlegel is drawing on the vocabulary of his theoretical articulation of *Symphilosophie* to point to the dialectical aspect of feminine withdrawal from the public. In *Lyceum*-fragment 112, Schlegel similarly associates "Heiligkeit" (holiness) with a plenitude of communication, one he calls "Symphilosophie oder Sympoesie." It is important, he says, that the poet does not want to impose a "bestimmte Wirkung" (particular impression) on the reader, but rather "tritt mit ihm in das heilige Verhältnis der innigsten Symphilosophie oder Sympoesie"[40] (enters with him into the sacred relationship of deepest symphilosophy or sympoetry).[41] Withdrawal itself will allow for a "heilig" relationship to the reader. The relationship he suggests here is one we find in both *Lucinde* and the essay "Über die Unverständlichkeit" (On Incomprehensibility): a kind of pulsating between comprehension and incomprehension, between harmony and disharmony.[42] "Laß auch die Worte oder die Menschen ein Mißverständnis zwischen uns erregen! Der tiefe Schmerz würde flüchtig sein und sich bald in vollkommenere Harmonie auflösen. Ich würde ihn so wenig achten, wie die liebende Geliebte im Enthusiasmus der Wollust die kleine Verletzung achtet"[43] (Let men or words try to bring misunderstanding between us! That deep pain would quickly ebb and soon resolve itself into a more perfect harmony. I'd pay as little attention to it as a woman in love does to the slight hurt she suffers in the heat of pleasure.)[44] Total withdrawal would foreclose on the kind of ambivalent "Wirkung" that could shift and pulsate and breathe in this way. The duty Schlegel suggests for the "Dichterin" is thus *both* to withdraw *and* to be present, to veil *and* to publicize.[45] Not

---

38 *KFSA*, II, 232.
39 Schlegel, *"Lucinde" and the Fragments*, 128.
40 *KFSA*, II, 161.
41 Schlegel, *"Lucinde" and the Fragments*, 157.
42 Keren Gorodeisky, "'No Poetry, No Reality': Schlegel, Wittgenstein, Fiction and Reality," in *The Relevance of Romanticism*, ed. Dalia Nassar (Oxford: Oxford University Press, 2014), 163–85 (171).
43 *KFSA*, V, 12.
44 Schlegel, *"Lucinde" and the Fragments*, 49.
45 Birgit Rehme-Iffert, *Skepsis und Enthusiasmus: Friedrich Schlegels philosophischer Grundgedanke* (Würzburg: Königshausen & Neumann, 2001), 90.

surprisingly, the sonnet concludes by suggesting a rather different relationship to "the world":

> Was du gedichtet, um ihr zu entfliehen,
> Das mußt du, weil du ihr allein es dankest,
> Der Welt zum Scheine scherzend wiedergeben.[46]

> (What you have written in order to escape it,
> You have to, since you owe it,
> Give back to the world in seeming jest.)

It is an ambivalent exhortation, to be sure: an encouragement that female authorship means not a retreat from the everyday world, but centrally an engagement with and a return to it. Schlegel here suggests that semi-private authorship is something to be avoided: to be a poet is to publish. Given that Dorothea had such immense qualms about putting her "child" out there, his insistence on ironizing publication, framing the act of addressing the world as "zum Scheine scherzend" (in seeming jest), seems meant to coax her out of her reticence, to loosen her control over her own output. In Freudian terms we could speak here of a hysteric mode played off against an anal-retentive one—Friedrich's advice to his wife is to be more hysterical.

At the same time, his advice comes with all the baggage that accompanies a man telling a woman to loosen up: for one thing, Schlegel frames his exhortation as a demand; this is one more duty Dorothea owes the world: "Das mußt du, weil du ihr allein es dankest, / Der Welt zum Scheine scherzend wiedergeben." For another, the "Scherz," which elsewhere he wants to posit as indistinct from seriousness, here hides secret seriousness—it is "Schein." The question of whether female writing is serious (i.e., done with a public and a profession in mind) or whether it is more of a lark (done for individual edification and emotional balance) is of course an overwhelming one for female writers around 1800—many, like Sophie Mereau, Karoline von Günderrode, and Bettina Brentano-von Arnim find their own very specific answers to it (so would Dorothea's own niece, the composer Fanny Mendelssohn, before long).[47] But in his opening poem to *Florentin*, Friedrich Schlegel wants to decide the question for her.

In the end he is unsuccessful. If Friedrich pushes his wife to publish more and to have publishing mean a more specific thing, she begins

---

46 *KFSA*, V, 172.
47 See for instance Françoise Tillard, *Fanny Mendelssohn* (Portland: Amadeus Press, 1996), 215.

to push her own mode of authorship onto him: a new reticence, a new care with insides and outsides, with seriousness and wit, whose outlines hint at religious preoccupations to come. In a letter of October 28, 1800, Dorothea writes to August Wilhelm Schlegel: "Der 'Florentin' wird·wirklich gedruckt zu meiner großen Angst. Wollte doch Gott, wir könnten daßselbe von der Lucinde sagen" (*Florentin* is actually getting printed, much to my terror. I wish to God we could have said the same about *Lucinde*).[48] What she owes the world of her art is a question that fills her with dread, and she wishes that Friedrich might similarly hesitate before putting his work out there.

"Anti-*Florentin*"

It is well known that *Florentin*, with its Romantic political pathos and its none-too-subtle anti-clericalism, would not represent its author's views very long. The book's fragmentary form, much like *Lucinde*'s, came to highlight the massive ideological reversals that would characterize its author's later life. Precisely because it was a fragment, and fragment of a whole she no longer believed in, *Florentin* hovered over Dorothea's subsequent writing career: "Ich wollte, ich hätte ihn damals fertig gemacht" (I wish I had finished him at that time), she wrote to Karoline Paulus in July 1805, "so könnte ich jetzt weit leichter einen Anti Florentin dichten" (then I could now much more readily compose an Anti-*Florentin*).[49] This was not true of the (equally fragmentary) *Lucinde*. Schlegel gradually moved away from his youthful positions—but if he ever wrote something that could be thought of as an "Anti-*Lucinde*," it was still safely in the future by 1805.

But if her own personal views shifted rather quickly away from those publicly expressed in her only novel, did her views on public expression shift alongside them? Deciding this question is made difficult by the fact that what exactly constitutes her public expression during this period is not altogether clear. She continued to write poetry, undertook a number of translation projects, and indeed claimed to have drafted that elusive sequel to *Florentin*—but her work continued to appear under Friedrich's name or editorship, and he appears to have had a heavy hand in shaping it. Conversely, his now-spouse seems to have retained her active role in editing *his* public expressions. Even if the charming chaotic ideology of *Lucinde* no longer guided them, they remained committed to switching roles.

---

48   Wieneke, *Briefwechsel*, 334.
49   Rudolf Unger, ed., *Der Briefwechsel von Dorothea und Friedrich Schlegel an die Familie Paulus* (Berlin: Behr, 1913), 63.

At the same time, Dorothea was the first to register discontent with their earlier modes of production. In the same 1805 letter to Karoline Paulus, Dorothea uses the phrase "mein Herz ist ihm [*Florentin*] bei meiner jetzigen Denkungsart ziemlich stiefmütterlich gesinnt" (given how I think today, my heart has come to feel towards [*Florentin*] in a rather stepmotherly manner).[50] It is surely not an accidental choice of words, given her earlier insistence on thinking of the novel as her child. Even though her mothering of it was never without a pronounced ambivalence, it is clear that her misgivings about *Florentin* are no longer those one necessarily has about blood relations. Rather, "stiefmütterlich" (stepmotherly) is probably to be taken quite literally: in *Florentin* she now worries she has raised someone else's child. It is clear that Dorothea was rethinking the mode of literary collaboration across gender lines that had brought both *Lucinde* and *Florentin* into being.

It is not as clear that Friedrich was rethinking it alongside her. Outwardly, both his modes of production and his reflections on them prolonged his strategies of the 1790s. In the 1806 *Poetisches Taschenbuch* (Poetic Booklet), Schlegel continued both the mode of production that had given rise to the *Athenäum*-fragments and the one that had inspired *Lucinde*—incorporating poems by other men (with their names appended after the poem), and a whole raft of unsigned poems, many of which are thought to be Dorothea's. Nor is there much evidence that he conceived of their cross-gender collaboration in terms radically different from those he employed in his dedicatory sonnet in *Florentin*.

The massive "Wechselgesang" (Antiphon) that Friedrich wrote during this period presents a dialogue between a "he" and a "she"—and in terms that seem directly taken from the 1801 dedicatory poem:

Und willst du, daß ich keinen Gott beneide,
Vergiß die strenge Sitt' und laß uns trinken,
Bis wir vom heitern Scherz berauscht sind beide.
Die Kunst ist leicht, nur folge meinen Winken![51]

(And if you wish that I should not feel envy for a god,
Forget strict customs and let us drink,
Until we're both inebriated by serene jest.
The art is easy, just follow my beckoning!)

When in the "Wechselgesang" the "he" speaks of "des Leichtsinns Pflichten" (the duties of levity), it clearly recalls "den hohen Leichtsinn

---

50 Unger, *Briefwechsel*, 63.
51 *KFSA*, V, 196.

unsrer Ehe" (the high levity of our marriage) from *Lucinde*'s "Dithyrambic Fantasy." When we are told that "So bleiben wir im allgmeinen Gleise, / Bis wir aus ihm in unser eignes lenken" (So we remain locked in the universal track / Until we pull from it into our own), then the notion of an always individualized sympoesy isn't far away.[52] Physical "beckoning" (Winke) guides us out of the world of duty, morals, and custom, spiritual chaos being dependent on or co-terminous with physical intoxication. In other words, Friedrich seems to understand his poeticized relationship to his wife, and its public-facing side (the poem itself) in much the same terms he employed in *Lucinde*. It was his wife's view that had changed. But rather than assert her view by publishing, she asserted it by acting upon what he was putting out into the world.

In 1806, Dorothea writes Friedrich with a long list of requests about specific poems to be included in his next collection. Her list includes one poem she calls "Wettgesang" (Competition Song)—most likely the aforementioned "Wechselgesang," which would appear in the *Gedichte*-edition of 1809. All of his poems appear to pass through her at this stage: those that she has read as copy-editor, and the ones that come from her pen but would be published under his name, or would be published with titles by him. Yet others she censors rather insistently: "Gegen die 'muthwilligen Gedichte' möchte ich, mein liebster Freund, in tiefster Demuth Einwendungen machen. Lasse sie doch ja nicht drucken, ebenso wenig als die 'Saturnalien.' Ich bitte Dich, lasse sie aus! Vollends den 'Weinberg'; doch nur ja diesen nicht. Es ist ja in dem 'Wettgesange' schon alles das angedeutet und viel schöner und graciöser" (I would like, my dear friend, to offer some solemn objections to including the "puckish poems." Please do not let them appear in print, any more than the "Saturnalia." I beg you, leave them out of the volume! This goes fully for the "Vineyard"; in particular that one. Everything is already alluded to in the "Wettgesang" and so much more beautifully and gracefully).[53] None of the poems Dorothea objected to ended up in the edition. In the context of the gendered collaborations of Friedrich and Dorothea, her reasons for rejecting them signal that she is, or perhaps they are, reconceiving the terms of that collaboration. She objects to the kind of explicitness that, in spite of the fact that it actually wasn't very explicit, critics had largely associated with *Lucinde*: in praising the "Wechselgesang," she insists on "Andeutung" (allusion), which she calls "schöner und graciöser" (more beautiful and graceful). Both her interventions and the kind of content they

---

52 *KFSA*, V, 197.
53 Schlegel, *Briefwechsel*, ed. Raich, 175.

permit are heavily gendered female: she prefers the more measured, the more graceful, the inexplicit, the slightly retiring. At the same time, she assigns Friedrich an implicitly female role: starting with the idea that *he*, not she, may have given birth to *Florentin*, she sees it as her role to police and structure his uncanny fecundity. In the terms of the "Dithyrambic Fantasy," she is man's "schonende Heftigkeit" (protective intensity) rather than the "anziehende Hingebung" (appealing devotion) of woman.

This emphasis on holding back, on erring on the side of undersharing, would come to dominate Dorothea's thinking for the rest of her life. As her letters to Friedrich during the long period of separation between 1818 and 1820 make clear, this extended far beyond her husband. The letters she writes him from Rome are full of chastisement: not for things he says and does, but for his lack of outrage at things that others say and do. The word "Skandal" is everywhere in these letters: Goethe's *West–östlicher Divan* (West–Eastern Divan) is "unser Skandal" (our scandal, February 5, 1820); the opening of a Protestant church in Rome is a "großer Skandal" (great scandal, July 21, 1819). Dorothea's religiosity, unlike Friedrich's, seems to assert itself at least in part in a great and fine-tuned readiness to be scandalized.

At the same time, she could push Friedrich into public intervention when she felt it was called for. When a negative review appeared in the *Allgemeine Zeitung* of the first Nazarene exhibition in Rome in July 1823, Dorothea relentlessly campaigned to have Friedrich (who had, unlike his wife, never seen the exhibition) express his public displeasure at the review. It was the sort of text she could have easily written; but it seemed important to her that it come from his pen. By September 1823, the paper published responses by the Nazarene artists themselves, including Dorothea's son, Philipp Veit.

But a sense of propriety, a sense for the lines that needed to separate inside from outside, were likely only one force pushing Dorothea towards a different publication ethic. The consequences of one's actions (including one's public utterances) began to preoccupy her. In the same 1800 letter to August Wilhelm in which she suggests that she wishes her husband shared her fear of publication, she mentions three poems Friedrich gave her for her birthday (her thirty-seventh): the two sonnets that would open *Florentin*, and "Der Welke Kranz" (The Wilted Wreath), which would be published in 1809: a poem on a wilted wreath of violets. "Ist es nicht wieder der ganze Friedrich, der mir unter einer großen Menge der herrlichsten Blumen Früchten, schönen Flammen, und Musik dieses rührende Andenken giebt? Ein Todten Opfer im vollsten blühenden Leben!" (Is it not again wholly typical of Friedrich that, in the great mass of the most gorgeous flowers, fruits, beautiful flames, and music, he picks out this touching memento for me? A sacrifice to the dead in the middle of flowering life).[54] Of the three poems, she chooses this rather morbid gift to include with the letter—the two exhortations to publish she treats gingerly, the *memento mori* she treats (and passes along) as "der ganze Friedrich" (wholly typical of Friedrich).

For Dorothea, the emphasis on responsibility and regret seems to have been identical with her preoccupation with propriety and privacy. The common denominator between both was an abiding concern with the awesome responsibility entailed in co-habitation, collaboration, and productivity. The kind of generative irresponsibility Friedrich goads her into manages to lay hold of her for only a few years. After escaping her first marriage in the late 1790s, she compares herself, in a letter to Karl Gustav von Brinckmann, to a shipwrecked person: she is marooned on her island, cast adrift (at least for a time) from friends, family, and even her children. Having escaped her "lange Sklaverei" (long enslavement) and the "Schiffbruch" (shipwreck) of her marriage to Simon Veit, she is alone and she likes it that way.[55] But this sense of joyous irresponsibility doesn't last long—and the first notes of care, of anxiety for a beloved object, sneak into her letters apropos of her written work, specifically *Florentin*.

As she begins drifting towards her religious conversion, Dorothea's faith clearly emerges in tandem with a pronounced regret: regret about how she has treated Simon Veit, regret perhaps also over what she is beginning to understand as a violation of sacrament. By 1808, she advises her son not to hurt her ex-husband's feelings and adds "mich reut jedes unsanfte Wort, das ich je gegen ihn ausgesprochen" (I regret every ungentle word I ever spoke against him).[56] The word "unsanft" (ungentle) is fraught in this context. Not only is it redolent of the kind of conventional femininity to which the "Dithyrambic Fantasy" is so strongly opposed ("Was Gewohnheit oder Eigensinn weiblich nennen, davon weißt du nichts"[57] [You are untouched by the faults that custom and caprice call female]);[58] it is also important that the Dorothea that emerges from her letters is not exactly gentle. She can be explosive, impetuous, badgering, nor does she express regret about her outbursts. So "unsanft" here seems to name a regret that begins and ends in her relationship to Veit.

---

54 Wienecke, *Briefwechsel*, 334.
55 Both quoted in Carola Stern, *"Ich möchte mir Flügel wünschen": Das Leben der Dorothea Schlegel* (Reinbek bei Hamburg: Rowohlt, 1990), 97.
56 Johann Michael Raich, ed., *Dorothea von Schlegel, geb. Mendelssohn und deren Söhne Johannes und Philipp Veit: Briefwechsel* (Mainz: Kirchheim, 1881), 305.
57 *KFSA*, V, 11.
58 Schlegel, *"Lucinde" and the Fragments*, 47.

In her final letter to Simon Veit (written on August 28, 1819), she entwines a sense of personal guilt and forgiveness and a theory of divine grace in a remarkable way. She opens by expressing how happy she is that he has "proven" to her that he forgives her: "Wie soll ich wohl mit Worten ausdrücken, was Dein Schreiben—der unwiderlegliche Beweis Deiner Verzeihung und treuen Freundschaft für Empfindungen in mir erregt" (How can I express in words what feelings your letter—the irrefutable testament to your forgiveness and devoted friendship—arouses in me).[59] But she turns out to be after more than Veit's forgiveness: she seeks to undo what has been done, expunge an injustice "for all eternity"—and this is something only achieved through prayer: "Ich habe alles Gott zu Füßen gelegt im Gebete, ich kann ja nichts tun, nur Er allein im Himmel, der Ewig-Allmächtige, kann geschehenes Unrecht, wenn wir es aufrichtig vor ihn bekennen, durch seine Allmacht für die Ewigkeit ungeschehen machen, kann Böses in Gutes verwandeln" (I have placed it all at God's feet in my prayers; after all, I cannot do anything. He alone in heaven, the Eternal-Almighty, can by his omnipotence undo an injustice done, so long as we openly confess it before him, for all eternity, can turn evil into good).[60] The gesture—not just to atone, but to undo, not just to set something right, but to set everything right—constitutes something of an echo of early Romantic *Naturphilosophie* (natural philosophy), but it has none of the confidence and ease with which the early Romantics communed with the cosmos. All Dorothea takes herself to have, for the moment, is a token of Veit's forgiveness, of Veit's acceptance of what has occurred, and that forgiveness in turn is the only possible stand-in for a greater redemption that will only come in the afterlife. Rather than expanding from something particular into the cosmos, Dorothea thinks that a more cosmic redemption may yet await, but for now she will have to make do with Veit's equally miraculous friendship. Totality is accessible for her only under negative premises: as the greater absolution yet withheld.

As Friedrich Schlegel's publication projects make clear, Dorothea's concerns eventually become his concerns. But the process by which this occurs can be difficult to trace. This is because it is not always clear which poems Dorothea authored and which were Friedrich's. The same letter Dorothea writes to Friedrich from Cologne in 1806 mentions a poem of hers. She calls it "Die Klage" (The Lament), but suggests that Friedrich retitle it. He appears to have done so, and there

---

59 *KFSA*, XXX, 164.
60 *KFSA*, XXX, 164.

is some confusion about which poem Dorothea is referring to. Franz Deibel suggests that it is "Der Stolze" (The Proud One), which indeed was included in the *Poetisches Taschenbuch* of 1806.[61]

If this is correct, then Dorothea engaged in, and Friedrich abetted, a remarkable poetic mimicry: "Der Stolze," both in title and in structure, very strongly resembles the other poems in the two cycles called *Ansichten* (Visions) and *Stimmen der Liebe* (Voices of Love). It would also suggest that Dorothea's poems took a more direct route to publication than many of Friedrich's own: "Der Welke Kranz," as mentioned above, was composed in 1800 and didn't see publication until 1809. If "Die Klage" is "Der Stolze," then Friedrich must not have done much editing other than to change the title. Her editorial knives were far sharper than his.

But Johann Michael Raich, who first edited the letters between Friedrich and Dorothea in the nineteenth century, makes a more provocative suggestion:[62] namely that "Die Klage" may have appeared as "Klagelied der Mutter Gottes" (Lament of the Virgin Mary) as the opening poem of Anton Passy's *Des Jünglings Glaube, Hoffnung und Liebe* (The Young Man's Faith, Hope, and Love) in 1821.[63] In this case, the "Klage" Dorothea mentioned back in 1806 would constitute something of a message in a bottle: starting with a cycle of poems she jotted down in her diary as "Der Sonntag-Morgen" (Sunday Morning) in 1806, Dorothea's poetry outpaces her public utterances and letters in terms of its open Catholicism. And it comes to anticipate strongly the sort of Catholicism that she would begin to practice upon her conversion in 1808.

"Das Klagelied der Mutter Gottes" epitomizes the Christian revision of the motifs of early Romanticism that seized hold of Schlegel's later devotional poetry. Whether or not it actually is Dorothea's work, it clarifies the extent to which the concerns that dominate her letters, diaries, and poems of the early 1800s have now taken over the couple's joint output: "dunkle Schleier" (dark veils), "Trauer" (mourning), and "Weinen" (crying). Longing has been replaced by regret, effusiveness by inwardness. The world-affirming pantheism of early Romanticism was deeply incompatible with a reactionary Catholicism that emphasized the fallenness of the natural world.

---

61 Franz Deibel, *Dorothea Schlegel als Schriftstellerin* (Berlin: Mayer & Müller, 1905), 104.
62 Raich, *Dorothea von Schlegel … und deren Söhne*, 175n.
63 Anton Passy, ed., *Des Jünglings Glaube, Hoffnung und Liebe: Ein Gedicht in drei Büchern, von Anton Passy. Mit einem einleitenden Gedichte von Friedrich von Schlegel* (Vienna: Jacob Mayer, 1821).

> Noch weint die Braut, und ruft vergebens
> Nach Ihm, dem vollen Quell des Lebens,
> Der herrlicher Sich stets enthüllt;
> Zu Ihm sehnt sich die Seele klagend,
> Bis Er die Arme um sie schlagend,
> Sie ganz mit Seiner Wonn' erfüllt.
>
> Noch deckt ein trüber Witwenschleier
> Der künftigen Vollendung Feier,
> Und Trauer hüllt die Schöpfung ein;
> Bis einst der Schleier wird gehoben,
> Muß ewig Klaggesang erhoben
> Von allem, was da atmet, sein.[64]
>
> (The bride cries and calls in vain
> For Him, the full Fount of Life,
> Who reveals Himself more beautifully still.
> The mournful soul strives far to find him,
> Until He, wrapping his arms around it,
> Fills it with His Joy.
>
> Still covers a turbid widow's veil
> The feast of future consummation,
> And Mourning veils all of Creation.
> Until one day the veil is lifted,
> Eternal mournful wail must ring
> By every living, breathing thing.)

The gestures are familiar from the cosmos of early German Romanticism (which may well argue for an 1806 provenance): a veil to be lifted, a source to which one wants to return, a future completeness towards which one strives. But the world before the veil is suffused with mourning, the life process that drives towards its lifting is pure "Klagegesang" (song of mourning). Being removed from the "Quell des Lebens" (source of life) is not mere transcendental homelessness, it is the mourning of the *Stabat mater*. The medieval hymn, which describes the Virgin Mary before her dying son on the cross, is about mourning and its transmission: the audience is asked to want to feel what Mary feels, to share in her sorrow, to cry her tears ("Fac me tecum pie flere" [Let me, pious one, weep with you]). Her sorrow is an object of our spectatorship, of our emulation.

---

64 *KFSA*, V, 421.

This "Klagegesang" (Mourning Song) turns to Mary not as object but as subject. Not a speaking subject, of course, but a subject capable of an act of mourning that exceeds what we can mimic. Nor is sorrow something we need to be taught to mimic: Schlegel's Mary presents a veritable litany, a compendium of pain—a Black Romantic version, almost a parody of early Romantic or Goethean pantheism. All of creation is gathered in mourning:

> Es geht ein allgemeines Weinen,
> So weit die stillen Sterne scheinen,
> Durch alle Adern der Natur;
> Es ringt und seufzt nach der Verklärung,
> Entgegenschmachtend der Gewährung,
> In Liebesangst die Kreatur.[65]

> (Universal sounds a lamentation,
> The whole of stellar illumination,
> Through every artery of nature.
> And sighing for transfiguration,
> Dying for an absolution,
> Struggles in loving fear the creature.)

And while the sorrow in the *Stabat mater* hymn is backward-looking —her pain is a reflection of Jesus' pain, while ours is supposed to be a reflection of hers—the pain in the "Klagegesang" is about the future. It anticipates a future, eternally deferred, in which suffering is transmuted into salvation: "Bis einst der Schleier wird gehoben, / Muß ewig Klaggesang erhoben / Von allem, was da atmet, sein." To breathe is to mourn, to love is a fearful drive towards "Verklärung," a ceaseless striving towards a dispensation that will only come when the veil is finally lifted in death.

This is the cosmos of Dorothea's final letter to Simon Veit; but at the same time, it's the kind of Black Romanticism that seems to animate "Der Welke Kranz," Friedrich's morbid gift for her thirty-seventh birthday. It is one the couple seems to have developed together—though each of them accentuates different aspects of it. His inclinations still seem to run towards the cosmic, hers to the careful observance of boundaries; he seems to emphasize the all-enveloping power of sorrow, she that of guilt and regret; both of them are fascinated with the power of motherhood, but each of them seems to take a different approach to the figure of the mother. In Friedrich Schlegel's final years, the question

---

65 *KFSA*, V, 414.

of faith would emerge as a point of common interest—what it knows and how it can be communicated. By that point Dorothea's role in guiding their communication was almost invisible—she contributed little to Schlegel's actual public output. But once again she would shape the modes of its publicness.

The Philosophy of Life

The summa of the late Catholic Schlegel's official philosophy is threefold: the set of articles he collected as *Signatur des Zeitalters* (Signature of the Age), which opened the first issue of the short-lived journal *Concordia* in 1820, and which occasioned the final break with his brother August Wilhelm; the lectures on the *Philosophie der Geschichte* (Philosophy of History, given in Dresden in 1828); and finally the fifteen lectures given in Vienna in 1827 that he collected as *Philosophie des Lebens* (Philosophy of Life). Questions of gender and family figure strongly in all of these (the family as a "Korporation" [corporation] for instance), but it is *Philosophie des Lebens* that most strongly hearkens back to the monistic precepts and argumentative strategies of Friedrich's and Dorothea's early work: The sexual relationship here emerges as a central axis along which rationality and the sensual can be reconciled, or rather their over-dichotomization overcome:

> Wenn nun aber das höchste Wissen und der göttliche Glauben innerlich und wesentlich eigentlich Eins sind, und in ihrem ewigen Anfang unzertrennlich zusammenhängen; so wird es nur auf das rechte Verhältniß, und auf die richtige Proportion zwischen den beiden Kräften und Elementen des menschlichen Daseins ankommen und davon abhängen, daß sie auch in der weitern Anwendung und im wirklichen Leben Eins bleiben, und nicht in feindlichen Gegensatz und Zwiespalt gerathen.[66]
>
> (If, however, highest knowledge and divine faith are, at their innermost and at their most essential, one and the same, and were interconnected indivisibly ever since their eternal beginning, then it depends on the right relation and the right proportion between these two forces and elements of human existence, and depends on the fact that the two are treated in all application and in real life as one, rather than being allowed to come into hostile opposition with and division from each other.)

There is little evidence that Dorothea was involved in co-writing these lectures. But in a way the lectures themselves furnish the terms for her

---

66 *KFSA*, X, 177.

invisibility. Schlegel turns to the concept of life to reconcile two "Kräften und Elementen des menschlichen Daseins" (forces and elements of human existence), namely the human drive for knowledge and the human need for faith. These two, he claims, are "innerlich und wesentlich eins" (at their innermost and at their most essential one and the same), but they risk coming into "feindlichen Gegesatz und Zwiespalt" (hostile opposition and division) in lived existence.[67]

While he avoids the vocabulary he would have used to describe this dynamic in his earlier writings, *Chaos, Verwirrung, Wechselwirkung* (chaos, confusion, reciprocal effects), this is recognizably an analogous process. The reason he may avoid them is that neither term—either faith or knowledge—is ever fully undone by its dynamization. In the *Athenäum*, Schlegel was fond of statements in which x turns out to be the true y, where the two terms, as *Lucinde* puts it, switch roles ("ob dir die schonende Heftigkeit des Mannes besser gelingt, oder mir die anziehende Hingebung des Weibes"[68] [whether you are better at imitating the protective intensity of the man, or I the appealing devotion of the woman]).[69] This is not the case here. Faith and reason are opposite impulses. Even though it is our job to combine them, their gendered associations serve to delineate them more clearly rather than confuse them or render them dynamic. Schlegel explicates this idea with a domestic simile, with gender dynamics. On first glance, it's Biedermeier kitsch of the worst kind:

> Die glaubende Seele soll als die Frau vom Hause, dort die erste Stelle behalten und behaupten; der wissende, oder nach dem Wissen strebende Geist, mag als der Mann in der innern Familie, auch außer dem Hause diesem oder jenem Geschäft nachgehen; nur aber soll er immer wieder an den heimathlichen Heerd zurückkehren, und sich dort an der rein empor steigenden Flamme der Andacht und der frommen Betrachtung oft von neuem erwärmen.[70]

> (The faithful soul is the Lady of the House, and shall retain and defend her position there; the Spirit, possessed by or searching for knowledge, can undertake his pursuits either as a man within the internal family, or outside of the home. But he must return again and again to the domestic hearth, to warm himself anew on the flames of devotion and faithful observance.)

---

67 *KFSA*, X, 177.
68 *KFSA*, V, 12.
69 Schlegel, *"Lucinde" and the Fragments*, 49.
70 *KFSA*, X, 177.

150 Gender, Collaboration, and Authorship

Female faith enables the striving exploits of male-gendered knowledge—so far, so bland. But Schlegel's simile suggests that reason—the man—has to have a faith of its own. The notion that, left to its own devices, reason will move beyond its proper boundaries had been a common one in German Idealism: implacable antagonists as they were otherwise, Friedrich Heinrich Jacobi and Immanuel Kant agreed on the importance of an outside limit on the roving of reason. According to Kant, the "land of truth" is an island, "umgeben von einem weiten und stürmischen Oceane, dem eigentlichen Sitz des Scheins, wo manche Nebelbank und manches wegschmelzendes Eis neue Länder lügt" (surrounded by a broad and stormy ocean, the true seat of illusion, where many a fog bank and rapidly melting iceberg pretend to be new lands). And he suggests that rather than rushing to sea, we "zuvor noch einen Blick auf die Karte des Landes werfen, das wir eben verlassen wollen, und ... fragen, ob wir mit dem, was es in sich enthält, nicht allenfalls zufrieden sein könnten oder auch aus Noth zufrieden sein müssen, wenn es sonst keinen Boden gibt, auf dem wir uns anbauen können"[71] (cast another glance at the map of the land that we would now leave, and ask, first, whether we could not be satisfied with what it contains, or even must be satisfied with it out of necessity, if there is no other ground on which we can build).[72] Kant's critical project, in other words, proceeds from the Humean proposition that it is better we never ship out in the same place. Jacobi meanwhile thought that we navigate this ocean using feeling and faith; use reason, and you will be shipwrecked. In this context, Schlegel's image entails a rather unusual claim: spirit, seeking knowledge, is under an ethical obligation to "immer wieder an den heimathlichen Heerd zurückkehren" (return again and again to the domestic hearth). This places an ethical limitation on cognitive processes, and it forces them not to stop before faith—as Jacobi and Kant had demanded—but to return to it out of their own volition to their "home." The contrast to early Romantic positions of "transcendental homelessness" could not be clearer: how does reason know how to return? What is it that compels it to?

The motivating force does not seem to be *eros*—it is here that Schlegel departs most clearly from Jacobi's fideism. Something in reason's progress appears to propel reason towards a return to its ground in faith. It

---

71 Immanuel Kant, *Kritik der reinen Vernunft* (Berlin: Königlich Preußische Akademie, 1911), B 294–5.
72 Immanuel Kant, *Critique of Pure Reason*, trans. Paul Guyer and Allen Wood (Oxford: Oxford University Press, 1998), 354.

Friedrich and Dorothea Schlegel 151

may have been the search for a force that might accomplish this feat that inaugurated the strangest cross-gender collaboration Friedrich Schlegel engaged in. In this collaboration Dorothea was no longer a direct partner, but rather a second-order partner—a custodian, a shaper of legacies. This would be Dorothea's and Friedrich's final collaboration, one that only took place after his death.

Friedrich Schlegel died on January 12, 1829; on the ninth anniversary of his death, January 12, 1838, Dorothea sent an unpublished manuscript of Friedrich's to the painter Ludwig Ferdinand Schnorr von Carolsfeld.[73] This manuscript was testament to a far stranger web of quasi-literary co-production, one that connected men and women, but one that largely seemed to exclude Dorothea. The way gender dynamics play themselves out in this hews much closer to the dialectical relationship of faith and knowledge Schlegel lays out in his 1827 lecture than to the gender roles that dominated the *Athenäum* years.

In the final decades of his life Schlegel explored a literalized *Symphilosophie* or *Sympoesie*. And while, during the *Athenäum* years, Schlegel's vision of co-productivity (especially with Schleiermacher) was intimately tied to a publicly visible (i.e., readable) product, the later-period Schlegel's cross-gender collaborations emphasized once again the incommunicable. Schlegel found himself in an odd collaborative relationship with sundry religious figures and upper-class ladies who explored telepathy and magnetism. He called these women his "Seelenschwestern" (soul sisters): he maintained an eight-year exchange of letters with the Augsburg aristocrat Christine von Stransky; advised the Countess Saint-Aulaire; and was in constant contact with Mater Agnes (Marianne Häcking, 1775–1829), an Ursuline nun. But the manuscript sent to Schnorr von Carolsfeld was the record of Schlegel's association with Countess Lesniowska, who lived in Vienna and whose dreams under the influence of magnetism Schlegel had chronicled for six years (May 1820 to April 1826).

What exactly did he believe the "Seelenschwestern" shared with him? Unlike in *Symphilosophie* it wasn't ideas, and unlike in *Sympoesie* it wasn't feelings—as Astrid Keiner puts it, "the immediate transmission, independent of and unadulterated by the medium of language, of thoughts 'with effects.'"[74] In practice, thoughts that are also actions concerned mostly religious devotion—Schlegel and his soul sisters would

---

73 Ursula Behler in *KFSA*, XXXV, xi.
74 Astrid Keiner, *Hieroglyphenromantik: Zur Genese und Destruktion eines Bilderschriftmodells und zu seiner Überforderung in Friedrich Schlegels Spätphilosophie* (Würzburg: Königshausen & Neumann, 2003), 163.

pray at the same moments, would chronicle dreams in which each other appeared religiously transfigured. But Keiner correctly points out that it is not hard to espy a theory of the sign behind this idea. The question is the one raised by *Lucinde*: How do you bring something that tends to exceed language into language?

For bring it into language they did: no public testimony of their thinking and experimentation emerged during Schlegel's lifetime, and even when Dorothea shared the Lesniowska diary, she did it only to help Schnorr von Carolsfeld with his own crank research into telepathy and mesmerism (the pages wouldn't see publication until the mid-twentieth century). But the diary existed, as did extensive letters: the moments of non-discursive communication were enframed by a truly staggering amount of discursive communication. Some of it had been published before Schlegel's death, though not under Schlegel's authorship: a record of visions and dreams, but also a record of his attempts to put in order the material obtained from his "Seelenschwester."

It is hard to read Schlegel's notes and not be put in mind of Freudian psychoanalysis—certainly most early-twentieth-century readers of the material tended to think Schlegel had anticipated a Viennese preoccupation by about sixty years. But especially when it comes to gender roles, the differences are as telling as the homologies. For one thing, Schlegel does not think of himself as an uninvolved observer—again and again he finds himself driven to visit Countess Lesniowska, sometimes by an "# Andeutung" (intuition), the "#" being his code for "magnetic."

For another, he is not simply an analyst or interpreter, he is in important respects a medium: he frames his mission as being "## befreyend" (freeing), meaning he and the countess release a kind of energy for each other that makes their visions possible or recoverable in the first place. Schlegel records several visits that proved abortive, because the number of visitors at the countess's destroyed their interpersonal magnetism. Most importantly, however, there exists no agentive, ordering role akin to that of the analyst that Schlegel claims for himself: magnetism, Schlegel seems to suspect, is about universal receptivity. In reading over the notes and letters between the soul siblings, one gets the suspicion, of course, that there is a great deal of spontaneity here, but the interlocutors all experience their impulses and associations as dictated by outside forces.

Religion suffuses these notes as much as a sense that religion might function here as a cover for other things. Schlegel and Lesniowska share real intimacy, but it is an intimacy entirely structured by religiosity. The raw, manic energy of Schlegel's earlier productions has transmitted itself to the visions, the magnetic impulses that buffet these two towards each other again and again. And it is the role of scripture to contain this energy, to find a hermeneutic home for it. Consider one visit in May 1825: The countess dutifully recalls a dream from the previous night, "welchen sie auch für mich aufgeschrieben zu haben glaubte." (which she believed she had written down for me somewhere).[75] In the end, she describes her vision for Schlegel—fiery letters, three interlocking triangles, and a black eagle—and he dutifully transcribes them. Schlegel appends a brief exegesis to his diary entry, in which he explains the motifs by referring them back to Bible passages.

Dorothea seems to have been largely left cold by the rather unconventional turn Friedrich's religiosity took during these final years. But after his death she used her stewardship of this rather strange, and for her possibly embarrassing, part of his cross-gender collaboration to mourn him. Even before the extent of the paper trail left by these mesmeric exercises became apparent in the mid-twentieth century, many analysts of Schlegel's work knew exactly what to call them: the women Schlegel grouped around him were unhappy hysterics, and he was really no different. Dorothea seems to have been quite familiar with her husband's theories; when she sent the documents to Schnorr von Carolsfeld, she made clear she'd read over them. Friedrich had spent his life oversharing; now Dorothea was oversharing for him.

But perhaps she let go of these records precisely because she understood that the mode of collaboration modeled here owed quite a bit to the mode that she had (often unsuccessfully) asked of Friedrich earlier in their writing relationship. This is after all a kind of intellectual project quite in keeping with the gender dynamics Schlegel laid out in his *Philosophie des Lebens*: a rationality that depends on, starts from, and returns into faith.

As science it's all perfectly wrong of course, and even as religion it's bunk. But it is hard not to credit Friedrich's exchanges with his soul siblings with a sincere faith, one that made their communication possible and that made their communication publishable. Schlegel's attentions to Countess Lesniowska have a distinctly amorous quality—and yet they seem driven by nothing so profane as sexual desire. One wonders what Dorothea thought setting the notes detailing this strange relationship on their tentative path towards a public. It was as much an act of oversharing as it was an act of showing that there was nothing to overshare here. And it wasn't a posthumous immortalization, with a view to securing Friedrich's legacy. If anything, it was a mortalization, a humanization—a record of Friedrich's farthest travels along the fog banks and melting ice of the Kantian seas.

---

75 *KFSA*, XXXV, 212.

Bibliography

Becker-Cantarino, Barbara. "Friedrich Schlegels *Lucinde* und Dorothea Schlegels *Florentin.*" In *Bi-Textualität: Zur Inszenierung des Paares*, ed. Annegret Heitmann, Sigrid Nieberle, Barbara Schaff, and Sabine Schülting, 131–41. Berlin: Erich Schmidt, 2001.
Becker-Cantarino, Barbara. *Schriftstellerinnen der Romantik*. Arbeitsbücher zur Literaturgeschichte. Munich: Beck, 2000.
Daub, Adrian. *Uncivil Unions: The Metaphysics of Marriage in German Idealism and Romanticism*. Chicago: University of Chicago Press, 2012.
Deibel, Franz. *Dorothea Schlegel als Schriftstellerin*. Berlin: Mayer & Müller, 1905.
Gorodeisky, Keren. "'No Poetry, No Reality': Schlegel, Wittgenstein, Fiction and Reality." In *The Relevance of Romanticism*, ed. Dalia Nassar, 163–85. Oxford: Oxford University Press, 2014.
Izenberg, Gerald. *Impossible Individuality: Romanticism, Revolution and the Origins of Modern Selfhood*. Princeton, NJ: Princeton University Press, 1992.
Kant, Immanuel. *Critique of Pure Reason*. Trans. Paul Guyer and Allen Wood. Oxford: Oxford University Press, 1998.
Kant, Immanuel. *Kritik der reinen Vernunft*. Berlin: Königlich Preußische Akademie, 1911.
Keiner, Astrid. *Hieroglyphenromantik: Zur Genese und Destruktion eines Bilderschriftmodells und zu seiner Überforderung in Friedrich Schlegels Spätphilosophie*. Würzburg: Königshausen & Neumann, 2003.
Lacoue-Labarte, Philippe and Jean-Luc Nancy. *The Literary Absolute*. Albany, NY: SUNY Press, 1988.
Passy, Anton, ed. *Des Jünglings Glaube, Hoffnung und Liebe: Ein Gedicht in drei Büchern, von Anton Passy. Mit einem einleitenden Gedichte von Friedrich von Schlegel*. Vienna: Jacob Mayer, 1821.
Plato. *The Dialogues of Plato*. Trans. Benjamin Jowett. Oxford: Clarendon Press, 1953.
Raich, Johann Michael, ed. *Dorothea von Schlegel, geb. Mendelssohn und deren Söhne Johannes und Philipp Veit: Briefwechsel*. Mainz: Kirchheim, 1881.
Rehme-Iffert, Birgit. *Skepsis und Enthusiasmus: Friedrich Schlegels philosophischer Grundgedanke*. Würzburg: Königshausen & Neumann, 2001.
Richards, Robert J. *The Romantic Conception of Life*. Chicago: University of Chicago Press, 2010.
Schlegel, Dorothea. *Dorothea Schlegel Briefwechsel*. Ed. Johann Michael Raich. Mainz: Kirchheim, 1881.
Schlegel, Dorothea. *Florentin: Ein Roman*. Berlin: Ullstein, 1987.
Schlegel, Friedrich. *Friedrich Schlegel's "Lucinde" and the Fragments*. Trans. Peter Firchow. Minneapolis: University of Minnesota Press, 1871.
Schlegel, Friedrich. *Kritische Friedrich Schlegel Ausgabe*. Ed. Ernst Behler, Jean Jacques Anstett, and Hans Eichner. Munich: Schöningh, 1958–.
Schleiermacher, Friedrich. *Briefwechsel 1800*. Berlin: De Gruyter, 1994.
Stern, Carola. *"Ich möchte mir Flügel wünschen": Das Leben der Dorothea Schlegel*. Reinbek bei Hamburg: Rowohlt, 1990.
Tillard, Françoise. *Fanny Mendelssohn*. Portland: Amadeus Press, 1996.
Unger, Rudolf, ed. *Der Briefwechsel von Dorothea und Friedrich Schlegel an die Familie Paulus*. Berlin: Behr, 1913.
Wieneke, Ernst, ed. *Briefwechsel von Caroline und Dorothea Schlegel*. Weimar: Kiepenheuer, 1914.

Six Holy Hermaphrodite
The Collaboration between Caroline and Friedrich de la Motte Fouqué

Eleanor ter Horst

Marked by shared intellectual and literary interests, the collaboration between Caroline and Friedrich de la Motte Fouqué placed them at the center of the Romantic movement. Though both authors are less well known today—Friedrich remembered chiefly for the novella *Undine*, and Caroline largely unrecognized—they were among the more prolific and well-known writers of their time, and closely connected to the larger group of Romantics, including Adelbert von Chamisso, Joseph von Eichendorff, E. T. A. Hoffmann, Wilhelm Schlegel, Friedrich Schleiermacher, and Karl August and Rahel Levin Varnhagen. Indeed, Caroline's family estate in Brandenburg, Nennhausen, was a gathering point for this group of Romantic writers.[1] After they were married—a second marriage for both of them—Caroline and Friedrich collaborated on the journals published by Friedrich, in which both of their works appeared. Despite her important individual and collaborative contributions to the Romantic literary scene, Caroline's literary endeavors were often judged negatively in comparison to Friedrich's, both by her contemporaries and by later critics. For example, Arno Schmidt, in his biography, *Fouqué und einige seiner Zeitgenossen* (Fouqué and Some of His Contemporaries), quotes E. T. A. Hoffmann's negative evaluation

---

1   Jean Wilde's biography of Caroline gives a sense of the lively scene at Nennhausen; see Jean Wilde, *The Romantic Realist: Caroline de la Motte Fouqué* (New York: Bookman Associates, 1955), 19–24. Arno Schmidt suggests that it was a literary center during the Romantic period (*Fouqué und einige seiner Zeitgenossen* [Zürich: Haffmans, 1993], 323); and Theodore Ziolkowski discusses the importance of the estate to Romantic literary production ("Nennhausen: Anregungsort romantischer Erzählkunst," *Jahrbuch für internationale Germanistik* 43 [2011]: 201–15 [201–4]).

of Caroline's novels, which implies that Caroline's work was derivative of Friedrich's, and provides as evidence for his claim the fact that her novel *Die Frau des Falkensteins* (The Lady of Castle Falkenstein) contains poems written by Friedrich.[2] More recently, however, Caroline has begun to receive attention independently of Friedrich, with a new critical edition of her works currently being published, and a number of scholarly books and articles devoted to her writings.[3] The focus of this recent criticism is, understandably, to establish Caroline's importance in her own right, as a writer engaged in the key issues of the Romantic movement, and to explore the notions of gender developed in her works.

Now that this process of reassessing Caroline's individual literary and theoretical contributions is under way, I believe that there is much to be gained from taking another look at the collaboration between Caroline and Friedrich, not for the purpose of elevating one member of the pair over the other, as Schmidt and others have done, but for the insight that such an approach can provide into the works of both authors, and into the development of the Romantic movement, which, despite its valorization of the individual creative genius, depended to a large extent on collaborative literary and philosophical efforts. My focus will be on a group of works by Caroline and Friedrich published around 1811–12, a period when both authors were well established as individual contributors to the Romantic movement. Central to my investigation will be Caroline's scholarly work *Briefe über die griechische Mythologie für Frauen* (Letters on Greek Mythology for Women, 1812), an examination of Greek mythology from historical, anthropological, and religious perspectives. Using Caroline's ideas as a framework opens new perspectives

---

2 See Schmidt, *Fouqué*, 167. Schmidt continues his negative assessment of Caroline, implying that Friedrich was unhappy in his marriage because Caroline played a dominant role in the relationship (168–70).
3 The 1990s saw a renewed interest in Caroline's literary and theoretical works, with a book-length study by Karin Baumgartner (*Public Voices: Political Discourse in the Writings of Caroline de la Motte Fouqué* [Bern: Lang, 2009]), and numerous articles focusing mostly on her historical novels. Other approaches include Sara Luly's focus on gender and the Gothic elements of Caroline's fiction ("Emasculating Fear: Gothic and Gender in Caroline de la Motte Fouqué's *Der Cypressenkranz*," *Monatshefte* 104, no. 2 ([Summer 2012]: 180–93), and Elisabeth Krimmer's examination of cross-dressing and gender transgressions ("Officer and Lady: Pants and Politics in Caroline de la Motte-Fouqué's *Das Heldenmädchen aus der Vendée* [1816]," *Studies in Eighteenth-Century Culture* 30 [2001]: 165–81). The scholarly edition of Caroline's works is being edited by Thomas Neumann; see Caroline de la Motte Fouqué, *Werke und Schriften*, ed. Thomas Neumann (Norderstedt: Books on Demand Ditzingen, 2006–).

on the uses of mythology in Friedrich's novella *Undine* (1811) and in Caroline's novel *Magie der Natur: Eine Revolutions-Geschichte* (Nature's Magic: A Story of Revolution, 1812). In both literary works, the recourse to mythology permits an exploration of permanence and change within history, as well as in individual relationships. The three works are connected by their examination of changing definitions of masculinity and femininity, as well as by their exploration of shifts in relationships between individual men and women. All three emphasize a hermaphroditic concept of gender, rather than sharp divisions between male and female, and all link creativity to the expression of both conventionally masculine and conventionally feminine qualities, as they draw on the concept of an originary femininity that encompasses both genders.

The works' embrace of hermaphroditic creativity suggests that both Caroline and Friedrich valued intellectual interaction between men and women, and that their marriage itself might be seen as an instance of hermaphroditic collaboration. Assessments of their relationship vary widely, with Schmidt, following Karl August Varnhagen, seeing Caroline as a negative influence on Friedrich,[4] and Wilde emphasizing the mutual support that they gave each other in literary and personal endeavors.[5] Evidence of their shared dedication to literary pursuits is provided not only by their joint editorship of journals such as *Die Jahreszeiten* (The Seasons), *Für müssige Stunden* (For Times of Leisure), and *Berlinische Blätter für deutsche Frauen* (Berlin Gazette for German Women), but also by Friedrich's own autobiography (*Lebensgeschichte*), which provides several examples of mutually beneficial literary discussions. In one instance, Friedrich recounts a scene of conversation with Caroline, during which he is giving her information about medieval French chivalric customs for a story that she is working on, while she remarks that he should try writing about this period in history, to which he is connected by his French ancestors.[6] This conversation marks the genesis of Friedrich's novel *Der Zauberring* (The Magic Ring). This

---

4 See Schmidt, *Fouqué*, 158–9. Varnhagen's and Schmidt's negative assessments of Caroline's role may be due, in part, to her transgressions against established gender norms. Varnhagen expresses both admiration and discomfort when he writes of her that "groß und schön gewachsen, in der Gesichtsbildung dem Apollo von Belvedere ähnlich, mußte sie für eine herrliche Erscheinung gelten, der man gezwungen war zu huldigen." Karl August Varnhagen von Ense, *Biographische Portraits* (Leipzig: Brockhaus, 1871), 120. As mentioned earlier, Schmidt emphasizes the dominant role that she played in her marriage (Schmidt, *Fouqué*, 159).
5 Wilde, *The Romantic Realist*, 42.
6 See Friedrich de la Motte Fouqué, *Lebensgeschichte des Baron Friedrich de la Motte Fouqué, aufgezeichnet durch ihn selbst* (Berlin: Hofenberg, 2015), 267.

autobiographical evidence, as well as accounts by Caroline's and Friedrich's contemporaries and assessments of later biographers, suggests that the Fouqués' collaboration was productive for their creativity but challenging for their contemporaries, as well as for later biographers and critics.

Caroline and Friedrich reassess categories of gender and social rank in the three works under discussion: *Briefe über die griechische Mythologie für Frauen*, *Undine*, and *Magie der Natur*, all written during a period of social and political upheaval between the French Revolution and the end of the Napoleonic Wars. Rather than assuming a linear influence, with one work giving rise to another, I focus on these three works as part of a web of dialogue, an ongoing process of collaboration. *Undine* was the first of the three to be published (in 1811 in the journal *Die Jahreszeiten*, and later that year as a book) and possibly the first to be written, although the genesis of each work is difficult to determine; according to Schmidt, Friedrich wrote *Undine* in 1809.[7] Caroline had completed *Briefe über die griechische Mythologie für Frauen* by March 1812, but this scholarly work would have taken considerable time to research and compose.[8] It was published in 1812, the same year as *Magie der Natur*. The three works show such remarkably similar preoccupations with gender distinctions, hermaphroditism, and theories of historical change and continuity as to suggest close collaboration and discussions between the two authors. Viewed together, they can be seen as reflections about the potential benefits of and barriers to male–female intellectual and creative collaboration.

Caroline's scholarly work on mythology, *Briefe über die griechische Mythologie für Frauen*, uses the epistolary form to establish dialogue, primarily with other women but also with male scholars, such as Friedrich Schlegel and Novalis, who addressed the importance of mythology to Romanticism's theories of creativity and spirituality.[9] With a different focus from that of these male thinkers, Caroline relates mythology to broad historical movements, as well as to spiritual practices, while

---

7   Schmidt, *Fouqué*, 186.
8   Varnhagen, *Biographische Portraits*, 136.
9   Novalis had planned a work entitled *Mythologie für Frauenzimmer*, of which only the introduction exists. Like Caroline, he stresses the continuity between Egyptian and Greek mythology; see Novalis, *Mythologie für Frauenzimmer*, in *Novalis Schriften: Die Werke Friedrich von Hardenbergs*, ed. Paul Kluckhohn and Richard Samuel (Stuttgart: Kohlhammer, 1998), VI.1, 152–3. Friedrich Schlegel emphasizes the central role of mythology for Greek art, and suggests that a new mythology is needed for progress in the contemporary arts; see Friedrich Schlegel, "Rede über die Mythologie," in *Kritische Friedrich Schlegel Ausgabe*, ed. Ernst Behler and Hans Dierkes (Paderborn: Schöningh, 2006), II, 311–22 (311).

emphasizing the change and continuity in women's and men's roles over time. Moving from a comparative study of creation myths, to the conflicts worked out in hero myths of ancient Greece, to a positing of unity between past and present through the rediscovery of an originary female divinity, Caroline asserts the necessity for a female voice amid the largely male-dominated discourses of classical studies, history, and comparative religion.[10] In so doing, she brings mythology into the contemporary, everyday world by asserting an unbroken link between ancient mythology and contemporary spiritual or creative endeavors, and by suggesting the possibility that women of her time might gain access to a buried female divine through the study of mythology and history.

While cognizant of cultural differences, Caroline emphasizes the continuity among Asian, Egyptian, Greek, and Hebraic mythologies, comparing their creation myths and demonstrating that various gods and goddesses possess similar attributes across historical and geographical demarcations. For example, she shows that the Mesopotamian goddess Astarte is closely related to the Egyptian Isis[11] and the Greek Io,[12] while the Phrygian Cybele was imported into Greece and became assimilated to Gaia[13] and Demeter.[14] Using mythology as a thread to connect seemingly disparate cultures, Caroline emphasizes the merging of male and female attributes in the earliest mythological figures, and in the creation myths: Chaos, the earliest state of the universe, was characterized by the intermingling of masculine and feminine traits.[15] This lack of gender differentiation extended to ancient divinities, such as Eros, whom Caroline, following ancient sources, such as Hesiod, places among the primordial deities, and designates as "die Liebe, die Weltseele, der heilige Geist"[16] (love, the world's soul,

---

10 Almut-Barbara Renger sees Caroline as using the epistolary form in order to make her incursions into male-dominated scholarship appear less threatening ("Zur Bestimmung von Genre und Geschlecht um 1800: Caroline Fouqués *Briefe über die griechische Mythologie*—ein Werk für Frauen?," *Jahrbuch der Fouqué-Gesellschaft Berlin-Brandenburg* [2003]: 47–60 [51–2]). Baumgartner emphasizes Caroline's strategy of employing religion, considered to be an appropriate subject of study for women, as an entry point into the male-dominated discourses such as history (*Public Voices*, 55–9).
11 Caroline de la Motte Fouqué, *Briefe über die griechische Mythologie für Frauen* (Berlin: Hitzig, 1812), 85 (hereafter *Briefe*).
12 *Briefe*, 304.
13 *Briefe*, 85.
14 *Briefe*, 139.
15 *Briefe*, 91.
16 *Briefe*, 83.

the divine spirit).[17] Similarly, the moon-goddess, Selene, incorporating "die höchste Idee weiblicher Naturkraft" (the most exalted idea of the feminine power of nature), was believed to have been originally both "männlich erzeugend" (engendering in the masculine manner) and "weiblich gebährend" (giving birth in the feminine manner).[18] The goddess Cybele appears as an important and paradoxical figure who, Caroline claims, represented "das mütterliche Prinzip des Lebens" (the maternal principle of life)[19] but was originally hermaphroditic, and was only later separated into a male and female principle. Attis, representing the male principle, emerged from Cybele who, falling in love with him, caused him to go mad and castrate himself.[20] Other gods, such as Hephaestus/Vulcan, partake of this originary hermaphroditism.[21] Caroline returns to this idea of undifferentiated genders towards the end of her work, pointing out that the cross-dressing Heracles[22] and the Amazons display the same hermaphroditic tendencies as Cybele/Attis, illustrating "die Ungeteiltheit göttlichen Wesens, welches sowohl männlichen als weiblichen Geschlechtes ist" (the indivisibility of the divine being, which partakes of both masculine and feminine genders).[23]

In emphasizing this originary hermaphroditism, Caroline affirms the theory of gender polarity, grounded in biology, which was becoming more prevalent in the nineteenth century, and, at the same time, allows for exceptions to the idea that men and women have separate, complementary roles based on their biological differences.[24] While validating the association of masculinity with the generative function, and femininity with the child-bearing function, she nonetheless stops short of implying a sharp distinction between male and female social roles based on these biological functions. For example, in the opening letter of *Briefe über die griechische Mythologie*, she establishes herself as a participant in a dialogue about ancient mythology, a field that was

---

17 All translations from the German are mine.
18 *Briefe*, 93.
19 *Briefe*, 72.
20 *Briefe*, 72–3.
21 *Briefe*, 165.
22 *Briefe*, 333.
23 *Briefe*, 325.
24 Karin Hausen advances the theory that men's and women's roles were becoming more polarized in the nineteenth century, as women were increasingly aligned with the domestic sphere, while men were said to be suited for engagement in the outside world; see Karin Hausen, "Die Polarisierung der 'Geschlechtscharaktere': Eine Spiegelung der Dissonanzen von Erwerbs- und Familienleben," in *Sozialgeschichte der Familie in der Neuzeit Europas*, ed. Werner Conze (Stuttgart: Klett, 1976), 367–93 (367).

traditionally a male province, and opens space for women to investigate and comment on the relevance of mythology to contemporary life. Noting that the exemplary (male) historian ("der Geschichtsschreiber") has erected a metaphorical wall preventing him from investigating the ancient world using the same historical methods employed with later periods, she calls for a rapprochement between the ancient and the modern worlds.[25] She disparages the contemporary historian's "unnatürlich Abreißen und Lossagen vom mütterlichen Schoße" ("unnatural rupture and separation from the maternal womb")[26] and favors a return to the originary feminine, suggesting that women are better equipped to effect the fusion of disciplines necessary for the study of mythology, because of their closeness to nature.[27] Associating mythology with "Naturgeschichte" (natural history) and "Religionsgeschichte" (history of religion),[28] she calls for a combination of traditionally masculine and traditionally feminine modes of understanding the world, a kind of hermaphroditic approach to intellectual investigation.

This mental hermaphroditism is grounded both in spirituality (the notion of an original, maternal divinity that nonetheless encompasses both genders) and in biology, not only in the human generative and maternal functions but also, more broadly, in the natural world of the elements. Caroline emphasizes the association of water with masculine traits in Greek mythology, in contrast to eastern mythological traditions, where it is gendered feminine. Although the Greeks associated water with male deities (Poseidon, Pontus, Nereus, Oceanus),[29] Caroline insists on its bi-gendered qualities: it is "Mannweib zugleich, und bewährt seine göttliche Ganzheit durch die Einigung des Entgegengesetzten" (at once masculine and feminine, and it preserves its divine unity by conjoining opposites).[30] Nature, as a reflection of the divine, encompasses traits that are thought to be mutually exclusive, bringing together not only characteristics of both genders, but also opposites such as life and death: associated with the "heilige Schooß" (sacred womb), water is also destructive of the very life that it brings forth ("ein Feind der eigenen Geburten" [enemy of its own progeny]), and encompasses both creation and destruction.[31]

---

25 *Briefe*, 2.
26 *Briefe*, 3.
27 *Briefe*, 4.
28 *Briefe*, 5.
29 *Briefe*, 126–7.
30 *Briefe*, 127.
31 *Briefe*, 127.

While water leads back to the origins of life, the element most closely related to the development of humanity is fire, which Caroline associates with Chaos and Eros, the primordial deities, both hermaphroditic. Like water, fire in Greek mythology is associated with the masculine principle (Helios, Hephaestus), but this masculinity emerges from an originary, undifferentiated element, which was then divided into masculine and feminine. Caroline gives the example of the Egyptian god Ptah, divided into sun and moon, whom she sees as a precursor of Zeus, the sun god, or "Himmelskönig" (king of heaven)[32] a thoroughly masculine deity who nonetheless leads back to the hermaphroditic origins of the divine. Zeus is characterized by contradiction, suggesting his original dual nature: "Nun tritt der Sonnengott sowohl als gewaltiger Zeus, Lenker, Order und Himmelskönig hervor, wie er sich uns kämpfend als leidender, schmachtender, sterbender Gott offenbarte" (Now the sun-god appears as mighty Zeus, ruler, bringer of order, just as he, struggling, revealed himself to us as a suffering, languishing, dying god).[33] In emphasizing the sun-god's suffering and mortality, Caroline may be referring to the attempt by Zeus's father, Chronos, to kill his son, but this passage also suggests that the Christian deity, split between a powerful father and a suffering, mortal son, derives from the hermaphroditic, originary feminine. Zeus "führt uns zugleich noch höher zu der Uridee des absolut weiblichen Prinzipes, der heilig ewigen, das Licht in sich tragenden Chaosnacht zurück"[34] (elevates us back to the originary idea of the absolute feminine principle, of the divine, eternal chaos-night that bears light within it).[35] Insisting on the bi-gendered qualities of an original divine, Caroline feminizes God the Father, and reconfigures the divine, as well as the creativity that it inspires, as female.

Caroline also associates human creativity with hermaphroditism. Drawing on the myth of Prometheus, who stole fire and gave it to humans, she defines the use of fire as the beginning of separation between humanity and divinity, since from this point forward humans became independent of the gods.[36] Prometheus himself is subject to the (human) cycle of rising and falling, life and death: first a powerful god, then captured and tortured by Zeus before being released and rising again: "daher ist der sterbende, scheidende Gott auch der Verklärte

---

32 *Briefe*, 238.
33 *Briefe*, 238.
34 *Briefe*, 238.
35 This concept of the feminine principle may anticipate Goethe's idea of "das Ewig-Weibliche" from *Faust*, II.
36 *Briefe*, 235–6.

und Gereinigte" (therefore the dying, departing god is also the transfigured and purified one).³⁷ Caroline sees this cycle of rising and falling as key to understanding the ancient tragedies, and she quotes at length from Sophocles' *Trachiniae*, which, exceptionally for Greek tragedies, places female experience at the center, as it features both a hero, Heracles, and a heroine, Deianira.³⁸ Tragic drama, a human creation, reflects the human and divine cycles of rising and falling, which Caroline also associates with masculine and feminine principles, respectively.³⁹ But male humans and deities can also embody the feminine principle, and females the masculine principle, as we have seen in the cases of Prometheus; Heracles; and associated primordial deities, such as Eros.⁴⁰ By showing that male gods and heroes reflect both masculine and feminine principles, Caroline makes a case for a link between divine hermaphroditism and creativity. Emphasizing that male heroes and gods, reflecting the originary female divine, contain both masculine and feminine traits, Caroline pairs Hyacinthus and Ganymede, two young human males desired by male gods, Apollo and Zeus, respectively. Hyacinthus, who turns into a flower, represents the earthly, falling, or feminine principle, while Ganymede, seized by Zeus in the form of an eagle and taken up to Olympus, represents the rising, or masculine principle.⁴¹ With a focus on these mythological figures involved in same-sex relationships, Caroline not only complicates the polarized gender paradigm of her time, which linked gendered traits to biological functions, but also suggests that a certain flexibility in gender identity and sexuality is a crucial component of creativity.

With Caroline's linking of hermaphroditism and creativity in mind, I would like to turn to two fictional works by Friedrich and Caroline, whose use of mythology complicates the nineteenth century's gender paradigms and understanding of marriage as a harmonious union of opposites. Concomitantly, these works explore the possibilities for male–female collaboration. Friedrich's *Undine* focuses on the myth of the water nymph and her connection to the natural world and humanity (male and female), while Caroline's *Magie der Natur: Eine Revolutions-Geschichte* explores the connection of women to nature that she posits in *Briefe über die griechische Mythologie*. Both fictional works feature a love triangle involving a man and two women. The two female characters in each work embody opposing principles, illustrating the

---

37 *Briefe*, 275.
38 *Briefe*, 337–9.
39 *Briefe*, 293.
40 *Briefe*, 275.
41 *Briefe*, 292–3.

idea of original hermaphroditism, or the dual nature of the female divine that Caroline elucidates in her study of Greek mythology.

Friedrich de la Motte Fouqué's *Undine* displays the duality of the feminine in its structure. In the first part of the novella, nature predominates and Undine's powers control the destiny of the knight, Huldbrand, and others who enter her domain. The setting of this section is a peninsula, which becomes an island once the water spirits cause the river to rise. Here, Undine resides with her foster parents, the fisherman and his wife; and the knight, Huldbrand, spends an extended period of time here, trapped by the rising waters, eventually marrying Undine and thereby allowing her to acquire a human soul. The second part of the novella shows the conflict between nature and culture, between Undine and Bertalda, the human female character. In this second section, Undine and Huldbrand leave the peninsula and journey to the city where Bertalda lives, then depart for Huldbrand's ancestral estate, Burg Ringstetten, where his affections begin to shift from Undine to Bertalda.

Undine derives much of its mythological material from *Liber de nymphis, sylphis, pygmaeis et salamandris et de caeteris spiritibus* (A Book on Nymphs, Sylphs, Pygmies, and Salamanders, and Other Spirits) by Paracelsus, the Renaissance physician, alchemist, and philosopher. Paracelsus associates four different types of spirits with the four elements—Undine is linked to water—and details their differences from humans, as well as their commonalities and the possibility of contact between humans and elemental spirits. The portions of *Undine* that focus on the marriage between the title character and the knight, Huldbrand, most likely derive their inspiration from Paracelsus, who lays out in detail how the (female) nymphs can acquire a soul through marriage with a human male. Paracelsus notes that the water nymphs are closest to humans of all the elemental spirits: they have the form of human beings and can mate with them, but they are separated from them by their lack of a soul.[42] This emphasis on the similarities and differences between humans and elemental spirits is made concrete in Friedrich's text through the opposition between Bertalda, a human female, and Undine, both of whom vie for Huldbrand's affections. As we have seen, Caroline's work on Greek mythology places a good deal of emphasis on the connections of various deities to the four elements, with particular attention to fire and water, but it is unclear whether she was also influenced by Paracelsus, or whether she is simply elucidating the elemental theory at the basis of Greek philosophy, which persisted in the alchemical theory of the Middle Ages and the Renaissance. In any

---

42 Paracelsus, *Liber de nymphis, sylphis, pygmaeis et salamandris et de caeteris spiritibus* (Bern: Francke, 1960), 22–7.

case, a similarity in approaches to gender, hermaphroditism, and the connection between the feminine principle and nature links the works of Caroline and Friedrich, apart from any Paracelsian influence.[43]

A natural setting displaying hermaphroditic traits is described in the opening passage of *Undine*. This setting is the home of Undine and her foster parents, the fisherman and his wife, and the natural elements that surround them evoke the relationship between Undine and Huldbrand, the knight whom she marries, while blurring gender distinctions:

> Der grüne Boden, worauf seine Hütte gebaut war, streckte sich weit in einen großen Landsee hinaus, und es schien ebensowohl, die Erdzunge habe sich aus Liebe zu der bläulich klaren, wunderhellen Flut in diese hineingedrängt, als auch, das Wasser habe mit verliebten Armen nach der schönen Aue gegriffen, nach ihren hochschwankenden Gräsern und Blumen und nach dem erquicklichen Schatten ihrer Bäume. Eins ging bei dem andern zu Gaste, und eben deshalb war jegliches so schön. Von Menschen freilich war an dieser hübschen Stelle wenig oder gar nichts anzutreffen, den Fischer und seine Hausleute ausgenommen. Denn hinter der Erdzunge lag ein sehr wilder Wald, den die mehrsten Leute wegen seiner Finsternis und Unwegsamkeit, wie auch wegen der wundersamen Kreaturen und Gaukeleien, die man darin antreffen sollte, allzusehr scheueten, um sich ohne Not hineinzubegeben.[44]

> (The green earth on which his hut was built extended into a large lake, and it seemed equally that the peninsula, out of love, had thrust its way into the blue, clear, marvelously bright water, and that the water, with amorous arms, had reached out to the beautiful meadow, to its tall, swaying grasses and flowers, and to the pleasant shadows of its trees. Each one visited the other, and for that very reason each was beautiful. In this pretty spot there were, however, few or no people to be found, except for the fisherman and the members of his household; for at the base of the

---

43 Gisela Dischner connects Friedrich's use of mythology with the larger Romantic project of incorporating myth into aesthetic theory, but does not refer to Caroline's work on Greek mythology; see Gisela Dischner, "Friedrich de la Motte-Fouqué: *Undine* (1811)," in *Romane und Erzählungen der deutschen Romantik: Neue Interpretationen*, ed. Paul Michael Lützeler (Stuttgart: Reclam, 1981), 264–84 (270–3).

44 Friedrich de la Motte Fouqué, *Undine: Eine Erzählung*, in *Werke: Auswahl in drei Teilen*, 3 vols. in 1, ed. Walther Ziesemer (Hildesheim: Olms, 1973), 52–119 (53) (hereafter *Undine*).

peninsula was a wild forest, which most people avoided except in case of dire necessity, because of its darkness and impassibility, and because of the wondrous creatures and illusions that one might encounter there.)

This passage emphasizes the intermingling of two elements, earth and water, in a situation reminiscent of Chaos in Greek mythology, the undifferentiated beginnings of existence. Even the compound words referring to the lake and the peninsula, "Landsee" and "Erdzunge," suggest a duality, the merging of two elements normally seen as separate. The elements are personified, with the earth described as insinuating itself into the water, and the water reaching out to grasp the land. There is also a hint of hermaphroditism, as typical distinctions between masculinity and femininity are rendered meaningless by the shifting grammatical genders associated with the two elements, and by the confusion of gender roles.[45] The earth and the water are characterized by a series of nouns with definite articles indicating different grammatical genders: masculine (*der*), feminine (*die*), and neuter (*das*). The earth is referred to as "der Boden," "die Erdzunge," "die Aue"; and the water is named "der Landsee," "die Flut," "das Wasser," all within a single sentence. Actions are also ambiguous: is the water reaching out to grasp the land, or is the land insinuating itself into the water? The passage makes clear, however, that the area's remoteness is what allows the primordial condition to flourish: the forest cuts the peninsula off from civilization, and very few humans venture into this area.

This lack of separation between earth and water, as well as the intermingling of male and female elements, is perhaps meant to mirror the relationship between Huldbrand—a human male connected to the land by his ancestral estate, Burg Ringstetten—and Undine, at home in the water. The association of Huldbrand with earth and the masculine

---

45 For Renate Böschenstein, the description of this landscape represents a fluid notion of gender ("Undine oder das fließende Ich," in *Sehnsucht und Sirene: Vierzehn Abhandlungen zu Wasserphantasien*, ed. Irmgard Roebling [Pfaffenweiler: Centaurus, 1992], 101–30 [122]). Some critics have perceived a gendered division in the narrative structure of the novella. Gonthier-Louis Fink associates the narrator with a sentimental attitude, the author with an implicit social critique ("Fouqués *Undine*: Die Diskrepanz zwischen Autor und Erzähler," in *Zwischen den Wissenschaften: Beiträge zur deutschen Literaturgeschichte*, ed. Gerhard Hahn and Ernst Weber [Regensburg: Pustet, 1994], 318–31 [331]). Andreas Solbach posits that Fouqué associates the text with the feminine, a challenge to the patriarchal order, and the author with the father, a representative of this order ("Immanente Erzählpoetik in Fouqués *Undine*," *Euphorion* 91, no. 1 [1997]: 65–89 [75–6]).

principle, and of Undine with water and the feminine principle, is, however, complicated by the role of Bertalda, Undine's human rival for Huldbrand's affections. Like the ancient goddesses described in *Briefe über die griechische Mythologie für Frauen*, who encompassed a duality, later split into a male and a female principle, the two female characters of *Undine* embody two notions of femininity. Bertalda is associated with the societal conventions of the Middle Ages, the setting of the novella. Sending Huldbrand on a quest into the woods adjoining the peninsula where Undine resides with her foster parents, Bertalda adheres to the conventions of medieval womanhood.[46] She is also highly aware of social rank: the foster daughter of nobility, she reacts with horror when Undine reveals that Bertalda's biological parents are none other than Undine's own foster parents, the fisherman and his wife. Undine, by contrast, embodies the Romantic association, developed in Caroline's work on Greek mythology, of woman and nature. Not only is she completely unaware of social categories such as rank—she thought that she would delight Bertalda with the revelation of her parentage, rather than cause her distress—Undine possesses an uncanny power over natural phenomena associated with water. Through her uncle, Kühleborn, she makes the river rise so that the peninsula becomes an island, and Huldbrand is trapped with Undine and her foster parents. To make this captivity more pleasant, Undine produces a barrel of wine from the river, varying the biblical story of the wedding in Cana by taking wine from the water. Undine's miraculous ability links her with the female deities described by Caroline in *Briefe über die griechische Mythologie für Frauen*. Friedrich's novella, however, displays ambivalence towards the elemental power associated with female divinity.

Huldbrand's ambivalence towards Undine's dual nature and power over the elements is first expressed in the dreams that he experiences on his wedding night:

Sooft er in der Nacht eingeschlafen war, hatten ihn verwunderlich grausende Träume verstört von Gespenstern, die sich heimlich grinzend in schöne Frauen zu verkleiden strebten, von schönen Frauen, die mit einem Male Drachenangesichter bekamen. Und

---

46 While focusing on the contrast between Undine and Bertalda, W. J. Lillyman emphasizes that both women, as well as Huldbrand, are under the control of the elemental spirits; see W. J. Lillyman, "Fouqué's *Undine*," *Studies in Romanticism* 10, no. 2 (1971): 94–104 (101–4). Edward Mornin states that Friedrich's nationalism causes him to favor the German Bertalda over the "foreign" Undine as a partner for Huldbrand ("Some Patriotic Novels and Tales by La Motte Fouqué," *Seminar* 11, no. 3 [1975]: 141–56 [154]).

wenn er von den häßlichen Gebilden in die Höhe fuhr, stand das Mondlicht bleich und kalt draußen vor den Fenstern; entsetzt blickte er nach Undinen, an deren Busen er eingeschlafen war und die in unverwandelter Schönheit und Anmut neben ihm ruhte. Dann drückte er einen leichten Kuß auf die rosigen Lippen und schlief wieder ein, um von neuen Schrecken erweckt zu werden.[47]

(Whenever he fell asleep during the night, strangely horrifying dreams disturbed him of secretly grinning ghosts that tried to disguise themselves as beautiful women, of beautiful women whose faces were suddenly transformed into dragons. And when he rose up, startled by the hideous sights, the moon shone pale and cold through the window. Horrified, he glanced at Undine, in whose arms he had fallen asleep and who rested next to him with unchanged beauty and charm. Then he pressed a light kiss on the rosy lips and fell asleep again, only to be awoken again by new terrors.)

Huldbrand's dreams of women revealed as monsters contrast with the reality of his beautiful bride, Undine, asleep next to him; yet the dreams suggest that the elemental powers of the woman he has married are uncanny and frightening to him, a reality that becomes apparent later, when Huldbrand realizes that Undine's acquisition of a human soul has not separated her from the natural world that she once inhabited. Undine's continued contact with the elemental spirits contributes to Huldbrand's eventual rejection of her in favor of Bertalda; yet this very connection to nature is what originally attracts him to Undine and wins her the admiration of both Huldbrand and Bertalda.

Indeed, it is the relationship between Bertalda and Undine, rather than Huldbrand's attachment to Bertalda, that initially loosens the ties of the married couple, Undine and Huldbrand. After the wedding they return to the city, where Bertalda, seeing Undine as her rival, nonetheless feels drawn to her: "In dieser gegenseitigen Neigung wußte die eine [Bertalda] bei ihren Pflegeeltern, die andre [Undine] bei ihrem Ehegatten den Tag der Abreise weiter und weiter hinauszuschieben; ja, es war schon die Rede davon gewesen, Bertalda solle Undinen auf einige Zeit nach Burg Ringstetten an die Quellen der Donau begleiten" (Bound by this mutual affection, both were able to continue postponing the day of their departure, the one [Bertalda] persuading her foster parents, the other [Undine] her husband; it was even discussed that

---

47 *Undine*, 79.

Bertalda might accompany Undine for a time to Ringstetten Castle at the source of the Danube).[48] The mutual affection between the two women rivals the affection between husband and wife, to the extent that Undine and Huldbrand delay their departure for Burg Ringstetten, and Bertalda thinks about accompanying them there. Of course, the plans change after Undine reveals Bertalda's parentage and Bertalda is rejected by her foster parents; yet Huldbrand and Undine take pity on her and bring her with them to Ringstetten, according to the initial plan. At Ringstetten, the love between the two women turns to rivalry, but after Bertalda flees into the dark forest and Undine saves her and Huldbrand from the power of her uncle Kühleborn, Undine regains the admiration of both Bertalda and Huldbrand, at least for a time. The manner in which Undine rescues her friend and her husband links her, once again, to ancient female divinities:

> Da scholl Undinens anmutige Stimme durch das Getöse hin, der Mond trat aus den Wolken, und mit ihm ward Undine auf den Höhen des Talgrundes sichtbar. Sie schalt, sie drohte in die Fluten hinab, die drohende Turmeswoge verschwand murrend und murmelnd, leise rannen die Wasser im Mondglanze dahin, und wie eine weiße Taube sah man Undinen von der Höhe hinabtauchen, den Ritter und Bertalden erfassen und mit sich nach einem frischen, grünen Rasenfleck auf der Höhe emporheben.[49]

> (Undine's charming voice resounded through the uproar, and when the moon emerged from the clouds, she became visible above the valley. She warned, she threatened the waters. The threatening, towering waves disappeared, grumbling and murmuring. The waters flowed softly away in the moonlight, and Undine, like a white dove, was seen diving from the peak, grasping the knight and Bertalda, and carrying them up with her to a fresh, green, grassy area above.)

The appearance of the moon ties Undine to Selene, the ancient, hermaphroditic goddess described by Caroline in *Briefe über die griechische Mythologie*, while the comparison of Undine to a white dove links her to other goddesses mentioned by Caroline, such as Ishtar, Astarte, and Aphrodite, as well as to the flood story of Genesis.

Undine's divine powers seem, for a time, to have restored peace among the three inhabitants of Ringstetten; yet the display of these

---

48 *Undine.*, 88.
49 *Undine*, 106.

powers during a voyage on the Danube occasions the final break between Huldbrand and Undine. The elemental spirits, hostile to Huldbrand and Bertalda, seize Bertalda's golden necklace, and Huldbrand prevents Undine from offering a replacement, cursing her for her continued contact with the spirit world. The curse forces Undine to leave the world of the humans and rejoin the element of water:

> Und über den Rand der Barke schwand sie hinaus.—Stieg sie hinüber in die Flut, verströmte sie darin, man wußt es nicht, es war wie beides und wie keins. Bald aber war sie in die Donau ganz verronnen; nur flüsterten noch kleine Wellchen schluchzend um den Kahn, und fast vernehmlich war's, als sprächen sie: "O weh, o weh! Ach bleibe treu! O weh!"[50]
>
> (And she disappeared over the edge of the boat.—she climbed over into the water, flowed away, you couldn't tell, it was like both and neither. Soon she had completely dissolved into the Danube; only small waves whispered, sobbing, around the boat, and it almost seemed that they spoke, "Alas, alas! O be faithful! Alas!")

This description of Undine's departure emphasizes her merging with the water. The phrase "es war wie beides und wie keins" makes Undine into a hermaphrodite, replacing her with a neuter pronoun, so that she is neither male nor female, neither water nor human. Her departure thus looks back to the undifferentiated Chaos of the novella's opening passage, and looks forward to the time when Undine rejoins Huldbrand at his funeral where, as a stream of water, she wraps herself around his grave: "Noch in späten Zeiten sollen die Bewohner des Dorfes die Quelle gezeigt und fest die Meinung gehegt haben, dies sei die arme, verstoßene Undine, die auf diese Art noch immer mit freundlichen Armen ihren Liebling umfasse" (In later times the inhabitants of the village were said to have pointed out the source and expressed conviction that this was the poor, rejected Undine who had found this way to hold her lover clasped in her arms).[51] The ending of the novella echoes the opening passage, in which the water reaches out "mit verliebten Armen" to embrace the land. This embrace, however, has proven to be deadly as well as loving: Undine was obligated by the laws of the elemental spirits to return to Ringstetten and kill Huldbrand, following his marriage to Bertalda. The duality of water, its life-giving and death-inducing characteristics, receives elaboration in Caroline's *Briefe über die*

---

50 *Undine*, 110.
51 *Undine*, 119.

griechische Mythologie, as we have seen. In *Undine*, the watery element reflects the duality of the originary female divine, bringing together male and female principles, life and death. Indeed, Huldbrand's marriage to Undine has caused not only his death but the extinction of his entire ancestral line, as the preparations for the funeral reveal: "[Huldbrand] sollte in einem Kirchdorfe begraben werden, auf dessen Gottesacker alle Gräber seiner Ahnherrn standen ... Schild und Helm lagen bereits auf dem Sarge, um mit in die Gruft versenkt zu werden, denn Herr Huldbrand von Ringstetten war als der letzte seines Stammes verstorben" ([Huldbrand] was to be buried in a church village, in whose cemetery all the graves of his ancestors stood ... His shield and helmet lay on the coffin to be lowered into the vault, for Sir Huldbrand of Ringstetten had died as the last descendant of his ancestral line).[52] By failing to produce offspring, Undine and Huldbrand have upset the social order of aristocratic inheritance, dependent on perpetuation through the male line. During the nineteenth century, men's and women's roles in reproduction increasingly defined their roles in society, so that a disruption of the procreative function also entailed a disturbance of conventional gender roles.

Despite its initial suggestion of a harmonious union between male and female elements, *Undine* presents a complex and ambivalent view of the possibilities of male–female interaction and collaboration. The connection of women to nature, and to an originary female divine, proves both attractive and threatening to a social order based on distinct biological roles. The connection between the duality inherent in the female divine and an overturning of the social order is explored more fully in Caroline's novel *Magie der Natur: Eine Revolutionsgeschichte*. Set in France during the revolutionary era, it explores the fate of an aristocratic family who flee their estate and native land, then return to a changed society following the passage of the revised French Constitution of 1795. Caroline's discomfort with the overturning of aristocratic privilege is apparent in this work, but she offers a more nuanced view of the Revolution than might be expected given her sympathies, as certain characters in the novel come to understand the necessity of adapting to changing political and personal circumstances, and as the novel treats characters who are social outcasts with some sympathy.[53]

---

52 *Undine*, 118.
53 Gerhart Hoffmeister emphasizes Caroline's negative assessment of the French Revolution, yet gives her credit for insight into the necessity of social change; see Gerhart Hoffmeister, "The French Revolution and the German Novel around 1800: Therese Huber's *Die Familie Seldorf* (1796) and Caroline de Fouqué's *Magie der Natur* (1812)," *European Romantic Review* 2 (1992): 163–71 (168–9).

The novel initially takes the perspective of the Marquis de Villeroi, a lone male figure whose wife has died in childbirth, and who sent away his twin daughters, Marie and Antonie, to be raised in a nunnery. His recourse to mesmerism may have contributed to his wife's death, but he continues to be drawn to the occult. Following the outbreak of the French Revolution, he retrieves his daughters from the nunnery with the intention of fleeing France, and narrowly escapes with them as the revolutionary *sans-culottes* burn his ancestral home. Exiled in Switzerland and Germany, the marquis and his daughters are joined by extended family and become part of a group of expatriates. Both daughters fall in love with the same man, Adalbert, and Antonie, following in her father's footsteps, uses mesmerism to try to win his love, but in the end sacrifices herself so that he and Marie can be together. The marquis rebuilds the family estate, Marie and Adalbert marry, and their child allows for the continuation of the family line and some stability amid changed historical and personal circumstances.

The love triangle, involving two women competing for a man's affections, serves a similar function as in Friedrich's *Undine*. Antonie and Marie, twin sisters representing different models of femininity, suggest even more strongly than Undine and Bertalda the duality of the originary female divinity. Like Undine, Antonie harnesses the powers of nature in order to draw Adalbert to her, while Marie, like Bertalda, adheres to cultural conventions. The duke, Adalbert's father and the brother of Marie's and Antonie's mother, makes a telling remark to his son about the differences between the two sisters, in connection with the political changes that have taken place in France. Expressing his acceptance of the changed country, as well as of his son's choice to marry Marie rather than Antonie, he describes Marie as "ein häuslich, bescheiden Weib" (a modest, domestic woman) and Antonie as "ein wunderbares Wesen von königlichem Stolz und hoher Entschlossenheit" (a wondrous being with regal pride and superb determination).[54] The duke connects Marie to the ideal of female domesticity and Antonie to an idea of female engagement in the wider world. Despite having preferred Antonie as a wife for his son, the duke finds Marie more suitable to the present social and political circumstances: "die stille heitere Marie paßt sich wohl für ein beschränktes Dasein, das unser aller Loos geworden ist" (the quiet, cheerful Marie is better suited for the limited existence that has become our collective fate).[55] The duke suggests that

---

54 Caroline de la Motte Fouqué, *Magie der Natur: Eine Revolutions-Geschichte* (1812). *BYU Scholars Archive: Sophie. Prose Fiction*, 52, http://scholarsarchive.byu.edu/sophiefiction/52, 92 (hereafter *Magie*).
55 *Magie*, 92.

ideas about what constitutes an ideal woman, at least from the male perspective, are not constant but vary in accordance with social and historical circumstances. The duality within the feminine, associated in *Briefe über die griechische Mythologie* with hermaphroditism, is explored through the characters of Marie and Antonie.

Women's roles and the scope of their activities are the subject of a discussion between the duke and Viktorine, a member of the expatriate group. The duke insists that women should restrict themselves to the domestic sphere and not involve themselves in politics, advancing the view that women "haben kein anderes Vaterland, als den engen Raum, welchen die vier Pfähle ihrer häuslichen Wirksamkeit einschließen. Die Welt mögen sie hier ahnden und fühlen, Liebes- und Lebensverhältnisse mögen sie hier begründen, aber Staatsverhältnisse werden sie nie begreifen" (have no other fatherland than the narrow space that the four pillars of their domestic activity enclose. Here they may sense and experience the world, establish love relationships and living conditions, but they will never understand affairs of state).[56] The idea that women should occupy themselves with the domestic sphere and affective relations was common in the nineteenth century, but Viktorine expresses an opposing view: "Niemals ... werde ich mich überzeugen, daß wir aus irgend einer Sphäre menschlicher Wirksamkeit ausgeschlossen seien. Wie häufig sind es grade Frauen, welche die Zügel des Staates geheim und sicher lenken, und nicht selten verdanken es die Männer nur ihnen, wenn sie auf ihrem rechtem Platze stehn" (Never ... will I convince myself that we are excluded from any sphere of human activity. How often women hold the reins of the state securely and discreetly, and not infrequently men fulfill their correct role only thanks to women).[57]

Viktorine's argument, that women already take some responsibility for guiding state affairs behind the scenes, seems to suggest that they are also capable of doing so openly. Despite his assertion of the opposing view, the duke expresses admiration for Antonie, a woman who resembles more closely the ideal described by Viktorine than the one that he himself proposes. The discussion is inconclusive: the German doctor, who plays the role of observer of the dramas played out among the exiles, grants that women possess extraordinary powers, and suggests that these were recognized in earlier times. He attributes to women "eine geheimnißvolle Gewalt über Dinge und Menschen,

---

56 *Magie*, 86.
57 *Magie*, 87–8.

welche selbst der gesellschaftliche Sprachgebrauch zauberisch nennt. Solch ein Zauber war von jeher anerkannt, die königlichen Frauen der Vorzeit übten ihn, mittelbar in das äußere Leben und dessen Gestaltung einwirkend" (a mysterious power over objects and people, which is conventionally called magical. Such magic was recognized in past times; the royal women of prehistory practiced it, intervening indirectly in external life and its organization).[58] The doctor alludes to Caroline's theory of an originary female divinity, now largely unrecognized but given a voice through women such as Viktorine. Antonie, intuiting a personal connection to the doctor's description of feminine spiritual power, asks him whether the stories of such women of ancient times are to be found in books. Rather than guiding her exploration, the doctor sees her curiosity as the sign of a sick mind, and advises her to concentrate on the living and the present time. This advice contrasts with Caroline's exploration of myth and history in *Briefe über die griechische Mythologie*, which she writes in order to facilitate women's connection with the ancient female divine. Perhaps, given access to such a work, Antonie might have experienced a productive life rather than being labeled as sick, and her "masculine" or hermaphroditic qualities would have been recognized as an aspect of femininity rather than seen as a violation of women's "natural" roles.

Like *Undine*, *Magie der Natur* is ambivalent about the possibility of integrating an ancient notion of femininity into contemporary society. Through the figure of Antonie, Caroline presents both the creative and the destructive potential of the mythological feminine, as Antonie harnesses but also violates natural law through her practice of mesmerism and the occult. While still in the convent, Antonie uncannily intuits that a young novice nun has a portrait of a man hidden under her garments. It later emerges that this young woman had been engaged to marry Adalbert, but her parents required her to enter the convent. Adalbert, not knowing of Antonie's involvement, later tells this story to Antonie and her family, stating that his beloved was wearing a necklace with his portrait. Antonie's reaction on hearing that she had inadvertently caused the sickness and death of Adalbert's fiancée is not regret, but a strengthening of her belief that she is Adalbert's guardian spirit ("Schutzgeist").[59] She interprets her connection to Adalbert as an unbreakable spiritual bond, and believes that she saved him from damnation by preventing his beloved from taking vows. She also reassesses her first encounter with the wounded Adalbert, during the family's journey across the Swiss Alps, as evidence of her ability

---

58 *Magie*, 88.
59 *Magie*, 84.

to heal him. Not only are other characters, including Adalbert, disturbed by Antonie's uncanny powers; the novel suggests that she, like her father, causes harm through her use (or misuse) of the power of nature. Nonetheless, the novel also implies that Antonie brings about destruction not because of inherent evil but because her capacities are ill suited to the era during which she is living, an era in which the female divine and women's connection to nature are largely unrecognized or seen as destructive of established social institutions such as marriage.[60]

The end of the novel shows Antonie increasingly beset by ill health and mental confusion, even as other members of the family regain a sense of normalcy. The marquis returns to the family estate, which was almost completely destroyed by the revolutionaries, and takes it upon himself to build a new residence in a style that reconciles the old and the new order ("die Bande zwischen Vor- und Mitwelt versöhnend zusammenhalte" [binds together and reconciles ancient with modern times]).[61] The new residence, less grandiose in design than the previous one, also unifies human habitation with the natural surroundings: "Vom alten Schloß sah man hier nichts. Das erneuete Gebäude lag zwischen heitern Pflanzungen, welche, noch ziemlich jung, der Raubsucht zu geringer Ausbeute dienend, unangetastet geblieben waren, und jetzt einen leicht gewundenen Pfad beschatteten, der sich an dem flacher werdenden Ufern des Stromes hinwand" (Nothing of the old castle could be seen. The renovated building stood between colorful plantings that, still fairly new, giving little motivation to plunder, had remained untouched, and now shaded a gently winding path, which lined the leveled shores of the river).[62] The marquis's acceptance of changing historical circumstances, and his willingness to integrate into the new society as well as into the natural surroundings, allow for the continuation of his family line. Marie, pregnant with Adalbert's child, delivers a

---

60 Todd Kontje emphasizes Antonie's unconventionality in light of Caroline's questioning of gender roles ("Nationalism or Cosmopolitanism? Women, the Novel, and German Identity 1815–1820," *Carleton Germanic Papers* 24 [1996]: 93–108 [98–101]). Mechthilde Vahsen, on the other hand, emphasizes Caroline's political and social conservatism, and connects Antonie's irrational embrace of her emotions with the irrationality of France's revolutionary excesses; see Mechthilde Vahsen, *Die Politisierung des weiblichen Subjekts: Deutsche Romanautorinnen und die Französische Revolution (1790–1820)* (Berlin: Schmidt, 2000), 138–43.
61 *Magie*, 109.
62 *Magie*, 109.

baby boy, but Adalbert himself is absent—he had departed for the war while the family was still in exile, in order to escape his involvement in the love triangle.

Adalbert's return to the marquis's ancestral residence also suggests a reconciliation between past and present. The former revolutionaries who had previously threatened the marquis's family and burned his castle are the ones who return their comrade in arms to his family. While the marquis and the other family members turn away from the past and reconcile themselves to present reality, Antonie remains fixated on the past. The marquis catches sight of her on the wall of the old castle. "Sie schlich wie ein Spuk an dem Schloßgemäuer hin, und sah verwirrend aus dem alten Leben herauf" (She crept like a ghost along the castle walls, and looked up confusedly from her former life).[63] Her attachment to the past and unwillingness to bend to changing circumstances prove fatal: the old ancestral estate is the site of her suicide by dagger. With this act she sets Adalbert free to marry Marie and permits the continuation of the old aristocratic order, under slightly changed circumstances.

As we have seen, the novel's attitude towards Antonie and the version of femininity that she represents is highly ambivalent. Some characters, such as the duke, express admiration for her, while others, like the baroness, Marie's and Antonie's aunt, make it clear that they consider Antonie's life and deeds to be an aberration, a disturbance of the natural order. As the baroness explains to Adalbert, "Ein Ausrenken oder Verzerren der schönen Naturverhältnisse kann nur durch einen Stoß oder Schlag in seine Ordnung zurückspringen. Der Schlag ist erfolgt. Sieh nun auf die heitere Ordnung des Lebens!" (A dislocation or deformation of nature's beautiful relationships can only return to order by means of a push or a blow. The blow has succeeded. Now look upon the serene order of life!)[64] The social order, which the baroness equates with the order of nature, can only be restored by Antonie's sacrifice, a suicide that, like her life, oversteps the usual bounds of femininity. Antonie's literary antecedents include Lessing's Emilia Galotti, who compels her father to kill her with a dagger in order to preserve her honor. Antonie, by contrast, acts alone and is excluded from the social order, unlike Emilia, who upholds the (formerly) aristocratic notion of honor in defiance of a corrupt and predatory aristocracy. Antonie's suicide also connects her to literary figures of the Romantic era, such as Karoline von Günderrode, who killed herself with a dagger in 1806, and Heinrich von Kleist, whose suicide by pistol in 1811 was possibly on

---

63 *Magie*, 110.
64 *Magie*, 115.

Caroline's mind when she wrote *Magie der Natur*.[65] Although Antonie is an outcast from conventional society, she is linked to literary characters and writers whose creativity co-existed with and may have derived from their inability to adhere to social norms. Her fate highlights the difficulty of accommodating a mythological and ancient notion of the female divine within contemporary society.

The novel's ending suggests that women's involvement in the maternal role, and their centrality to family life, can compensate for the loss of their ancient, mythological power: "Die alten Wunder waren von der Erde verschwunden, aber die Liebe schuf täglich neue. Die Magie ihres Familienstammes blühete in Marien auf so eigene reizende Weise wieder auf, daß sie ihres Gatten Herz in stets unauflöslichern Banden an sich zog" (The ancient miracles had disappeared from the earth, but love created new ones daily. The magic of her ancestral line blossomed in Marie in such an enchanting manner that she drew her husband's heart closer to her in ever more indissoluble bonds).[66] This affirmation of Marie's domesticated experience of femininity contrasts with the originary female divine that Caroline explores in *Briefe über die griechische Mythologie*. Yet the centrality of Antonie's experience to the novel suggests that the ancient myths, though marginalized, have not been completely suppressed.

Caroline's mythological study affirms the importance of establishing a connection, in the present, to ancient views of the female divine, and suggests that the originary notion of femininity encompassed both male and female traits. Her work on mythology indirectly challenges the idea that men and women should inhabit separate spheres, instead opening the door to intellectual and political collaboration between men and women. The fictional works of both Caroline and Friedrich, however, display considerable ambivalence towards the aspect of femininity that Caroline associates with the female divine. Friedrich's Undine and Caroline's Antonie threaten social conventions by drawing on an ancient, mythological concept of femininity as hermaphroditic, preceding the separation of humanity and divinity into male and female. The wall between the ancient and the modern worlds, which Caroline attempts to scale in *Briefe über die griechische Mythologie für Frauen*, remains stubbornly standing. The fictional works of Caroline and Friedrich elucidate both the difficulties and the potential rewards of bringing ancient models of the feminine into contemporary culture,

---

65 Jean T. Wilde ("Heinrich von Kleist's Suicide: Two Unpublished Letters by Caroline de la Motte Fouqué," *Germanic Review* 26, no. 3 [October 1951]: 192–5) reproduces two emotional letters that Caroline wrote shortly after the suicide.
66 *Magie*, 116.

and may reflect the misunderstandings that they faced from their contemporaries as a hermaphroditically collaborative couple. Although the individual works of fiction express doubts about the integration of mythological, hermaphroditic notions of gender into contemporary society, the three texts, viewed as a whole, give a sense of how this integration might be possible in a creative context. *Briefe über die griechische Mythologie*, *Undine*, and *Magie der Natur* establish among themselves a rich dialogue about the roles of men and women, and the possibility of change through a juxtaposition of the ancient and the modern. Viewed as contributions to a collaborative work, rather than isolated individual expressions, they realize Caroline's vision, expressed in *Briefe über die griechische Mythologie*, of a hermaphroditic approach to creativity and intellectual investigation.

Bibliography

Baumgartner, Karin. *Public Voices: Political Discourse in the Writings of Caroline de la Motte Fouqué*. Bern: Lang, 2009.

Böschenstein, Renate. "Undine oder das fließende Ich." In *Sehnsucht und Sirene: Vierzehn Abhandlungen zu Wasserphantasien*, ed. Irmgard Roebling, 101–30. Pfaffenweiler: Centaurus, 1992.

Dischner, Gisela. "Friedrich de la Motte-Fouqué: *Undine* (1811)." In *Romane und Erzählungen der deutschen Romantik: Neue Interpretationen*, ed. Paul Michael Lützeler, 264–84. Stuttgart: Reclam, 1981.

Fink, Gonthier-Louis. "Fouqués *Undine*: Die Diskrepanz zwischen Autor und Erzähler." In *Zwischen den Wissenschaften: Beiträge zur deutschen Literaturgeschichte*, ed. Gerhard Hahn and Ernst Weber, 318–31. Regensburg: Pustet, 1994.

Fouqué, Caroline de la Motte. *Briefe über die griechische Mythologie für Frauen*. Berlin: Hitzig, 1812.

Fouqué, Caroline de la Motte. *Magie der Natur: Eine Revolutions-Geschichte* (1812). *BYU Scholars Archive: Sophie. Prose Fiction*. 52. http://scholarsarchive.byu.edu/sophiefiction/52 (accessed March 2, 2019).

Fouqué, Caroline de la Motte. *Werke und Schriften*. Ed. Thomas Neumann. Norderstedt: Books on Demand Ditzingen, 2006–.

Fouqué, Friedrich de la Motte. *Lebensgeschichte des Baron Friedrich de la Motte Fouqué, aufgezeichnet durch ihn selbst*. Berlin: Hofenberg, 2015.

Fouqué, Friedrich de la Motte. *Undine: Eine Erzählung*. In *Werke: Auswahl in drei Teilen*. 3 vols. in 1. Ed. Walther Ziesemer, 52–119. Hildesheim: Olms, 1973.

Hausen, Karin. "Die Polarisierung der 'Geschlechtscharaktere': Eine Spiegelung der Dissonanzen von Erwerbs- und Familienleben." In *Sozialgeschichte der Familie in der Neuzeit Europas*, ed. Werner Conze, 367–93. Stuttgart: Klett, 1976.

Hoffmeister, Gerhart. "The French Revolution and the German Novel around 1800: Therese Huber's *Die Familie Seldorf* (1796) and Caroline de Fouqué's *Magie der Natur* (1812)." *European Romantic Review* 2 (1992): 163–71.

Kontje, Todd. "Nationalism or Cosmopolitanism? Women, the Novel, and German Identity 1815–1820." *Carleton Germanic Papers* 24 (1996): 93–108.

Krimmer, Elisabeth. "Officer and Lady: Pants and Politics in Caroline de la Motte-Fouqué's *Das Heldenmädchen aus der Vendée* (1816)." *Studies in Eighteenth-Century Culture* 30 (2001): 165–81.
Lillyman, W. J. "Fouqué's *Undine*." *Studies in Romanticism* 10, no. 2 (1971): 94–104.
Luly, Sara. "Emasculating Fear: Gothic and Gender in Caroline de la Motte Fouqué's *Der Cypressenkranz*." *Monatshefte* 104, no. 2 (Summer 2012): 180–93.
Luly, Sara. "The Horror of Coming Home: Integration and Fragmentation in Caroline de la Motte Fouqué's 'Der Abtrünnige.'" *Goethe Yearbook* 24 (2017): 175–95.
Mornin, Edward. "Some Patriotic Novels and Tales by La Motte Fouqué." *Seminar* 11, no. 3 (1975): 141–56.
Novalis. *Mythologie für Frauenzimmer*. In *Novalis Schriften: Die Werke Friedrich von Hardenbergs*. Vol. VI.1. Ed. Paul Kluckhohn and Richard Samuel. Stuttgart: Kohlhammer, 1998.
Paracelsus. *Liber de nymphis, sylphis, pygmaeis et salamandris et de caeteris spiritibus*. Bern: Francke, 1960.
Renger, Almut-Barbara. "Zur Bestimmung von Genre und Geschlecht um 1800: Caroline Fouqués *Briefe über die griechische Mythologie*—ein Werk für Frauen?" *Jahrbuch der Fouqué-Gesellschaft Berlin-Brandenburg* (2003): 47–60.
Schlegel, Friedrich. "Rede über die Mythologie." In *Kritische Friedrich Schlegel Ausgabe*. Vol. 2, ed. Ernst Behler and Hans Dierkes, 311–22. Paderborn: Schöningh, 2006.
Schmidt, Arno. *Fouqué und einige seiner Zeitgenossen*. Zürich: Haffmans, 1993.
Solbach, Andreas. "Immanente Erzählpoetik in Fouqués *Undine*." *Euphorion* 91, no. 1 (1997): 65–98.
Vahsen, Mechthilde. *Die Politisierung des weiblichen Subjekts: Deutsche Romanautorinnen und die Französische Revolution (1790–1820)*. Berlin: Schmidt, 2000.
Varnhagen von Ense, Karl August. *Biographische Portraits*. Leipzig: Brockhaus, 1871.
Wilde, Jean T. "Heinrich von Kleist's Suicide: Two Unpublished Letters by Caroline de la Motte Fouqué." *Germanic Review* 26, no. 3 (October 1951): 192–5.
Wilde, Jean T. *The Romantic Realist: Caroline de la Motte Fouqué*. New York: Bookman Associates, 1955.
Ziolkowski, Theodore. "Nennhausen: Anregungsort romantischer Erzählkunst." *Jahrbuch für internationale Germanistik* 43 (2011): 201–15.

Seven Concepts of Collaboration
Märchenomas, the Woman Writer, and the Brothers Grimm

Julie L. J. Koehler

Let me "uns [versetzen] ... zurück in die Zeiten der Riesen, Feen, Hexen und Kobolde" (transport us ... back to the times of giants, fairies, witches, and kobolds), writes the anonymous but presumed female author of the 1801 collection *Feen-Mährchen: Zur Unterhaltung für Freunde und Freundinnen der Feenwelt* (Fairy Tales: For the Entertainment of Friends of the Fairy World).[1] An exciting offer is made all the more enticing when the author informs her readers that the source of these tales is a "bejahrte Tante" (aged aunt) who once shared "Ströme von Weisheit" (streams of wisdom) with the author and her cousins as children. As with many collections in the period, the depiction of an older woman telling fairy stories adds authenticity to the text. In many texts of the eighteenth and nineteenth centuries, a description of a *Märchenoma*, or fairy-tale grandma, sharing her stories with a group of children in private space prefaced the stories within.[2] A decade later, the Brothers Grimm would depict their own sources for *Kinder- und Hausmärchen* (Children's and Household Tales) (hereafter *KHM*) in a strikingly similar way.[3] There is, however, an important difference

---

1 Anon., *Feen-Mährchen: Zur Unterhaltung für Freunde und Freundinnen der Feenwelt*, ed. Ulrich Marzolph (New York: G. Olms, 2000 [1801]), 3. All translations are my own, unless otherwise noted.
2 Shawn C. Jarvis and Jeannine Blackwell, ed. and trans., *The Queen's Mirror: Fairy Tales by German Women, 1780–1900* (Lincoln: University of Nebraska Press, 2001), 89. Blackwell and Jarvis identify the author as presumably female, and she is treated as such in earlier scholarship.
3 Jacob Grimm and Wilhelm Grimm, *Kinder- und Hausmärchen*, ed. Heinz Rölleke, 2 vols. (Cologne: Diederichs, 1982 [1819]), I, x. The Grimms' first depiction of their *Märchenoma* source appears in the second edition of their text in 1819.

between the source of the *Feen-Mährchen* and the *KHM*. The aged aunt is an admitted fiction, while the Brothers Grimm's *Märchenomas* were living contributors. While many nineteenth-century authors invoked the *Märchenoma* to grant their work a romanticized authenticity, men and women collaborated with *Märchenomas* (both fictional and living) in distinctly different ways that reflected tensions around dualisms of gender and culture in the period. For male scholars and writers, such as the Grimms, the *Märchenoma* was a passive vessel of German culture, and this collaboration was in truth an appropriation of creative female work to serve the concept of the male *Autor*. In nineteenth-century German, the word *Autor* (author) was connected closely with concepts of individual genius. Within nineteenth-century *Geschlechtscharaktere* (gender characteristics) and gendered dualisms, this construction fit the most neatly: an active male *Autor* and a passive female vessel. Women writers, however, leveraged this supposed partnership to subvert, resist, and replace these reductive dualisms that made true collaboration between creative women and men appear impossible.

There is, of course, a long tradition of an old storytelling woman in Europe. Marina Warner traces the concept back to the second century in *From the Beast to the Blonde* (1996).[4] One of the earliest collections of fairy tales in Europe, Giambattista Basile's 1636 *Tale of Tales*, features a parade of elderly female storytellers in the frame narrative.[5] In the French tradition, Charles Perrault wrote of Mother Goose.[6] In the late eighteenth century, collections of *Kunstmärchen*, or literary fairy tales, became popular in the German states, with authors such as Christoph Martin Wieland citing as inspiration *Ammen-Märchen* (nursemaid's tales).[7] In each of these cases, as in *Feen-Mährchen*, the *Märchenoma* is a

---

There were seven main editions of *Kinder- und Hausmärchen* between 1812 and 1857. The Grimms made substantial changes across editions. I will reference the first (1812) and second edition (1819) when discussing these changes, as many of the substantial changes happened between these volumes. If referencing the text in general, I will refer to the final edition (1857). In addition, I will reference the 1810 manuscript version of the collection where necessary.

4   Marina Warner, *From the Beast to the Blonde: On Fairy Tales and Their Tellers* (New York: Noonday Press, 1996), 14. Apuleius used the Latin term "anilis fabula," or old woman's tale, to describe the predecessor to "Beauty and the Beast" in his tale "Cupid and Psyche" (Warner, *From the Beast to the Blonde*).
5   Giambattista Basile, *Giambattista Basile's "The Tale of Tales; or, Entertainment for Little Ones,"* ed. Nancy Canepa (Detroit: Wayne State University Press, 2007).
6   Christine A. Jones, *Mother Goose Refigured: A Critical Translation of Charles Perrault's Fairy Tales* (Detroit: Wayne State University Press, 2016).
7   Christoph Martin Wieland, *C. M. Wielands Sämmtliche Werke*, ed. J. G. Gruber (Oxford: Oxford University Press, 1828), VI, 354.

fiction or a nameless reference. Although her tradition is honored, the authors, often male or assumed to be male, published and profited from her stories without naming her. Jacob and Wilhelm Grimm are the first, however, to create a collection of fairy tales in which they name (some) sources and even place a picture of their most beloved, Dorothea Viehmann, in the frontispiece of their second edition.[8]

The interaction between the Grimms and their sources is often romanticized as a moment of collaboration. The poor and uneducated women have treasured stories to share and the Grimms have the knowledge and position to bring their stories to a broader public. This depiction is, however, as much a fiction as any of the references above. The vast majority of the Grimms' sources were relatively well-educated, upper-middle-class and noble women.[9] The Grimms and other collectors in the period treated their sources, whether noble or peasant, not as collaborators, but rather as passive vessels of German culture from which they could gather raw materials. The storytellers, whether peasants such as Viehmann, published authors such as Karoline Stahl, or noble-born young ladies such as the sixteen-year-old Annette von Droste-Hülshoff, were given no autonomy or ownership over their tales, and once the tales were extracted, the Grimms went on to edit, embellish, or remove the stories as they saw fit.

In some ways, the Grimms struggled with the concept of the *Märchenoma*, which conflicted with concepts of authorship and *Genie* (genius) in the period. In order to maintain the role of the *Autor*, the Grimms could not depict their sources as active story-creators, only as passive storytellers. So too, many authors in the period emphasize the inspiration of *Volksmärchen* (folktales), in their *Kunstmärchen*. In more recent scholarship the term *Buchmärchen* (book fairy tales) has been used to describe collections such as the Grimms'. These stories are not proper folktales, from a modern folklorist's perspective, because of the practices of the Grimms, but they are not exactly literary fairy tales either. There was and is a fine line to walk when considering a folktale as authentic. For the Grimms, their desire for authenticity contradicted how they viewed their own position as *Autor* of the text.

Women writers, however, rejected both the concept of the *Märchenoma* as passive resource and the masculine subject of the genius *Autor*. Droste-Hülshoff, for instance, while relating a story to Wilhelm Grimm, quite literally took the pen out of his hand and began to record

---

8   Jacob Grimm and Wilhelm Grimm, *Kinder- und Hausmärchen*, ed. Heinz Rölleke, 3 vols. (Göttingen: Vandenhoeck & Ruprecht, 1986 [1812]), frontispiece.
9   John M. Ellis, *One Fairy Story Too Many: The Brothers Grimm and Their Tales* (Chicago: University of Chicago Press, 1983).

the tale herself. When asked to gather a tale for the Grimms, Bettina Brentano-von Arnim described a conversation with, instead of a collection from, a *Märchenoma*. Neither Droste-Hülshoff's nor Brentano-von Arnim's tales would make the collection. For these writers, the *Märchenoma* and the *Märchen* itself were a space in which the binaries of the period could be softened, if not broken, and the women writers could find a place outside the strict, gendered dualisms of the nineteenth century.

Benedikte Naubert, a consultant of the Grimms, devoted one-third of her "Der kurze Mantel" (The Cloak) to a lengthy first-person narrative of a *Märchenoma* whose story is one not of cultural heritage, but of personal experience and wisdom. Thirty years after the first edition of *KHM*, Adele Schopenhauer turned the Grimm model on its head in her tale "Waldmärchen" (Forest Fairy Tale), where a fictional male fairy-tale author is silenced at the outset of the frame narrative, and the audience is instead guided to the feet of a female storyteller, orally telling the original. These authors gave birth to their own mentors in fictional depictions of *Märchenomas*. For these sources, associates, consultants, and contemporaries of the Grimms, the *Märchenoma* is not a passive inspiration or a resource to be mined; instead she is a representative of both the true legacy of creative, intelligent women story-creators and the absent public mentor that many women writers or *Autorinnen* deeply needed in a period of growing female authorship and growing public disdain for the professional woman. The *Märchenoma* as depicted and described by these women writers directly contradicted gendered dualisms of the period and concepts of individual genius, in light not only of folklore, but of all literature. Instead of simply imagining a woman in the masculine position of the genius *Autor*, these women writers developed conceptions of creative men and women that both contradicted the gendered dualisms and acknowledged a space for creativity outside the strict gender characteristics of the period.

Geschlechtscharaktere and Gendered Dualism

In the nineteenth-century German states, women writers numbered in the hundreds. Just the century before, there were only a handful of published women authors. A number of factors contributed to this shift, but as female readership broadened, women also became editors and even publishers in a few cases, making way for more in the field.[10] The concept of the *Autorin* (female author), however, was considered

---

10 Jeannine Blackwell and Susanne Zantop, eds., *Bitter Healing: German Women Writers from 1700 to 1830. An Anthology* (Lincoln: University of Nebraska Press, 1990), 22–4.

unfeminine and deviant, as Ruth-Ellen Boetcher Joeres describes in her text *Respectability and Deviance*.[11] Joeres also examines how women writers both emulated and strongly disagreed with talented male writers who often felt women had no place in the public sphere. Some authors reflected on their struggle with male mentors in their writing; the proto-feminist author Hedwig Dohm, for example, wrote a short story in which an energetic and creative older woman is killed by a marble bust of Nietzsche that falls in a gust of wind.[12] Others invented their own fictional female mentors within their writing. As Lisabeth Hock explains in *Replicas of a Female Prometheus*, Bettina Brentano-von Arnim wrote the character of Goethe's mother, Frau Rath, as a conceptual female intellectual mentor whom Brentano-von Arnim could have relied on in her youth.[13]

The disdain for the *Autorin* in German society had much to do with the way in which gender roles and characteristics were defined in the long nineteenth century. From the Reformation on, the role of women rapidly changed, but this period was a critical time for the development of strict *Geschlechtscharaktere*. Ute Frevert's *Mann und Weib, und Weib und Mann* (Man and Wife, and Woman and Man) looks specifically at this period between the 1780s and the 1820s and demonstrates how definitions of women developed from brief physiological descriptions or explanations of duties specific to certain situations (merchants' wives, for instance) to long, complex analyses of women's physical, mental, and spiritual traits and how they compared to and complemented those of men.[14] Karin Hausen also analyzes this period, and describes how polarized sexual character descriptions were solidified.[15] Towards the end of this important period and into the first two decades of the nineteenth century, the character of women became associated primarily with domesticity, and women's work was relegated primarily to the home and to the roles of wife and mother.

---

11 Ruth-Ellen Boetcher Joeres, *Respectability and Deviance: Nineteenth-Century German Women Writers and the Ambiguity of Representation* (Chicago: University of Chicago Press, 1998).
12 Joeres, *Respectability and Deviance*, 142.
13 Lisabeth Hock, *Replicas of a Female Prometheus: The Textual Personae of Bettina von Arnim* (New York: Peter Lang, 2000), 31.
14 Ute Frevert, *"Mann und Weib, und Weib und Mann": Geschlechter-Differenzen in der Moderne* (Munich: Beck, 1995).
15 Karin Hausen, "Family and Role-Division: The Polarisation of Sexual Stereotypes in the Nineteenth Century—an Aspect of the Dissociation of Work and Family Life," trans. Cathleen Catt, in *The German Family: Essays on the Social History of the Family in Nineteenth- and Twentieth-Century Germany*, ed. Richard J. Evans and W. Robert Lee (London: Croom Helm, 1981), 51–83 (57–8).

To frame this discussion, I will use the theoretical framework of feminist eco-critic Val Plumwood. In *Feminism and the Mastery of Nature*,[16] Plumwood explores dualisms that affiliate women with nature, animality, emotion, the private realm, and repetition and reproduction. Men are therefore associated with reason, culture, humanity, intellect, the public realm, and creative and intellectual production.[17] Within this gendered construction, however, Plumwood warns against simply imagining a reversal or ascribing the male characteristics to the female, for that would require women to embody their oppressor. Societies will not, according to Plumwood, easily accommodate women who step into a cultural role that has been defined in direct opposition to all that is feminine.[18] Instead, Plumwood argues the only solution is to break the dualisms altogether: "For women, the real task of liberation is not equal participation or absorption in such a male dominant culture, but rather subversion, resistance and replacement."[19]

Within the realm of the fairy tale, we see demonstrations of Plumwood's dualisms in assertions from authors of the late eighteenth century, such as Christoph Martin Wieland, who praises the stories of the *Märchenoma* for offering inspiration, but insists that "gedruckt werden müßten sie nicht" (they ought not to be published).[20] In this way, the work of women was relegated to the background and considered a part of the environment that Plumwood describes, in which "male 'achievement' takes place."[21] This continued through the Romantic period as the *Kunstmärchen* blossomed into a popular genre. In the early decades of the nineteenth century, however, Jacob and Wilhelm Grimm began to see the stories of women as more than simply inspiration and sought to publish a collection of fairy tales. The Grimms treat their *Märchenomas*, however, more as resources than collaborators, reducing their living, breathing sources to what Plumwood calls a "terra nullius, a resource empty of its own purposes ... available to be annexed for ... the purposes of reason and intellect."[22] Later in the period, philosophers such as Georg Hegel and Arthur Schopenhauer discuss women as lesser evolved beings than men and therefore more closely related to nature. As Schopenhauer writes, women are "eine Art Mittelstufe, zwischen dem Kinde und dem Manne, als welcher der

---

16 Val Plumwood, *Feminism and the Mastery of Nature* (New York: Routledge, 1993).
17 Plumwood, *Feminism and the Mastery of Nature*, 43.
18 Plumwood, *Feminism and the Mastery of Nature*, 59.
19 Plumwood, *Feminism and the Mastery of Nature*, 31.
20 Wieland, *Sämmtliche Werke*, VI, 354.
21 Plumwood, *Feminism and the Mastery of Nature*, 21.
22 Plumwood, *Feminism and the Mastery of Nature*, 4.

eigentliche Mensch ist" (a sort of intermediate stage between the child and the man, who is truly a human).[23]

In the eighteenth and nineteenth centuries, the individual creativity of the writer was deeply connected to the concept of Genie, as Jochen Schmidt carefully follows in his text *Die Geschichte des Genie-Gedankens 1750–1945* (A History of Thought on Genius 1750–1945).[24] Schopenhauer's conception of man was also closely related to the way in which he wrote about the genius. Just as he associated women with nature and animals, so, too, did he feel that genius required man to rise above natural instincts. For Schopenhauer, nature represented "Mangel, Ungenügen, unselige Triebspannung" (lack, insufficiency, disastrous impulsive stress).[25] Here Schopenhauer applies genius to man and culture, placing nature (and therefore women) as its opposite. Concepts of the male *Autor* as genius were closely bound up in the tensions between *Märchenoma* and *Autorin*. The Grimms, Ludwig Achim von Arnim, and Clemens Brentano, among others, recognized a sort of collective genius in folklore that they tried to capture in their collections.[26] Still, Wilhelm Grimm clarified his position that "Volkspoesie lebe gleichsam im 'Stand der Unschuld,' während die Kunstpoesie ein Produkt Bewußtseins und der Bildung sei" (folklore lives in a sort of state of innocence, while literature is the product of consciousness and education).[27] Although Grimm acknowledges the genius of the *Märchenoma*, it is not her own, but that of the collective culture that rests inside her. On the other hand, individual genius is associated with education, knowledge, and the creation of literature.

Here is the crux of the problem for women writers, for they can play neither the role of the *Märchenoma* nor that of the male genius author in the dualisms of the period, and yet, they were producing literature and collaborating with men on folklore projects, *Kunstmärchen*, and even operas. Engelbert Humperdinck would use Elisabeth Ebeling's play *Dornröschen* for the libretto of his 1902 opera, for example, in much the same way that the Grimms claimed the published work of Karoline Stahl as an anonymous folktale in their collection.[28] Particularly in

---

23 Arthur Schopenhauer, "Ueber die Weiber," in *Parerga und Paralipomena* (Berlin: A. W. Hayn, 1851), II, 365.
24 Jochen Schmidt, *Die Geschichte des Genie-Gedankens 1750–1945*, 2 vols. (Darmstadt: Wissenschaftliche Buchgesellschaft, 1985), I, xiii.
25 Quoted in Schmidt, *Die Geschichte des Genie-Gedankens*, I, 471.
26 Schmidt, *Die Geschichte des Genie-Gedankens*, II, 214.
27 Quoted in Schmidt, *Die Geschichte des Genie-Gedankens*, 214.
28 Engelbert Humperdinck and Elisabeth Ebeling, *Dornröschen: Märchen in einem Vorspiel und drei Akten*, musical score (Leipzig: M. Brockhaus, 1902).

the field of fairy tales, there were many creative projects in which men and women worked together, or works that men openly acknowledged were inspired by the creative work of women, but for which the man frequently received credit as the author. The women's contributions had to be backgrounded (to use Plumwood's term) to allow the individual genius of the male *Autor*. While the male writers represent the *Märchenoma* neatly within the gendered dualisms, women writers in the period seek to do just as Plumwood describes: subvert concepts of creative women and creative work; resist appropriation by male writers and collectors; and replace gendered binaries that praise the *Märchenoma*, but dismiss the *Autorin*, with a new concept of a creative, intelligent, productive woman in society, distinct from male-dominated concepts of the *Autor* and the genius.

The Brothers Grimm: Collaboration as Extraction

Although the Grimms had great respect for the *Märchenoma* as a concept, in practice they failed to treat the *Märchenoma* as a creative individual. In general, their identification of their sources is spotty at best. Often they list only a first name, initials, or simply a location. "Nach drei Erzählungen aus Hessen" (from three accounts out of Hesse), reads the first line of notes on "Aschenputtel" (Cinderella), a typical reference for a source.[29] Of their most famous older female sources, the ambiguous records of one, Alte Marie (Old Marie), have led scholars to claim that she was a complete fabrication, and the identity of another unnamed source, the Marburger Märchenfrau (Marburg Fairy Tale Woman), continues to be debated to this day.[30] The Grimms wrote quite a bit,

---

29 Jacob Grimm and Wilhelm Grimm, *Kinder- und Hausmärchen: Jubiläumsausgabe mit den Originalanmerkungen der Brüder Grimm*, ed. Heinz Rölleke, 3 vols. (Stuttgart: P. Reclam, 1984 [1857]), 46.
30 Heinz Rölleke, "Die 'stockhessischen' Märchen der 'Alten Marie': Das Ende eines Mythos um die frühesten KHM-Aufzeichnungen der Brüder Grimm," in *"Nebeninschriften": Brüder Grimm—Arnim und Brentano—Droste-Hülshoff. Literarische Studien* (Bonn: Bouvier, 1980), 1–15. A discussion of the mythology behind the creation of Alte Marie can be found here and in Ellis, *One Fairy Story Too Many*, esp. 25–30. A thorough counter-argument to Rölleke's and Ellis's claims can be found in Herman Rebel, "Why Not Old Marie?… or Someone Very Much like Her?," *Social History* 13 (1988): 1–27 (9–12). On the Marburger Märchenfrau, see Heinz Rölleke, "'Die Marburger Märchenfrau': Zur Herkunft der KHM 21 und 57," *Fabula* 15 (1974): 87–94. See also Siegfried Becker, "Gab es Marburger Beiträger zu den 'Kinder- und Hausmärchen'? Zur Frage der Lokalisierung von Märchenfiguren und Märchenerzählern," in *Die Brüder Grimm in Marburg*, ed. Andreas Hedwig, Schriften des Hessischen Staatsarchivs Marburg 25 (Marburg: Hessisches Staatsarchiv Marburg, 2013), 57–88 (63).

however, about their most beloved storyteller, Dorothea Viehmann, as she represented the sort of authentic source that they sought. An older woman living in Hesse, she was the descendant of French Huguenots and a widowed mother of seven when the Grimms first met her in the early 1800s.[31] The Grimms were so taken with Viehmann that they had an illustration of her placed in the frontispiece of their second edition in 1819. In addition, they added a description of her to the preface, saying of her that she is "noch rüstig ... hat ein festes Gesicht, blickt hell und scharf aus den Augen, und ist wahrscheinlich in ihrer Jugend schön gewesen" (still spry, has a firm face, looks clear and sharp in the eyes, and was likely beautiful in her youth).[32] The Grimms claimed that she had told "die meisten und schönsten Märchen" (most of the tales, and the most beautiful tales) of their second edition, but today scholars have used the Grimms' notes and manuscripts to link her name to only a couple of dozen of the 210 fairy tales in the collection.[33] Since Viehmann represented an ideal *Märchenoma* for the Grimms—a lower-class, Hessian, older woman—they attempted to depict her and those like her as their primary sources.

The way in which the Brothers Grimm discussed these sources, however, reveals their clear understanding of these women as a *terra nullius*, much like Plumwood describes. As noted above, the Brothers Grimm often identified anonymous or perhaps even fabricated *Märchenomas*, including Alte Marie and the Marburger Märchenfrau. When they included a story from a male source, they provided a name and location, but then qualified the story as coming from the man's nursemaid or mother.[34] In contrast to Wieland, they felt that these women's stories could be published, but as an academic endeavor in the service of a study of German culture. The women themselves were seen only as vessels of traditional knowledge. They write that Dorothea Viehmann "bewahrt diese alten Sagen fest in dem Gedächtnis" (preserved these old sagas firmly in her memory).[35] Here her memory is where the stories are stored, and Viehmann is given credit only for her ability to

---

31 Peter K. Taylor, *Indentured to Liberty: Peasant Life and the Hessian Military State, 1688–1815* (Ithaca, NY: Cornell University Press, 1994), 238.
32 Grimm and Grimm, *Kinder- und Hausmärchen* (1982 [1819]), I, x.
33 Quotation from Grimm and Grimm, *Kinder- und Hausmärchen* (1982 [1819]), I, x. The attribution of tales to Viehmann is found in Rölleke's commentary in Grimm and Grimm, *Kinder- und Hausmärchen* (1982 [1819]), II, 543.
34 Johannes Bolte and Jiří Polívka, eds., *Anmerkungen zu den Kinder- u. Hausmärchen der Brüder Grimm: Neu bearbeitet*, 5 vols. (Hildesheim: G. Olms, 1963), III, 457. In this note to "Der heilige Joseph im Walde," the Grimms describe their source as a young student, but clarify that he originally heard the story from his nanny.
35 Grimm and Grimm, *Kinder- und Hausmärchen* (1982 [1819]), I, x.

remember and to repeat. For instance, they claim "niemals änderte sie bei einer Wiederholung etwas in der Sache ab, und bessert ein Versehen, sobald sie es bemerkt" (she never changed a single element in each repetition, and corrected an error as soon as she noticed it).[36] There is an emphasis on her ability to repeat without change, and even a judgment on changes themselves. Rather than viewing a change in a story as perhaps an alteration for context or an improvisation—actions that folklorists recognize we all do in everyday storytelling—the Grimms have labeled it as a *Versehen* (mistake).[37]

This undermines Viehmann's work and ability in two ways. On the one hand the Grimms have removed her autonomy as a storyteller, reducing her to merely a repeater. On the other hand, they have taken the position that the story itself is an unchanged whole and that mistakes can be made. This attitude also gave the Grimms license to make changes themselves to Viehmann's stories. Their changes, unlike Viehmann's, were seen not as mistakes, but rather as corrections. Ruth Bottigheimer's 1987 *Bad Girls and Bold Boys* demonstrates how the Grimms' edits led to passive, quiet heroines and active, vocal villainesses across the seven main editions of the collection.[38] Many of Viehmann's stories in particular were changed significantly over the course of the Grimms' seven editions. Their edits of her stories, including "Aschenputtel" and "Die zwölf Brüder" (The Twelve Brothers), show a silencing of heroines and additional direct speech given to negative female characters. Regardless of their motives, in this way the Grimms further silenced the expression of their most treasured source. Certainly, *KHM* is the result of work by both men and women, but for the Grimms to play the role of the *Autor* the creative contributions of women had to be backgrounded, in order to make room for male achievement. In Viehmann's case, the very elements that made her the ideal source in the Grimms' eyes (her class, gender, and lack of education), also denigrated her work to that of only source material, instead of recognizing it as a creative contribution of her own intellect.

The Grimms applied this logic not only to the oral tales of peasant women, but also to published women writers. One of the most beloved and well known of the over 400 women who published fairy tales in the nineteenth century, Karoline Stahl published collections of fairy tales

---

36 Grimm and Grimm, *Kinder- und Hausmärchen* (1982 [1819]), I, x.
37 Joan Newlon Radner, *Feminist Messages: Coding in Women's Folk Culture* (Urbana: University of Illinois Press, 1993), 9.
38 Ruth Bottigheimer, *Grimms' Bad Girls and Bold Boys: The Moral and Social Vision of the Tales* (New Haven, CT: Yale University Press, 1987).

for children.[39] Anticipating the Grimms' own movement towards a children's audience for *KHM* later in the nineteenth century, Stahl wrote what a period lexicon describes as "sehr fruchtbare und gern gelesene" (very productive and enjoyably read) didactic children's literature.[40] Stahl experimented and mixed motifs from French and German tales, like other authors discussed below.[41] The Grimms admired her inspiration, saying she worked with "großenteils echte, aus mundlicher Überlieferung gesammelte Märchen" (mostly genuine fairy tales gathered from oral tradition) in her work, but they found her writing "nicht ausgezeichnet, aber doch einfach und ohne Überladung" (not exceptional, but still simple and without embellishment).[42]

The Grimms selected one of her tales, "Der undankbare Zwerg" (The Ungrateful Dwarf), for their 1837 edition. The story had been published already in two editions of Stahl's *Fabeln, Mährchen, und Erzählungen für Kinder* (Fables, Fairy Tales, and Stories for Children) in 1818 and 1821, but she is only referenced as a source in the Grimms' notes. They renamed the tale "Schneeweisschen und Rosenrot" (Snow White and Rose Red) and attempted to reframe it in a way that would indicate it came from oral tradition.[43] The tale became one of the best-loved tales in Germany, but is rarely attributed to Stahl.[44] There is no record of any oral tradition connected with it or any other variant of the tale prior to Stahl's own publication in 1818.[45] Still, within the field of fairy-tale studies today it is not unusual to see the tale attributed to the Grimms and analyzed as an anonymous folktale.[46] The attitudes and actions of the Grimms not only affected women writers in their own time period, but have had a lasting effect on their place in scholarship.

---

39 Shawn Jarvis, *Im Reich der Wünsche: Die schönsten Märchen deutscher Dichterinnen* (Munich: C. H. Beck, 2012), 320.
40 Anon, "Karoline Stahl," in Carl Herloßsohn, ed., *Damen Conversations-Lexikon* (Leipzig: 1837), IX, 389.
41 Karoline Stahl, "The Wicked Sisters and the Good One: A Fairy Tale," trans. Shawn C. Jarvis, *Marvels & Tales* 14, no. 1 (2000): 159–64 (159).
42 Grimm and Grimm, *Kinder- und Hausmärchen* (1984 [1857]), III, 345.
43 Marijana Hameršak, "A Never Ending Story? Permutations of 'Snow White and Rose Red' Narrative and Its Research across Time and Space," *Narodna umjetnost: Croatian Journal of Ethnology and Folklore Research* 48, no. 1 (2011): 146–60.
44 Walter Scherf, *Das Märchenlexikon* (Munich: C. H. Beck, 1995), II, 1042.
45 Scherf, *Das Märchenlexikon*, II, 1042.
46 Cristina Bacchilega, "Fairy-Tale Adaptations and Economies of Desire," in *The Cambridge Companion to Fairy Tales*, ed. Maria Tatar (Cambridge: Cambridge University Press, 2015), 79–96. This is an example of an article from a well-respected fairy-tale scholar that analyzes "Schneeweisschen und Rosenrot" but does not acknowledge Stahl as the author or the tale as her own creation.

192 Gender, Collaboration, and Authorship

Subversion: Bettina Brentano-von Arnim and the *Märchenfrau* Lehnhardt

The concept of *Märchenomas* as vessels of German culture rather than creative storytellers is best depicted, however, in the language used to discuss another *Märchenoma*, known only as Frau Lehnhardt, and her interaction with a young Bettina Brentano-von Arnim.[47] Frau Lehnhardt had been the nursemaid of Friedrich Carl von Savigny, the Grimms' friend and mentor.[48] Savigny wrote the Grimms in 1808 that she had stories to share, and was growing ill.[49] In the same period, Clemens Brentano and Ludwig Achim von Arnim were also working on a collection of folk culture, *Des Knaben Wunderhorn* (The Boy's Wonderhorn).[50] There was a collaboration among the two groups to meet with Frau Lehnhardt while she still lived. Achim von Arnim wrote to his future wife, Brentano's sister—then Bettina Brentano—explaining that the Grimms had written him about Frau Lehnhardt and asking Bettina Brentano to visit her. Each of these men discusses Lehnhardt as a resource to be exploited, but ultimately Bettina Brentano-von Arnim would gather tales with a different approach. Instead of a recording, Brentano-von Arnim describes a discussion and even a collaboration between herself and Lehnhardt in storytelling.

Jacob Grimm wrote to Savigny in 1808 that he hoped to have a few days free "aus der Frau Lenhardin für mich Vorteil zu ziehen" (to extract from Frau Lehnhardt a benefit for myself).[51] He was unable to find the time to make it to Frankfurt, where Lehnhardt lived, however, so he contacted Achim von Arnim. Achim von Arnim wrote to Bettina Brentano-von Arnim that he recognized "den heimlichen Schatz, der in der Frau Lehnhardtin verborgen" (the holy treasure that conceals itself within Frau Lehnhardt).[52] Again, as with Viehmann, a male collector

---

47 Frau Lehnhardt's name is spelled a number of ways, including Lehnhart, Lenhard, and Lenhart, and she is sometimes referred to in the feminine, Lehnhardtin and Lenhardin. I will use Lehnhardt in my discussion.
48 Heinz Rölleke, "Bettines Märchen," in *Herzhaft in die Dornen der Zeit greifen: Bettine von Arnim*, ed. Konrad Feilchenfeldt and Christoph Perels (Frankfurt am Main: Freies Deutsches Hochstift, 1985), 225–31 (225–6).
49 Rölleke, "Bettines Märchen," 226.
50 Ludwig Achim von Arnim and Clemens von Brentano, *Des Knaben Wunderhorn: Alte deutsche Lieder*, ed. Willi August Hoch (Munich: Winkler, 1957 [1805–8]).
51 Jacob Grimm to Friedrich Carl von Savigny, March 25, 1808, in Jacob Grimm, Wilhelm Grimm, and Friedrich Carl von Savigny, *Briefe der Brüder Grimm an Savigny*, ed. Wilhelm Schoof (Berlin: Erich Schmidt, 1953), 40.
52 Ludwig Achim von Arnim to Bettina von Arnim, April 2, 1808, in Ludwig Achim von Arnim and Bettina Brentano-von Arnim, *Arnim und Bettine: Briefe der Freundschaft und Liebe*, Vol. I, ed. Otto Betz and Veronika Straub (Frankfurt am Main: Knecht, 1986), 198.

has reduced his source, here Lehnhardt, to a container in which fairy tales are stored. The quote goes on, however, to elaborate more clearly on this perspective, as he continues, "O wäre ich ein guter Bergknappe und -steiger um diese Kindermärchen aus ihr loszuhauen" (Oh, if only I were a good mountain climber and miner, I would carve these fairy tales out of her).[53] In the clearest example of woman as *terra nullius*, Achim von Arnim equates Lehnhardt's mind to a mountain, and himself to a miner. In an uncomfortable depiction of the extraction, he uses the verb *hauen* (to cut, to chop, or to carve) to describe how he would take the stories from her. Far from a collaboration, Achim von Arnim views himself as the only active participant in this process. Lehnhardt is merely a mountain to be climbed, a resource to be mined. Lehnhardt's stories are the treasure within, not the creative products of an intelligent woman.

Neither the Brothers Grimm nor Achim von Arnim were able to climb this mountain, however, and Bettina Brentano-von Arnim took on the task. Bettina Brentano-von Arnim and the Grimms were lifelong friends. As a young woman, Bettina Brentano-von Arnim assisted on *Des Knaben Wunderhorn* and in the initial collection of *KHM*, and may have submitted her own stories as well.[54] The Grimms honored her work and friendship by dedicating all seven of the main editions of *KHM* to her. Bettina Brentano-von Arnim did not approach her meeting with Frau Lehnhardt as one of extraction, however, and the story she chooses to share with Achim von Arnim and the Grimms is quite different from those that appear in *KHM*.

She writes to Achim von Arnim, explaining how she had written Frau Lehnhardt and how she had "wegen der Mährlein [sie] geplagt" (pestered [Frau Lehnhardt] about the little story).[55] Here Bettina Brentano-von Arnim implies that her source may be bothered, treating Frau Lehnhardt as the respected authority of whom Bettina Brentano-von Arnim seeks a favor, rather than as merely a source to be accessed. When she eventually gathers a tale, it is not to the liking of the Grimms or Achim von Arnim, however. The tale, "Hans ohne Bart" (Beardless Hans) is a story of a young man whose mother breastfeeds him into adulthood.[56] This gives him incredible strength, but he is insensitive and destructive, unable to feel empathy. The ending of the tale is a bit ambiguous. Arnim wrote to the Grimms, "nun weiß

---

53 Arnim and Brentano-von Arnim, *Arnim und Bettine*, 198.
54 Rölleke, "Bettines Märchen," 225–6.
55 Röllecke, "Bettines Märchen," 226.
56 Bettina Brentano-von Arnim, "Hans ohne Bart," in *Märchen der Bettine, Armgart, und Gisela von Arnim*, ed. Gustav Konrad (Frechen: Bartmann, 1965), 10–12.

es die Frau Lehnhart nicht weiter, sie meint, es endigt sich mit einer Schatzgräbergeschichte, daß der Teufel ihm viel Geld gibt" (now Frau Lehnhardt does not know how it goes on; she thinks it ends with a treasure-hunter story, in which the devil gives him much money).[57]

While the Grimms and others emphasized that a *Märchenoma* should be able to remember and repeat verbatim, Arnim remarkably describes Lehnhardt as unable to remember the exact ending. The story cannot, therefore, reside in a perfect whole in her memory. Instead, Arnim shares that Lehnhardt has thought of an ending, suggesting that she has the ability to do such a thing. Here, Lehnhardt is able to improvise, and creatively apply an ending that may work. Arnim goes on to write, "Mir gefällt am besten, daß er die Irrwische immer erwischt" (I like it best, that he [the devil] always catches the little rascals).[58] Instead of extracting the stories like a good miner, it appears that Arnim has had a conversation in which Lehnhardt shared a story, and a possible ending, and then Arnim even offered her opinion of a different ending. Here we see a collaboration between collector and storyteller, or woman writer and *Märchenoma*, as they imagine how the story could end. This is a more realistic representation of how the work of folklore gets done, but not a scenario that fit comfortably into nineteenth-century conceptions of authorship. The story was not included in *Des Knaben Wunderhorn* or *KHM*.

Brentano-von Arnim also subverted the extraction of tales by seeking to collaborate. In her work on *Des Knaben Wunderhorn* and *KHM*, she more often played the role of collector and scholar, and she wrote her own literary fairy tales as well. Unlike other *Kunstmärchen* in the period, such as Fouqué's *Undine* or Goethe's *Das Märchen* (The Fairy Tale), Brentano-von Arnim's work is closer in length and style to *Volksmärchen* or a contribution from a *Märchenoma*, and does not contain complex, overarching allegories. In this way, she honors the product of the *Märchenomas* as literature as well, but her story confused her future husband, Achim von Arnim. Bettina Brentano-von Arnim wrote Achim von Arnim later in 1808 with an original story entitled "Der Königssohn" (The Prince) that she hoped might be published in the Heidelberg Romantic paper *Zeitung für Einsiedler* (Newspaper for Hermits).[59] Achim von Arnim, however, wrote back excitedly asking, "Das Märchen ist recht artig, hast Du es unverändert so von der Frau

---

57 Brentano-von Arnim, "Hans ohne Bart," 12.
58 Brentano-von Arnim, "Hans ohne Bart," 12.
59 Bettina Brentano-von Arnim, "Der Königssohn," in Konrad, *Märchen der Bettine*, 7–10. Rölleke, "Bettines Märchen," 228. Rölleke describes Brentano-von Arnim's intention for the piece to be published here.

Lenhardt?"(The fairy tale is quite good. Do you have it unchanged from Frau Lehnhardt?).[60] She responded, "Das Märchen ist von mir, daß es Dir etwas Dunkel vor schwebt wird wohl seyn, weil ich Dir einmal sprach daß ich ein solches schreiben wollte, die letzte Hälfte schrieb ich grad so in Deinen Brief" (The fairy tale is by me; if this is unclear to you it is probably because I told you that I wanted to write something like this, [and] I wrote the second half right into your letter).[61] The story was never published in *Zeitung für Einsiedler*, as it folded soon after this. Bettina Brentano-von Arnim's disbelief indicates a frustration with Achim von Arnim's obsession with *Märchenomas* and his concept of literature.

Although the Grimms knew the story, they did not include it in their collection. It was first published over a century later in 1913, in Reinhold Steig's *Achim von Arnim und die ihm nahe standen* (Achim von Arnim and Those Close to Him). As this title reveals, even 100 years later, in the genre of fairy tales Bettina Brentano-von Arnim was really only appreciated in her relationship to male writers. She was the sister of Clemens, the friend of Wilhelm and Jacob, and the wife of Achim, and her contributions were characterized in that context. Although she collaborated in the position of collector on *KHM* and *Des Knaben Wunderhorn*, and wrote her own creative tales, she was never considered their equal and always viewed as a subordinate in each relationship. Grimm scholar Heinz Rölleke writes: "It remains nonetheless an enticing question, whether the Brothers Grimm would have even respected the fairy tales recorded by Bettina."[62]

Resistance: Annette von Droste-Hülshoff, Anti-*Märchenfrau*

As a collector, albeit a subordinate one, and friend of the Grimms, Brentano-von Arnim was in a position to partially control the way in which a *Märchenoma* was treated and how her story was gathered. The young Annette von Droste-Hülshoff was in a very different place in relationship to the Grimms, as a talented and ambitious future author to whom the Grimms came for stories. She did not, it would appear, desire to be a source so much as an author, and she actively resisted her work's appropriation. We have records that the Grimms were familiar with the talented author when she was a girl in the early 1800s; scholars have long been frustrated, however, by the lack of information about the interaction of the writers who would become such important

---

60 Ludwig Achim von Arnim to Bettina Brentano-von Arnim, April 26, 1808, in Armin and Brentano-von Armin, *Arnim und Bettine*, I, 25.
61 Bettina Brentano-von Arnim to Ludwig Achim von Arnim, April 27–9, 1808, in Arnim and Brentano-von Arnim, *Arnim und Bettine*, I, 232.
62 Rölleke, "Bettines Märchen," 225–6.

figures in nineteenth-century literature.⁶³ Save a few mentions in letters from each, and reports from Droste-Hülshoff's sister Jenny, there is very little documentation of their interactions.⁶⁴ We have a description of the first meeting between the Grimms and Droste-Hülshoff in July of 1813, in which Wilhelm Grimm describes Droste-Hülshoff as the most knowledgable of the Haxthausen family, but writes, "es ist schade daß sie etwas vordringliches und unangenehmes in ihrem Wesen hat" (it is a shame that she has something urgent and unpleasant in her constitution).⁶⁵ He explains to his brother that Droste-Hülshoff was born premature, and therefore had "etwas frühreifes bei vielen Anlagen. Sie wollte beständig brillieren" (something precocious in many facilities. She constantly wanted to be brilliant).⁶⁶ Droste-Hülshoff's youth, ambition, and unattractive appearance place her in contrast to the older, modest, and beautiful Viehmann.

Although we have letters from Droste-Hülshoff's young aunt Ludowine von Haxthausen that claim to send stories and riddles in Droste-Hülshoff's hand, there are very few available to scholars today. Of those in the Grimms' documents, none was published or commented on save one, "König Einbein" (King One-Leg).⁶⁷ In the handwritten document, the story is recorded in both Wilhelm Grimm's and Annette von Droste-Hülshoff's hands. Karl Schulte-Kemminghausen, the first scholar to write on the story in 1936, describes it as a collaboration between the two.⁶⁸ Jeannine Blackwell depicts, however, a conflict between the collector and the author when describing the shared pen.⁶⁹ The record begins in Wilhelm Grimm's handwriting, but towards the middle of the story the pen changed hands and most of the latter half is written in Droste-Hülshoff's hand. At the very end of the story, the pen returns to Grimm, but he does not complete it, and it ends in a

---

63 Jeannine Blackwell, "German Fairy Tales: A User's Manual. Translations of Six Frames and Fragments by Romantic Women," in *Fairy Tales and Feminism: New Approaches*, ed. Donald Haase (Detroit: Wayne State University Press, 2004), 108.
64 Karl Schulte-Kemminghausen, "Volksüberlieferung aus dem Nachlaß der Brüder Grimm," *Westdeutsche Zeitschrift für Volkskunde* 33 (1936): 41–50 (41). As access to the Grimms' archives can be difficult to secure, I have relied on Schulte-Kemminghausen's transcript of the contents there both relating to Droste-Hülshoff and in her hand.
65 Quoted in Schulte-Kemminghausen, "Volksüberlieferung," 42.
66 Quoted in Schulte-Kemminghausen, "Volksüberlieferung," 42.
67 Schulte-Kemminghausen, "Volksüberlieferung," 42. For some examples of stories that bear Droste-Hülshoff's name, see Heinz Rölleke, *Märchen aus dem Nachlaß der Brüder Grimm* (Bonn: Bouvier, 1977), 100. It is not clear if the stories Rölleke mentions are the same as those that were included in the letter from her aunt.
68 Schulte-Kemminghausen, "Volksüberlieferung," 42.
69 Blackwell, "German Fairy Tales," 118.

sentence fragment. The Grimms never published the tale; the only note written beneath it by Wilhelm Grimm and again above it once received by Jacob Grimm is "usw. ich halte es für gemacht" (and so on, I consider it contrived).[70]

The strange note could have several meanings, but in an 1814 letter, from Jacob to Wilhelm, this is clarified. He writes: "Bei der Aulnoy ist auch gut das Märchen von Prinz Einbein ... (was dir einmal bei Haxthausens erzählt wurde und Dir natürlich schlecht vorkam)" (There is also a good fairy tale of Prince One-Leg from Aulnoy ... [which you were once told by one of the Haxthausens and naturally you found it wanting]).[71] So "Konig Einbein" was written off for its similarity to a tale by Marie-Catherine d'Aulnoy, the famous French fairy-tale writer of the seventeenth century. The Grimms were known for their aversion to references to French culture, and often edited out motifs and even words with French roots.

Schulte-Kemminghausen details how Westphalian fondness for France, and their tradition of employing French governesses, may have affected this reaction, but this hardly accounts for the dismissal.[72] Droste-Hülshoff had a German governess, and was no lover of Napoleon, even penning a celebration poem following his fall from power.[73] In addition, the beloved Viehmann had a much stronger connection to France, as a native French speaker and the descendant of Huguenots. She often included clear references to French variants in her tales, which the Grimms quietly removed from later editions. Moreover, in the same letter, Jacob Grimm also wrote about the possibility of a German variant of the same tale: "Vermutlich also auch in Deutschland und, wenn wirs echt bekommen, gewiß ein schönes" (Presumably there is also one in Germany and, when we receive a real one, it will certainly be a beauty.)[74] They hope to find a German variant of the d'Aulnoy tale, and yet they are unwilling to accept the d'Aulnoy-like variant they received from German-speaker Droste-Hülshoff as that artifact.

Unlike Viehmann, Droste-Hülshoff would not allow for a passive extraction of a tale from her memory, but instead took control of the pen herself. Like Brentano-von Arnim, Droste-Hülshoff creatively produces her own story based on her knowledge of other tales. There is nothing to say that Viehmann and other *Märchenomas* did not do something similar orally, and certainly we see evidence of Viehmann's familiarity with

---

70 Schulte-Kemminghausen, "Volksüberlieferung," 47.
71 Schulte-Kemminghausen, "Volksüberlieferung," 43.
72 Schulte-Kemminghausen, "Volksüberlieferung," 44–5.
73 Schulte-Kemminghausen, "Volksüberlieferung," 43.
74 Schulte-Kemminghausen, "Volksüberlieferung," 43.

Perrault in many variants, but the Grimms' own language demonstrates their rigid understanding of the stories as unchanged wholes merely residing within the quarry of a *Märchenoma*'s mind. Droste-Hülshoff's creation stands in stark contrast, as did her appearance and ambition. As Wilhelm Grimm described her, she was a young woman who wanted to be brilliant. She would not be recorded, but preferred instead to write herself, and she resisted being placed in the position of *Märchenoma*. The very creativity and ambition that put off the Grimms, and that placed her in a position outside of period dualisms, would lead to her success as an author. The Grimms were not interested in such stories, however, and they saw creative retellings as a sort of sacrilege, tainting the treasure they sought to uncover in the German folk.[75]

Droste-Hülshoff wrote her own report of her interactions with the Grimms in this period many years later in a letter of 1844 to her friend Elise Rüdiger: "Wilhelm Grimm hat mir durch sein Mißfallen jahrelang den bittersten Hohn und jede Art von Zurücksetzung bereitet, so daß ich mir tausendmal den Tod gewünscht ... ich war damals sehr jung, sehr trotzig und sehr unglücklich" (Wilhelm Grimm showed me his disapproval through years of bitter scorn and every form of affront, so that I wished myself dead a thousand times ... I was so young then, and very defiant and unhappy).[76] Droste-Hülshoff appears to have desired the approval of Grimm, and may have seen him as mentor, but as with many women writers, her mentor was unwilling to play such a role to an ambitious woman. Heinz Rölleke describes how the Grimms' opinion of Droste-Hülshoff's work varied from "characteristically reserved to dismissive."[77] As Joeres has discussed, the male writer as mentor simply could not work within period conceptions of women's and men's work.[78] Droste-Hülshoff was not an ideal *Märchenoma*, nor did she fit into the dualisms of the period as an ambitious, productive, and talented woman writer. Still, she resisted being placed in the role of *Märchenoma*, a passive vessel of culture, and sought instead to represent a story of her own creation, in relation to the long tradition of women telling fairy tales with which she was familiar. Her later works also included references to folklore and legend. She might

---

75 G. Ronald Murphy, *The Owl, the Raven and the Dove: The Religious Meaning of the Grimms' Magic Fairy Tales* (New York: Oxford University Press, 2000). An in-depth analysis of the Grimms' religious relationship to the fairy tale, *The Owl, the Raven and the Dove* offers a more complete look at how the Grimms equated fairy tales with religious relics.
76 Schulte-Kemminghausen, "Volksüberlieferung," 43.
77 Rölleke, "Bettines Märchen," 225.
78 Joeres, *Respectability and Deviance*, 26.

have been a great collaborator or colleague to the Grimms, had they given her the chance to do so.

Replacement I: Benedikte Naubert's Fictional *Märchenoma* in "Der kurze Mantel"

When Brentano-von Arnim and Droste-Hülshoff sought to collaborate with the Grimms, both were quite young and neither were published authors. At the time, there were, however, women who had published collections of tales in the same period as the Grimms. Among them were the anonymous author of *Feen-Mährchen* mentioned in the introduction, Benedikte Naubert, and Karoline Stahl. The Grimms were well aware of all three, and mention them often in their notes. All three had much in common with Droste-Hülshoff, as they tended to include motifs from the French tradition in their texts, especially from women writers of the salon period, such as d'Aulnoy. This is something the Grimms, naturally, disliked, calling Naubert's work in particular "bearbeitete eigentliche Volkssagen" (true folk sagas reworked).[79]

Benedikte Naubert was already well established in the field decades before the Grimms came on the scene. She published her collection of literary fairy tales, *Neue Volksmärchen der Deutschen* (New Folktales of the Germans), in 1789. In the period, several authors, including Wieland, quoted earlier, published popular collections featuring long, literary fairy tales based on folk tradition. Naubert was writing as an anonymous man. Although her publisher pushed her to use the feminine form "Verfasserin," she made clear that she preferred to be known as a masculine "Verfasser."[80] Many great authors of the period cite her collection as an inspiration, including Schiller, Tieck, Fouqué, Kleist, and Hoffmann. As Shawn C. Jarvis clearly lays out in "The Vanished Woman of Great Influence," however, "the reception of Benedikte Naubert falls into two distinct periods which roughly coincide with the period of her anonymity and the unveiling of her identity."[81] Following this unveiling in 1817, her work was relegated to that of *Trivialliteratur* (trivial literature), even as the texts of male authors whom she inspired began to take their place in the German canon.[82]

---

79 Grimm and Grimm, *Kinder- und Hausmärchen* (1984 [1857]), III, 325.
80 Laura Martin, *Benedikte Nauberts "Neue Volksmärchen der Deutschen": Strukturen des Wandels* (Würzburg: Königshausen & Neumann, 2006), 15.
81 Shawn C. Jarvis, "The Vanished Woman of Great Influence: Benedikte Naubert's Legacy and German Women's Fairy Tales," in *In the Shadow of Olympus: German Women Writers around 1800*, ed. Katherine Goodman and Edith Josefine Waldstein (Rochester: State University of New York Press, 1992), 189–209 (191).
82 Jarvis, "The Vanished Woman," 192–3.

The Grimms learned her identity nearly a decade earlier and consulted her for their collection, but kept her identity secret. They were particularly taken with her depiction of "Frau Holle" in her tale "Der kurze Mantel" (The Cloak). This is the first example of a reference to the tale in German. The Grimms would publish three variants in their collection, and Stahl featured one in hers as well. Interestingly, in "Der kurze Mantel," Naubert depicts a *Märchenoma* as well, but instead of representing her story as a pure treasure of German culture, Naubert depicts the *Märchenoma*'s story as one of personal experience and female wisdom. In what Tatiana Korneeva describes as a "narrative cross dress," the *Märchenoma*'s first-person tale is situated within an assumed male third-person narration. The tale takes up one-third of the text, allowing Naubert to, in a manner, publish the very type of tale that Wieland and others thought should remain in the private realm, while at the same time contesting the concept of the *Märchenoma* as merely a vessel of German folk culture.[83] Naubert takes us into the private realm and represents how these tales are more than just inspiration, but have a wisdom and purpose of their own. In this way, she removes the *Märchenoma* from the background of female inspiration and brings her tale directly into the male narration. Her work represents a kind of collaboration between the male third-person narrator and the female first-person storyteller, as together they bring the narrative to fruition. Moreover, Naubert imagines in the role of the *Märchenoma* Frau Rose, a creative storyteller who contradicts and complicates the dualisms of the period, and by doing so, imagines a female mentor for herself and other women writers.

In "Der kurze Mantel," the orphan Genelas, exiled from King Arthur's very corrupt court, is taken in by a kind old woman, Frau Rose, who teaches her to spin. While they spin, Frau Rose tells the story of her life, in which she plays the role of the Kind Girl in "Frau Holle." In Rose's story, Frau Hulla (Naubert's spelling) makes her a great spinner, but Rose's jealous cousin Magdalene and her own husband Martin thwart Frau Hulla's good will, calling it sorcery, leaving her ultimately alone and impoverished. In the frame story, Frau Hulla provides Genelas and Rose yarn with which they spin a cloak that reveals a woman's faithfulness. Back at the court, the cloak redeems Genelas's honor. She marries a knight, and they move with Frau Rose to Scotland.

Naubert demonstrates the power of a woman's oral tale over a male written narrative, for it is only through Rose's story that Genelas learns what she needs to know to be victorious at court. She also depicts a

---

83 Tatiana Korneeva, "Cross-Dressing Strategies in Benedikte Naubert's Fairy Tale Novella *Der kurze Mantel*," *German Life and Letters* 65, no. 3 (2012): 281–94 (287).

successful collaboration between a peasant woman and a noble woman (and a goddess) as they create the cloak together. As Frau Hulla tells Genelas at the end of the story, "vergiß nie, daß die Faden, aus welchen dein Ehrenkleid gewebt ward von deiner eignen Hand zur Zeit des Kummers gesponnen" (never forget that the threads from which your cloak of honor was woven were spun by your own hand in your time of suffering).[84] In contrast to a structure such as Wieland's, in which the man makes the story into proper literature, or a structure such as the Grimms', in which the men properly categorize, cut, and polish their mined treasures, Naubert lays bare the woman's oral tale (albeit a fictional one) within the text and then allows the power of such a tale to influence events within the male-narrated frame. In "From Woman to Woman," Anne Thiel points out that because Rose tells her story in the first person, she can describe the motivations and thought-processes behind her actions and frame her story as one about personal, as opposed to universal, wisdom.[85] In this way, although Naubert wrote as a man, she was able to depict a *Märchenoma* who was much more than a vessel of cultural tradition. Her complex *Märchenoma* is both productive and emotional: her work takes place in the private realm, but has an effect in the public world of the court as well. She is a replacement for reductive *Märchenoma* rhetoric and she stands outside the gendered dualisms and characteristics of the period. Frau Rose's tale is a worthwhile product of the hard work of her own lived experience, just like the cloak. The character of Genelas redeems herself with the knowledge from an oral, unedited, first-person account of "Frau Holle," decades before the tale would appear in the Grimms' collection. In this way, Naubert also imagines possible mentors for female creators outside the world of men, both in the storytelling and weaving of Frau Rose, and in the magical Frau Hulla, as she reinvents the concepts of an ideal *Märchenoma*.

Replacement II: Adele Schopenhauer's *Märchen-Jungfrau* in "Waldmärchen"

Years after the Grimms' first edition, but still over a decade before their final edition, Adele Schopenhauer's 1844 "Waldmärchen" (Forest Fairy Tale) also features a lengthy fictional tale from a *Märchenoma*, and critiques the failed collaboration between female source and male

---

84 Benedikte Naubert, *Neue Volksmärchen der Deutschen*, ed. Marianne Henn, Paola Mayer, and Anita Runge, 4 vols. (Göttingen: Wallstein, 2001), I, 160.
85 Anne Thiel, "From Woman to Woman: Benedikte Naubert's 'Der kurze Mantel,'" in *Harmony in Discord: German Women Writers in the Eighteenth and Nineteenth Centuries*, ed. Laura Martin (Bern: Peter Lang, 2002), 125–44 (130).

academic. Schopenhauer's own history put her in an interesting position to reflect on this relationship. As discussed above, her estranged brother, Arthur Schopenhauer, held his own problematic theories about the role of women, who he felt were not as evolved as men, since "sie selbst kindisch, läppisch und kurzsichtig, mit einem Worte, Zeit Lebens große Kinder sind" (they are themselves childish, foolish, and short-sighted; in a word, they are big children for their whole lives).[86] According to Arthur Schopenhauer and others, women were less evolved than men, and therefore they were closer to nature, acted on intuition, and could not control their emotions. The *Märchenoma* fits neatly into this depiction as a being who instinctually reproduces the same tales her mother and grandmother did before her. Just as the Grimms treated their sources as mere repeaters, a few steps removed from the genius of the *Autor*, Arthur Schopenhauer treated woman as a being a step removed from culture and man, the only "eigentliche Mensch" (true human).[87] Plumwood identifies that humanity has been associated with men, while women are described as more connected to animals and nature.[88] Adele Schopenhauer would play on this association and replace it with a more complicated picture of women, men, and nature.

Adele Schopenhauer was not only a fully evolved human, but was also an author, something of which her brother did not approve. Her own life contradicted his conception of woman, as she lived and worked amongst a group of creative women in Bonn, including Ottilie von Goethe, Goethe's daughter-in-law and editor; Annette von Droste-Hülshoff, mentioned earlier; and Adele Schopenhauer's lover, archaeologist Sibylle Mertens-Schaafhausen. The discussion in Schopenhauer's "Waldmärchen" demonstrates the conflict between well-respected male authorship and female inspiration, and investigates the concept of woman as a natural resource. In it a *Märchenoma* has heard her story not from another woman, but from nature itself. The story has then been adapted (within the text) by a male academic. While critiquing the appropriation of women's stories for male achievement, Schopenhauer also depicts an example of how men and women can work together, as it is a man who beckons the audience to the parlor to hear a woman's story, and within her story she depicts a man closely connected to nature. In this way, Schopenhauer's male and female characters contradict and complicate the gendered dualism, and she imagines a replacement for gendered concepts of the *Märchenoma*, the *Autor*, and nature.

---

86 Schopenhauer, "Ueber die Weiber," 365.
87 Schopenhauer, "Ueber die Weiber," 365.
88 Plumwood, *Feminism and the Mastery of Nature*, 43.

The frame story opens with the sentence "Die Vorlesung war beendet" (The reading came to an end), and this is as close as we come to hearing the voice of the male author in that reading.[89] The nameless *Autor* never speaks in the text, but the private audience instead springs into conversation following the ending of his reading of what all assume was a fairy tale, all except one young man who questions the genre: "Ein Märchen? ... Ich hätte das eher für eine Allegorie gehalten" (A fairy tale? I had thought it was more of an allegory).[90] This is perhaps an acknowledgment of heavily allegorical *Kunstmärchen*, such as Goethe's "Das Märchen." Still, the audience argues that the two are not mutually exclusive. This leads to a discussion of the nature of fairy tales themselves. An older woman, a critic, a professor, and a poet each take a turn at defining the fairy tale, but the young man still insists that the *Autor*'s tale was more literary. Finally, it is the handsome young son of the house who chimes in: "ich denke mir aber, es ist mit dem Märchen wie mit der Liebe, die auch kein Weiser richtig definiert: jeder denkt sich etwas anderes darunter" (I think instead it is with the fairy tale as with love, which also cannot properly be defined by wise men; everyone thinks of it as something else).[91] This explanation brings the argument to a close, and also changes the discussion from one of genre to one of emotion. The fairy tale is a feeling rather than a form of literature.

In the dualisms of the period, it would then follow that it belonged more to the world of women. Following this the young man invites the audience: "kommt lieber mit mir ins Vorzimmer: da sitzt meine Schwester Linda unter den Kindern, die heute nicht in die Gesellschaftszimmer dürfen, und erzählt ihnen auch Märchen" (please come with me into the next room, where my sister Linda is sitting with the children who are not allowed in the parlor today, and is telling them fairy tales too).[92] As the group moves into the next room, they find a group of eager children listening to Linda. The *Märchen* that she tells is called "Quellenmärchen." Since the German word *Quelle* (source, spring) is used to describe the source material for an adaptation, *Quellenmärchen* could describe the source of the nameless male author's tale that opened the scene. The *Quelle* here, however, is more literal, as the children set the scene for the tale: "Die Glühwürmchen zünden ihre Laternchen an, und der Quell beginnt sein Märchen" (The glowworms light their lanterns, and the spring begins his fairy tale).[93] So the source of the fairy tale is a

---

89 Adele Schopenhauer, *Haus-, Wald- und Feldmärchen*, ed. Karl Wolfgang Becker (Hanau: Werner Dausien, 1987 [1844]), 5.
90 Schopenhauer, *Haus-, Wald- und Feldmärchen*, 5.
91 Schopenhauer, *Haus-, Wald- und Feldmärchen*, 6.
92 Schopenhauer, *Haus-, Wald- und Feldmärchen*, 6.
93 Schopenhauer, *Haus-, Wald- und Feldmärchen*, 7.

literal *Quell* or well that whispers a story to those who listen. This frame tale disrupts the issue of the original. The scene opens with the ending of the nameless male author's tale. In a reversal of the real-world politics of fairy tales, the reader does not hear the author's tale or his name. Here it is the male author/editor, a Grimm equivalent, whose actual tale is never printed and whose name is unimportant. And the oral female storyteller is a named young woman, Linda, who has a rapt public audience, and the opportunity to share her story verbatim. It is noteworthy that here the man uses his position in the house (and society) to bring attention to the oral story of a woman. Rather than extracting the story and adding it to a collection, as the nameless *Autor* might have done, the young man of the house uses his influence to give prominence to the work of a woman.

As in Naubert's "Der kurze Mantel," instead of the edited, scholarly tale, the audience is given an oral tale. Instead of the creative product of a woman, however, this tale has a source that reaches beyond that of the female oral storyteller, back to nature itself, back to the *Quell*. That Linda has gotten her story from a natural well would, at first, appear to be a trope similar to early eco-feminist writing. Linda, as a woman, is more connected to nature and therefore can bring forth the most beautiful story born from the whispering of the well. In light of nineteenth-century conceptions of the *Märchenoma*, however, this is a step removed. For Linda is here the collector of the tale, not the resource itself that must be mined. In addition, the story that she tells is curiously one about a young man who is closely bound to nature. A young man who is the last of his line returns to his ancestral lands as a woodsman's apprentice. The young man always "tat das Notwendige am letzten; dagegen liebte er das Schöne und Wunderbare im Walde, pflegte und schonte die Blumen am Rain und freute sich der jüngsten Bäumchen" (completed the essential tasks last; for he loved the beauty and wonder in the forest, attended to and preserved every flower on the ridge, and took joy in the youngest sapling).[94] The hero of her tale cares for nature, rather than mining it. Schopenhauer replaces the concept of the male scholar who would extract what he needed with a nurturing man, living in harmony with nature. The relationship between man or woman and nature itself is represented as a collaboration.

This depiction of storytelling, occurring in a private room, told to children, and gathered from nature itself, may seem to fit within the feminine dualism of the period. Linda's story itself, however, calls on men, not women, to find a closer connection to nature in order truly to serve the land and their people. Linda is also not an older, lower-class

---

94 Schopenhauer, *Haus-, Wald- und Feldmärchen*, 8.

woman by the fireside, but someone much more similar to the true source of the Brothers Grimm, an aristocratic young woman in a parlor. As Schopenhauer imagines a more perfect collaboration among nature, men, women, and literature, she also represents each of the players of the Grimm collection as worthy, literary, and connected to the mystery of the fairy tale. The direct connection to the land itself continues the Grimm framework of tales belonging to the German land and empowering the concept of a German nation. *Autor*, *Märchenoma*, and the land itself work together to share the story, demonstrating the power and tradition of this conceptual collaboration that both critiques the extraction model and replaces it with a more collaborative and open structure.

Conclusion

Schopenhauer's and Naubert's representation of *Märchenomas* differs greatly from that of the Grimms. Instead of being instinctual repeaters of tales, these *Märchenomas* are telling stories based on their own experience, from sources of their own. By representing a natural source, Schopenhauer points out the flawed narrative of woman as resource, and points towards a more natural man as the key to the German states' survival. The language of the Grimms, Arthur Schopenhauer, Achim von Arnim, and others, however, reflects a very different understanding of what the female mind is capable of. The Grimms show great respect, admiration, and love for Viehmann, but are unable to see her work as anything other than the product of an excellent memory. Stahl's own published creative work was to them no different, and they felt free to take a story of hers as their own finding. Their treatment of Frau Lehnhardt depicted most clearly that they felt women were only vessels of knowledge to be collected. From these interactions, relationships, and inspirations, the Grimms and other collectors in the period demonstrate an understanding of the *Märchenoma* as *terra nullius*, with resources that were theirs for the taking.

Women writers in the period, however—Brentano-von Arnim, Droste-Hülshoff, Naubert, and Adele Schopenhauer among them—not only did not fit into the dualisms of the period, but actively subverted, resisted, and replaced them, to use Plumwood's construction. They leveraged the appropriative relationship between the male *Autor* as genius and the *Märchenoma* as inspiration in order both to critique the inconsistencies in such depictions of creative men and women, and to speak to the collaborative and complex nature of fairy tales, folklore, and literature itself. These women subverted this relationship, revealing the inadequacy of gendered dualisms; they resisted reductive concepts of the *Autor* and the *Märchenoma*; and they replaced them with new conceptions of creative women, supportive men, female mentors, and art as collaboration.

Bibliography

Anon. *Feen-Mährchen: Zur Unterhaltung für Freunde und Freundinnen der Feenwelt.* Ed. Ulrich Marzolph. New York: G. Olms, 2000 [1801].

Arnim, Ludwig Achim von and Bettina Brentano-von Arnim. *Arnim und Bettine: Briefe der Freundschaft und Liebe.* Vol 1. Ed. Otto Betz and Veronika Straub. Frankfurt am Main: Knecht, 1986.

Arnim, Ludwig Achim von and Clemens von Brentano. *Des Knaben Wunderhorn: Alte deutsche Lieder.* Ed. Willi August Hoch. Munich: Winkler, 1957 [1805–8].

Bacchilega, Cristina. "Fairy-Tale Adaptations and Economies of Desire." In *The Cambridge Companion to Fairy Tales,* ed. Maria Tatar, 79–96. Cambridge: Cambridge University Press, 2015.

Basile, Giambattista. *Giambattista Basile's "The Tale of Tales; or, Entertainment for Little Ones."* Ed. Nancy Canepa. Detroit: Wayne State University Press, 2007.

Becker, Siegfried. "Gab es Marburger Beiträger zu den 'Kinder- und Hausmärchen'? Zur Frage der Lokalisierung von Märchenfiguren und Märchenerzählern." In *Die Brüder Grimm in Marburg,* ed. Andreas Hedwig. Schriften des Hessischen Staatsarchivs Marburg 25, 57–88. Marburg: Hessisches Staatsarchiv Marburg, 2013.

Blackwell, Jeannine. "German Fairy Tales: A User's Manual. Translations of Six Frames and Fragments by Romantic Women." In *Fairy Tales and Feminism: New Approaches,* ed. Donald Haase, 73–111. Detroit: Wayne State University Press, 2004.

Blackwell, Jeannine and Susanne Zantop, eds. *Bitter Healing: German Women Writers from 1700 to 1830. An Anthology.* Lincoln: University of Nebraska Press, 1990.

Bolte, Johannes and Jiří Polívka, eds. *Anmerkungen zu den Kinder- u. Hausmärchen der Brüder Grimm: Neu bearbeitet.* 5 vols. Hildesheim: G. Olms. 1963.

Bottigheimer, Ruth. *Grimms' Bad Girls and Bold Boys: The Moral and Social Vision of the Tales.* New Haven, CT: Yale University Press, 1987.

Brentano-von Arnim, Bettina. "Hans ohne Bart." In *Märchen der Bettine, Armgart, und Gisela von Arnim,* ed. Gustav Konrad, 10–12. Frechen: Bartmann Verlag, 1965.

Brentano-von Arnim, Bettina. "Der Königssohn." In *Märchen der Bettine, Armgart, und Gisela von Arnim,* ed. Gustav Konrad, 7–10. Frechen: Bartmann, 1965.

Ellis, John M. *One Fairy Story Too Many: The Brothers Grimm and Their Tales.* Chicago: University of Chicago Press, 1983.

Frevert, Ute. *"Mann und Weib, und Weib und Mann": Geschlechter-Differenzen in der Moderne.* Munich: Beck, 1995.

Grimm, Jacob and Wilhelm Grimm. *Die älteste Märchensammlung der Brüder Grimm: Synopse der Handschriftlichen Urfassung von 1810 und der Erstdrucke von 1812.* Ed. Heinz Rölleke. Cologny: Fondation Martin Bodmer, 1975.

Grimm, Jacob and Wilhelm Grimm. *Kinder- und Hausmärchen.* Ed. Heinz Rölleke. 2 vols. Cologne: Diederichs, 1982 [1819].

Grimm, Jacob and Wilhelm Grimm. *Kinder- und Hausmärchen.* Ed. Heinz Rölleke. 3 vols. Göttingen: Vandenhoeck & Ruprecht, 1986 [1812].

Grimm, Jacob and Wilhelm Grimm. *Kinder- und Hausmärchen: Jubiläumsausgabe mit del Originalanmerkungen der Brüder Grimm.* Ed. Heinz Rölleke. 3 vols. Stuttgart: P. Reclam, 1984 [1857].

Grimm, Jacob, Wilhelm Grimm, and Friedrich Carl von Savigny. *Briefe der Brüder Grimm an Savigny.* Ed. Wilhelm Schoof. Berlin: Erich Schmidt, 1953.

Hameršak, Marijana, "A Never Ending Story? Permutations of 'Snow White and Rose Red' Narrative and Its Research across Time and Space." *Narodna umjetnost: Croatian Journal of Ethnology and Folklore Research* 48, no. 1 (2011): 146–60.

Hausen, Karin. "Family and Role-Division: The Polarisation of Sexual Stereotypes in the Nineteenth Century—an Aspect of the Dissociation of Work and Family Life." Trans. Cathleen Catt. In *The German Family: Essays on the Social History of the Family in Nineteenth- and Twentieth-Century Germany*, ed. Richard J. Evans and W. Robert Lee, 51–83. London: Croom Helm, 1981.

Herloßsohn, Carl, ed. *Damen-Conversations-Lexikon*. Vol. IX. Leipzig: Volckmar, 1837.

Hock, Lisabeth. *Replicas of a Female Prometheus: The Textual Personae of Bettina von Arnim*. New York: Peter Lang, 2000.

Humperdinck, Engelbert and Elisabeth Ebeling. *Dornröschen: Märchen in einem Vorspiel und drei Akten*. Musical score. Leipzig: M. Brockhaus, 1902.

Jarvis, Shawn C. *Im Reich der Wünsche: Die schönsten Märchen deutscher Dichterinnen*. Munich: C. H. Beck, 2012.

Jarvis, Shawn C. "The Vanished Woman of Great Influence: Benedikte Naubert's Legacy and German Women's Fairy Tales." In *In the Shadow of Olympus: German Women Writers around 1800*, ed. Katherine Goodman and Edith Josefine Waldstein, 189–209. Rochester: State University of New York Press, 1992.

Jarvis, Shawn C. and Jeannine Blackwell, ed. and trans. *The Queen's Mirror: Fairy Tales by German Women, 1780–1900*. Lincoln: University of Nebraska Press, 2001.

Joeres, Ruth-Ellen Boetcher. *Respectability and Deviance: Nineteenth-Century German Women Writers and the Ambiguity of Representation*. Chicago: University of Chicago Press, 1998.

Jones, Christine A. *Mother Goose Refigured: A Critical Translation of Charles Perrault's Fairy Tales*. Detroit: Wayne State University Press, 2016.

Korneeva, Tatiana. "Cross-Dressing Strategies in Benedikte Naubert's Fairy Tale Novella *Der kurze Mantel*." *German Life and Letters* 65, no. 3 (2012): 281–94.

Martin, Laura. *Benedikte Nauberts "Neue Volksmärchen der Deutschen": Strukturen des Wandels*. Würzburg: Königshausen & Neumann, 2006.

Murphy, G. Ronald. *The Owl, the Raven and the Dove: The Religious Meaning of the Grimms' Magic Fairy Tales*. New York: Oxford University Press, 2000.

Naubert, Benedikte. *Neue Volksmärchen der Deutschen*. Ed. Marianne Henn, Paola Mayer, and Anita Runge. 4 vols. Göttingen: Wallstein, 2001.

Plumwood, Val. *Feminism and the Mastery of Nature*. New York: Routledge, 1993.

Radner, Joan Newlon. *Feminist Messages: Coding in Women's Folk Culture*. Urbana: University of Illinois Press, 1993.

Rebel, Herman. "Why Not Old Marie? … or Someone Very Much like Her?" *Social History* 13 (1988): 1–27.

Rölleke, Heinz. "Bettines Märchen." In *Herzhaft in die Dornen der Zeit greifen: Bettine von Arnim*, ed. Konrad Feilchenfeldt and Christoph Perels, 225–31. Frankfurt am Main: Freies Deutsches Hochstift, 1985.

Rölleke, Heinz. "'Die Marburger Märchenfrau': Zur Herkunft der *KHM* 21 und 57." *Fabula* 15 (1974): 87–94.

Rölleke, Heinz. *Märchen aus dem Nachlaß der Brüder Grimm*. Bonn: Bouvier, 1977.

Rölleke, Heinz. "Die 'stockhessischen' Märchen der 'Alten Marie': Das Ende eines Mythos um die frühesten *KHM*-Aufzeichnungen der Brüder Grimm." In *"Nebeninschriften": Brüder Grimm—Arnim und Brentano—Droste-Hülshoff. Literarische Studien*, 1–15. Bonn: Bouvier, 1980.

Scherf, Walter. *Das Märchenlexikon*. Vol. II. Munich: C. H. Beck, 1995.

Schmidt, Jochen. *Die Geschichte des Genie-Gedankens 1750–1945*. 2 Vols. Darmstadt: Wissenschaftliche Buchgesellschaft, 1985.

Schopenhauer, Adele. *Haus-, Wald- und Feldmärchen*. Ed. Karl Wolfgang Becker. Hanau: Werner Dausien, 1987 [1844].

Schopenhauer, Arthur. "Ueber die Weiber." In *Parerga und Paralipomena*, II, 362–71. Berlin: A. W. Hayn, 1851.

Schulte-Kemminghausen, Karl. "Volksüberlieferung aus dem Nachlaß der Brüder Grimm." *Westdeustche Zeitschrift für Volkskunde* 33 (1936): 41–50.

Stahl, Karoline. *Fabeln, Mährchen und Erzählungen für Kinder*. Nuremberg: Tampe, 1821.

Stahl, Karoline. "The Wicked Sisters and the Good One: A Fairy Tale." Trans. Shawn C. Jarvis. *Marvels & Tales* 14, no. 1 (2000): 159–64.

Taylor, Peter K. *Indentured to Liberty: Peasant Life and the Hessian Military State, 1688–1815*. Ithaca, NY: Cornell University Press, 1994.

Thiel, Anne. "From Woman to Woman: Benedikte Naubert's 'Der kurze Mantel.'" In *Harmony in Discord: German Women Writers in the Eighteenth and Nineteenth Centuries*, ed. Laura Martin, 125–44. Bern: Peter Lang, 2002.

Warner, Marina. *From the Beast to the Blonde: On Fairy Tales and Their Tellers*. New York: Noonday Press, 1996.

Wieland, Christoph Martin. *C. M. Wielands Sämmtliche Werke*. Ed. J. G. Gruber. Vol. VI. Oxford: Oxford University Press, 1828.

Eight A Meeting of Minds?
The Dialogue between Voices Female and Male in the Poems of the West–Eastern Divan

Charlotte Lee

Johann Wolfgang von Goethe's *West–östlicher Divan* (West–Eastern Divan) is, by its nature, dialogic. The collection, composed between 1814 and 1819, is an extended, imaginary conversation with the fourteenth-century poet Hafiz—one of Iran's most revered writers, whose own *Divan* had appeared in German in 1812–13, translated by the Austrian diplomat and orientalist Joseph von Hammer-Purgstall. Although Hafiz is the key influence, the collection also expresses a lifelong fascination on Goethe's part with Islam, and draws on a range of Asian and Middle Eastern cultural traditions. In addition to this imagined exchange, the *Divan* was also founded in part on a real dialogue between Goethe and the young poet and actress Marianne von Willemer (1784–1860). Their shared passion animated the *Buch Suleika* (Book of Suleika) in particular, one of the twelve "books" that constitute the *Divan*. This section, which has the most developed dialogic structure in the cycle, contains several poems written by Marianne herself. Both the *Book of Suleika* as a whole and Marianne's own poems are collaborative, the result of mutual inspiration. The history of the partnership between Goethe and Marianne has become somewhat mired in controversy, however, and this can cast a shadow over the gender dynamics that develop *within* the work. There are two related, but distinct, questions that need to be asked of the *Book of Suleika*: first, whether the work *was* a "joint venture"; and second, whether it is also *about* a joint venture—that is to say, whether it depicts a genuine partnership, a collaboration between two persons assumed to be equal.

The answer to the first question ought to be simple. Those poems by Marianne that appear in the *Book of Suleika* were not simple imitations of Goethe's writing, produced, as if in some passive dream, by a vessel filled with inspiration from a greater source. Her work attests, rather, to a robust talent and personality, one fully able to participate in the sophisticated game of poetic shape-shifting that is the *Divan*. Marianne was a good technician, her skills in verse honed through numerous compositions that predate her exchanges with Goethe. More than this, though, there is a "poetological dimension" to her work.[1] This self-consciousness suggests an independence of mind, which is the prerequisite for interesting (as opposed to merely competent) poetry, and is the first reason why it is important to understand Marianne's presence in the *Divan* as an active one. The second reason is that she in fact did a good deal to nourish Goethe's developing passion for eastern themes and motifs. He was still composing poems for the *Divan* during his stay with Marianne and her husband in Frankfurt between May and September 1815, and she became the living inspiration for the cycle.[2] In the evenings, Goethe would read his work to the Willemers and to Sulpiz Boisserée, and Marianne would perform musical settings of his earlier poems. He also gave Marianne a copy of Joseph Hammer's translation of Hafiz; she read it, and took up Goethe's interest. She lent the celebrations for his sixty-sixth birthday an eastern theme, and the Turkish military decoration emblazoned with a sun and moon that she purchased for him at the Frankfurter Messe (Frankfurt Trade Fair) later gave rise to the poem "Die Sonne kommt!" (The sun appears!). Goethe's muse she undoubtedly was, but she was also his interlocutor, and an active contributor at various stages of the *Divan* venture. Moreover, their dialogue continued beyond the completion of that work. Goethe continued to exchange letters with both the Willemers until his death in 1832.[3] These include plenty of social and domestic details, but there are a number of examples of a reprise of the *Divan* spirit by both parties. The exchange of November and December 1822, for instance, contains a number of references to the cycle, as well as two new poems—one by Goethe, and a response by Marianne—that enact a repartee characteristic of the *Book of Suleika*.

---

1 See Markus Wallenborn, *Frauen. Dichten. Goethe: Die produktive Goethe-Rezeption bei Charlotte von Stein, Marianne von Willemer und Bettine von Arnim* (Tübingen: Niemeyer, 2006), 177.
2 Wallenborn, *Frauen. Dichten. Goethe*, 187–8.
3 See Johann Wolfgang Goethe, *Johann Wolfgang Goethe: Briefwechsel mit Marianne und Johann Jakob Willemer*, ed. Hans-J. Weitz (Frankfurt am Main: Insel, 1986 [1965]) (hereafter *Goethe–Willemer Briefwechsel*). See also Carl Hammer, Jr., "Goethe and Marianne: After the 'Divan,'" *South Central Bulletin* 28, no. 4 (1968): 134–8.

Viewing the *Divan* as a joint project is anything but straightforward, however. Goethe did not acknowledge Marianne as the author of the poems in the published version of the work; nor is it possible to say beyond all doubt precisely which poems are hers. Since 1869, when her involvement in the collection was first brought into mainstream public awareness by Herman Grimm, the debate has veered between two extremes: heightened defensiveness of Goethe on the one hand and, on the other, an exaggeration of Marianne's role in the *Divan*. Marianne herself claimed in a letter from 1856 that "außer dem Ost- und Westwinde habe ich nichts auf meinem Gewissen als allenfalls noch: 'Hochbeglückt in deiner Liebe' und 'Sag, du hast wohl viel gedichtet,' habe allerdings manches andere angeregt, veranlasst und erlebt'[4] (apart from the poems of the East and West Wind [i.e., 'How interpret this emotion' ('Was bedeutet die Bewegung') and 'Ah, West Wind, your moist wings gliding' ('Ach um deine feuchten Schwingen')], I have nothing on my conscience besides, at most, 'By your love I am elated' and 'Say, you have so much perfected'; but I inspired, instigated and also experienced many other things).[5] On the basis of this, T. J. Reed has argued that only the "East Wind" and "West Wind" poems can be attributed "with any kind of certainty" to Marianne.[6] Owing to poor record-keeping and, in the case of "By your love" and "Say, you have so much perfected," the absence of original copies in Marianne's hand, absolute certainty on the matter is out of the question. Reed concludes that we may take Marianne at her word, but with due caution and precision.[7] This means understanding the extent of her involvement in the *Divan* as the "small, but by no means insignificant canon"[8] of the poems of the East and West Wind and, perhaps ("allenfalls" [at most], as she herself put it) "By your love" and "Say." This is a reasonable approach, especially given that Marianne did not produce her responses to Goethe's evolving *Divan*

---

4 See Herman Grimm and Marianne von Willemer, *Im Namen Goethes: Der Briefwechsel Marianne von Willemer und Herman Grimm*, ed. Hans Joachim Mey (Frankfurt am Main: Insel, 1988), 230.
5 I quote, by kind permission of Professor Joachim Whaley, excerpts and titles of the poems from John Whaley's translation: Johann Wolfgang Goethe, *West-östlicher Divan/West-eastern Divan*, trans. John Whaley (Munich: Deutscher Taschenbuch, 1979 [1974]). Except where stated, all other translations, including this extract from Marianne's letter, are my own.
6 T. J. Reed, "Was hat Marianne wirklich geschrieben? Skeptische Stimmen aus England," in *Liber amicorum: Katharina Mommsen zum 85. Geburtstag*, ed. Andreas Remmel and Paul Remmel (Siegeburg: Bernstein, 2010), 465–83 (478).
7 Reed, "Was hat Marianne wirklich geschrieben?", 478.
8 Reed, "Was hat Marianne wirklich geschrieben?", 478.

with the express intention of being included in it, even though that is the context in which we most frequently encounter her work today.[9]

The question remains, though, of whether Goethe had the right, first, to publish her poems in his cycle without explicitly acknowledging her authorship, and second, to undertake minor, but significant, alterations to them (which continue to be reflected in standard editions of the *Divan*). On the first point, a defense of sorts might be the desire for privacy, to shield his relationship with Marianne (whatever its true nature) from the prying eyes and overactive tongues that, given Goethe's fame, would have remained hungry well into the preparation of the *Ausgabe letzter Hand*, the final and definitive edition of his works. Corroboration for this might be found in Goethe's handling of their epistolary exchange: shortly before he died in 1832, he returned a packet of Marianne's letters to her, "der Brust, der sie entquollen" (to the breast from which they sprang),[10] and the exchange was not published in full until 1877. In addition, his letters were generally addressed either to Marianne's stepdaughter, Rosine Städel, or to her husband, but never to her individually; and Goethe's record in his journal of messages sent and received tends simply to refer to "Willemers," that is, to both partners.[11] Yet, although the wish to fend off gossip is understandable, other aspects of Goethe's use of the material are less easily justified. Wallenborn echoes other critics in deploring in particular the alteration of the fourth strophe of the "East Wind" poem. The version most commonly printed reads thus: "Und mir bringt sein leises Flüstern / Von dem Freunde tausend Grüße; / Eh noch diese Hügel düstern / Grüßen mich wohl tausend Küsse" (Its soft whispering my lover / Sends a thousand times to greet me; / Fore the dusk these hills can cover / His kiss thousandfold shall meet me).[12] Yet Marianne's original is less fulsome, more restrained: the "thousands" in lines 2 and 4 of Goethe's version are absent, and the strophe closes with the speaker imagining herself sitting quietly at the feet of her beloved. Wallenborn is sharp in his criticism of Goethe's interference, arguing that he thereby appropriated wholesale a poem that was written for him, out of love and of admiration, and turned Marianne's work into another song of "his" Suleika.[13]

---

9 Wallenborn, *Frauen. Dichten. Goethe*, 189.
10 See *Goethe–Willemer Briefwechsel*, 270, 275: the little poem "Vor die Augen meiner Lieben," composed in 1831, marks this act.
11 *Goethe–Willemer Briefwechsel*, ix.
12 See the *Münchner Ausgabe* (Munich Edition): Johann Wolfgang Goethe, *Sämtliche Werke nach Epochen seines Schaffens* (hereafter *MA*), Vol. XI.1.2, ed. Karl Richter with Katharina Mommsen and Peter Ludwig (Munich: Hanser, 1998), 86; Goethe, *West–östlicher Divan*, trans. Whaley 134–5.
13 Wallenborn, *Frauen. Dichten. Goethe*, 194.

This uncomfortable set of questions lingers on without any wholly satisfactory answer, and it might seem inappropriate to suggest that the *Divan* can be viewed as a joint venture, given that one party did not receive due credit for her contribution. Nor would it seem to augur well for the construction of female roles and the depiction of cross-gender collaborations *within* the work. Yet there is, perhaps, a parallel with the Orientalism debate. This, too, turns on the issue of appropriation, and of respecting the integrity of the other. Opinion is divided on whether Goethe's *Divan* represents a genuine ability to step outside a "western" mindset, but Todd Kontje proposes an interesting compromise. The inevitable aspect of Eurocentrism in Goethe's outlook is tempered, Kontje argues, by his ability to relativize his own position: "It is not so much a question ... of Goethe's generous understanding of the East, but more of his ironic awareness of the Western desire for Oriental origins that casts a kinder light on his imperial imagination."[14] I would like to suggest an equivalent approach to the issue of gender and female authorship in the *Divan*. Rather than expecting an ideal level of understanding of women, we might detect an "ironic awareness" of (to the poet's mind) the incompleteness of men without them.

This is not without parallel in Goethe's oeuvre. In her essay on Goethe and the feminist reader, Gail K. Hart points to the reversal, or at least the problematization, of the stereotypical male–female/active–passive dichotomy at points throughout *Faust*: from Gretchen's refusal to be escorted home in Part I, to the "leading" role that she, in her heavenly incarnation as one of the "Büsserinnen" (holy penitent women), plays at the end of Part II.[15] Suleika is a different character. Whereas Gretchen leads, or refuses to follow, out of an instinctive sense of what is morally right (and, in Part I, perhaps also an element of teenage rebellion), Suleika does so because she is using her mind. It is worth noting that Goethe's decision to reformulate "Sitz ich still zu seinen Füßen" (I shall sit quietly at his feet) *increases* the autonomy of the female voice: as the editors of the *Münchner Ausgabe* (Munich Edition) observe, the action also enabled him to discard an element of devotion in the original that did not quite fit with the game between equals which his couple plays in love and in poetry.[16] In the display of intellectual reciprocity as well

---

14 Todd Kontje, *German Orientalisms* (Ann Arbor: University of Michigan Press, 2004), 132.
15 Gail K. Hart, "Errant Strivings: Goethe, *Faust* and the Feminist Reader," in *From Goethe to Gide: Feminism, Aesthetics and the French and German Literary Canon 1770–1936*, ed. Mary Orr and Lesley Sharpe (Exeter: University of Exeter Press, 2005), 7–21 (20).
16 See commentary to *MA*, XI.1.2, 636.

as sensual enjoyment that is the *Book of Suleika*, we can discern genuine respect for women's capacity to think. The issue of Goethe's appropriation of Marianne's work remains problematic, and, as will become clear later, there are deficiencies in the role that he carves out for women in the *Divan*. Yet—thanks not least to Marianne's inspiration and example—Goethe has deliberately constructed this highly sophisticated literary experiment so that it not only includes, but indeed requires, an active, independent, female voice.

Marianne's poems are offshoots of a real-life exchange, and when placed alongside the work of her conversation partner they form a further dialogue, a new one in poetry. The interplay of "life" and "art" in the *Divan* is notoriously complex, and this famous "failed" rhyme in Goethe's "Locken! haltet mich gefangen" (In the circle of her features) from the *Book of Suleika* might be called the point of tangency between the two:[17]

> Du beschämst wie Morgenröthe
> Jener Gipfel ernste Wand,
> Und noch einmal fühlet Hatem
> Frühlingshauch und Sommerbrand.[18]

> (You make blush, like red of morning,
> This high summit's dour retreat,
> And once more there comes to Hatem
> Breath of spring and summer's heat.)

"Hatem" is the pseudonym adopted by the male poet, and this piece marks the culmination of teasing allusions (such as the frequent mention of an age difference) to the affair between the "real-life" Hatem and Suleika: for, by the scheme of the alternating rhymes, the word "Morgenröthe" (red of morning) would fit much better with another name—Goethe. Yet, as has often been observed, trying to read the *Book of Suleika* as autobiography with a light coating of fiction will lead us up a blind alley. For one thing, it is pointless: enjoyable though it is to speculate, we can never know for sure whether the relationship between Goethe and Marianne was a meeting of more than hearts and minds. More importantly, though, such an approach would be reductive. Role play, the artful trying on of different masks and personae, is central to the entire conception of the *Divan*. That gentle poetic irony is particularly pronounced in the *Book of Suleika*: both writers produce poetry

---

17 MA, XI.1.2, 79–80; Goethe, *West–östlicher Divan*, trans. Whaley, 122–5.
18 MA, XI.1.2, 80; Goethe, *West–östlicher Divan*, trans. Whaley, 123, 125.

about poetry, and the dialogic element heightens the knowingness of their activity still further.

Marianne's poems participate fully, then, in the self-conscious play of this section of the *Divan*. In "Was bedeutet die Bewegung" ("How interpret this emotion," also known as the "Ostwind," or "East Wind") and "Ach um deine feuchten Schwingen" ("Ah, West Wind, your moist wings gliding," or simply "Westwind"), Marianne adopts motifs from her reading of Hafiz, such as the East Wind and the dust as bearers of messages of affection. In the first poem, the lyric voice anticipates the arrival of news of her beloved on the wings of the East Wind, while, in the second, she entreats the West Wind to carry her love back to him. The two pieces, therefore, strike the same mode as Goethe's poems for this section of the *Divan*: they share in the loving exchange between a woman and a man, and in the cross-fertilization of east and west, which is the overarching scenario of the *Book of Suleika*. Yet, perhaps more interestingly, these two poems, written at most within a month of each other, also form a dialogue with one another, or of the poet with herself: for the movement from one to the other entails a revision of the poet's perspective, an examination of the shifting tonalities of her own moods.[19] The element of dialogue in what is really a monologue is a further indicator of the poetic self-awareness of these pieces. Taken as a pair, they can be regarded as variations on a theme, as a compositional experiment by a highly skilled practitioner of the art form. The poems are given here in Marianne's original wording:[20]

WAS BEDEUTET die Bewegung?
Bringt der Ostwind frohe Kunde?
Seiner Schwingen frische Regung
Kühlt des Herzens tiefe Wunde.

Kosend spielt er mit dem Staube,
Jagt ihn auf in leichten Wölkchen,
Treibt zur sichern Rebenlaube
Der Insekten frohes Völkchen.

---

19 The date of "Was bedeutet die Bewegung" has been estimated as September 23, 1815, on the basis of Goethe's papers. In the same source, "Ach um deine feuchten Schwingen" is dated September 26, 1815, though Marianne herself later claimed to have composed the poem in October. See *MA*, XI.1.2, 635, 638–9; and *Goethe–Willemer Briefwechsel*, 342.

20 I have used John Whaley's translations with the exception of the fourth strophe of the "East Wind": this I have adapted to give an (albeit clumsy) reflection of Marianne's original wording.

Lindert sanft der Sonne Glühen,
Kühlt auch mir die heißen Wangen,
Küßt die Reben noch im Fliehen
Die auf Feld und Hügel prangen.

Und mich soll sein leises Flüstern
Von dem Freunde lieblich grüßen,
Eh noch diese Hügel düstern
Sitz ich still zu seinen Füßen.

Und du magst nun weiter ziehen,
Diene Frohen und Betrübten,
Dort wo hohe Mauern glühen
Finde ich den Vielgeliebten.

Ach, die wahre Herzenskunde,
Liebeshauch, erfrischtes Leben
Wird mir nur aus seinem Munde,
Kann mir nur sein Atem geben.[21]

(HOW INTERPRET this emotion?
Brings the East Wind news that pleases?
How its wings' refreshing motion
My heart's wound with coolness eases.

Fondles, chases helter skelter
Dust in playful cloud formations,
Drives to vineyard's leafy shelter
Joyous insect populations.

Makes the sun's glow mild and tender,
Coolness to my hot cheeks blowing,
Flees and kisses vines in splendour
Over field and hillside growing.

With its soft whispering my lover
Means me affectionately to greet;
Fore the dusk these hills can cover
Silent at his feet I'll sit.

Once more on your way now wander!
Serve the loving and dejected,
By those high walls glowing yonder
Soon I'll find my heart's elected.

---

21 *Goethe–Willemer Briefwechsel*, 335–6.

Ah, true touch in heart's recesses,
Breath of love, fresh animation,
These his mouth alone expresses,
Breathes alone his inspiration.)

ACH! UM DEINE feuchten Schwingen
West wie sehr ich dich beneide,
Denn du kannst ihm Kunde bringen,
Was ich durch die Trennung leide.

Die Bewegung deiner Flügel
Weckt im Busen stilles Sehnen,
Blumen, Augen, Wald und Hügel
Stehn bei deinem Hauch in Thränen.

Doch dein mildes sanftes Wehen
Kühlt die wunden Augenlider;
Ach, für Leid müßt ich vergehen,
Hofft ich nicht, wir sehn uns wieder.

Geh denn hin zu meinem Lieben,
Spreche sanft zu seinem Herzen,
Doch vermeid ihn zu betrüben
Und verschweig ihm meine Schmerzen.

Sag ihm nur, doch sag bescheiden,
Seine Liebe sei mein Leben,
Freudiges Gefühl von beiden
Wird mir seine Nähe geben.[22]

(AH, WEST WIND, your moist wings gliding
Stir my envious admiration:
For to him you bring this tiding
How I grieve in separation!

Your wings' motion has such power,
Yearning through my heart it presses;
Hill and forest, field and flower
Fill with tears from your caresses.

Yet your mild and gentle blowing
Soothes and cools my eyelids burning:
I had died from pain so glowing
But for hope of his returning.

---

22 *Goethe–Willemer Briefwechsel*, 342–3.

Hurry then to meet my lover,
Softly to his heart appealing;
Yet you must not cloud him over,
And my pain must keep concealing.

Tell him, though with modest voice:
That his love is my life's essence,
In them both I shall rejoice
When again I feel his presence.)

The "Ost-" and "Westwind" poems share certain motifs and pieces of vocabulary—"Schwingen" (rendered as "gliding" in the second translation, "motion" in the first), "Kunde" (tidings), "Bewegung"/"Regung" (both of which can be rendered as "motion")—but they strike a different tone. The keynote of "Ostwind" is given by the word "frisch" (rendered as "refreshing") in line 3. Although the poem opens with two questions, "Was bedeutet die Bewegung? / Bringt der Ostwind frohe Kunde?," in the main the atmosphere is one of confidence. The questions seem to expect an answer, the scaldings of passion are "cooled" and "soothed," and yet a sensuous energy also recurs: "Kosend spielt er mit dem Staube, / Jagt ihn auf in leichten Wölkchen," or "Küßt die Reben noch im Fliehen / Die auf Feld und Hügel prangen." "Westwind," by contrast, is more muted and wistful, more introverted. Little has changed about the essential situation, that of separation from the beloved, but the opening strophe, instead of expressing excitement, is framed by the words "Ach!" and "durch die Trennung leide" ("grieve in separation"). Yet, although the anxiety of isolation is brought more fully into relief in "Westwind," here, too, the poet is able to draw comfort and healing from her aerial messenger: this time, it is "dein mildes sanftes Wehen" ("your mild and gentle blowing") rather than "[s]einer Schwingen frischer Regung" ("its wings' refreshing motion") that "cools" her sore eyes. Both poems draw strength and inspiration from the unique bond with the beloved, which crosses any distance. In some ways, the ending of "Westwind" is still more affirmative than that of its counterpart: "Kann mir nur sein Athem geben" ("Breathes alone his inspiration"), which was the closing line of "Ostwind," modulates into "Wird mir seine Nähe geben" ("When again I feel his presence"). The poetic voice also speaks with dignity: even the more exuberant "Ostwind" opens up moments of quiet reflection, as in the line (in Marianne's original) "Sitz ich still zu seinen Füßen" ("Silent at his feet I'll sit"). There is great sincerity about "Ostwind" and "Westwind," yet the mirroring and changing of elements between them is beautifully judged, and executed with poetic awareness. Marianne's input, while thoroughly imbued with the common purpose of the *Divan*, guarantees the presence of an independently minded female voice in the Hatem–Suleika exchange.

Exchange is a central theme in the *Book of Suleika*, but if anything, it is even more highly developed on the structural level than on that of content. The sheer conversational energy of this section marks it out from the rest of the work: even the dialogues in the *Book of the Inn* (*Schenkenbuch* in the original German) and the *Buch des Paradieses* (Book of Paradise) are written on a much smaller scale. The (imagined) interlocutor who gives life to the entire collection—that is, Hafiz—is given a voice only once, in a few lines at the beginning of the *Buch Hafis* (Book of Hafiz). Suleika, by contrast, is not only the focus of the poet's attention in the book that bears her name, but is herself a vocal presence throughout. This might seem of limited significance, given that her voice is, to an extent, a product of Goethe's imagination (many of the Suleika poems were genuinely his own work); but, as we have seen, the conversation is not *solely* on the level of fantasy, thanks to the presence of those poems by Marianne. Suleika is also accorded a striking autonomy of tone, even within the state of mutual dependence that this part of the *Divan* celebrates. Her voice is variegated, involving different colors and moods from poem to poem, and she is a robust interlocutor. In its depictions both of poetry and of love, the *Book of Suleika* edges towards the dynamic that, for the art historian John Berger, distinguishes portrayals of the sexual encounter in non-European artistic traditions: an encounter, that is, which takes place "between two people, the woman as active as the man, the actions of each absorbing the other."[23]

Suleika's first entry, in "Hochbeglückt in deiner Liebe" ("By your love I am elated")[24]—one of the poems sometimes attributed to Marianne—both echoes and alters the words of the previous poem, "Nicht Gelegenheit macht Diebe" ("Thieves occasion does not make"),[25] spoken by Hatem; she "talks back," as it were. The meter and verse form are carried over from "Nicht Gelegenheit," but the order of the opening alternate rhyme is reversed (to "Liebe"/"Diebe" [love/thieves] from "Diebe"/"Liebe" in the previous poem), and an additional strophe is placed at the end. This gives visual reinforcement to the sense, evident from the first word, "Hochbeglückt," of a speaker brimming with confidence. The theme has modulated from the dependency born of desire, which Hatem explores, to the energy generated by love, and to the ability of lovers to shape events. The notion of *erneuern* (to renew), advanced at the end of Hatem's poem only once he has worked his

---

23 John Berger, *Ways of Seeing* (London: Penguin, 2008), 53.
24 MA, XI.1.2, 69; Goethe, *West–östlicher Divan*, trans. Whaley, 104–7.
25 MA, XI.1.2, 68; Goethe, *West–östlicher Divan*, trans. Whaley, 104–5.

way through *verarmen* (to impoverish), rushes through Suleika's verses. The boldness expressed in "Hochbeglückt" may have as much to do with youth as it does with gender: reminders of Hatem's relative maturity are planted at intervals throughout this section, and may account in part for the disparity in outlook between "Nicht Gelegenheit" and "Hochbeglückt." Yet the question of age is only implicit. In this pair of poems, at least, Suleika seems to have the ascendancy in terms of energy and optimism. It is her voice that gently contradicts the male interlocutor: "Schelt ich nicht Gelegenheit" ("With occasion find no faults"),[26] "Scherze nicht! Nichts von Verarmen!" ("Do not jest! No thought of alms").[27] It is she who professes confidence in the notion of free will: "Gieb dich mir aus freyer Wahl" ("Give yourself with open eyes"), "Meine Ruh', mein reiches Leben / Geb' ich freudig, nimm es hin" ("All my peace, rich life, my all / I give gladly; all is yours!"). In this scene, finally, it is her strength that is expressed in their embrace: "Halt ich dich in meinen Armen" ("When I hold you in my arms").

The repartee is similarly intricate in the next of the poems possibly composed by Marianne, "Sag du hast wohl viel gedichtet" ("Say, you have so much perfected").[28] Here, Suleika challenges Hatem, in a teasing way, about the authenticity of his love: each of those earlier passionate poems must have been a "Liebespfand," a deposit or pledge, for other women. Hatem concedes, but, in a deft move, ends the poem with the assertion that all the others were but avatars in whom she, Suleika, was "[p]rophezeyt" (foretold). The piece is a delightful reflection on the theme of authenticity, which toys overtly with its own artificiality by its liberal use of "eastern" motifs: "Moschusduftend Lockenschlangen, /

---

26 *MA*, XI.1.2, 69; Goethe, *West–östlicher Divan*, trans. Whaley, 105.
27 *MA*, XI.1.2, 69; Goethe, *West–östlicher Divan*, trans. Whaley, 107.
28 *MA*, XI.1.2, 72; Goethe, *West–östlicher Divan*, trans. Whaley, 110–11. Criticism has been rather disparaging about the likelihood of the version of "Sag du hast wohl viel gedichtet" that we have in the *Ausgabe letzter Hand* being her original work. See for example the commentary in the *Münchner Ausgabe*: "Kann ein so spielerisch-artistisch anmutendes Gedicht von Marianne gedichtet worden sein? Sie selbst hat die Urheberschaft in vorsichtig einschränkenden Wendungen zugeschrieben ... Schließt man eine frühere Gedichtversion von ihrer Hand nicht aus, ist eine um so entschiedenere und freiere Überarbeitung durch G. anzunehmen" (*MA*, XI.1.2, 610). We have seen that "playful artistry" was absolutely within Marianne's capability, so this on its own will not do as evidence that the poem was not hers. Given the absence of a manuscript, however, for this poem, as for "Hochbeglückt in deiner Liebe," there is little purpose in speculating on the extent of Goethe's involvement. A more productive approach is to treat all the poems—those we know to be Goethe's and those we know to be Marianne's, and those in between—as rhetorical constructs, and to analyze them on that basis.

Augenwimpern reizumhangen" (Perfumed with musk, curls confounded / Eyelashes with charms surrounded).[29] It is playful, but perfectly formed and balanced. In his response, Hatem adopts the rhyme scheme that Suleika has initiated (*aabaabab*) and inserts different sounds, thereby echoing and varying her text in equal measure, just as she had done with his in "Hochbeglückt in deiner Liebe." In addition, the poem enacts a flirtatious verbal swordfight. Suleika's tone is gently mocking: there is something dismissive about "Hin und her dein Lied gerichtet" ("Here and there your song directed"), and even "[s]chöngeschrieben" ("written beautifully") and "[p]rachtgebunden" ("bound so fine") could contain an element of derision. Hatem parries her thrust with a rather brazen "Ja!" and moves through a brief series of fantasies, implicitly inviting her and us to join in the imaginative spectacle; at last, he relinquishes his own teasing by making her the embodiment and summation of the delights that he has just enumerated. Granted, this particular skirmish ends in a victory for the man, and with the objectification of the woman; but in "Sag du hast wohl," as in the *Book of Suleika* as a whole, both speakers bear responsibility for ensuring that the dialogue remains both sensuous and intellectually taut.

Such a partnership could never be completely and consistently level: relationships are always shifting, and too often loaded with desire and interest, however progressive the social, cultural, or political context. Yet the *Book of Suleika* offers a picture of relative parity between the genders in the making of love and the making of poetry. In Goethe's "Behramgur,"[30] for example, the poet recalls the legend of the invention of rhyme: Behramgur "sprach entzückt aus reiner Seele Drang" ("Pure soul compelled [him] to cast delight in sound"), and his beloved Dilaram "Erwiderte mit gleichem Wort und Klang" ("Same words and tone held fast and answer found"). He then draws a parallel with—but also, subtly, a distinction from—his own situation: his poetry emerges, as it were, from a weave of reciprocal gazes and conversations: "Denn was ich froh, aus vollem Herzen, sprach, / Das klang zurück aus deinem holden Leben, / Wie Blick dem Blick, so Reim dem Reime nach" ("For all that I from full and glad heart spoke / From your own gracious life reverberated / As look the look, so rhyme the rhyme awoke"). In both cases it is the male figure who is charged with the intellectual task of "inventing" the rhyme; but the

---

29 The poem is given in a slightly different version in John Whaley's edition: "Moschusduftend" is given as "Wimpern-Pfeilen," which he translates as "darting lashes," which is followed by "Hals und Brust" (neck and breast), rather than "Augenwimpern." The "confounded"/"surrounded" rhyme, which I have adopted in my text, is his.
30 *MA*, XI.1.2, 84–5; Goethe, *West–östlicher Divan*, trans. Whaley, 130–3.

addressee of this poem is, perhaps, afforded a little more autonomy in the venture than Behramgur's Dilaram, who, we are told, responded with the same words and tone ("mit gleichem Wort und Klang"). The speaker's beloved does echo him, as we have already seen, but the lines quoted above are preceded by the words "Hast mir dieß Buch geweckt, du hast's gegeben" ("In me you roused this book, by you donated"). While the first part of the sentence could imply the standard role of a muse, the second formulation, with its use of "gegeben" ("donated"), is more interesting. His inspiration is in her gift, and he cherishes his dependence. The same is true in "Die schön geschriebenen" ("These lovely manuscripts"):[31] their love affair is compared to a ball game, in which she throws him her "Leidenschaft" ("passion") and he returns his "gewidmetes Ich" ("dedicated self"). Here, too, the poet and his beloved are relatively equal partners: once again, she initiates the activity in this section of the poem, and there is an element of challenge—"Daß ich ihn fange" ("So that I catch it") introduces a note of strain, suggesting that he has to concentrate or he might drop the ball. In both poems, then, the beloved is far from a passive screen onto which the poet projects his ambitions, literary or erotic.

In its final form, the *Book of Paradise* (the final section of the *Divan*) is the book that, of all in the cycle, comes closest to the dynamics of the *Book of Suleika*. This book was not originally conceived as an exchange, but in 1820 Goethe added four lyric dialogues between the poet and a houri. These profoundly altered the shape and the tone of the section, once again creating space for a female voice. In the Islamic paradise, the figure of the houri is a virgin companion to the male faithful; she turns out in Goethe's version to be an avatar of Suleika, much as, in the strange other-world of "Bergschluchten" (Mountain Gorges) at the end of *Faust*, II, one of the penitent women was "formerly called Gretchen."[32] As we see in "Vorschmack" ("Foretaste")[33] the paradise in the *Divan* is, true to the models of Islamic utopia, very much a world created for the pleasure of men: "Auf meinem Schoos, an meinem Herzen halt ich / Das Himmels-Wesen, mag nichts weiter wissen" (Upon my lap, against my heart I press / The heavenly being, seek to know no further); but it is made clear that the spell cast by female charms still has the ability to render men powerless, however briefly. Although the houri is there for his delectation—"Du aber bist mir beschieden" ("You though to me

---

31 *MA*, XI.1.2, 75–6; Goethe, *West–östlicher Divan*, trans. Whaley, 116–17.
32 *MA*, XVIII.1, ed. Gisela Henckmann and Dorothea Hölscher-Lohmeyer (Munich: Hauser, 1991), 350.
33 *MA*, XI.1.2, 117–18; Goethe, *West–östlicher Divan*, trans. Whaley, 178–9.

are imparted")[34]—the poem "Einlass" (Admittance) implies that she must be sufficiently impressed by him before she submits to his desires. Moreover, she continues some of the gentle teasing familiar from the *Book of Suleika*. In "Anklang" (Resonances), for example, she refers to his poetry—which she has heard from her watch at the gates of paradise—as something rather tentative and unsure of itself: "Da hört ich ein wunderlich Gesäusel, / Ein Ton- und Sylbengekräusel, / Das wollte herein" ("I heard a peculiar strange rustling, / Of sounds and syllables tussling, / It wanted to stay"). Only later does she concede: "Sing' mir die Lieder an Suleika vor: / Denn weiter wirst du's doch im Paradies nicht bringen" (Sing me those songs to Suleika once more: / For here in Paradise you still won't do it better).[35] The decision to put the words "ein wunderlich Gesäusel" and "Sylbengekräusel" in the mouth of the female interlocutor signals the continuation of that "ironic awareness" of the poet's incompleteness that emerged in the *Book of Suleika*.

Ultimately, however, the *Book of Paradise* does not offer quite the same display of female agency. In both books, the female interlocutor is unambiguously the object of male desire, but the alternative role—that of *intellectual* partner—is not as developed for the houri as it is for Suleika. That is not to say that respect for women is lacking in the *Book of Paradise*. Katharina Mommsen has demonstrated convincingly that, in this section, Goethe mounts a challenge to the notion of woman as a being of inferior status, which is sometimes an aspect of Islam, as it is of the other Abrahamic religions.[36] In Mommsen's interpretation, Goethe first exposes misogynist attitudes in poems such as "Auserwählte Frauen" ("Chosen Women")[37] or, in the *Buch der Betrachtungen* (Book of Observations), "Behandelt die Frauen mit Nachsicht!" (Treat women with care),[38] and then counters them by giving women a voice in his *Divan*, and—in an implicit rejection of the notion of paradise as accessible to men only—emphasising their heavenly qualities. Mommsen writes: "That women should be at such evident spiritual and eschatological disadvantage appeared to Goethe so characteristic of Islam that he chose to call attention to them in an arresting way."[39] Even so, the terms in which

---

34 "Anklang" (Resonances), line 35, in MA, XI.1.2, 118–19; Goethe, *West–östlicher Divan*, trans. Whaley, 184–7.
35 Both quotations are from "Anklang," in MA, XI.1.2, 118–19.
36 Katharina Mommsen, *Goethe and the Poets of Arabia*, trans. Michael M. Metzger (Rochester, NY: Camden House, 2014), esp. 174, 179. German original: Katharina Mommsen, *Goethe und die arabische Welt* (Frankfurt am Main: Insel, 1989), 362, 371.
37 MA, XI.1.2, 116–17; Goethe, *West–östlicher Divan*, trans. Whaley, 182–3.
38 MA, XI.1.2, 42; Goethe, *West–östlicher Divan*, trans. Whaley, 60–3.
39 Mommsen, *Goethe and the Poets of Arabia*, 179.

Goethe honors women perhaps require more thorough critical treatment than Mommsen gives. Just as it is reductive to make them into the object of desire, so an excessive tendency to idealize can also be confining. This remark from Goethe to Eckermann is quoted by Mommsen as evidence of his support for women, but it also makes plain the problems inherent in the idealizing approach: "Frauen sind das einzige Gefäß, was uns Neueren noch geblieben ist, um unsere Idealität hinein zu gießen. Mit den Männern ist nichts zu tun. Im Achill und Odysseus, dem Tapfersten und Klügsten, hat der Homer alles vorweggenommen" ("Women are the only vessel into which we moderns can pour our sense of the Ideal. Nothing can be done with the men. In Achilles and Odysseus, the bravest and cleverest, Homer has pre-empted every possibility").[40] The notion of woman as a "vessel" into which men can pour their own ideals is far removed from the active female voice that "talks back" in the *Book of Suleika*. The extent of the role accorded to the imaginary woman in that book was, perhaps, a unique moment in the *Divan*, one made possible by the "real" female voice that resounds through it.

Of course, the *Divan* is not a piece about gender norms, and its purpose is neither to challenge nor to confirm them. Rather, it is about the loving creation of poetry. In the *Book of Suleika*, the exchange between the male and female interlocutors is a precondition for creativity, just as it was during Goethe's stay in Frankfurt in 1815. Gail Hart observes, in relation to *Faust*, that "[t]his is neither emancipatory nor oppressive writing and Goethe did not, in any case, work along these particular axes".[41] This rings true for the *Divan* also: Suleika is neither a trailblazer for women's independence, intellectual or otherwise, nor does she speak with the subservience generally expected of women in Goethe's time.

Perhaps the last word should be given to Goethe's poem "Abglanz" ("Reflection")[42] in the *Book of Suleika*, which captures something of the significance of women (and, perhaps, one woman in particular) for this phase of his poetry. The curiously haunting middle strophe has the poet seeing his beloved first in the mirror, then in his poems:

Wenn ich nun vorm Spiegel stehe,
Im stillen Wittwerhaus,
Gleich guckt, eh' ich mich versehe,
Das Liebchen mit heraus.

---

40 Goethe to Eckermann, July 5, 1827; quoted in Mommsen, *Goethe und die arabische Welt*, 364; Mommsen, *Goethe and the Poets of Arabia*, 175 (Metzger's translation of Goethe is used here).
41 Hart, "Errant Strivings," 19.
42 *MA*, XI.1.2, 91–2; Goethe, *West–östlicher Divan*, 142–5.

Schnell kehr' ich mich um, und wieder
Verschwand sie die ich sah
Dann blick ich in meine Lieder,
Gleich ist sie wieder da.

(When I stand before the mirror
In quiet house bereaved
She peeps, 'fore I see the error,
Beloved's face perceived,
I turn quickly round, in vain,
She vanished, she I saw;
I look in my songs again,
At once she's there once more.)

It is not clear whether "das Liebchen," the beloved, is the same person whose absence has turned his surroundings into a "house bereaved," or whether she has captured his imagination more recently; but the reference to the rupture of death gives this essentially playful poem a certain fragility. Her flitting presence is both a game of hide-and-seek and a more solemn reminder of the transience of all things. Yet she is also a life-giving force, and a guarantor of permanence. In the context of the intensive exchange between partners in the *Book of Suleika*, the image of the poet's beloved staring back at him from the mirror suggests a deep intimacy, a meeting of minds. The third strophe is concerned with the enduring presence of this "Liebchen" in the poet's work: a presence that sustains it; improves it; and, crucially, enables him to express himself more truly:

Die schreib' ich immer schöner
Und mehr nach meinem Sinn,
Trotz Krittler und Verhöhner,
Zu täglichem Gewinn.
Ihr Bild in reichen Schranken
Verherrlichet sich nur,
In goldnen Rosenranken
Und Rämchen von Lasur.

(More beautiful I'm writing
And more in my own sense,
The scornful critics spiting,
For daily recompense.
Fine bound her image poses,
Exalts alone her fame,
In golden scrolls of roses
And pretty azure frame.)

The poem can be read as a tribute to a feminine influence that, though not always there in physical form, offers inspiration so powerful for the poet that it enables his poetry to renew itself. The continuation of the correspondence between Goethe and Marianne, long after his sojourn in Frankfurt had ended and the *Divan* had been published, attests to the lasting power of the relationship between the "real-life" pendants of the figures in the *Book of Suleika*. The use of the mirror motif in "Abglanz," with its sense of "now you see her, now you don't," also offers an apt— and, perhaps, poignant—image of how history has dealt with Marianne's own contribution to the *Divan*. But, despite all the difficulties attendant on Goethe's use of Marianne's material, I contend that the *Book of Suleika* both derives from and depicts a genuine partnership: and that it was, therefore, a joint venture in the truest sense.

Bibliography

Berger, John. *Ways of Seeing*. London: Penguin, 2008.
Goethe, Johann Wolfgang. *Johann Wolfgang Goethe: Briefwechsel mit Marianne und Johann Jakob Willemer*. Ed. Hans-J. Weitz. Frankfurt am Main: Insel, 1986 [1965].
Goethe, Johann Wolfgang. *Sämtliche Werke nach Epochen seines Schaffens*. Vol. XI.1.2. Ed. Karl Richter with Katharina Mommsen and Peter Ludwig. Munich: Hanser, 1998.
Goethe, Johann Wolfgang. *Sämtliche Werke nach Epochen seines Schaffens*. Vol. XVIII.1. Ed. Gisela Henckmann and Dorothea Hölscher-Lohmeyer. Munich: Hanser, 1991.
Goethe, Johann Wolfgang. *West–östlicher Divan / West–eastern Divan*. Trans. John Whaley. Munich: Deutscher Taschenbuch, 1979 [1974].
Grimm, Herman and Marianne von Willemer. *Im Namen Goethes: Der Briefwechsel Marianne von Willemer und Herman Grimm*. Ed. Hans Joachim Mey. Frankfurt am Main: Insel, 1988.
Hammer, Carl, Jr. "Goethe and Marianne: After the 'Divan.'" *South Central Bulletin* 28, no. 4 (1968): 134–8.
Hart, Gail K. "Errant Strivings: Goethe, *Faust* and the Feminist Reader." In *From Goethe to Gide: Feminism, Aesthetics and the French and German Literary Canon 1770–1936*, ed. Mary Orr and Lesley Sharpe, 7–21. Exeter: University of Exeter Press, 2005.
Kontje, Todd. *German Orientalisms*. Ann Arbor: University of Michigan Press, 2004.
Mommsen, Katharina. *Goethe and the Poets of Arabia*. Trans. Michael M. Metzger. Rochester, NY: Camden House, 2014.
Mommsen, Katharina. *Goethe und die arabische Welt*. Frankfurt am Main: Insel, 1989.
Reed, T. J. "Was hat Marianne wirklich geschrieben? Skeptische Stimmen aus England." In *Liber amicorum: Katharina Mommsen zum 85. Geburtstag*, ed. Andreas Remmel and Paul Remmel, 465–83. Siegeburg: Bernstein, 2010.
Wallenborn, Markus. *Frauen. Dichten. Goethe: Die produktive Goethe-Rezeption bei Charlotte von Stein, Marianne von Willemer und Bettine von Arnim*. Tübingen: Niemeyer, 2006.

Nine The Correspondence of Rahel Levin Varnhagen and Ludwig Robert

Epistolary Writing as a Space for *Symphilosophieren*

Laura Deiulio

Despite the German Romantics' emphasis on *Symphilosophieren* and collaborative thinking, the model of the genius author often dominates scholarly views of the period. But female writers in particular, constrained by social convention from publishing under their own names, rarely conformed to this model of the author, with the result that their work has often been forgotten or trivialized. The intellectual and salonnière Rahel Levin Varnhagen (1771–1833) provides a crucial case study of the value of collaborative work and of the limitations of the model of author as genius. The example of Rahel's interactions with her brother, the playwright Ludwig Robert (1778–1832), is particularly illuminating because their lifelong relationship uncovers many different elements of the collaborative mode of working.

Rahel's intellectual ideas took shape primarily in interactions with other people: in the two salons she hosted in Berlin prior to 1806 and during the 1820s, respectively; in conversations with her vast network of literary acquaintances; and in the thousands of personal letters she exchanged with family, friends, and intellectual interlocutors. By definition, this work was collaborative, for personal letters are composed for an addressee, while conversations require one or more partners. In a sense, then, Rahel took the Romantic concept of *Symphilosophieren* seriously, becoming an intellectual; a literary figure; and, in the words of Barbara Hahn, a writer "without a work."[1]

---

1 Barbara Hahn, *"Antworten Sie mir!" Rahel Levin Varnhagens Briefwechsel* (Basel: Stroemfeld/Roter Stern, 1990), 11.

What does it mean to be a writer without a work? Rahel was a highly respected figure on the literary scene during her lifetime and thereafter, and recent research has only underscored the depth of her influence.[2] Scholars also generally agree that she was aware of the value of her epistolary writing at quite a young age, and she pseudonymously published excerpts of her writings beginning in her forties.[3] Ursula Isselstein's extensive research in the Varnhagen archives has revealed that Rahel, with her husband Karl August Varnhagen (1785–1858), collated and prepared numerous letters for posthumous publication, work that had previously been attributed to him alone.[4] So there can be no doubt that Rahel was actively engaged in creating and disseminating her ideas. At the same time, she resisted participation in the system of formal authorship by choosing not to write or publish in conventional genres.

Rahel herself was well aware of the unusual nature of her choice to write in unstructured forms, telling Friedrich de la Motte Fouqué in 1829: "Nennen Sie ja meinen Namen nicht! Nicht, daß ich nicht willig, ja gerne, eine Schriftstellerin wäre. Ich schämte mich nicht, ein Neutonisches Werk über Sternkunde, oder Mathematik zu schreiben: aber *kein Werk* hervorbringen zu können, und doch drucken zu lassen, da wandelt mich Scheu an" (Do not mention my name! Not that I wouldn't willingly, even gladly, be a writer. I would not be ashamed to write a Newtonian work about astronomy, or mathematics: but to produce

---

2   In a recent article, Renata Fuchs has used materials held in the Varnhagen Collection in the Jagiellonian Library in Kraków, Poland, to support her contention that Rahel enjoyed international public influence. See "'Soll ein Weib wohl Bücher schreiben; Oder soll sie's lassen bleiben?': The Immediate Reception of Rahel Levin Varnhagen as a Public Figure," *Neophilologus* 98 (2014): 303–24 (309). Dagmar C. G. Lorenz too notes that Rahel's fame did not begin to fade until the 1840s; see *Keepers of the Motherland: German Texts by Jewish Women Authors* (Lincoln: University of Nebraska Press, 1997), 27.
3   One frequently cited piece of evidence for Rahel's views on the import of her own writing is an 1800 letter to Wilhelmine von Boye, in which she exhorts Boye: "und sterb' ich—such' *alle* meine Briefe ... Es wird eine Original-Geschichte und poetisch" (July 1, 1800). See Rahel Levin Varnhagen, *Rahel: Ein Buch des Andenkens für ihre Freunde*, ed. Barbara Hahn, 6 vols. (Göttingen: Wallstein, 2011) (hereafter *BDA*), I, 215. All the texts published by Rahel during her lifetime have been collected into Rahel Varnhagen von Ense, *"Ich will noch leben, wenn man's liest": Journalistische Beiträge aus den Jahren 1812–1829*, ed. Lieselotte Kinskofer, Forschung zum Junghegelianismus 5 (Frankfurt am Main: Peter Lang, 2001).
4   Ursula Isselstein, "Rahels Schriften I: Karl August Varnhagens editorische Tätigkeit nach Dokumenten seines Archivs," in *Rahel Levin Varnhagen: Die Wiederentdeckung einer Schriftstellerin*, ed. Barbara Hahn and Ursula Isselstein, *Zeitschrift für Literaturwissenschaft und Linguistik* Beiheft 14 (Göttingen: Vandenhoeck & Ruprecht, 1987), 16–36 (18).

no work, and yet to publish—at that thought, shyness overcomes me).[5] Excerpts of Rahel's writings appeared in Fouqué's journal *Berlinische Blätter für deutsche Frauen* (Berlin Pages for German Women) in 1829,[6] and this passage is clearly a plea for him to maintain her anonymity, even though many acquaintances in her circle might nonetheless have recognized her texts. Yet she states that she would gladly be a writer, implying that if she could produce a standard scientific work, she would publish it under her own name. What embarrasses her is the thought that she might print writings, such as letters, that did not conform to standard genres, and nonetheless claim credit for such a publication. This is of course an extremely odd position: first, because she did not write about science or express the ambition to be a scientist, and moreover, because publishing her epistolary writing was precisely what she was doing here. Despite her avowed modesty, Rahel was consciously resisting the single-author model while remaining cognizant of the value of her contributions.

What then does her way of working tell us about the alternative spaces of Romanticism? How does it challenge received notions of authorship while creating new modes of collaborative interaction? This chapter explores these questions using the letters she exchanged with Ludwig Robert. Of course, Rahel enjoyed collaborative exchanges with many other correspondents, including the statesman Friedrich Gentz; the Swedish diplomat Karl Gustav von Brinckmann; and not least, her husband, who became her editor and helped her to shape her legacy. But the correspondence with her brother is particularly insightful for two reasons. First, he became a published literary author and he actively sought out her advice and input on his writing. Second, as siblings, they experienced together the various stages of their lifelong development into German intellectuals of Jewish descent.

During his lifetime, Ludwig Robert achieved some of the external success that eluded his (today much more famous) sister. After serving an apprenticeship in business as a young man, Robert—in contrast to his two brothers—decided to change his profession and pursue a literary life.[7] Although he subsidized his income with proceeds from the siblings' inheritance, he did achieve modest success as a professional

---

5   June 17, 1829, *BDA*, V, 278. Unless otherwise noted, all translations are my own.
6   See the note on Friedrich de la Motte Fouqué in *BDA*, VI, 197. Rahel's article is reprinted in Varnhagen von Ense, *"Ich will noch leben,"* 143–77.
7   The Levin family had five children, of whom Rahel was the oldest, and Ludwig Robert (born Liepmann Levin) was the third child and second son. Following their father's death in 1790, Mordechai Levin (later Marcus Theodor Robert-Tornow) took responsibility for the family's financial affairs; both he

playwright, journalist, and critic. He composed a number of plays, poems, at least two texts with accompanying music by Carl Maria von Weber, and was a regular correspondent for the *Morgenblatt für gebildete Stände* (Morning Paper for the Educated Classes). Although never one of the elite poets of the age—and mostly forgotten today—Ludwig Robert did succeed in living the life of the mind.

Robert's relationship with his sister is documented in the 300 surviving letters that have been collected and edited by Consolina Vigliero in Volume II of the critical *Edition Rahel Levin Varnhagen*.[8] As with much personal correspondence, the letters create a challenge for the interpreter by combining seemingly quotidian news about family and friends with fascinating comments on current events and social issues. Well before the publication of the correspondence in 2001, Vigliero proposed that a key to analyzing their relationship lay in Robert's designation of his sister as "mein lieber Schwester-Freund" (my dear sister-friend). Vigliero argues that while a familial bond unites the two siblings, another, more intellectual, bond allows Rahel to evolve as a critic, co-author, and financial patron of Robert's work as well as supportive sister.[9]

Taken in this light, one can read the letters not as mere "supporting" documents in a broader project of publishing texts for the book market,

---

and, eventually, the youngest brother, Meier Levin (later Moritz Robert-Tornow), regulated the family's finances until well into their siblings' adulthoods. As adults, Marcus and Moritz enjoyed successful business careers in Berlin, while their younger sister, Rose, moved to Amsterdam at age nineteen to marry Carel Asser, a member of the Jewish community there. The family originally had hoped that Ludwig Robert would pursue a career in business as well, so his decision to become a professional writer allowed a special bond to form between him and his salonnière sister.

8   Almost all of the letters exchanged between Rahel and her brother are held today by the Varnhagen Collection, along with most of Rahel's other papers. Originally bequeathed to the Prussian Royal Library (today the Berlin State Library), the Varnhagen Collection was moved to Silesia for safekeeping during the Second World War. Following the war the archive was considered lost until the late 1970s, when it was rediscovered at the Jagiellonian Library. A team of international researchers initiated the critical *Edition Rahel Levin Varnhagen* in the 1990s (hereafter *ERLV*); the letters between Rahel and Robert appear in Vol. II, *Briefwechsel mit Ludwig Robert*, ed. Consolina Vigliero (Munich: C. H. Beck, 2001).

9   See Consolina Vigliero, "'Mein lieber Schwester-Freund': Rahel und Ludwig Robert in ihren Briefen," in Hahn and Isselstein, *Wiederentdeckung*, 47–55 (50–2). Vigliero also identifies "eine Vielzahl von Handlungssträngen" in her afterword to the edited letters. See Consolina Vigliero, "'Setzen sich da Polonius und Pilades und Iphigenie (Vater Freund und Schwester) hin und schreiben an Ludwig Robert': Der Briefwechsel von Rahel Levin Varnhagen und Ludwig Robert," *ERLV*, II, 931.

but as a form of working in their own right. In the private space of the letters, Rahel is able to contribute to her brother's publishing endeavors; serve as a kind of ideal reader for him; and, together with him, develop an identity as a German-Jewish intellectual in a rapidly evolving society. The letters become, then, a space of collaborative work, in which two writers create a form of text outside of the authorial system, a semi-public space for experimental thinking.

Rahel and Published Texts

Although Rahel did not receive any formal higher education or work in conventional genres, Robert was very aware of his sister's talents and regarded her most highly. In 1797 he tells her:

> Wundere Dich nicht, daß ich ausführlicher, und in gewißen Sin, klüger zu Dir schreibe, als ich zu Dir sprach. Du warst mir immer zu überlegen, als daß es in Person hätte geschehen können, den es gehört eine *verzweifelte Contenance* dazu, wenn man keine Prétension auf Ansprüche haben kan, sich *Dich* zu näheren; wenn man auch gleich Dein Bruder in optima forma ist.[10]
>
> (Do not be amazed that I write to you with more detail, and in a certain sense, with more wisdom, than I spoke to you. You were always too superior to me, so that it could not happen in person, for a certain desperate quality, when one does not presume to make any claims, is required to approach you, even when one is your brother in best form.)

Later that year he reinforces this sentiment when he says: "Wie *sehr* ich Dich liebe, wie *sehr* ich glücklich bin, dadurch daß Du meine Schwester bist, wie *unglücklich* mir alle Leute die ich auf der Straße begegne vorkommen, weil Sie *nicht* eine *solche* Schwester, *nicht* eine *solche* Freundin haben, das brauche ich Dir nicht zu sagen" (August 31, 1797, ERLV, II, 35) (How *much* I love you, how *very* happy I am because you are my sister, how *unhappy* all the people whom I meet on the street appear to me, because they do *not* have *such* a sister, *not such* a friend—that I do not need to tell you). Rahel's letters to Robert prior to 1801 have not been preserved, but the positive tone of her letters up until his death in 1832 demonstrates that she had a high opinion of him and his talents. Far from the model of a male intellectual creating works

---

10 January 20, 1797, in *ERLV*, II, 21. In the critical edition, all spelling irregularities found in the manuscripts are retained. Throughout the chapter, all emphases in quotations from *ERLV* are in the original.

of genius in a vacuum, then, the correspondence between Rahel and Robert showcases two interlocutors who saw each other as esteemed partners in an ongoing intellectual exchange.

Given his admiration for his sister, it is not surprising that throughout his career, Robert would seek out Rahel's opinion of his writing projects. For instance, in 1817 he writes of some satirical poems he has composed: "Daß die Müllerxenien Dir gefielen, ist mir sehr angenehm gewesen; aber wenn ich Dein Urtheil überhaupt wissen wollte, so war ich doch nicht so unbescheiden über diese Lumperei eine so detallirte Rezension zu begehren, für die ich aber gehörig danke und zum Dank hier vier Sonette beilege auf Jaïk der Madam Fischer verstorbenen Affen in Berlin"[11] (That you liked the satirical poems about Müller was very pleasing to me; but even though I wanted to know your judgment in general, I was not so immodest about this dirty trick as to desire so detailed a review, for which I, however, thank you as is appropriate and, out of thanks, include here four sonnets to Jaik, the deceased monkey of Madam Fischer in Berlin). While this exchange appears to be simply a lighthearted show of support for a fun personal project, during the next decade Robert would begin to seek much more substantive feedback for his journalistic writings.

Miriam Sambursky notes that around the time of the modest success of Robert's play *Die Macht der Verhältnisse* (The Power of Circumstances) at the Royal Theater in Berlin in late 1815, Robert began to contribute articles about the Berlin theater to Johann Friedrich Cotta's influential periodical *Morgenblatt für gebildete Stände*.[12] Robert continued to write articles for Cotta's journal even after relocating to southern Germany, an activity that certainly must have been an important source of income for him. During the 1820s we see Robert not only consulting his sister on his journalistic writing, but also allowing her to edit drafts or even to send him passages that he then published under his own name. For instance, almost as an afterthought, Robert concludes a long letter to his sister of April 22 and 28, 1825 with the request: "Wenn Du mal Zeit hast, schreibe doch etwas über Spontinische Musik. Ich mögte gern einen ausführlichen Aufsatz über ihn schreiben und drucken lassen" (*ERLV*, II, 434) (If you have time, write something about Spontini's music. I would like to write and publish a detailed essay about him).

---

11 January 18, 1817, *ERLV*, II, 155. The satirical poems in question were directed against Adam Müller and, per the editor of the Ludwig Robert correspondence, survive in the Varnhagen Collection. See *ERLV*, II, 681–2 n. 6.
12 Miriam Sambursky, "Ludwig Roberts Lebensgang," *Bulletin des Leo Baeck Instituts* (Neue Folge) 15, no. 52 (1976): 1–22 (12).

In her response, Rahel first states: "wie oft spreche ich 3. viertel Stunden lang über Spontini: und nun Du mich danach fragst weiß ich grade nichts; oder äußerst wenig" (May 12, 1825, *ERLV*, II, 434) (how often do I speak for three-quarters of an hour about Spontini: and now that you ask me about him I suddenly know nothing, or very little). She then writes a long passage describing the music of Spontini and its emotional effect on the listener. She mentions that her husband has copied the passage and would ideally like to publish it as well ("wollte es einrüken laßen" [*ERLV*, II, 436] [wanted to place it in a publication]), but since Robert has requested the passage first she is giving it to him. He did publish an edited version of part of Rahel's letter in the *Morgenblatt*.[13]

The tenor of this letter—as well as her emphasis on the fact that her husband also wanted to publish her remarks on Spontini—suggests that Rahel did indeed want her ideas to be known, even if indirectly, by the reading public. As far as the articles in the *Morgenblatt* are concerned, her motivation will have been at least partly to provide financial assistance: following her marriage to Varnhagen, Rahel's finances were more stable while Robert needed income from his journalistic publications. Rahel was no doubt aware that by providing him the raw material for such publications she was assisting him in his efforts to make a living. Legally speaking, one might consider this practice a form of ghostwriting, which Gunter Nitsche clearly differentiates from plagiarism, since ghostwriters grant permission for their work to be published under a patron's name.[14] Ghostwriting as Nitsche describes it here is primarily an economic act—the ghostwriter provides his or her work to a patron in exchange for compensation, although in Rahel's case she waives compensation.[15] But at some level, she must have felt pride that her ideas were worthy of being developed for publication. Although she resisted professionalization and economic compensation, Rahel used her collaborative relationship with Robert to create a space for her ideas to enter into circulation.

---

13 See *ERLV*, II, 819. The article itself is reprinted in Varnhagen von Ense, "*Ich will noch leben*," 131–4.
14 Gunter Nitsche, "Plagiat und Urheberrecht," in *Plagiat, Fälschung, Urheberrecht im interdisziplinären Blickfeld*, ed. Dietmar Goltschnigg, Charlotte Grollegg-Edler, and Patrizia Gruber, with contributions from Victoria Kumar (Berlin: Erich Schmidt, 2013), 77–88 (79).
15 Two of Rahel's twentieth-century editors, Konrad Feilchenfeldt and Rahel E. Steiner, contend that during her lifetime, it was an accepted journalistic practice to rework personal correspondence for publication. See "Rahel Varnhagens 'Werke,'" in Rahel Levin Varnhagen, *Rahel Bibliothek. Rahel Varnhagen: Gesammelte Werke* (hereafter *GW*), ed. Konrad Feilchenfeldt, Rahel E. Steiner, and Uwe Schweikert (Munich: Matthes & Seitz, 1983), X, 80.

Rahel's contributions to Robert's journalistic career occurred in the context of several collections of her letter excerpts that she and her husband edited and published, and at the same time as the preparations they made for publications that would not appear until many years after her death. These activities suggest that while Rahel developed the ambition to formulate her views in publishable form, she never gained the confidence to publish openly under her own name. We must read her writings in the light of this double, even paradoxical, status: a writer who did not participate in the literary market.

A letter of January 15, 1819 clearly depicts the simultaneous eagerness and trepidation with which Rahel participates in the editing of a text by Robert. The day before, he had sent her a letter to Cotta that accompanied a review he had written for the "Korrespondenz-Nachrichten" (Correspondence-News) column of the *Morgenblatt*. He tells her: "Schreibe mir, wie Du zufrieden bist; und schicke den Brf sogleich auf die Post" (*ERLV*, II, 219) (Write to me whether you are satisfied, and send the letter to the post office at once). In her response of January 15, she goes through each of her reactions, point by point. In particular, she objects to his use of the phrase "rothhaarige Grundsätze" (red-haired principles), a reference to the intrigues of Secretary Wurm in Schiller's play *Kabale und Liebe* (Intrigue and Love). Rahel does not feel that this reference is clear in the context of Robert's review, and starts her letter by stating that she does not dare allow herself to amend it, but he could write to Cotta himself and change the reference. In the course of her letter, however, she realizes that the manuscript needs to be sent on to Cotta quickly, and she begins to formulate her correction herself. She asks her brother: "Streich' ich rothhaarige Grundsätze? Ja! was setz' ich aber dafür? 'Mit Grundsätzen des Rothhaarigen aus Kab: und Liebe? Ich weiß es noch nicht zu drehen. Du! Ich habe gestrichen!!! und gesetzt 'mit Grundsätzen des [des] schlechten Sekretairs aus Kabal' und Liebe.' Bist Du böse? Es ist geschehen!" (January 15, 1819, *ERLV*, II, 221) (Do I strike "red-haired principles"? *Yes!* but what do I put in its place? "With principles of the red-haired man from *Intrigue and Love*"? I still don't know how to polish it. Listen! I have crossed it out!!! and put "with principles of the bad secretary from *Intrigue and Love*." Are you angry? It is done!).[16] Rahel's correction of Robert's word choice in this example might seem relatively modest, and in the event, her phrasing does not appear in the version of Robert's review published in the

---

16 In the critical edition, square brackets around a word indicate that it was crossed out by the writer of the original manuscript.

Morgenblatt on February 1, 1819.[17] Yet, her articulation of her thought process makes clear how nervous she was at the thought of interpolating her ideas into Robert's publication. Simultaneously, the fact that she does actually insert her correction and then forward his letter to Cotta demonstrates her desire to participate in the project.

It is clear to us what Ludwig Robert gained from the publishing relationship with his sister: a source of great advice; constructive criticism; and, quite literally, texts that he could use to further his own career. But it is clear that Rahel also benefited from the relationship. By allowing her brother to use her ideas and her words, she had the satisfaction of knowing that they were reaching a wider audience, while not taking the intellectual risk of publication fully on her own. One finds this sentiment clearly expressed in a letter of September 19, 1825. Rahel believes her brother to be visiting France on this date, and she devotes most of her letter to an analysis of a recent performance of Gioachino Rossini's opera *L'italiana in Algeri* (The Italian Girl in Algiers). While this production has created great enthusiasm in Berlin, Rahel has a more nuanced reaction and says of her opinion: "Drum ich's Dir [schreibe, L. D.] mein Freund—nach Frankreich. Vielleicht kannst Du's etwas zubereitet von dort aus in ein deutsches Journal senden. Es drängt die Brust das auszusprechen, was wir für wahr halten müssen, und worüber prachtvoller Wahn *herrscht*" (September 19, 1825, *ERLV*, II, 443) (This is why I [am writing] it to you my friend—to France. Perhaps you can send it from there, somewhat edited, to a German journal. My heart urges me to articulate that which we must consider to be true, and about which magnificent madness *reigns*). Robert apparently found Rahel's review convincing, for in a letter of September 27 he reports that he has already prepared her text for the *Morgenblatt*.

In *Sich einen Namen machen* (Making a Name for Oneself), her book on anonymous and pseudonymous publications around 1800, Susanne Kord points out that since the 1970s, scholars have developed theories to explain how women wanted to leave traces of themselves in the historical record, while simultaneously participating in the gender discourse that silenced them.[18] Rahel's desire to have her voice heard while

---

17 See anon. [Ludwig Robert], "Korrespondenz-Nachrichten," *Morgenblatt für gebildete Stände* 13, no. 27 (February 1, 1819): 107–8. Ludwig Robert's name does not appear as a byline. See Hathi Trust Digital Library, https://babel.hathitrust.org/cgi/pt?id=umn.31951001899530t;view=1up;seq=119.

18 Susanne Kord, *Sich einen Namen machen: Anonymität und weibliche Autorschaft 1700–1900*, Ergebnisse der Frauenforschung 41 (Stuttgart: J. B. Metzler, 1996), 23–7.

maintaining her anonymity can be understood in these terms. Further, issues of originality and copyright that began to surface around 1800 complicate her ambivalent attitude towards publishing her work.[19] Two theoretical points are of interest here. First, as Ronald Bettig argues in a broad-based analysis, copyright law may have developed more to protect the financial investment of book publishers than to preserve authors' rights.[20] Under this perspective, copyrighted works enter the capitalist system as financial investments or commodities—meaning that Rahel's contribution to Robert's publications was a form of pre- or extra-capitalist writing. Second, Heinrich Bosse and other scholars have theorized that the concept of the "author" emerged precisely in the Romantic period in order to anchor the commodity system by which an "author" sold his work for profit even while a book achieved the status of "work" only if created by an "author."[21] In other words, the author function ensured that the publisher, who was making the monetary investment, had the right to receive a return on this investment.[22] Such a model, then, implies that the "author as genius" is dependent on the author as owner of intellectual property in the form of a marketable work. Rahel, of course, was a brilliant thinker, conversationalist, and letter writer, but as we have noted did not produce "works"—meaning that her literary production existed outside the commodified copyright system.

Several additional instances, however, point to Rahel's pride of ownership in her ideas. In the early months of 1827, the correspondents react to a review Rahel had read in the Parisian *Courrier français* that had favorably compared Alexandre Duval's *Le Tasse* (Tasso) to Goethe's *Torquato Tasso*. In a letter that is no longer extant, Rahel asks her brother to

---

19 Copyright laws emerged piecemeal in the German-speaking lands prior to 1871. Baden was the first German state to introduce a copyright law, in 1806. Prussia promulgated such a law in 1837, four years after Rahel's death. But laws do not emerge out of nothing: the gradual legal shift suggests that writers' and readers' attitudes were evolving, as well.
20 Ronald V. Bettig, "Critical Perspectives on the History and Philosophy of Copyright," *Critical Studies in Mass Communication* 9, no. 2 (1992): 131–55 (138–9, 149–50).
21 Heinrich Bosse, *Autorschaft ist Werkherrschaft: Über die Entstehung des Urheberrechts aus dem Geist der Goethezeit*, new edn., with foreword by Wulf D. v. Lucius (Paderborn: Fink, 2014). Throughout this book, Bosse develops his contention that an author retains some rights when he sells a work, and that this system of author's rights underpins copyright law (see esp. 93).
22 See Jacob Norberg's summary of Bosse's arguments in his review essay on the second edition of *Autorschaft ist Werkherrschaft* and other works: "Authorship and Ownership," *German Studies Review* 39, no. 2 (2016): 353–63 (355). Peter Jaszi, too, considers how the Romantic concept of authorship is intertwined with the legal system. See "Toward a Theory of Copyright: the Metamorphosis of 'Authorship,'" *Duke Law Journal* 41 (1991): 455–502.

compose an essay for the *Morgenblatt*, clearly favoring Goethe in what Robert would later describe as "scharfen Phrasen" (critical phrases) (January 12, 1827, *ERLV*, II, 483). Robert does develop these ideas into a published article, even asking her to forward his review to Goethe if she liked it.[23] However, when Rahel reads the final version she is not completely satisfied, complaining in a letter of February 23, 1827 that he left out two "Wesentlichkeiten" (relevant points) and critiquing the article's general tone (February 23, 1827, *ERLV*, II, 497–8). She did, however, ask an actor going on tour to make Ottilie von Goethe aware of the review, thus demonstrating her overall agreement with the ideas Robert had articulated at her behest.[24]

In another case, when Robert is preparing a number of his literary verses for publication, she asks that in the poem cycle "Promenaden eines Berliners in seiner Vaterstadt" (Promenades of a Berliner in His Home City) her name be inserted into the following line: "Die *Schwester*, nannte mich oft so" (My *sister* often called me thus).[25] She tells her brother: "ich will auch genannt seyn! Es sind's weit schlechtere Leute und ich komme in Deinem Leben oft genug vor: so will ich auch in einem Gedicht stehn!" (*ERLV*, II, 436) (I also want to be named! Far worse people are named and I appear in your life often enough: thus I want to be in a poem as well!).

Indeed, the publishing relationship between Rahel and Robert did not work solely in one direction. In 1821, after Goethe's novel *Wilhelm Meisters Wanderjahre* (Wilhelm Meister's Journeyman Years) had appeared, the siblings discussed the book at length in their letters. On June 5, 1821 Rahel writes to her brother:

> so beginne ich doch wieder einen Neuen [Brief, L. D.] heute: und das blos wegen Göthens Wanderjahre dies ist ein großes Ewenement ... Je mehr Einer durch Gaben, Leben, und Denken bereitet ist, je mehr hat er an diesem [Buch] Werk: es selbst ist ein resumé aller Götheschen Werke: die selbst nichts anders sind als eben so viel geistige Gesichtspunkte, des ganzen irdischen Daseyns, [mit inbegriffen des Menschlichen] die Betrachtung über des Menschen Geist[s] mit inbegriffen.
> (June 5, 1821, *ERLV*, II, 346)

---

23 See *ERLV*, II, 487 and 496. The reprinted article can be found in Varnhagen von Ense, "*Ich will noch leben*," 187–94.
24 See *ERLV*, II, 855–6 n. 102 for the reference to Ottilie von Goethe. Feilchenfeldt and Steiner also read Rahel's comments on February 23 as evidence that she felt she was a co-author of Robert's published text. See *GW*, X, 79–80.
25 May 12, 1825, *ERLV*, II, 436.The published version reads: "Die Schwester Rahel nannte mich oft so" (*ERLV*, II, 820 n. 130).

> (so I begin yet another new [letter] today: and that simply on account of Goethe's *Wanderjahre* this is a great event ... the more one is prepared through gifts, life, and thinking, the more one can gain from this work: it itself is a summation of all Goethe's works, which are themselves nothing more than just so many intellectual perspectives, on the entire earthly existence, including the consideration of the human spirit.)

She continues for over two pages with insightful comments about the novel, concluding with the request that Robert write and send her a passage about the *Wanderjahre* for a collection she would like to publish. He complies with her request in his next letter, and Rahel later publishes the collection pseudonymously in the periodical *Der Gesellschafter; oder, Blätter für Geist und Herz* (The Conversationalist; or, Pages for Spirit and Heart).[26] This publication is but one piece of evidence that supports the view that Rahel, while she did not write "works" or publish openly, was well aware of the value of her ideas. Although she did not choose conventional genres for her writing, Rahel was nonetheless driven by the desire to give voice to her ideas outside of the system of professionalized publication.

Rahel as Ideal Reader

Despite the evidence that Rahel did at times contribute to Robert's journalistic writings, their projects cannot be defined as collaborative in the traditional sense. I have not found any instances where Rahel made direct contributions to Robert's plays or poetry, and even her contributions to his journalistic writing did not stem from an intention to co-author publications. Rather, the specific editorial interventions seem representative of an underlying relationship that, as documented in the letters, does fit the term collaborative. Over their lifetime, they shared ideas and contributed to each other's development.

The collaborative nature of Robert's relationship with his sister is also manifest in her role as his ideal reader. In Rahel, Robert knows he will always have a sympathetic audience, who can understand and appreciate his ideas and serve as a source of respected advice. We see this in 1825, when for the first time she attended a production of his play *Die Macht der Verhältnisse* (The Power of Circumstances), which had premiered over ten years earlier. In a letter of April 13, 1825 she praises the play's conversational tone, the structure of the scenes, and the characters and their portrayal. In his answering letter of April 22, he affirms:

---

26 The article is also reprinted in Varnhagen von Ense, *"Ich will noch leben,"* 76–98.

Außerordentlich ist Deine Auffassung meines Stückes und für mich um so belohnender, da ich wollte, daß der Kunstverständige gerade das in der Arbeit sehen sollte, was Du darin gesehen hast: die festvermauerte Folge der Scenen, die Sprache die aus den Begebenheiten hervorgeht und sie wieder aus sich hervorgehen läßt, die selbstbewußte Entsagung alles Zierraths und Verschmähung lyrischen Pomps, die Natürlichkeit der Theater-Coups—dies hinsichtlich der Form; und hinsichtlich des Stoffes: die große Tragödie unserer dicht neben uns an sich blähenden und selbst die Bessern beherrschende Nichtigkeit.
(April 22, 1825, *ERLV*, II, 426–7)
(Your view of my play is extraordinary and all the more rewarding for me since I wanted the connoisseur to see in the work exactly that which you saw: the firmly cemented sequence of scenes, the language that stems from the events and allows them to emerge from it anew, the self-confident renunciation of all ornamentation and the disdain for lyrical pomp, the naturalness of the *coups de théâtre*—this in light of the form; and in light of the material: the great tragedy of our nothingness, which puffs itself up right under our noses and rules even the elite.)

In this passage, Robert admits that his sister had perceived in the play exactly the structure and elements that he had hoped would be apparent. Although the topic here is a work that has already been completed, and thus would not be altered by Rahel's commentary, we are once again reminded that Rahel's critical voice, combined with a deep understanding of the theater, make her an invaluable reader of Robert's work.

In 1820, another example occurs that does affect, if not the composition of a text, at least the theater where Robert would attempt to place it. After writing a play entitled *Kassius und Phantasus; oder, Der Paradiesvogel* (Kassius and Phantasus; or, The Bird of Paradise), Robert sends it to his siblings in Berlin, with a request for their opinion. As he tells Rahel in a letter on January 8, 1820: "Ich schicke auch heute Ohme mein Stück. Lies es und zeige mir an, wo Longueurs sind, die nirgend so sehr, als im Lustspiel zu fürchten sind" (January 8, 1820, *ERLV*, II, 269) (I am also sending Ohme my play today. Read it and point out to me where there are extraneous passages, which are nowhere to be feared as much as in a comedy).[27] Rahel responds about a month later:

---

27 Ohme was the nickname of Rahel's and Robert's brother Marcus Theodor Robert-Tornow.

> Gestern las ich mit größter Aufmerksamkeit den Paradiesvogel Mich hat es unendlich unterhalten. Mir scheint das Stück auch kurtz, und in dieser Hinsicht gut zur Aufführung. Ob aber eine hiesige Direktion es nehmen kann ist die Frage. Der erste kleine Akt muß gewiß verkürtz werden; die andern kleinen sind gar nicht zu lang ... Gewiß werden sie auch viele Witze die da treffen könnten, und um die es sehr Schade wäre, weil das Ganze nur aus Solchen besteht, weglaßen wollen. Mir persönlich ist aufgefallen, daß der Jude eine zu große, ja einzige Rolle spielt; und daß man sich das in seinem Dialecte nicht möchte gefallen laßen.
>
> (February 8, 1820, *ERLV*, II, 270–1)
>
> (Yesterday I read the Bird of Paradise with the greatest attention. It entertained me to no end. The play even seemed short to me, and in this regard good for performance purposes. But the question is whether a local theater administration could take it on. The first short act must certainly be shortened; the other short ones are not too long at all ... Certainly they will want to leave out many jokes that could be relevant, which would be a pity, because the whole thing is composed of just such jokes. I personally noticed that the Jew plays a role too large, yes unique; and that one may not take kindly to the part in his dialect.)

Even though Rahel describes here her view of the play, she also informs Robert that she and her husband have made plans to get together with the families of her other two brothers for a dramatic reading of his work. Three days later she writes again, reporting:

> Gestern nämlich, nachdem wir es einzeln jeder für uns gelesen hatten, lasen wir es bey Ohme zusammen laut. Er, ich, die Frau die Kinder, V: [Varnhagen, L. D.]; Moriz hatte es bey sich gelesen, und war auch derselben Meinung: wir alle gleicher: jeder nach seiner Persönlichkeit nüancirt. *Ich* nämlich, glaube, in Wien, in Leipzig, auf einem Theater wo Einer wie Kaibel ist, *kann* es mit Abänderungen gegeben werden.
>
> (February 11, 1820, *ERLV*, II, 273)
>
> (Yesterday, namely, after each of us had read it for ourselves, we read it out loud at Ohme's house. He, I, his wife, the children, Varnhagen; Moritz had read it at home and was of the same opinion: we were all of the same opinion, each one nuanced according to his personality. *I* namely, believe it *can* be produced with some alterations in Vienna, in Leipzig, at a theater where there is someone like Kaibel.)[28]

---

28 Karl Ludwig Kaibel was a successful actor.

As she goes on to detail, she essentially thinks the anti-Jewish atmosphere in Berlin is currently too strong for the play, although she does like the work. In Robert's letter of thanks, he states:

> Ihr habt mich vollkommen überzeugt, daß das Stück in Berlin weder eingereicht, noch gegeben werden kann. Oder vielmehr, es *ist* bereits gegeben ausgepfiffen und in den Berliner Blättern rezensirt. Ihr seyd mir so wie Ihr da zusammen saßest, ein Mikroberlinischpublikum; was kann ich also von dem Makropublikum erwarten, wo noch oben ein übler vorbedachter Wille gegen mich nicht ausbleiben wird.
> (Mid-February 1820, *ERLV*, II, 277)
> (You have completely convinced me that the play can be neither submitted nor performed in Berlin. Or rather, it *has* already been performed, booed, and reviewed in the Berlin papers. You are for me, as you sat together there, a micro-Berlin audience; what can I therefore expect from the macro audience, where a negative prejudicial will against me will still not be lacking.)

Although he has faith that his play is a work of quality,[29] after receiving the reaction of his siblings, Robert decides not to send the play to the director of the Berlin theater. While not a direct collaboration, interactions such as this suggest how familial and social context could shape a writer's work.[30]

This type of group reading and discussion—what the Romantics might have called *Symphilosophieren*—seems to have been fairly widespread in Rahel's circle. In 1821, during an extended stay in Dresden, she writes a letter to her brother in which she describes a visit from their mutual friend Ludwig Tieck. First, Tieck's wife, Amalie, and a family friend came by for a half hour or so, and then Tieck himself joined them. Amalie Tieck and the friend left to call on someone else, but Tieck stayed for more than five hours and read the first third of his manuscript for *Der Aufruhr in den Cevennen: Eine Novelle in vier Abschitten* (The Rebellion in the Cevennes: A Novella in Four Sections) aloud to Rahel, Varnhagen, and another guest.[31] After describing her positive reaction to the project,

---

29 The play was later performed at least once each in Karlsruhe and Vienna, as Vigliero reports in *ERLV*, II, 738–9 n. 25.
30 Isselstein goes so far as to characterize the family's influence in this case as a kind of "Vorzensur" (pre-censorship). See Ursula Isselstein, "Emanzipation wovon und wofür? Das Beispiel der Familie Levin aus Berlin," in *Jüdinnen zwischen Tradition und Emanzipation*, ed. Norbert Altenhofer and Renate Heuer, *Jahrbuch des Archivs Bibliographia Judaica* 2/3 (1986/7) (Bad Soden: A. & V. Woywod, 1990), 80–113 (98).
31 Only the first two sections of *Der Aufruhr in den Cevennen* were published, in 1826.

Rahel particularly highlights that Tieck was seeking a critical response from his listeners: "Tiek war so glüklich als wir, solche Zuhörer und Beurtheiler zu haben. Er las es uns eigenst um auf Verfehltes aufmerksam gemacht zu werden" (October 12, 1821, *ERLV*, II, 366) (Tieck was as happy as we were to have such listeners and evaluators. He read it to us especially in order to be made aware of anything incongruous). In addition, Tieck relates that he had recently read the manuscript to other friends, and they not only didn't understand it, but *mis*understood it. From this we can glean that Rahel and her circle formed particularly critical, albeit appreciative, listeners.

To be sure, Rahel Levin Varnhagen, with her intellectual gifts and her wide circle of literary friends, may have been a unique example of an informed reader or listener. However, her experiences in providing feedback both to her brother and to Tieck sharply differentiate her from the more typical Romantic model of women as passive audience to male authors' texts. Rahel's example suggests a more nuanced model of literary interaction in which women played a role more critical than that of passive reader. In the next section we shall consider how such interaction shaped the identities of both Rahel and her brother.

German-Jewish identity

The Levin children were born into the Berlin Jewish community at a time when it did not yet have full civil rights but when it was beginning to transition into fuller membership in modern German society.[32] Despite her success as a salonnière, Rahel often lamented her status as a double outsider—a woman and a Jew. As a man, Robert may have enjoyed more freedoms, but he too struggled to establish himself in a social context that discriminated against those of Jewish origin. Faced with the dilemma of developing an identity in a culture that did not fully accept them, both Rahel and Robert turned to their interest in leading examples of German culture as a means of articulating shared beliefs and values. In a sense, then, the two siblings became collaborators in constructing themselves as intellectuals of Jewish heritage in a culture marked by an emerging sense of itself as a German nation.

The siblings' shared admiration for the German poet Johann Wolfgang von Goethe forms a recurring theme in their correspondence and

---

32 Steven M. Lowenstein points to the Haskalah, or Jewish Enlightenment, as well as changing economic patterns, as bringing reform to the Berlin Jewish community. Particularly sweeping changes, including the call for assimilation, began upon the death of Frederick II in 1786, meaning that the Levin siblings' youth would have witnessed the beginnings of such change. See Steven M. Lowenstein, *The Berlin Jewish Community: Enlightenment, Family, and Crisis, 1770–1830* (New York: Oxford University Press, 1994), 29–33, 43–54, 69–73.

was also foundational in their intellectual identities.³³ On the personal level, common admiration for a major author must certainly have strengthened their own bond. But as Silke Schlichtmann has suggested, many Jews of Rahel's generation identified with Goethe's work as a strategy to further a desired assimilation into secular German society.³⁴ As we have seen, one result of Robert's and Rahel's years-long discussion of Goethe's ideas was her edited collection of texts on Goethe's novel *Wilhelm Meisters Wanderjahre* that appeared in the *Gesellschafter* in 1821. Vigliero notes that Goethe later thanked Rahel for this publication in the *Morgenblatt* and in his journal *Über Kunst und Altertum* (On Art and Antiquity) (see *ERLV*, II, 779 n. 124). Goethe's reaction and the success of her project prompt Rahel to tell her brother in 1822 that she feels as if she has won the Order of the Black Eagle, the highest Prussian order. In the same letter, she continues: "Mein Leben ist an seine Adresse gelangt. Daß *dieser* Mann *erlebe* von seinen Zeitgenossen, daß er vergöttert, anerkannt, studirt, begriffen, mit dem einsichtigsten Herzen geliebt würde, war der Gipfel all meiner Erdenwünsche und Kommission!" (February 9, 1822, *ERLV*, II, 395) (My life has arrived at its address. That *this* man should *learn* from his contemporaries that he is idolized, recognized, studied, understood, loved with the most insightful heart, was the summit of all my earthly wishes and commission!).

---

33 Many scholars have discussed the influence of Goethe on Rahel's thought, including Käte Hamburger in her essay "Rahel und Goethe" (first published in 1968, the essay is reprinted in *GW*, X, 179–204) and Hannah Arendt throughout her biography of Rahel (see *Rahel Varnhagen: The Life of a Jewess*, ed. Liliane Weissberg, trans. Richard Winston and Clara Winston, 1st complete edn. [Baltimore, MD: Johns Hopkins University Press, 1997]). Barbara Hahn has analyzed not only how Rahel and other Jewish women of her generation read Goethe, but also their interactions with him. See in particular "Demarcations and Projections: Goethe in the Berlin Salons," in *Goethe in German-Jewish Culture*, ed. Klaus L. Berghahn and Jost Hermand (Rochester, NY: Camden House, 2001); "Goethe Lesen—über Goethe Schreiben: Briefe und Aufzeichnungen deutscher Jüdinnen um 1800," in *Lektüren und Brüche: Jüdische Frauen in Kultur, Politik und Wissenschaft*, ed. Mechthild M. Jansen and Ingeborg Nordmann (Königstein/Taurus: Helmer, 2000), 48–71; and "Mit Goethe im Bad. Begegnungen im Exterritorialen: Rahel Levin, Sara und Marianne Meyer," *Monatshefte* 92, no. 3 (2000): 336–50. Numerous references to the Weimar poet in the Rahel–Robert correspondence show that Robert shared his sister's enthusiasm for Goethe's work.
34 The thesis of Schlichtmann's essay is that Shakespeare played a role similar to that of Goethe in Rahel's thinking, but she first evaluates the significance of Goethe for Rahel and demonstrates how he, as representative of German culture, indirectly mediated Rahel's role in secular society. See Silke Schlichtmann, "Deutsch werden mit Tasso und Hamlet: Rahel Levin Varnhagens Goethe- und Shakespeare-Lektüren als Akkulturationsversuche," *Shakespeare-Jahrbuch* 141 (2005): 51–65 (54–7).

This juxtaposition of a sense that it was her destiny to admire Goethe ("mein Leben ist an seine Adresse gelangt") with the type of pride that winning a patriotic order would produce underscores Schlichtmann's point that study of a major cultural icon such as Goethe was linked to the process of assimilation. By establishing her reputation as an interpreter of the Weimar poet, Rahel in particular was able to create a secular, German intellectual identity for herself.

The way in which studying a German intellectual's ideas stems from a desire to assimilate becomes even clearer, I will argue, when one considers the two siblings' also very enthusiastic admiration for the philosopher Johann Gottlieb Fichte. In addition to his academic success, Fichte was also active as what today we might call a public intellectual, giving lectures on a variety of topics in Jena and Berlin. Many members of the Berlin Jewish community, including Rahel and Robert, eagerly engaged with the ideas Fichte presented in his lectures.[35] Fichte must have displayed considerable personal charisma in his public speaking, for Rahel frequently refers to him as an inspirational teacher. On February 3, 1807 she tells her brother that Fichte "hat mein bestes Herz herausgekehrt, befruchtet, in Ehe genommen; mir zugeschrieen 'Du bist nicht allein' und mit seinen gewaltigen Klauen im Kopf, die rohe Menge bezwungen, so bald sie sich nur stellt" (February 3, 1807, *ERLV*, II, 77) (enticed forth, pollinated, and accepted into marriage my best heart; called out to me "you are not alone" and, with the powerful claws in his head, conquered the coarse crowds as soon as they faced his challenge). Rahel's statement reveals not only that she felt Fichte's ideas helped her develop into her best self, but also that they made her feel part of a (German) community: "Du bist nicht allein."

In 1807–8 Fichte gave his famous public lectures *Reden an die deutsche Nation* (Addresses to the German Nation) in Berlin. These lectures seek to establish German uniqueness and to trace how individuals develop into members of the German community through education (*Erziehung*); as such, they are today often held to be the foundation of an aggressive form of German nationalism. Fichte argues that the German language, which he sees as stemming in an uninterrupted line from its origins, contains the symbolic and spiritual identity of the nation. In the fourth speech, he declares:

---

35 See Liliane Weissberg, "Kann ein Jude ein Romantiker sein?," in *Romantische Religiösität*, ed. Alexander von Bormann (Würzburg: Königshausen und Neumann, 2005), 265–83 (277). In her article, Weissberg argues that Fichte's lectures influenced Robert's and Rahel's patriotic feelings, and she interprets Robert's play *Die Tochter Jephthas* in light of such patriotism.

Es ist vom übersinnlichen Theile der Sprache die Rede, vom sinnlichen zunächst und unmittelbar gar nicht. Dieser übersinnliche Theil ist in einer immerfort lebendig gebliebenen Sprache sinnbildlich, zusammenfassend bei jedem Schritte das ganze des sinnlichen und geistigen, in der Sprache niedergelegten Lebens der Nation in vollendeter Einheit, um einen, ebenfalls nicht willkührlichen, sondern aus dem ganzen bisherigen Leben der Nation nothwendig hervorgehenden Begriff zu bezeichnen, aus welchem, und seiner Bezeichnung, ein scharfes Auge die ganze Bildungsgeschichte der Nation rückwärtsschreitend wieder müßte herstellen können.[36]

(Here we are directly concerned in the first place with the supersensuous and not the sensuous part of language. In a language that has remained continuously living this supersensuous part is symbolical; it summarises at every step the totality of the sensuous and spiritual life of the nation as it is embedded in language in perfect unity, in order to designate a concept that is likewise not arbitrary but necessarily goes forth from the entire previous life of the nation. From this concept and from its designation a keen eye, moving backwards, ought to be able to reconstruct the entire cultural history of the nation.)[37]

This link between linguistic and cultural history, however speculative, may have been attractive to Fichte's listeners in 1807, for it justified a pride in German cultural achievements directly after the French occupation of Prussia in 1806. It also helps to explain why the Levin siblings felt such great admiration for this particular philosopher, despite the fact that in other contexts he rejected equal rights for Jews and women. After all, both siblings had worked to perfect their German-language skills, and to develop their intellectual faculties, as a means of integrating into the society around them.

As residents of Berlin during the French occupation, Rahel and her brother would have been attracted to Fichte's emphasis on German cultural achievements. Several years later, in a letter to Varnhagen shortly after Fichte's untimely death at age fifty-one, Rahel lamented that the Wars of Liberation would conclude but Fichte would not be able to experience the rebuilding of the German nation. She writes:

---

36 Johann Gottlieb Fichte, *Reden an die deutsche Nation*, in *Gesamtausgabe der Bayerischen Akademie der Wissenschaften*, Vol. I.10, *Werke 1808–1812*, ed. Reinhard Lauth, *et al.* (Stuttgart-Bad Cannstatt: Frommann-Holzboog, 2005), 154.
37 Johann Gottlieb Fichte, *Addresses to the German Nation*, ed. with an introduction and notes by Gregory Moore (Cambridge: Cambridge University Press, 2008), 57.

Fichte konnte also nicht erleben, daß sich die Länder vom Krieg erholten, Zäune wieder aufgebaut würden, dem Bauer geholfen, den Gesetzen nachgeholfen, daß die Schulen sich wieder herstellten und füllten, daß gewitzigte Staatsleute ihnen von den Fürsten Schutz verschafften! daß Gesetze erfunden und ausgetheilt würden, daß die Denker frei, ohne den Augenblick zu schaden, sie Volk und Regenten zur Geistesprüfung vorlegen dürften; dies selbst ein Glück, zu aller Zukunft Glück!

(February 14, 1814, *BDA*, III, 69)

(And so Fichte was unable to experience the fact that states would recover from the war, fences would be rebuilt, the peasant would be helped, laws would be helped along; that schools would be reestablished and filled; that seasoned statesmen would obtain protection for them from the princes! that laws would be created and promulgated, that thinkers, without harming the moment, would be allowed freely to present them for intellectual testing to the people and the regents; this itself is a joy, a joy for the whole future!)

While this citation is not from the letters Rahel wrote to her brother, it nonetheless sheds light on the thoughts she shared with him. The emphasis in this passage is on the very real, concrete work—such as rebuilding fences—that took place in the wake of the war with France. But one very quickly realizes that she is speaking metaphorically of something far greater: the building of a modern culture as the German-speaking lands entered the nineteenth century. While not involved in nation building, both Rahel and her brother comment frequently on social issues in their writings. They may have seen parallels in the German attempt to rebuild their society following the war and their own attempts to participate in the developing intellectual community.

The Levin siblings' Jewish heritage, of course, formed a major part of their identities and required constant reflection as they evolved as German intellectuals. In contrast to many of Rahel's other correspondences, the letters she exchanged with Ludwig Robert have German-Jewish identity as a major theme, as scholars such as Heidi Thomann Tewarson, Liliane Weissberg, Consolina Vigliero, and Lothar Kahn have discussed.[38] Neither Rahel nor Robert participated in the organized

---

38 See Heidi Thomann Tewarson, "German-Jewish Identity in the Correspondence between Rahel Levin Varnhagen and her Brother, Ludwig Robert: Hopes and Realities of Emancipation 1780–1830," *Leo Baeck Institute Yearbook* 39, no. 1 (1994): 3–29; Weissberg, "Kann ein Jude Romantiker sein?"; Vigliero's afterword in *ERLV*, II, esp. 932; and Lothar Kahn, "Ludwig Robert: Rahel's Brother," *Leo Baeck Institute Yearbook* 18, no. 1 (1973): 185–99.

practice of Judaism, and both were baptized in their early forties. But clearly, the mere fact of being baptized did not erase their connection to Jewish culture. On the contrary, the question of their cultural background remains of utmost concern to them throughout their lives, making their correspondence into a private space in which they can wrestle with the intricacies of their German-Jewish identity.[39]

While neither correspondent views their Jewish background as a strictly negative condition, both of them frequently feel themselves to be at a social disadvantage because of it. Even at a young age, Robert was constantly aware of the fact of his Jewishness. In 1797, while working as an apprentice in Hamburg, Robert tells his sister: "*Du* weißt doch am besten wie einem Juden in der Geselschaft zu Muthe, und auch selbst dann, und vielleicht dann am mehrsten, wenn man für keinen, gemeinen, gehalten wird. Besonders konnte *ich* mißmütig werden, oder *ich* vielmehr gar nicht, da ich es schon war" (February 14, 1797 *ERLV*, II, 28) (*You* know best of all how a Jew in society feels: even then, and perhaps then most of all, when people do not think he is a common one. *I* especially could get bad-tempered, or rather *I* not at all, for I already felt that way). Despite the grammatical infelicity of this (no doubt quickly composed) private letter, the intent is clear: Robert as a Jew is always aware of his differentness in society—even when he is not treated as a "common" ("gemeinen") Jew—and this leads to a chronic state of feeling ill-tempered ("mißmütig").

Yet, both Rahel and Robert waited until shortly before their respective marriages to be baptized (which allowed them legally to marry their spouses): it does not seem that other personal or religious preferences motivated this choice. Following baptism, they both continued to feel affinity for members of the Jewish faith, and, in the case of the anti-Semitic Hep-Hep riots of 1819, outrage. Furthermore, both writers recognize that baptism is a complicated step. In May 1813, only about a year before her own baptism, Rahel writes to her brother about having met with their much older, well-respected cousin in Breslau. She tells Robert the two had discussed the baptism of Ferdinand, the son of Rahel's youngest brother Moritz: "Auch von der Taufe Ferdinands sprach er; nicht heftig; ich ganz ehrlich. Wenn man nur gejüdischt ist, meint er; taufen schadet nichts. Darauf sagte ich, man müsse nicht nur Religion haben, sondern die Religionen studirt haben: dies verstand er sehr gut—viel!" (May 12, 1813, *ERLV*, II, 113) (He also spoke of the baptism of Ferdinand; not

---

39 Even Lothar Kahn, who underscores the sincerity of Robert's conversion to Christianity ("Ludwig Robert," 191, 197), concedes that Robert's Jewish heritage continued to influence him throughout his life (198).

heatedly; I completely honestly. If one is only "jewished," he opined; baptism does not do any harm. At that I said, one must not only have religion, but rather have studied religions: this he understood very well—much!). In the German cultural context—in which converted Jews often found that they did not escape social prejudice even after the often difficult decision to change their religion—the phrase "baptism does not do any harm" may strike one as almost hilariously ironic. What the cousin clearly means here is that if one comes from a Jewish cultural background, the mere fact of baptism cannot erase this important part of a person's identity. Rahel takes an intellectual stance here, saying that "one has to have studied religions"—implying that the selection of one's religion is ideally a conscious choice following careful reflection.

Nonetheless, Robert seems to have a bit of trepidation when he tells Rahel in 1819 of his own decision to be baptized in preparation for his marriage:

> Aus unserer Individualität können wir nun ein Mal nicht heraus. Sey übrigens versichert, daß ich mir keine *Fremde* aufdringen oder anreden lasse; und wenn mir Glaube nothwendig ist, so sey überzeugt, daß es von jeher *mein* Bedürfniß war—Deine innere Demuth ist ja auch Glaube; und eben der echte ... Daß dieser Schritt und meine Liebe eine große Veründrung in mir hervorgebracht haben ist wahr; eben so wahr ist es, daß diese Veründrung nicht ohne Kampf bewirkt wurde—Der einzelne Mensch hat *auch* seine Geschichtsepochen.
> (Late March 1819, *ERLV*, II, 235–6)
> (We cannot escape our individuality once and for all. Rest assured, by the way, that I will not myself be forced or talked into a *foreign* one; and if faith is necessary to me, so be convinced that it has always been *my* need—your inner humility is also faith; and precisely the genuine one ... That this step and my love have brought forth a great change in me is true; it is just as true that this change did not come about without a struggle—The individual person *also* has his historical epochs.)

The reference to historical epochs makes it clear that for Robert, personal development was an ongoing struggle, part of the joint undertaking of becoming a German-Jewish intellectual that he shared with his sister. Following baptism, the work continued, for neither sibling suddenly became a conventional Christian. Instead, Robert could be very critical of people who claimed to be Christians without, in his opinion, truly acting morally.

Rahel's and Robert's struggles with what it meant to be an emancipated German Jew show them leaving the traditional Jewish community and entering a newer, modern world as baptized, middle-class, German intellectuals. While their discussions of Goethe, or Fichte, or German culture in general did not usually result in publications or other scholarly products, they demonstrate the extent to which their individual development was embedded in their familial context.[40] The correspondence between Ludwig Robert and his sister suggests a way of thinking and working that existed outside of the sphere of professionalized authorship. In his literary production, Robert moved with some success towards a newer, professionalized way of writing, but his *Symphilosophieren* with his sister clearly remained of vital importance to him. Rahel, although she began to publish excerpts from her letters in mid-life and would work with her husband to prepare many others for publication, continued to practice a form of intellectual production that is difficult to categorize using terms such as "professional" and "author."[41]

Conclusion

Rahel Levin Varnhagen's chosen genre consisted of personal letters, texts that are most often accorded value when the person who wrote them has done or written something else that is famous. Her work as a whole thus highlights the problem that the co-written *Morgenblatt* texts represent in miniature: that the writing process is long and complicated and that too often the prevailing model of the genius author discounts the contributions of female or marginalized writers. What gets lost when one ignores the voices of unpublished and unacknowledged collaborators?

Bettig (citing Arnold Hauser) reminds us that in ancient Greek oral culture, poets saw their work as a collective achievement.[42] This observation can help us better to understand the import of collaborative work, for collaboration is also often oral and thus ephemeral. In the case of Ludwig Robert, he most likely could have achieved professional success without his sister's input, but from their correspondence we can see that her support and inspiration were a lifelong part of his intellectual identity. In the case of Rahel Levin Varnhagen, the fact that scholarly interest in her writing remains alive today suggests

---

40 Ursula Isselstein argues that as Rahel and her brothers made the transition from the Jewish to the Christian world, they turned to their family for the support they felt was lacking in the broader community. See "Emanzipation," 92.
41 Clearly, Rahel shared the lack of access to the discourse of professionalism with most of the female writers of her age. See Kord, *Sich einen Namen machen*, 84.
42 Bettig, "Critical Perspectives," 134.

that she achieved lasting influence—on Robert and on many other conversation partners—despite working in a manner that is not considered canonical.

By expanding our view of ways of working to include collaborative patterns, we are creating a more nuanced picture of German Romanticism. While the other members of the Robert-Tornow family did not pursue intellectual careers, they remained active members of Rahel's cultural circle. We can glean a sense of their influence from a long letter of 1821, when Robert concludes a passage about the theater with the remark: "Wenn man mir doch einen Monathl Bericht über das Theater Berlins schreiben wollte; ich würde daraus einen Bf für das Morgenbl fabriziren. Es müßten aber zu diesem Berichte sämtliche Familienglieder Ihr Scherflein beitragen" (November 26, 1821, *ERLV*, II, 384) (If only someone wanted to write me a monthly report about the theater of Berlin; I would fabricate a letter for the *Morgenblatt* out of it. But all family members would have to make their small contribution to this report). To my knowledge, this project never came to fruition. But the image of three siblings in Berlin sending their collective opinions to a brother in Karlsruhe for publication in a national newspaper provides a hypothetical example of how *Symphilosophieren* could bear practical fruit.

The context in which Rahel Levin Varnhagen worked, marked by collaboration and in the absence of strict copyright laws, suggests a disavowal of the single-author model. Neither Rahel nor her brother experienced moral qualms about his claiming her work for his publication projects, while she herself insisted that her own texts be published without her name attached to them. Rahel's writings emerged from a gendered, non-capitalist means of production, and thus challenge common assumptions of intellectual ownership. For this reason, they are worthy of study, precisely because they suggest an alternative to the "genius" model of authorship.

Bibliography

Anon. [Ludwig Robert]. "Korrespondenz-Nachrichten." *Morgenblatt für gebildete Stände* 13, no. 27 (February 1, 1819): 107–8. Hathi Trust Digital Library. https://babel.hathitrust.org/cgi/pt?id=umn.31951001899530t;view=1up;seq=119 (accessed November 2, 2018).

Arendt, Hannah. *Rahel Varnhagen: The Life of a Jewess*. Ed. Liliane Weissberg, trans. Richard Winston and Clara Winston. 1st complete edn. Baltimore, MD: Johns Hopkins University Press, 1997.

Bettig, Ronald V. "Critical Perspectives on the History and Philosophy of Copyright." *Critical Studies in Mass Communication* 9, no. 2 (1992): 131–55.

Bosse, Heinrich. *Autorschaft ist Werkherrschaft: Über die Entstehung des Urheberrechts aus dem Geist der Goethezeit*. New edn., with foreword by Wulf D. v. Lucius. Paderborn: Fink, 2014.

Fichte, Johann Gottlieb. *Addresses to the German Nation*. Ed. with introduction and notes by Gregory Moore. Cambridge: Cambridge University Press, 2008.
Fichte, Johann Gottlieb. *Gesamtausgabe der Bayerischen Akademie der Wissenschaften*. Vol. I.10, *Werke 1808–1812*. Ed. Reinhard Lauth, et al. Stuttgart-Bad Cannstatt: Frommann-Holzboog, 2005.
Fuchs, Renata. "'Soll ein Weib wohl Bücher schreiben; Oder soll sie's lassen bleiben?': The Immediate Reception of Rahel Levin Varnhagen as a Public Figure." *Neophilologus* 98 (2014): 303–24.
Hahn, Barbara. *"Antworten Sie mir!" Rahel Levin Varnhagens Briefwechsel*. Basel: Stroemfeld/Roter Stern, 1990.
Hahn, Barbara. "Demarcations and Projections: Goethe in the Berlin Salons." In *Goethe in German-Jewish Culture*, ed. Klaus L. Berghahn and Jost Hermand, 31–43. Rochester, NY: Camden House, 2001.
Hahn, Barbara. "Goethe Lesen—über Goethe Schreiben: Briefe und Aufzeichnungen deutscher Jüdinnen um 1800." In *Lektüren und Brüche: Jüdische Frauen in Kultur, Politik und Wissenschaft*, ed. Mechthild M. Jansen and Ingeborg Nordmann, 48–71. Königstein/Taurus: Helmer, 2000.
Hahn, Barbara. "Mit Goethe im Bad. Begegnungen im Exterritorialen: Rahel Levin, Sara und Marianne Meyer." *Monatshefte* 92, no. 3 (2000): 336–50.
Hahn, Barbara and Ursula Isselstein, eds. *Rahel Levin Varnhagen: Die Wiederentdeckung einer Schriftstellerin. Zeitschrift für Literaturwissenschaft und Linguistik* 14. Göttingen: Vandenhoeck & Ruprecht, 1987.
Isselstein, Ursula. "Emanzipation wovon und wofür? Das Beispiel der Familie Levin aus Berlin." In *Jüdinnen zwischen Tradition und Emanzipation*, ed. Norbert Altenhofer and Renate Heuer, 80–113. *Jahrbuch des Archivs Bibliographia Judaica* 2/3 (1986/7). Bad Soden: A. & V. Woywod, 1990.
Isselstein, Ursula. "Rahels Schriften I: Karl August Varnhagens editorische Tätigkeit nach Dokumenten seines Archivs." In *Rahel Levin Varnhagen: Die Wiederentdeckung einer Schriftstellerin*, ed. Barbara Hahn and Ursula Isselstein, 16–36. *Zeitschrift für Literaturwissenschaft und Linguistik* 14. Göttingen: Vandenhoeck & Ruprecht, 1987.
Jaszi, Peter. "Toward a Theory of Copyright: The Metamorphosis of 'Authorship.'" *Duke Law Journal* 41 (1991): 455–502.
Kahn, Lothar. "Ludwig Robert, Rahel's Brother." *Leo Baeck Institute Yearbook* 18, no. 1 (1973): 185–99.
Kord, Susanne. *Sich einen Namen machen: Anonymität und weibliche Autorschaft 1700–1900*. Ergebnisse der Frauenforschung 41. Stuttgart: J. B. Metzler, 1996.
Lorenz, Dagmar C. G. *Keepers of the Motherland: German Texts by Jewish Women Authors*. Lincoln: University of Nebraska Press, 1997.
Lowenstein, Steven M. *The Berlin Jewish Community: Enlightenment, Family, and Crisis, 1770–1830*. New York: Oxford University Press, 1994.
Nitsche, Gunter. "Plagiat und Urheberrecht." In *Plagiat, Fälschung, Urheberrecht im interdisziplinären Blickfeld*, ed. Dietmar Goltschnigg, Charlotte Grollegg-Edler, and Patrizia Gruber, with contributions from Victoria Kumar, 77–88. Berlin: Erich Schmidt, 2013.
Norberg, Jacob. "Authorship and Ownership." Review of Heinrich Bosse, *Autorschaft ist Werkherrschaft: Über die Entstehung des Urheberrechts aus dem Geist der Goethezeit* (Paderborn: Fink, 2014) and other works. *German Studies Review* 39, no. 2 (2016): 353–63.

Sambursky, Miriam. "Ludwig Roberts Lebensgang." *Bulletin des Leo Baeck Instituts* (Neue Folge) 15, no. 52 (1976): 1–22.

Schlichtmann, Silke. "Deutsch werden mit Tasso und Hamlet: Rahel Levin Varnhagens Goethe- und Shakespeare-Lektüren als Akkulturationsversuche." *Shakespeare-Jahrbuch* 141 (2005): 51–65.

Tewarson, Heidi Thomann. "German-Jewish Identity in the Correspondence between Rahel Levin Varnhagen and her Brother, Ludwig Robert: Hopes and Realities of Emancipation 1780–1830." *Leo Baeck Institute Yearbook* 39, no. 1 (1994): 3–29.

Varnhagen, Rahel Levin. *Edition Rahel Levin Varnhagen.* Vol. II, *Briefwechsel mit Ludwig Robert.* Ed. Consolina Vigliero. Munich: C. H. Beck, 2001.

Varnhagen, Rahel Levin. *Rahel Bibliothek. Rahel Varnhagen: Gesammelte Werke.* Ed. Konrad Feilchenfeldt, Rahel E. Steiner, and Uwe Schweikert. Vol. X. Munich: Matthes & Seitz, 1983.

Varnhagen, Rahel Levin. *Rahel: Ein Buch des Andenkens für ihre Freunde.* Ed. Barbara Hahn. 6 vols. Göttingen: Wallstein, 2011.

Varnhagen von Ense, Rahel. *"Ich will noch leben, wenn man's liest": Journalistische Beiträge aus den Jahren 1812–1829.* Ed. Lieselotte Kinskofer. Forschung zum Junghegelianismus 5. Frankfurt am Main: Peter Lang, 2001.

Vigliero, Consolina. "'Mein lieber Schwester-Freund': Rahel und Ludwig Robert in ihren Briefen." In *Rahel Levin Varnhagen: Die Wiederentdeckung einer Schriftstellerin,* ed. Barbara Hahn and Ursula Isselstein, 47–55. *Zeitschrift für Literaturwissenschaft und Linguistik* 14. Göttingen: Vandenhoeck & Ruprecht, 1987.

Weissberg, Liliane. "Kann ein Jude Romantiker sein?" In *Romantische Religiösität,* ed. Alexander von Bormann, 265–83. Würzburg: Königshausen und Neumann, 2005.

Ten Reflexive Authorship in Bettina Brentano-von Arnim's *Die Günderode*
Narrative Disunity, Hölderlin, and Günderrode

Karen R. Daubert

An Enigmatic Author

An avid reader, salon host, correspondent, conversationalist, novelist, and "epistolary and dialogic strategist,"[1] Bettina Brentano-von Arnim (1785–1859) purposefully defied limitations unjustifiable to her mind.[2] Proving in her defiance of boundaries to be "somewhat vagabond-like," she had a wide circle of friends and correspondents.[3] As an informally educated widow, she wrote on public matters to King Friedrich Wilhelm IV of Prussia.[4] Brentano-von Arnim refused "false alternatives," not consenting "to be an ineffective outsider on the one

---

1   Wolfgang Bunzel, Kerstin Frei, and Mechtild M. Jansen, "Vorwort," in *"Mit List und ... Kühnheit ... Widerstand leisten": Bettine von Arnims sozialpolitisches Handeln zwischen Privatheit und Öffentlichkeit*, ed. Wolfgang Bunzel, Kerstin Frei, and Mechtild M. Jansen (Berlin: Saint Albin, 2010), 7–10 (9). All translations are mine unless otherwise noted.
2   Scholars have not formed a consensus around this writer's name, as a quick glance at secondary sources reveals. I follow Frederiksen and Goodman's precedent. See Elke P. Frederiksen and Katherine R. Goodman, eds., *Bettina Brentano-von Arnim: Gender and Politics* (Detroit: Wayne State University Press, 1995), 32 n. 2.
3   Hildegund Keul, "Brot teilen nach Recht und Gerechtigkeit: Bettine von Arnims 'Schwebe-Religion' und ihre sozial-politische Bedeutung," in Bunzel *et al.*, *"Mit List und ... Kühnheit,"* 77–90 (79).
4   "Ludwig Geiger's publication in 1902 of the correspondence between King Friedrich Wilhelm IV and Bettine von Arnim ... was the first work that altered the image of von Arnim as the naïve, emotional, childlike author of *Goethes Briefwechsel mit einem Kinde* (1835)." Edith Waldstein, *Bettine von Arnim and the Politics of Romantic Conversation* (Columbia, SC: Camden House, 1988), 3.

hand or a well-adjusted philistine on the other."⁵ She "emerges in a field of tension between existential contrasts. She presents herself simultaneously as in tune with nature and socially revolutionary, maternal and eccentric, steady and nimble."⁶ Spanning and connecting eras also, a young Bettina Brentano (especially via her correspondence in 1801–3 with her older brother Clemens Brentano) plays an observer role in early German Romanticism, while the mature writer Brentano-von Arnim, "celebrated by the Young Germany movement," contributes to keeping the flame of romantic tension burning into the second half of the nineteenth century.⁷

Brentano-von Arnim's epistolary novels have proved puzzling because of their radical inclusiveness (i.e., defiance of boundaries). *Goethes Briefwechsel mit einem Kinde* (Goethe's Correspondence with a Child, 1835), *Die Günderode* (Günderode, 1840), *Clemens Brentanos Frühlingskranz* (Clemens Brentano's Spring Wreath, 1844), and *Ilius Pamphilius und die Ambrosia* (Ilius Pamphilius and Ambrosia, 1848), while earning some fame, have in general frustrated "fact hunters" and irritated "judges of art."⁸ The former denounce her inexact presentation of historical documents and people, which are simultaneously incorporated into playful, ahistorical, and synthetic artworks. The latter decry her art as "too uncontrolled, too uncritical,"⁹ and produced by a "crazy and unique writing-machine" that produces "only wastepaper."¹⁰ The enigma that her writing poses is to a degree unsurprising, on account of her creative commitment to open and fluid works of art, as well as

---

5   Christa Wolf, "Your Next Life Begins Today: A Letter about Bettine," trans. Jan Van Heurck, in Frederiksen and Goodman, *Gender and Politics*, 35–67 (39).
6   Keul, "Brot teilen," 77. The quotation continues, "Ihr Leben und Schreiben verbindet Romantik und Religion, Mystik und Politik, Natur und Kunst ... Durch ihre Heirat gehört sie dem Adel an, setzt sich dann aber konsequent für die Armen und Marginalisierten ihrer Gesellschaft sowie für sozial-politische Veränderungen ein."
7   Keul, "Brot teilen," 77.
8   Ursula Liebertz-Grün, *Ordnung im Chaos: Studien zur Poetik der Bettine Brentano-von Arnim* (Heidelberg: Carl Winter, 1989), 2. See also Frederiksen and Goodman, *Gender and Politics*, 31: "The long, but sparse tradition of scholarship on Bettina Brentano-von Arnim has been plagued by its desire—and inability—to distinguish between 'reality' and 'fiction.'"
9   Bettina Brentano-von Arnim, *Bettine Brentano von Arnim: Aus meinem Leben*, collected with commentary by Dieter Kühn (Frankfurt am Main: Insel, 1982), cited in Liebertz-Grün, *Ordnung im Chaos*, 2.
10 Friedrich Kittler, "Writing into the Wind, Bettina," *Glyph* 7 (1980): 32–69 (35). Quoted by Patricia Anne Simpson, "Letters of Sufferance and Deliverance: The Correspondence of Bettina Brentano-von Arnim and Karoline von Günderrode," in Frederiksen and Goodman, *Gender and Politics*, 269.

to the as yet little analyzed originality and complexity of her texts. Pursuing a pioneering approach to literature and history, to memoir and elegy, Brentano-von Arnim presents past and future, fact and fiction, history and imagination, as inseparable, imbricated phenomena.

Following groundbreaking rediscovery work in the years 1969–80 by Ingeborg Drewitz, Gisela Dischner, and Christa Wolf,[11] a handful of studies appeared that shed light specifically on Brentano-von Arnim's novels; useful for my purposes are Edith Waldstein's 1988 *Bettine von Arnim and the Politics of Romantic Conversation* and Ursula Liebertz-Grün's 1989 *Ordnung im Chaos: Studien zur Poetik der Bettine Brentano-Von Arnim* (Order in Chaos: Studies on the Poetics of Bettine Brentano-von Arnim). Waldstein provides useful and thorough historical and bibliographic material, and situates the epistolary novels along a continuum between salon conversations and targeted political engagement, the latter including Brentano-von Arnim's conversational novels *Dies Buch gehört dem König* (The King's Book, 1843) and *Gespräche mit Dämonen* (Conversations with Daemons, 1852). Liebertz-Grün offers in-depth readings and textual analysis, emphasizing the artistry of Brentano-von Arnim's literary structures and the complexity of the works' thematic content. Further, Liebertz-Grün highlights Brentano-von Arnim's playful use of literary traditions and the usefulness of this play in eluding censorship and challenging her readers.

Die Günderode, in Liebertz-Grün's study, reveals productive tensions in a subtle and complex friendship; Waldstein sees the novel as "an experiment with a truly dialogic mode of perception and expression."[12] In this chapter, I analyze productive tensions in *Die Günderode* by focusing on telling moments of Brentano-von Arnim's purposeful narrative arrangements, with a special emphasis on the techniques she uses to create a model of authorship in which the authority of a single writer splits into unstable relationships among multiple entities that work together. My term for this model is reflexive authorship.[13] Reflexive authorship, although not functioning as a direct collaboration

---

11 Ingeborg Drewitz, *Bettina von Arnim: Romantik, Revolution, Utopie* (Düsseldorf: Diederichs, 1969); Gisela Dischner, *Bettina von Arnim: Eine weibliche Sozialbiographie aus dem 19. Jahrhundert* (Berlin: Wagenbach, 1978); Bettina Brentano-von Arnim, *Die Günderode: Briefroman*, ed. with an afterword by Christa Wolf (Leipzig: Insel, 1980).
12 Waldstein, *Bettine von Arnim*, 57.
13 Though mentions of "reflexive authorship" are not to be found, Malcolm Ashmore's *The Reflexive Thesis: Wrighting Sociology of Scientific Knowledge* (Chicago: University of Chicago Press, 1989) engages reflexivity in scholarly writing. Helen Swift, "The Ghost(s) of the Author(s) Past, Present, and Future: A Literary-Reflexive Perspective on Authorship in the Poems of Jean de Meun

in the traditional sense, facilitates an indirect collaborative interaction by incorporating multiple voices and by destabilizing the authorial voice. Traditional literary collaboration produces simulated, negotiated voices; Brentano-von Arnim's work offers an implicit theory of collaboration.

Disunity, Time, and Narrative

In *Die Günderode*, a complex system of unstable relationships comes to light through a variety of disunities. Brentano-von Arnim mines the potential of these disunities to ignite the effectiveness of textual personae and to ally them to each other. One disunity appears between Brentano-von Arnim and a persona of, we presume, her younger self, called in the text simply Bettine. Similarly, the Günderode of the title, appearing within the text most often as Karoline, is non-identical to the writer Karoline von Günderrode (1780–1806), who under the pseudonym Tian published two books of poetry and single works in periodicals during her lifetime. Brentano-von Arnim's choice to spell Günderode differently than the family's preferred Günderrode adds to the disunities. Among the allies she fashions for Bettine and Karoline, Brentano-von Arnim gives prominence to the figure Hölderlin, a split persona encompassing the well-known poet Friedrich Hölderlin (1770–1843) and a fictional Hölderlin.

The multiple entities at work in *Die Günderode*, disunited in themselves, are also fragmented among places and times. This feature is inherent in the division between the fictional perspectives of the personae Bettine, Karoline, and Hölderlin and the retrospective perspective of Brentano-von Arnim, writing in the Berlin of the 1830s as she looks back to social circles that she participated in around 1800 and to her friendship with Karoline von Günderrode in the Frankfurt am Main of 1802–6.[14] Brentano-von Arnim employs the ambiguity introduced by distance to create an unstable proximity connecting the figures of Bettine, Karoline, and Hölderlin.

Brentano-von Arnim creates in *Die Günderode* a time that is neither bound to external markers of chronology nor confined to an internal plot-driven or psychological sequence. In Bettine, she crafts an identity stemming directly from such an open temporal structure. In the conclusion to his *Temps et récit* (Time and Narrative, 1983–85), Paul Ricoeur

---

and Martin Le Franc," *Medium Aevum* 73, no. 2 (2004): 235–59, brings the intersection of reflexivity and intertextuality to light. Swift speaks of a "slippery polyphony" (244) that may encompass a writer's past and present voices as well as the "person of the author of a previous work" (235).

14 See Frederiksen and Goodman, *Gender and Politics*, 15; and Dischner, *Eine weibliche Sozialbiographie*, 61.

sums up in structural relationship to one another two of his fundamental concepts, "third time" and "narrative identity," which summary provides a reference point for Brentano-von Arnim's work.

> The mimetic activity of narrative may be schematically characterized as the invention of a third-time constructed [as] ... an interweaving of the respective referential intentions of history and fictional narrative ... The fragile offshoot issuing from the union of history and fiction is the assignment to an individual or a community of a specific identity that we can call their narrative identity.[15]

Ricoeur's structure, though meant to apply broadly in theory, sheds light on the specific model of reflexive authorship I am attributing to Brentano-von Arnim.

Ricoeur describes an interweaving of history and fiction into a third time whose offshoot, narrative identity, "rests on a temporal structure that conforms to the model of dynamic identity arising from the poetic composition of a narrative text."[16] The mimetic activity in *Die Günderode* interweaves history (real times, places, and people) and fiction (an independent depiction of imaginary interconnections) into unstable, dynamic interrelationships of poetic entities. *Die Günderode*'s personae Hölderlin and Karoline (and others) refer to historical individuals and represent reinvented textual figures. At the intersection of these disunities, a space opens for implied authorship, an activity performed collaboratively with Bettine. For Ricoeur, what is important about the framing temporal structure and its outcome narrative identity is that together "[t]hey constitute a meaningful constellation, without for all that forming a binding chain."[17] For Brentano-von Arnim, the freedom to create meaningful narrative identity motivates her commitment to an open, irreducible disunity.

Construction

Of Brentano-von Arnim's ingenious works, *Die Günderode*, in particular, seems to raise especially high obstacles to understanding: "There are few texts that are so difficult to decipher as *Günderode*."[18] For one thing, *Die Günderode*, with a subtitle of *Briefe aus den Jahren 1804–1806* (Letters

---

15 Paul Ricoeur, *Time and Narrative*, Vol. III, trans. Kathleen Blamey and David Pellauer (Chicago: University of Chicago Press, 1988), 245–6. My reading of Ricoeur is indebted to William C. Dowling's *Ricoeur on Time and Narrative: An Introduction to "Temps et récit"* (South Bend, IN: University of Notre Dame Press, 2011).
16 Ricoeur, *Time and Narrative*, 246.
17 Ricoeur, *Time and Narrative*, 274.
18 Liebertz-Grün, *Ordnung im Chaos*, 37.

from the Years 1804–1806), is indeed formed in part from redacted actual letters, constituting German literature's first published correspondence between two women. It is also the initiating moment in the publication history of Günderrode's letters. Owing to the socio-historical import of these facts, as well as to the fascinating light they shed on the transmission of correspondence, scholars are tempted to approach the book as an edition of letters in the service of history, memoir, or biography, rather than as the innovative text it is. Secondly, *Die Günderode* features a "free and equal" exchange and "reciprocal enrichment"[19] between Karoline and Bettine, which Bettine intentionally extends to other key figures—of special interest here, Hölderlin. Such reciprocity is absent in Brentano-von Arnim's other epistolary novels. Unlike the other fictionalized correspondences, *Die Günderode* cannot be read as an apotheosis; the power relationships are not clear. The novel's purpose, construction, and genre have posed questions from its publication to today.

The title persona of *Die Günderode* stands in a tradition of eponymous characters of well-known epistolary novels, among which we find Johann Wolfgang von Goethe's Werther and Hölderlin's Hyperion. Surprisingly, and in contrast to tradition, the book is not focused on the eponymous character, but is chiefly concerned with her correspondent, Bettine. Additionally, in Brentano-von Arnim's book, letter-writing is not a rhetorical device that serves to set out a linear story, as in *Die Leiden des jungen Werthers* (The Sufferings of Young Werther). Indeed, *Die Günderode* begins, continues, and ends *in medias res*; it has no plot, and no action-driven climax.[20] Its epistolary genre serves a formal purpose, that of foregrounding an intermediary space by means of a continuous oscillation between distance and connection.[21] The epistolary form ensures disunity of time and place.

Brentano-von Arnim constructs *Die Günderode* as an aggregate of many variously sized, interconnected parts, arranged at different levels. Most fundamentally, it takes the form of sixty letters (some short, some extensive, some with enclosures) divided into two volumes. The

---

19 Waldstein, *Bettine von Arnim*, 38, 56.
20 See also Frederiksen and Goodman, *Gender and Politics*, 26–7. In describing Brentano-von Arnim's approach to her works in general, they note her "tendency not to write *on* or *about* anything or anyone, without writing herself into the relationship. This is less an egoistic trait than a sign of moral responsibility, since it does not objectify the subject or establish a distance between subject and author ... It is not academic; Bettina Brentano-von Arnim always writes in media [*sic*] res."
21 On the genre's functions as mediator and as a bridge and/or barrier, and on the temporal polyvalence of epistolarity, see Janet G. Altman, *Epistolarity: Approaches to a Form* (Columbus: Ohio State University Press, 1982), especially Chapter 1, "Epistolary Mediation," 13–15, 42–3; also 129–41, 185–212.

whole that is formed from the letters could be pictured as an eccentrically designed puzzle, having "the structure of a picture puzzle made from little mosaic stones."[22] Or perhaps, to accommodate the varying sizes of the pieces, one could picture a stage-set constructed of expansive scaffolds containing in variously sized sections various characters and sub-settings.

Most prominent are the two core epistolary voices, Bettine and Karoline, who soliloquize, converse, and retell conversations that they have had with one another, as well as with others. Housed within other levels of scaffolding appear personae such as "Großmama" (grandmama), referring to Sophie von La Roche; Clemens, Gunda, and Melina (Clemens, Kunigunda, and Magdalena Brentano, siblings to Bettine); and Savigny, Nees, and St. Clair (Friedrich Carl von Savigny, Elisabetha Nees von Esenbeck, and Isaac von Sinclair, friends). In still other parts of the work's structure are found characters from dialogues by Günderrode (presented in the novel as conversations between Bettine and Karoline reworked into stylized, titled products).[23] One such dialogue features a teacher and a pupil, while "Wandel und Treue" (Change and Loyalty) presents Violet and Narcissus.

Haunting the labyrinth of names on the pages of *Die Günderode* are shadows of the historical persons referred to. It is difficult to approach this complex text without inadvertently conflating the characters and the historical persons. While there is no clear, bright line of separation, it is important to distinguish the majority of the text, in which we are dealing with Brentano-von Arnim's invention, from the external reference to historical writers such as Hölderlin and Günderrode and their works as mediated by other sources. Otherwise, we might conflate the knowledgeable, seasoned Brentano-von Arnim in her mid-fifties with the protected young teenager who was intimate with Karoline von Günderrode, thereby erasing the purposeful artistry of the former.

As she writes, Brentano-von Arnim puts into her characters' formulations verbatim quotations from extant letters or previously published, separately transmitted works, seamlessly followed by paraphrase of source material or entirely invented text. She treats in this manner letters, poems, and prose pieces by Günderrode, as well as parts of letters from other correspondences and quotations from other writers.[24] Brentano-von

---

22 Liebertz-Grün, *Ordnung im Chaos*, 37.
23 "Die Manen" and "Wandel und Treue" appeared in Günderrode's first book, *Gedichte und Phantasien* (1804).
24 The transmission of Günderrode's works is complex. The definitive edition to date is *Karoline von Günderrode: Sämtliche Werke und Ausgewählte Studien*, ed. Walter Morgenthaler (Frankfurt am Main: Stroemfeld/Roter Stern, 1990). Eleven of the fifteen works attributed to her in *Die Günderode* had been previously published in

Arnim neither documents the quotations from others, nor makes a differentiation between external sources and her own invention. Yet, she does not fuse the multiple voices; she performs an exploit of collaboration. *Die Günderode*'s (almost) ahistorical fluidity complements a structure in which disparate voices create together.

The work's use of historical, well-known names, its paraphrasing of previously published works and extant letters, and its aggregate structure result in a multiplication of voices. Brentano-von Arnim occasionally employs the subjunctive of indirect discourse as a technique not only to highlight the intentional profusion of voices but also to enact their disunities. In one such long passage, Bettine repeats to Karoline the words of a friend.[25] This retelling overlaps with Bettine's report of that friend repeating to Bettine the words of another mutual friend. The subjunctive mode remains throughout the passage, making clear that Bettine here is reporting other voices, yet also revealing slippage between speakers. The purport is passed on through a duet, then a trio. To the extent that "der dichtende Gott" (the poeticizing god [Härtl, II, 267]) and "der Geist [der] sich rhythmisch ausdrükken könne" (the mind that can express itself rhythmically [266]) add more parts, the multiple voices function chorally. In subjunctive passages and throughout the novel, the multiple entities co-creating *Die Günderode* pass narrative parts and thematic roles from one to another. Writer personae, readers of each, interlocutors, even dream figures take the stage.

Multiple voices working together in crafted, unstable relationships, combined with Brentano-von Arnim's refusal to reify utterances, writings, or moments, make *Die Günderode* radically open in form. "The most striking thing about this book is the easiest thing to overlook, because it is not explicitly formulated: the statement made by the book's structure."[26] The construction of *Die Günderode*, by giving visibility to disunities and multiplicities, directly contributes to Brentano-von Arnim's creation of reflexive authorship.

Gedichte und Phantasien and *Poetische Fragmente*. Of the other four, two are considered "Zweifelhaft" by Morgenthaler, and the other two he considers not Günderode's. No edition of collected letters of Günderrode has appeared. In order to obtain access to reliable editions of her letters, one must consult numerous publications. See Karen R. Daubert, "The Denouement of the Ideal: Genre as Philosophical Action in Hölderlin, Günderrode, and Kleist," PhD dissertation (Princeton University, 1998), Appendix I, "Sources of Günderrode's Letters," 238–9.

25 Bettina von-Arnim Brentano, *Bettine von Arnim: Werke*, on behalf of the Nationale Forschungs- und Gedenkstätten der klassischen deutschen Literatur in Weimar, Vol. II, *Die Günderode/Clemens Brentanos Frühlingskranz*, ed. Heinz Härtl (Berlin and Weimar: Aufbau, 1989), 265–9 (herafter Härtl).

26 Wolf, "A Letter about Bettine," 59.

Multiplicity

Brentano-von Arnim's construction of *Die Günderode* informs and is informed by thematic and figural multiplicities. Connected by the persona of Bettine, the figures Hölderlin and Karoline represent powerful poets, involuntary outsiders, and inspiring mentors. In the novel, Hölderlin and Karoline fragment into interrelated elements of a productive instability.

According to Bettine, Hölderlin is poet par excellence, poet as singer, and poet as intimate lover of language.[27] Karoline represents poet as crafter of language and poet as truth teller. As poets, the status assigned to each by Bettine could not be higher. Yet, through indistinct depictions of Hölderlin's illness and isolation in Homburg and Karoline's impoverished, unmarried seclusion in the *Damenstift* (home for gentlewomen), these cherished poets are beyond convenient, conventional accessibility. Through correspondence and reading, Bettine brings them close. With Karoline, Bettine exchanges poems and essays, as well as critiques of each, and together they create and hone ideas. Bettine adores reading Hölderlin; in her letters she cites and paraphrases the historical Hölderlin's *Hyperion*, lyric poems, and *Ödipus der Tyrann* (Oedipus Tyrannus).[28] Together highlighting an unconventionality that desires to mitigate social restrictions, and emphasizing an immersion in poetical and philosophical activity, Karoline and Hölderlin act as comrades to Bettine.

Brentano-von Arnim depicts Bettine writing multiple, interrelated tropes that evoke the novel's aggregate construction and suggest a platform for implicit collaboration. At one point early in *Die Günderode*, Brentano-von Arnim shows Bettine making rhetorical use of Plato's Academy—his circle of conversational mentorship in Attic Greece, inspired by Socrates. Each rhetorical role assigned by Bettine is flexible enough to figure pupil or teacher. Bettine writes to Karoline:

> Weißt Du was, Du bist der Platon ... und ich bin Deiner liebster Freund und Schüler Dion ... Es ist ein Glück—ein unermeßliches, zu großen heroischen Taten aufgefordert sein. Für meinen Platon, den großen Lehrer der Welt ... mit meinem Leben einstehen! Ja so will ich Dich nennen künftig, Platon! —und einen Schmeichelnamen will ich Dir geben, Schwan will ich Dir rufen, wie Dich Sokrates genannt hat, und Du ruf mir Dion.
>
> (Härtl, II, 43–4)

---

27 Bettine writes to Karoline of Hölderlin's relationship to language: "Er war mit ihr verbündet, sie hat ihm ihren heimlichsten, innigsten Reiz geschenkt ... So wahr! er muß die Sprache geküßt haben" (Härtl, II, 146–7). Simpson, in her "Letters of Sufferance," profiles the image of the kiss in *Die Günderode* (265–8).

28 Härtl outlines Brentano-von Arnim's use of Friedrich Hölderlin's texts (II, 849–53).

(You know, you are Plato ... and I am your dearest friend and pupil Dion. ... It is a stroke of luck—an inestimable one, to be called upon to do great heroic deeds. To defend my Plato, the great teacher of the world ... with my life! Yes, thus I intend in future to call you Plato! —and it's my wish that you have a pet name; I'll call you Swan, as Socrates named you, and you call me Dion.)

Within this context of dramatized friendship and self-sacrifice, Bettine's persona aligns first with Dion (pupil of Plato) and then with Socrates (teacher of Plato). Karoline is addressed as Plato (teacher of Dion) and as Swan (pupil of Socrates), introducing role exchanges and inverting hierarchy. Each persona represents complex disunities.

Moving from allusion to abstract speculation, Brentano-von Arnim has Bettine continue the passage by introducing additional slippages. "Ich denk, ob einer mit seinem eignen Geist reden kann?—Der Dämon des Sokrates, wo ist der geblieben?—Ich glaub jeder Mensch könnte einen Dämon haben, der mit ihm sprechen würde ... Was Du mir sagst, scheint mir auch vom Dämon durch Dich gemeldet" (Härtl, II, 53, 55) (I ponder whether one can converse with one's own mind? —The daemon of Socrates, where did he live?[29] I believe every person could have a daemon, who would speak with him. —Whatever you say to me appears to me also to be made known through you by the daemon). Bettine perceives Karoline as medium to a daemon. It's left ambiguous whose daemon is referred to at the end of the passage, Karoline's or Bettine's. Perhaps it is shared. As *Die Günderode* continues, Brentano-von Arnim develops such ambiguity, as well as an ambiguity embodied in the notion of semi-divinity.

At a highpoint of metaphysical speculation, Bettine repeats to Karoline a report of a Hölderlinian description portraying a disunity of art and life, of human and divine. "Einmal sagte Hölderlin, alles sei Rhythmus, das ganze Schicksal des Menschen sei *ein* himmlischer Rhythmus, wie auch jedes Kunstwerk ein einziger Rhythmus sei, und alles schwinge sich von den Dichterlippen des Gottes, und wo der Menschengeist dem sich füge, das seien die verklärten Schicksale, in denen der Genius sich zeige" (Härtl, II, 269; emphasis in original) (Once Hölderlin said all is rhythm, the entire destiny of a person is one heavenly rhythm, as also each work of art is its own rhythm, and all arch

---

[29] Bettine is referring to "Socrates' *daimonion*, the voice that prevented Socrates from engaging in certain courses of action from time to time." Alexander Nehamas, *The Art of Living: Socratic Reflection from Plato to Foucault* (Berkeley: University of California Press, 1998), 36.

from the poeticizing lips of the god, and wherever the human mind falls into line with that, those are the transfigured destinies in which genius show itself.) Rhythm, like Socrates' daemon, speaks human destiny. At the same time, rhythm, like the ambiguous daemon speaking from Karoline to Bettine, reveals human genius. It is as if divine poeticizing lips issue a coin of creation with two sides. Rhythm, here, could be seen as both teacher (poeticizing lips of god) and pupil (falling into line). Per Hölderlin (and Bettine), one's self, one's mind, daemon, or rhythm branches into shared teaching, learning, or speaking poetically. In asymmetrical yet somehow balanced relationships, it is these entities that together produce the aggregate narrative *Die Günderode*.[30]

Intellectual Reciprocity
Moving deeper into an exploration of the novel on a thematic level, we find Karoline in her first letter laying a foundation of collaborative common ground with Bettine. She observes that she finds "einen gewissen Zusammenhang" (a certain coherence [Härtl, II, 11]) between her own dreams and Bettine's expressed thoughts. This observation is further elaborated in an enclosed stylized dialogue between teacher and pupil, in which the teacher at one point describes a mechanism for productive disunity: "Ähnliche Gedanken verschiedener Menschen, auch wenn sie nie von einander wußten, ist in geistigem Sinn schon Verbindung" (II, 14)[31] (Similar thinking by distinct individuals, even if they never knew of each other, is in an intellectual sense already connection). This mechanism of connection recalls the inherent distance and defiant intimacy of a daemon. The possibility opens (perhaps in a third time interweaving

---

30 A constellation of concepts encompassing doubtful agency, teaching/learning, and semantic ambiguity has much to do with irony. Brentano-von Arnim frequently employs and alludes to irony (for example, by repeated references to Socrates). Her use of irony accounts for yet another source of the difficulty that her texts present, as well as affording a strong connection to early German Romanticism. Alexander Nehamas argues that irony is neither honesty (an easily decipherable rhetorician's trope) nor fraud (intentional deceptiveness), but rather leaves questions open. "Irony often communicates that only part of a picture is visible to an audience, but it does not always entail that the speaker sees the whole. Sometimes, it does not even imply that a whole picture exists. Uncertainty is intrinsic, of the essence" (Nehamas, *Art of Living*, 67). Brentano-von Arnim's irony works with the other elements of her style to support reflexive authorship.
31 The attributed text slightly reworked by Brentano-von Arnim differs from Günderrode's 1804 published work, entitled "Die Manen" (The Spirits), which has: "ein ähnlicher oder gleicher Gedanke in verschiedenen Köpfen, auch wenn sie nie von einander wußten, ist im geistigem Sinne schon eine Verbindung" (Günderrode, *Sämtliche Werke*, 1:33).

history and fictional narrative) for two such "verschiedene Menschen," Bettine and Hölderlin, or Karoline and Hölderlin, to work together as related entities. Brentano-von Arnim the writer thus has the poet/correspondent Karoline make assertions regarding a category of *Zusammenhang* or *Verbindung* that allows for a theoretical conversational context occurring outside of usual cultural conventions and societal structures.

Building on this, Brentano-von Arnim depicts a type of work, reflexive self-definition, that can be done through "connection in an intellectual sense." Its depiction unfolds as a complex set of tropes, beginning where Karoline posits an intentional sense of belonging (reminiscent of the iconic biblical story of Ruth), resulting in the freedom of an independently formed loyalty, which she calls "Fundamentaltreue" (foundational loyalty [Härtl, II, 35]). Karoline describes intentional, chosen loyalty as a dreamlike, habitual action that occurs "in der Zeiten Raum" (in a space [spanning] ages). This action—"uns da zu finden, einander die Hand zu bieten" (finding one another there, offering each other our hands [II, 36])—signifies reflexive self-definition. Via Karoline, Brentano-von Arnim takes this notion further, positing that cooperative, near-and-far loyalty supports mutually reinforcing independent life paths. "[Die Gewohnheit] wird den Baum der Treue in uns pflegen, daß er als selbständiges Leben von uns beiden ausgehe und stark werde" (II, 36) (That habitual action will nurture the tree of loyalty in us, so that as independent life it comes from us both and becomes strong). The tree of loyalty branches in analogy to the form of the Dion/Plato/Socrates allusion and shares the formal effect of the ambiguously shared daemon described by Bettine; it partakes of the unstable splitting of reflexivity. Mutually independent intent nurtures the tree, which in turn forks into reciprocal, independent efficacy.

Thematic threads of reciprocity appear throughout the correspondence.[32] At a high point in the novel, Bettine elucidates reciprocity as shared purpose. "Wir wollen nicht umsonst zusammengetroffen haben in dieser Welt—laß uns eine Religion stiften für die Menschheit ... Warum sollten wir nicht zusammen denken über das Wohl und Bedürfnis der Menschheit?" (Härtl, II, 162, 166) (We intend not to have met one another in this world in vain—let us establish a religion for humanity ... Why should we not think together about human welfare and needs?). The epistolary persona of Bettine articulates to her reader/correspondent a considered intention to collaborate by means of *zusammen denken*.

---

32 Writing to Karoline, for example, Bettine formulates in the context of a discussion of harmony "was unsere Sinne bewegt—zum Mitleben, Mitschaffen, das ist Leben, das ist Wollust—wirkend sein! ... daß du zur Entfaltung des Harmonienstroms mitwirken kannst" (Härtl, 115–16).

Bettine underlines the potential transformative efficacy of such mutual intent: "Aber ganz verstanden sein, das deucht mir die wahre alleinige Metamorphose, die einzige Himmelfahrt" (II, 158) (But to be completely understood, that seems to me the sole true metamorphosis, the only assumption into heaven). The intense reciprocity posited by Bettine is made possible by the fact that each thinker remains independent, removed from the other; like the tree of loyalty, each preserves disunity within collaboration.[33]

Further developing the concept of *zusammen denken* and reinforcing the essential distance needed for (mutual) self-definition, Karoline depicts her exchange with Bettine as an "Ineinandergreifen" (meshing together) that ought "uns auch frei machen von jeder kleinlichen Eigensucht, und wir sollten wie die Jüngliche, während sie nach dem Ziel laufen, nicht uns Zeit gönnen, an was anders zu denken, als im schwebenden Lauf auszuharren" (Härtl, II, 37) (also to make us independent from every petty selfishness, and we ought to be like youths who run to the finish line, and not allow ourselves time to think in the floating course of the race about anything else except holding out). Karoline imagines two athletes running in parallel towards a common goal, and as they run, experiencing a motivating indeterminacy, "im schwebenden Lauf." This image reinforces Bettine's notion of reciprocity as shared purpose, and it resonates with Bettine's proposed shorthand for the religion that she aspires to establish with Karoline, "unsere schwebende Religion" (our hovering religion [II, 181]), a religion functioning in indeterminacy.[34]

To these considerations of an indeterminacy that motivates, Brentano-von Arnim adds Hölderlin's voice (as recycled by Bettine and St. Clair) describing a reciprocal creative process. "Und nur die Poesie verwandle aus einem Leben ins andre, die freie nämlich ... Die Zäsur sei eben jener lebendige Schwebepunkt des Menschengeistes, auf dem der göttliche Strahl ruhe ... [U]nd diesen Augenblick müsse der Dichtergeist festhalten und müsse ganz offen, ohne Hinterhalt seines Charakters sich ihm hingeben" (Härtl, II, 268) (And only Poetry,

---

33 Brentano-von Arnim's "thinking together" anticipates Baier's investigation into "the commons of the mind" and her assertion that "right reason" is "reasoning together." Annette C. Baier, *The Commons of the Mind*, The Paul Carus Lecture Series 19 (Chicago: Open Court, 1997), 1, 19.

34 This irreducible religion, viewed both seriously and ironically in the correspondence, resurfaces as a vital notion in *Dies Buch gehört dem König* and remains integral in *Die Günderode*. Keul notes that the theme of "Religionsstiftung" is found also in Novalis and Schleiermacher, and remarks, "Nichts ist dem Schriftstellerin in Religionsfragen mehr zuwider als Unbeweglichkeit, Starrheit, ein Sich-Verschanzen hinter Mauern und Barrikaden" ("Brot teilen," 81).

namely unfettered Poetry, transforms from one life into another ... The caesura is exactly that lively hover point of the human mind, on which the divine beam rests ... And the poetic mind is obliged to hold onto that moment and is obliged to abandon itself to that moment without withholding its individuality). This process depends on indeterminacy, as "Begeisterung" (enthusiasm) brings the mind "ins Schwanken" (into fluctuation [II, 268]). Pointing to reciprocity in complementary ways, Bettine's "schwebende Religion," Karoline's "im schwebenden Lauf," and Hölderlin's "Schwebepunkt" work together.

Brentano-von Arnim seems to have discovered in her apprehension of Hölderlin what one Hölderlin interpreter characterizes as "a kind of thinking beyond antithesis—a responsiveness to the dimension that holds entities together and makes them graspable through the opposition that distinguishes them."[35] Metaphorically running in parallel towards the same goal, simultaneously holding on and letting go, the caesura (the rest, turning point) paradoxically demands activity and passivity; it connects. What for Hölderlin may be "an act of ascetic self-disowning"[36] is for the personae in *Die Günderode* an act of reflexive self-disowning. An interval between letters, an effort to remember or to understand, an uncommitted moment that can determine meter and meaning, these spaces in time provide an opportunity to think together.

Hölderlin and Günderrode

In Brentano-von Arnim's work, indirect interactions depicted within the narrative posit a mediated affinity between Karoline and Hölderlin. In this section, I will show that, by crafting in parallel two self-reported reader responses of Bettine's, positioned strategically, Brentano-von Arnim creates an implicit collaboration between Karoline and Hölderlin. Brentano-von Arnim frames each response (each of Bettine's readings) in a similar structure of curved trajectory, puts the diction of each in resonance with the other, and expresses the persona Bettine's worldview by weaving it into the legacies of the historical Günderrode and Hölderlin as reported in the correspondence. The protagonist and reader Bettine, as created by Brentano-von Arnim the survivor, provides a medium of reflexivity.

The following telling passage provides a preview of Bettine's two readings. It asserts the indestructible efficacy of intellectual reciprocity as it simultaneously asserts the significance of Hölderlin to Bettine's project.

---

35 Stanley Corngold, *Complex Pleasure: Forms of Feeling in German Literature* (Stanford: Stanford University Press, 1998), 60.
36 Corngold, *Complex Pleasure*, 74.

Vom Hölderlin hab ich auch erzählen hören, aber lauter Trauriges ... ach, auch er hat gesagt: *Wer mit ganzer Seele wirkt, irrt nie!* Ja, wer unzerstreut und mit ganzer Seele dabei wär, der könnte wohl Tote erwecken, drum will ich mich sammeln und an Dich denken, daß ich Dich mir wach erhalte, daß Du mir nicht stirbst.

(Härtl, II, 434–5)

(Of Hölderlin I have heard accounts, but all utterly lamentable ... Ah, it was he who said: *Whoever acts with heart and soul never errs!* Yes, he who would be undistracted, and present in heart and soul, could well wake the dead; that's why I intend to collect myself and think of you, so that I may keep you awake to me, so that for me you die not.)

Bettine pivots from the Hölderlin quotation[37]—*Wer mit ganzer Seele wirkt, irrt nie!*—to an interpretative application of these words bearing on her interdependence with Karoline. The semantic sequence that turns on "drum" (that's why) indicates between Hölderlin and Karoline "a certain coherence," albeit a speaking silence, effected through Bettine herself. It is unspoken (in Christa Wolf's words "not explicitly formulated"), yet opens a caesura for Bettina and for her implied readers.[38] This short passage figures Brentano-von Arnim's narrative strategy—her own version of Friedrich Schlegel's famous *Symphilosophie*—in microcosm.[39]

Brentano-von Arnim implements reflexive authorship also in the macrocosm of the novel's construction. The first strategically placed reader response comes to light in Volume I's centerpiece letter. Bettine describes to Karoline her intellectual and emotional engagement as she studies Hölderlin's *Ödipus der Tyrann*. Her "thinking together" with Hölderlin and empathy with Sophocles' tragic hero partake of the unstable multiplicity and productive disunity that define the novel.

---

37 Härtl notes a discrepancy between Brentano-von Armin's text and Hölderlin's *Hyperion*. "Hyperion in seinem zweiten Brief an Diotima im zweiten Band von Hölderlins Roman *Hyperion*: 'Wer nur mit ganzer Seele wirkt, irrt nie'" (II, 903 n. 434).

38 Wolf, "A Letter about Bettine," 59.

39 "Der synthetische Schriftsteller konstruiert und schafft sich einen Leser, wie er sein soll ... Er will keine bestimmte Wirkung auf ihn machen, sondern er tritt mit ihm in das heilige Verhältis der innigsten Symphilosophie oder Sympoesie." Friedrich Schlegel, *Charakteristiken und Kritiken I (1796–1801)*, ed. Hans Eichner, Vol. II, Part I of *Kritische Friedrich-Schlegel-Ausgabe, Kritische Neuausgabe*, ed. Ernst Behler, Jean J. Anstett, and Hans Eichner (Zürich: Thomas, 1967), 161.

[W]as erst im griechischen Dichter in seinen schärfsten Regungen durch den Geist zum Lichte trat und jetzt durch diesen schmerzlichen Übersetzer zum zweitenmal in die Muttersprache getragen, mit Schmerzen hineingetragen—dies Heiligtum des Wehtums—über den Dornenpfad trug er es, schmerzlich durchdrungen ... Und das nährt mich, stärkt mich ... [D]en Klaggesang, den sing ich abends auf dem Dach vom Taubenschlag aus dem Stegreif, und da weiß ich, daß auch ich von der Muse berührt bin and daß sie mich tröstet.

(Härtl, II, 147)

(What first came to light by means of a Greek poet's mind in its sharpest emotions and now is borne by this painful translator a second time into our mother tongue, borne across with pain—this relic of the realm of suffering—he carried it over a path of thorns, painfully permeated ... And it nurtures me, strengthens me. I sing the lament [of Oedipus] impromptu from the roof of the pigeon loft, and then I know that I, too, have been touched by the muse and that she comforts me.)

Brentano-von Arnim has Bettine repeat a form of *Schmerz* (pain) three times for emphasis. Through Bettine's creative participation, she connects Sophocles' depiction of pain with Hölderlin's empathetic translation. Then, at an intense and complex epistolary transition, Brentano-von Arnim places a subtle pivot, indicating an arc of interpretation. Bettine's distress turns to understanding, as adulation of Hölderlin's dedication in assimilating and translating anguish strengthens and inspires her. From a distance of displaced intimacy, Karoline's correspondent Bettine sings with Hölderlin, following a trajectory leading from a challenging reading experience, to despair, through an interpretative process, to a moment of "intelligibility dawning."[40] Brentano-von Arnim creates a multi-voiced, disunited disclosure via destabilization.

This interpretation of a "relic of the realm of suffering" mirrors the presentation of Bettine's reader response to the final letter attributed to Karoline. In *Die Günderode*, Karoline's farewell letter displaces both the end of the two women's friendship and the historical Karoline von Günderrode's suicide. At the time of her death, the third book of poetry by Tian, *Melete*, was ready for publication, but suppressed. Its deferred publication did not occur until 1906. Though not belonging to *Die Günderode*, these mournful contextual facts cannot be fully ignored by any reader of Brentano-von Arnim's *Goethes Briefwechsel mit*

---

40 Corngold, *Complex Pleasure*, 12.

einem Kinde—which directly addresses Günderrode's suicide—or anyone familiar with Karoline von Günderrode's biography. Brentano-von Arnim devises Karoline's farewell letter as a deferral; it casts a vague shadow of prophecy and defies clarity despite its tone of admonition.

Initiating the novel's elaborate and lengthy closing, Bettine's response indicates that she reads, even studies, Karoline's letter as she did Hölderlin's translation. Indeed, her reading is portrayed as a translation. Initially, Karoline's ambiguous letter, resigned in tone, causes Bettine to experience foreboding. "Dein Brief kam mir wie Nebel vor—ja, wie Nebel" (Härtl, II, 458) (Your letter seemed to me like fog—yes, like fog). Bettine then follows an eccentric interpretative process, involving accumulated displacements. First, she relies on memory, in this case remembering the deaths of each of her parents, when as a child she actively interpreted and processed her grief. Second, she shares the letter with a friend, introducing into her interpretation a conversational context. Ephraim, Bettine's instructor in Hebrew and mathematics and, like Hölderlin and Karoline, a mentor and an outsider, balances with the presence of face-to-face interaction the distances inherent in correspondence and reading.

Juxtaposing distance and proximity, Bettine fashions her own persona into an intermediary entity—indeed, a divine herald, a "Botschaft Gottes" (messenger of God [II, 460]). Bettine, as metaphorical translator between heaven and earth, taps into an ability to collaborate via correspondence with her poet-mentor. In interpreting Karoline's letter, Bettine moves beyond desolation and feels able to affirm the inspiration of her childhood, which she links directly to affirmation and joy in Karoline. The fog and confusion disappear, and she comes again to an intelligible disclosure. As Bettine created a multi-voiced interpretation through her active response to reading *Ödipus* in Hölderlin's translation, so through her active reading of Karoline's closing letter she effects productive intellectual reciprocity.

In the Volume I centerpiece passage above, Bettine uses the metaphor of a "Dornenpfad" (path of thorns) to indicate the writer's trials in translating heroic pain from Greek to German. In the Volume II farewell exchange, Karoline describes Bettine as active, not passive—her impetus "[n]icht Mitleid, sondern Energie" (not compassion, but energy). Bettine agrees, paraphrasing Karoline's observation, "Ich kann nicht teilnehmen, mich treibts, die Dornen aus dem Pfad zu reißen" (Härtl, II, 460) (I cannot share [someone's pain], I'm driven to tear the thorns from the path). Brentano-von Arnim connects the Volume I and Volume II passages with two images of thorny paths, whose resonance serves additionally to indicate Bettine's character development. Taking another's part not through sympathy but through being moved to positive action, Bettine models "foundational loyalty": intricately interdependent, yet retaining active, analytical distance.

Brentano-von Arnim employs for her depiction of indirect interaction between Karoline and Hölderlin the tools that the novel's correspondents have articulated: paradoxically near-and-far cooperation (*Fundamentaltreue*), thinking together at a distance (*zusammen denken*), and simultaneous epiphany and metamorphosis in spaces in and/or out of time (*Ineinandergreifen* and *Zäsur*). *Die Günderode* enacts a narrative third time through its idealized representation of the historical writers Günderrode and Hölderlin and their reader Bettine. Brentano-von Arnim establishes Karoline and Hölderlin as key reference points for the protagonist Bettine's journey of self-development. In crafting her book, she twines the representations of a direct relationship with Karoline and an indirect connection to Hölderlin, associating them within Bettine's fictionalized narrative identity.

Productive Disunity

Die Günderode is imbued with a prickly and non-transparent yet pervasive purposefulness. Brentano-von Arnim describes the character of her style as "herzhaft in die Dornen der Zeit zu greifen" (to reach heartily into the thorns of the age)[41] and "mit List und auch mit grader offner Kühnheit ... Widerstand leisten" (to resist with cunning and also with forthright, frank boldness).[42] It takes tenacity and tricky candor to create a dynamic, synthetic artwork informed by a philosophical inclination towards irreducibility.

The principal difficulty that *Die Günderode* poses stems directly from Brentano-von Arnim's rejection of conventional insistence on separations—whether past from present, internal from external, or immediate from mediated—in favor of productive disunity. Bold cunning provides dexterity to connect quotations, paraphrases, and original texts into an epistolary novel. *Die Günderode* emphasizes liminal forms—correspondence, translation, and conversation—and thereby ensures a mercurial flexibility, allowing a complementarity of voices and a radical openness. By design, the attribution of agency remains opaque throughout.

Die Günderode portrays multiple perspectives that interconnect along axes of disclosed affinity. Brentano-von Arnim's project moves the

---

41 Brentano von-Arnim, *Der Briefwechsel Bettine von Arnims mit den Brüdern Grimm 1838–1841*, ed. Hartwig Schultz (Frankfurt am Main: Insel, 1885), 77. Quoted by Keul, "Brot teilen," 78.
42 Brentano-von Arnim, *Briefwechsel mit den Brüdern Grimm*, 110. Quoted by Angela Thamm, "Heilsames Schreiben: Empathie, Strategie und politisches Handeln bei Bettine von Arnim geb. Brentano," in Bunzel *et al.*, "Mit List und ... Kühnheit," 139–54 (142).

separated writers Friedrich Hölderlin and Karoline von Günderrode into a circle of reciprocity. Without making sequential arguments about what their works may or may not have in common, her text itself illuminates the two writers' thinking together. Brentano-von Arnim's epistolary novel attends to the two historical poets' legacies, while simultaneously delineating previously cloudy connections that suggest similarities between the poetics of the two writers as well as an affinity between those similarities and the poetics and worldview posited through the character Bettine.

In *Die Günderode*, the model of the single-author genius passes through a prism. Through a sophisticated construction of intimacy through accumulated displacements, Hölderlin and Karoline remain remote yet within reach. Exploring radical alternatives to the inherited model, Brentano-von Arnim integrates the personae Hölderlin and Karoline into the character Bettine's perspective on and approach to the world. Brentano-von Arnim challenges normative views on authorship, documentary history, and literary transmission by means of reflexive authorship. *Die Günderode*'s theoretically based aggregate structure, its commitment to intellectual reciprocity, and its creation of indirect yet productive interactions work together to offer an implicit theory of collaboration.

Bibliography

Altman, Janet G. *Epistolarity: Approaches to a Form*. Columbus: Ohio State University Press, 1982.
Ashmore, Malcolm. *The Reflexive Thesis: Wrighting Sociology of Scientific Knowledge*. Chicago: University of Chicago Press, 1989.
Baier, Annette C. *The Commons of the Mind*. The Paul Carus Lecture Series 19. Chicago: Open Court, 1997.
Brentano von-Arnim, Bettina. *Bettine Brentano von Arnim: Aus meinem Leben*. Collected with commentary by Dieter Kühn. Frankfurt am Main: Insel, 1982.
Brentano von-Arnim, Bettina. *Bettine von Arnim und Friedrich Wilhelm IV: Ungedruckte Briefe und Aktenstücke*. Ed. Ludwig Geiger. Frankfurt am Main: Rütten und Loening, 1902.
Brentano von-Arnim, Bettina. *Bettine von Arnim: Werke*. On behalf of the Nationale Forschungs- und Gedenkstätten der klassischen deutschen Literatur in Weimar. Vol. II, *Die Günderode/Clemens Brentanos Frühlingskranz*. Ed. Heinz Härtl. Berlin and Weimar: Aufbau, 1989.
Brentano von-Arnim, Bettina. *Der Briefwechsel Bettine von Arnims mit den Brüdern Grimm 1838–1841*. Ed. Hartwig Schultz. Frankfurt am Main: Insel, 1985.
Brentano von-Arnim, Bettina. *Die Günderode: Briefroman*. Ed. with an afterword by Christa Wolf. Leipzig: Insel, 1980.
Bunzel, Wolfgang, Kerstin Frei, and Mechtild M. Jansen, eds. *"Mit List und ... Kühnheit ... Widerstand leisten": Bettine von Arnims sozialpolitisches Handeln zwischen Privatheit und Öffentlichkeit*. Berlin: Saint Albin, 2010.
Corngold, Stanley. *Complex Pleasure: Forms of Feeling in German Literature*. Stanford: Stanford University Press, 1998.
Daubert, Karen R. "The Denouement of the Ideal: Genre as Philosophical Action in Hölderlin, Günderrode, and Kleist." PhD dissertation. Princeton University, 1998.

Dischner, Gisela. *Bettina von Arnim: Eine weibliche Sozialbiographie aus dem 19. Jahrhundert.* Berlin: Wagenbach, 1978.
Dowling, William C. *Ricoeur on Time and Narrative: An Introduction to "Temps et récit."* South Bend, IN: University of Notre Dame Press, 2011.
Drewitz, Ingeborg. *Bettina von Arnim: Romantik, Revolution, Utopie.* Düsseldorf: Diederichs, 1969.
Frederiksen, Elke P. and Katherine R. Goodman, eds. *Bettina Brentano-von Arnim: Gender and Politics.* Detroit: Wayne State University Press, 1995.
Frederiksen, Elke P. and Katherine R. Goodman, eds. "Introduction." In *Bettina Brentano-von Arnim: Gender and Politics*, ed. Elke P. Frederiksen and Katherine R. Goodman, 11–34. Detroit: Wayne State University Press, 1995.
Günderrode, Karoline von. *Karoline von Günderrode: Sämtliche Werke und Ausgewählte Studien.* Ed. Walter Morgenthaler. Frankfurt am Main: Stroemfeld/Roter Stern, 1990.
Keul, Hildegund. "Brot teilen nach Recht und Gerechtigkeit: Bettine von Arnims 'Schwebe-Religion' und ihre sozial-politische Bedeutung." In *"Mit List und … Kühnheit … Widerstand leisten": Bettine von Arnims sozialpolitisches Handeln zwischen Privatheit und Öffentlichkeit*, ed. Wolfgang Bunzel, Kerstin Frei, and Mechtild M. Jansen, 77–90. Berlin: Saint Albin, 2010.
Kittler, Friedrich. "Writing into the Wind, Bettina." *Glyph* 7 (1980): 32–69.
Liebertz-Grün, Ursula. *Ordnung im Chaos: Studien zur Poetik der Bettine Brentano-von Arnim.* Heidelberg: Carl Winter, 1989.
Nehamas, Alexander. *The Art of Living: Socratic Reflection from Plato to Foucault.* Berkeley: University of California Press, 1998.
Ricoeur, Paul. *Time and Narrative.* Vol. III. Trans. Kathleen Blamey and David Pellauer. Chicago: University of Chicago Press, 1988.
Schlegel, Friedrich. *Charakteristiken und Kritiken I (1796–1801).* Ed. Hans Eichner. Vol. II, Part I of *Kritische Friedrich-Schlegel-Ausgabe, Kritische Neuausgabe*, ed. Ernst Behler, Jean J. Anstett, and Hans Eichner. Zürich: Thomas, 1967.
Seyhan, Azade. *Representation and Its Discontents: The Critical Legacy of German Romanticism.* Berkeley: University of California Press, 1992.
Simpson, Patricia Anne. "Letters of Sufferance and Deliverance: The Correspondence of Bettina Brentano-von Arnim and Karoline von Günderrode." In *Bettina Brentano-von Arnim: Gender and Politics*, ed. Elke P. Frederiksen and Katherine R. Goodman, 247–77. Detroit: Wayne State University Press, 1995.
Swift, Helen. "The Ghost(s) of the Author(s) Past, Present, and Future: A Literary-Reflexive Perspective on Authorship in the Poems of Jean de Meun and Martin Le Franc." *Medium Aevum* 73, no. 2 (2004): 235–59.
Thamm, Angela. "Heilsames Schreiben: Empathie, Strategie und politisches Handeln bei Bettine von Arnim geb. Brentano." In *"Mit List und … Kühnheit … Widerstand leisten": Bettine von Arnims sozialpolitisches Handeln zwischen Privatheit und Öffentlichkeit*, ed. Wolfgang Bunzel, Kerstin Frei, and Mechtild M. Jansen, 139–54. Berlin: Saint Albin, 2010.
Waldstein, Edith. *Bettine von Arnim and the Politics of Romantic Conversation.* Columbia, SC: Camden House, 1988.
Wolf, Christa. "Nun ja! Das nächste Leben geht aber heute an. Ein Brief über die Bettine." In Christa Wolf, *Lesen und Schreiben: Neue Sammlung*, 284–318. Darmstadt: Luchterhand, 1980.
Wolf, Christa. "Your Next Life Begins Today: A Letter about Bettine." Trans. Jan Van Heurck. In *Bettina Brentano-von Arnim: Gender and Politics*, ed. Elke P. Frederiksen and Katherine R. Goodman, 35–67. Detroit: Wayne State University Press, 1995.

Eleven "Where Words Are Not Enough"
Audience and Authorship in the Marriage Diaries of Robert and Clara Schumann

Brian Tucker

September 13, 1840 was an important day for Clara Schumann, née Wieck. Her first day of married life as well as her twenty-first birthday, it was the date on which she assumed the roles of both spouse and fully fledged adult. On this day, Robert inaugurated their marriage with a proposal—namely, that they would document their time together in a shared diary.[1] They maintained this jointly written marriage diary over several years, through several notebooks. Although first written for the couple's private use, the diary today offers a model that challenges received notions of audience and authorship.

Robert outlines in the first, quasi-contractual entry a detailed vision for the diary's format and composition. As he explains, they will work on the diary separately, taking turns, each for a week at a time. At the end of each week, one spouse will present the diary to the other to read and begin the next entry. A meticulous recorder of everyday life even before the marriage, Robert describes its purpose, writing, "es soll ein Tagebuch werden über Alles, was uns gemeinsam berührt in unserem Haus- und Ehestand; unsre Wünsche, unsre Hoffnungen sollen darin aufgezeichnet werden" (it shall be a diary about everything that touches us mutually in our household and marriage; our wishes, our hopes shall be recorded therein).[2] The Schumanns' marriage diary was thus

---

1 A critical edition of the Schumanns' marriage diaries was first made available in 1987, and an English translation followed in 1993. See Robert Schumann, *Tagebücher*, ed. Gerd Nauhaus (Leipzig: Deutscher Verlag für Musik, 1987); and *The Marriage Diaries of Robert and Clara Schumann*, ed. Gerd Nauhaus, trans. Peter Ostwald (Boston, MA: Northeastern University Press, 1993). I refer throughout to the Ostwald translation, and on the few occasions where I have substituted my own wording, the emendations are indicated in the text with brackets.
2 Schumann, *Tagebücher*, II, 99; Schumann and Schumann, *Marriage Diaries*, 3.

intended to fulfill a fairly typical role, to register the events of their lives, as well as their plans and hopes for the future. But it is clear from the outset that this collaborative endeavor was also meant to have a novel, dialogic function within the marriage. Robert writes, "auch soll es sein ein Büchlein der Bitten, die wir an einander zu richten haben, wo das Wort nicht ausreicht; auch eines der Vermittlung und Versöhnung … kurz ein guter wahrer Freund soll es uns sein, dem wir Alles vertrauen" (it should also be a little book of requests that we direct toward one another [where words are not enough]; also one of mediation and reconciliation … in short, it shall be our good, true friend, to whom we entrust everything).[3] When Robert notes the insufficiency of language in this passage, he imagines a limit to the efficacy of spoken words and face-to-face conversation. In these instances, the diary will step in as an intermediary and supplemental form of communication. He imagines the diary as a beloved, mutual friend, one with whom he will be able to share the things that he cannot say to his wife directly. Clara agrees and indicates that she accepts the project's terms by countersigning this first entry.

Robert uses the word *Tagebuch* (diary) to describe their jointly written text, and there is probably no better term for a private book comprising a series of dated entries about one's own life. Sidonie Smith and Julia Watson define the diary as a "form of periodic life writing" that "records dailiness in accounts and observations of emotional responses."[4] Indeed, many aspects of the Schumanns' collaborative life writing—its stated beginning, its dated entries, its discontinuity and selectivity—conform to the most common genre conventions of the diary.[5] And yet, at the same time, one already sees from these initial passages that the Schumanns' co-authored text is not a typical example of a diary. It begins with a different structure, a different purpose, and a different audience.

If the marriage diaries have often served as a window onto the Schumanns' personal life, or as a document of Robert Schumann's fluctuating

---

3   Schumann, *Tagebücher*, II, 99; Schumann and Schumann, *Marriage Diaries*, 3.
4   Sidonie Smith and Julia Watson, *Reading Autobiography: A Guide for Interpreting Life Narratives* (Minneapolis: University of Minnesota Press, 2001), 193. In the same discussion, Smith and Watson note that some scholars differentiate diary and journal through the fact that diaries are more private and intimate, whereas journals are more public. Without subscribing to this distinction, I follow the standard translation of *Ehetagebücher* as "marriage diaries" and use the term "diary" throughout this essay.
5   On the nature of diaries, see further Philippe Lejeune, *On Diary*, ed. Jeremy Popkin and Julie Rak, trans. Katherine Durnin (Manoa: University of Hawai'i Press, 2009), especially the section "Theory," 147–210; and Peter Heehs, *Writing the Self: Diaries, Memoirs, and the History of the Self* (New York: Bloomsbury, 2013), 6–9.

mental state, to tell the story of a mad artistic genius in the mold of Hölderlin or Baudelaire, in this chapter I aim to approach the diaries from a different angle, as an unusual embodiment of collaborative writing and an example of male–female co-authorship in the late Romantic era.[6] Simply by being the product of two authors, their writing departs from the standard form of the diary, which is perhaps the most personal and intimate form of life writing and the mode most clearly tied to a singular narrative self or "I." What happens when the "I" of the diary's narrative voice is split over two selves? In what ways does a dialogic diary differ from those with a single narrative voice and an audience of one? Answering such questions reveals how the Schumanns' collaborative project challenges and undermines the conventions of diary writing. At the same time, the marriage diaries also evince an unusual model of shared authorship, one that is ultimately quite different from the work of two people producing together a text for publication or a broader audience.[7]

Forms of life writing, including published autobiographies, as well as private journals and diaries, bring to the fore the relationship of the self to language. Beginning perhaps with post-structural approaches of the late twentieth century, scholars have questioned the received wisdom that an autobiographical text such as a diary is necessarily the

---

[6] Few studies are devoted exclusively to the marriage diaries, though all the biographical works cited here rely on the Schumanns' diaries as primary documents. One early and important example of the tendency to read the diaries as evidence of Robert Schumann's mental condition is Peter Ostwald, *Schumann: The Inner Voices of a Musical Genius* (Boston, MA: Northeastern University Press, 1985). See further John O'Shea, who discusses the Schumanns' marital issues as well as the possibility that Robert suffered from syphilis, bipolar disorder, or even schizophrenia. John O'Shea, *Music and Medicine: Medical Profiles of Great Composers* (London: J. M. Dent, 1990), 124–39. Norman Currie, who also views Robert Schumann's mental health through the lens of his diaries and letters, sees an artist who was able to function at a high level until the final stages of his illness. Norman Currie, "Another Perspective on Robert Schumann's Personality," *Journal of Musicological Research* 30 (2011): 131–63.

[7] One might object that, because the Schumanns never intended to distribute or publish their diaries, their writing does not qualify as true authorship. Indeed, Michel Foucault's canonical essay "What Is an Author?" suggests by analogy that a private text such as a diary would not be characterized by an "author function": "A private letter may well have a signer—it does not have an author." Michel Foucault, "What Is an Author?," in *Aesthetics, Method, and Epistemology*, ed. James D. Faubion, trans. Robert Hurley et al. (New York: New Press, 1998), 205–22 (211). I nonetheless describe the marriage diaries in terms of authorship and author function. Though they began as private documents, Clara preserved the diaries throughout her life, and the Schumanns clearly saw themselves as writing not only for each other but for posterity as well.

product of a unified, coherent self. Reversing the direction of cause and effect, they suggest instead that the act of writing constructs the sense of a coherent self. Paul de Man asks in this vein, "We assume that life *produces* the autobiography as an act produces its consequences, but can we not suggest, with equal justice, that the autobiographical project may itself produce and determine the life … ?"[8] Paul Eakin revisits this passage in an insightful reflection on self-invention in writing. Returning to the question of whether the self precedes language or vice versa, Eakin avoids the typically dichotomous responses, preferring instead "to conceptualize the relation between the self and language as a mutually constituting interdependency."[9] This sense of interdependency is what ultimately makes the Schumanns' marriage diary a rich case study in collaborative writing. If a typical diary can be seen as an attempt to invent a version of the self in language, to depict life and shape it at the same time, then the Schumanns' collaborative marriage diary is also, in an important sense, an attempt to invent their marriage through the act of writing. Following de Man, we might say not only that the beginning of the Schumanns' joint diary coincides with the first day of their marriage, but also that their marriage truly begins with the opening of the diary. With its joint authorship and dual audience, the Schumanns' diary both reflects the nature of their shared life and attempts to fashion that shared life according to their needs and ambitions.

In many ways, we recognize the Schumann's marriage diaries as belonging comfortably to the history of the personal diary, whose origin Philippe Lejeune traces to late-eighteenth-century Europe. By keeping a diary, the Schumanns participate in a form of private, personal life writing that had gained widespread popularity within the previous century. Lejeune defines the diary as "a series of dated traces" and argues that "the diary begins when traces in a series attempt to capture the movement of time."[10] The salient features of the marriage diaries accord with this definition. For Lejeune, dating the entries and thereby

---

8 Paul de Man, *The Rhetoric of Romanticism* (New York: Columbia University Press, 1984), 69.

9 Paul Eakin, *Fictions in Autobiography: Studies in the Art of Self-Invention* (Princeton: Princeton University Press, 1985), 8. The discussion of de Man's take on autobiography comes in Chapter 4, "Self-Invention in Autobiography: The Moment of Language," 185–7. On the interdependency of self and language, see further Margo Culley, who writes that, "the persona in the pages of the diary shapes the life lived as well as the reverse." Margo Culley, "Introduction to *A Day at a Time: Diary Literature of American Women, from 1764 to 1985*," in *Women, Autobiography, Theory: A Reader*, ed. Sidonie Smith and Julia Watson (Madison: University of Wisconsin Press, 1998), 217–21 (219).

10 Lejeune, *On Diary*, 179.

marking the time of writing is an essential aspect of a personal diary, and the Schumanns are careful to date each entry, not only with the calendar date but also, at least through the first year, with the number of weeks of married life. The ordinal numbering of weeks indicates clearly not only that these entries are dated, but also that they exist within a series of documents that aim to register the passage of time.

The marriage diaries are furthermore typical in that they are often redundant and selective. The entries are usually restricted to a few facets of the Schumanns' lives, mostly to their social life and the visitors with whom they interact, as well as to concerts and other musical events.[11] Like many personal diaries, the Schumanns' marriage diaries record the mundane aspects of daily life, even if in their case dinner guests might well include the likes of Felix Mendelssohn or Franz Liszt.

In other ways, though, the Schumanns' diary project differs from a conventional personal diary. I have already suggested that the dialogic element leads to a different model of writing; in addition, as a joint venture, the marriage diaries depart from conventional ideas of audience as well. A diary typically has only one audience: oneself, the author who is both writer and reader. In this sense Lejeune characterizes the rise of the personal diary as an inward or solipsistic turn. He describes a radical turning point: everyone communicated happily with friends and family "up until the day when people realized they could do it without others." Diary writing, he says, is "the incredible idea of taking a sheet of paper to write to no one, to write to oneself, to write the self."[12] On this view, the diary is primarily a monologue, or at best, a solipsistic dialogue—a present self recording experiences for the benefit of a future self. In fact, Lejeune is so committed to the diary's function as a replacement for human interaction that he suggests the return of a human audience would eliminate the necessity of the diary (or the self) as audience. He writes, "The 'end' of a diary can come simply because this problem has been resolved: you meet a person with whom you can talk or with whom you can write," and he imagines a young woman who gives up her diary once she meets her future husband.[13] Of course, the example of the Schumanns, who initiate a diary at the outset of their marriage, contradicts this hypothesis. Here, securing an audience for

---

11 In a typical entry from November 1840, for instance, Clara writes, "*Sonnabend d. 21* machten wir *Theresen* [Schumann] unseren Gegenbesuch. Sie scheint glücklich zu sein, und ist ihr nicht zu verdenken.... Der *Sonntag d. 22*, war ein unruhvoller Tag, wie immer der Tag, wo man Tischgäste hat, wenn es auch noch so einfach ist" (Schumann, *Tagebücher*, II, 126).
12 Lejeune, *On Diary*, 335.
13 Lejeune, *On Diary*, 194.

one's thoughts and feelings does not render the personal diary obsolete. On the contrary, the marriage union becomes a point of departure for a new kind of diary that builds in the life partner as audience and in turn shapes the very relationship it depicts.

With its two writers (and readers), the Schumanns' marriage diary thus turns the established notion of the diary's audience on its head. The diary, in their hands, is no longer a letter addressed to no one, or to a future version of oneself, and meant to be read decades later. From the outset, Robert and Clara Schumann address their entries to each other, with the expectation that what they write will be read by the other person after just a few days. David Ferris observes that the marriage diary's "hybrid nature" makes it "not so much a private diary as a mode of communication between husband and wife."[14] In fact, Robert begins the diary by addressing the initial entry to "My dearly beloved young wife," and then goes on to explain the format of a diary intended to facilitate communication when spoken words alone will not suffice.[15] If the written word typically allows an author to communicate in spite of distance, spatial or temporal, here the Schumanns turn to writing in spite of proximity. Unlike other forms of writing—unlike letters for instance—their marriage diary is not meant to replace an absent voice. Instead, it supplements face-to-face communication; it does and says what the voice alone cannot. Nancy Reich points out that, "For the Schumanns ... such a venture was particularly apt, since both had difficulty expressing their feelings in speech."[16] In other words, Robert apparently had good reason to believe that face-to-face conversation alone would not suffice, and the shared diary provides a textual supplement to their reticence in speaking.

Of course, the entries also give the impression that, although neither spouse is often away from home, Robert's voice is nonetheless absent when he is immersed in composing. Two months into their marriage, Clara closes an entry, writing, "Du mußt mir schon manchmal ein kleines schriftliches Gespräch mit Dir erlauben, denn, ich kann Dich den ganzen Tag über nicht viel habhaft werden" (occasionally you must let me have a little written conversation with you, because during the whole day I can't get ahold of you often enough).[17]

---

14 David Ferris, "The Fictional Lives of the Schumanns," in *Rethinking Schumann*, ed. Roe-Min Kok and Laura Tunbridge (Oxford: Oxford University Press, 2011), 357–94 (366).
15 Schumann, *Tagebücher*, II, 99; Schumann and Schumann, *Marriage Diaries*, 3.
16 Nancy Reich, *Clara Schumann: The Artist and the Woman* (Ithaca, NY: Cornell University Press, 2001), 80.
17 Schumann, *Tagebücher*, II, 121; Schumann and Schumann, *Marriage Diaries*, 29–30.

The passage captures succinctly the diary's function in this relationship as a supplement to speaking in person. Although the formulation "written conversation" sounds contradictory, Clara uses the diary for precisely this purpose, to convey her thoughts and feelings to Robert when she does not want to interrupt his work with a face-to-face conversation.

This dialogic function—this conviction that they are writing for each other—is evident throughout the marriage diaries. Many of the entries begin and conclude with notes of affection explicitly addressed to the other person. Moreover, Robert imagined the diary as a way to present requests to each other, and Clara uses it to do just that. An apparent point of tension early in their marriage was deciding how much to travel in support of Clara's career as a concert pianist. Perhaps it was a difficult topic to discuss, or maybe their conversations had hit a dead end, but Clara repeatedly turns to the diary to create a workable arrangement for their shared life. She first mentions Robert in the third person but then shifts to address him in the first person: "Könnte ich nur den Robert bewegen mit mir nach Holland und Belgien zu reisen, damit ich doch nächsten Winter benutze … Ueberlege es Dir doch noch einmal, mein lieber Mann!" (If only I could persuade Robert to travel with me to Holland and Belgium, so that use can be made of next winter … Think it over [once again], my dear husband!)[18] One sees here the slippage from one kind of diary writing to another. The thought begins in the mode of classic diary writing, with Clara pouring out her frustration to the page, to herself, or to no one in particular. But she knows that Robert is the entry's actual audience and that he will be reading these words, and in the next sentence, she addresses him directly with her request. The diary thus serves as a kind of mediator as Clara and Robert invent a way to balance their dual careers.

The marriage diaries furthermore function as a dialogue in that the entries occasionally respond to each other and create the sense of a conversation. When Robert feels unable to produce new music, Clara confesses to the diary, "Daß Robert meint, jetzt Nichts schaffen zu können, und dies ihn schwermütig stimmt, betrübt mich sehr" (It troubles me greatly that Robert believes he cannot create anything now, and that this depresses him). Once again, she begins the paragraph as a conventional diarist would, writing about her husband in the third person and sharing her emotions with the blank pages of a journal. But the knowledge that he will read her entry pulls her towards a second-person address, and she asks him directly, "Oder glaubst Du etwa, weil Du mich nun

---

18 Schumann, *Tagebücher*, II, 110; Schumann and Schumann, *Marriage Diaries*, 16.

zur Frau hast, nun ginge es nicht mehr? oder hast Du sonst Sorgen durch mich? ... Du sagst, 'ich weiß wohl, woher es kommt'—warum sprichst Du Dich nicht deutlicher aus? nächste Woche bitte ich Dich, daß Du es mir sagst" (Or do you believe it couldn't happen anymore because now you have me for a wife, or do you have other worries because of me? ... You say, "I know well where that comes from"— why don't you express yourself more clearly? Next week I shall ask you please to tell it to me).[19] Note that when Clara describes her own thoughts and feelings, she engages in more conventional diary writing. But when Robert's thoughts and feelings are at issue, it makes sense to exchange monologic speculation for direct inquiry. To understand better her husband's situation, she even cites here a passage from his last entry, so that the entries exist not just in a series but in an interconnected web. One Socratic complaint about writing (as opposed to speech) is that writing affords no opportunity for dialogue: even when its words are unclear, the written text cannot answer questions, explain itself further, or defend itself.[20] And yet Clara's questions and entreaties show that the give-and-take of the Schumanns' marriage diaries allows for a more dialogic form of writing. Precisely because the diary will return to Robert's hands, it mitigates against some of the most long-standing complaints about writing's shortcomings—namely the inability to follow up or elaborate on what has been written.[21] Furthermore, one sees here that the diary does not merely report or depict their married life. Through the give-and-take of the diary, the Schumanns work to construct, in writing, a version of an intimate relationship that will play out in real life.

The marriage diaries are also noteworthy for their novel form of authorship. Of course, the simple fact that two authors share the work of writing in itself departs from the conventions of the personal diary. Reich notes that, in the nineteenth century, co-authored diaries were uncommon but not unheard of.[22] The Schumanns' close friends Felix and Cécile Mendelssohn, for example, also shared a diary for a period

---

19 Schumann, *Tagebücher*, II, 114; Schumann and Schumann, *Marriage Diaries*, 22.
20 See Plato, *Phaedrus*, in *Euthyphro, Apology, Crito, Phaedo, Phaedrus*, ed. Jeffrey Henderson, trans. Harold North Fowler (Cambridge, MA: Harvard University Press, 1914), 564–5, 275e.
21 It is interesting, though, that Robert's next entry does not respond to Clara's questions. He just ignores them. In this instance at least, his text still resembles the writing about which Socrates complains. Like the images of a painting, his words appear "like living beings, but if one asks them a question, they preserve a solemn silence" (Plato, *Phaedrus*, 565, 275e).
22 Reich, *Clara Schumann*, 80.

of time.[23] Such exceptions notwithstanding, in a typical diary the narrative "I" is both the subject and object of writing. The self narrates itself to itself. When two writers work jointly on the diary, though, it cannot have as its topic the life and experiences of a singular self or "I." One sees in the marriage diaries how the collaborative project shifts the focus to the shared aspects of their lives—to their family, their mutual friends, and their shared interests and endeavors in music. Indeed, one could go so far as to say that the condition of possibility for the conjointly written diary is a shared life. The collaborative project works mainly because the Schumanns share the same passions, interests, and social events.

In contrast, their particular kind of collaborative diary writing starts to break down when Robert and Clara are apart, when their lived experiences do not overlap. In March and April of 1842, for example, Clara undertook a concert tour of northern Germany and Copenhagen. Robert accompanied her only as far as Hamburg and then spent the remainder of the time in Leipzig with their young daughter Marie.[24] When Clara returns home in May, she retrospectively recounts the details of her trip, adding dated entries such as, "*Sonntag d. 3* endlich gab ich mein erstes Concert im Königl[ichen] Theater. Volles Haus—viel Jubel! einige Hervorrufungen, da capo's, gute Einnahme" (On *Sunday the 3rd* [of April, 1842] I finally gave my first concert in the Royal Theater. Full house—big celebration! Several requests for encores, *da capos*, good return).[25] Clara gives a day-by-day account of her travels, but when she

---

23 Robert in fact expresses his pleasure at having a diary project in common with the Mendelssohns. "Freude machte es mir, v. Mendelssohn zu hören, daß er in d. ersten Jahre s[einer] Verheirathung ein ähnliches Tagebuch mit seiner Frau geführt, wie wir, daß sie es aber später vernachläßigt" (Schumann, *Tagebücher*, II, 155; Schumann and Schumann, *Marriage Diaries*, 70). Although the Schumanns will not abandon their diary so quickly, the entries—especially Robert's—do become less frequent after the first year of marriage. They eventually give up the jointly written diary in spring of 1844.
24 On this period of the Schumanns' life, see further Martin Geck, *Robert Schumann: The Life and Work of a Romantic Composer*, trans. Stewart Spencer (Chicago: University of Chicago Press, 2012), 140–1; and Veronika Beci, *Die andere Clara Schumann* (Düsseldorf: Droste, 1997), 80–5. Geck and Beci have differing views regarding the nature of the Schumanns' marriage and collaborative work. While Geck sees the relationship as mainly happy, with some scattered conflicts, Beci sees it as mostly unhappy and contentious. Both authors cite the diaries for supporting evidence. I prefer to set aside as potentially undecidable this question of emphasis—i.e., whether the marriage was mostly happy or mostly contentious—to focus instead on how the Schumanns employ the diary as a tool to shape their relationship.
25 Schumann, *Tagebücher*, II, 220; Schumann and Schumann, *Marriage Diaries*, 142.

and Robert are apart, neither person's account could do justice to their marriage or married life; each perspective remains incomplete. Thus, one finds Robert, as he reads Clara's long entry, adding notes about his own experiences in the margins. Alongside Clara's descriptions of sights, soirées, concerts, and profits, Robert inserts the record of his own melancholy days, spent alone: "d. 20. Miserables Leben. Viel im Contrapunct u. der Fuge geübt diese Zeit über" (the 20th. Miserable life. Much practicing of counterpoint and fugues during this time).[26] As long as the Schumanns lead overlapping lives, one person can write on behalf of both. When they go their separate ways, however, the single narrative voice of most entries gives way to a polyphonic diary writing, with two voices describing the same span of time from different perspectives. In this case, the difference in perspective lies in the contrast between Clara's excitement over successful performances and Robert's despondent emotional state.

This atypical dual-voiced entry from 1842 recalls the other noteworthy aspect of the diary's authorship: what is novel in the Schumanns' marriage diary is not simply that it is a collaborative endeavor; rather, the novelty lies also in the particular nature of that collaboration. The Schumanns decided to keep a joint diary by taking turns with the responsibility of writing. One could just as easily imagine a co-authored diary written entirely in the style of the two-voice entry described above, in which two spouses both record their individual experiences, so that the hypothetical diary would include two—often intertwined—records of each day or week. Or two people who sit down together at some appointed time and decide collaboratively what to write in the diary. But the Schumanns go about it differently. They choose from the outset to write alone, one at a time, and to give each spouse full responsibility for recording a week's worth of life with each entry. This turn-taking style of collaboration might seem like an unusual way to produce a marriage diary, but it accomplishes two things. First, it strikes a compromise between the collaborative nature of a shared marriage diary and the solitude of conventional diary writing. Yes, theirs is a co-authored diary, but it consists primarily of entries composed by an individual who writes alone. Each spouse gets to be the diary's sole author for a week at a time. Second, and perhaps more important, the turn-taking structure of composition reflects the tensions in the Schumanns' marriage and the kind of collaborative arrangements they negotiated in other aspects of their lives.

---

26 Schumann, *Tagebücher*, II, 215; Schumann and Schumann, *Marriage Diaries*, 346 n. 33.

As composers and professional musicians, the Schumanns were frequent collaborators, not only on the marriage diary but in their personal and professional lives. Robert was the genius Romantic composer and Clara the virtuoso pianist, an arrangement that often worked out well, since Robert had in Clara a reliable performer who could present his new work to the public according to his wishes. In March 1841, for instance, the Schumanns organized a collaborative concert. It was to be Clara's first performance as Clara Schumann as well as the debut of Robert's first symphony, his *Spring Symphony* in B-flat major (op. 38). Robert recounts the concert in the diary, writing, "Glücklicher Abend, der uns unvergeßlich sein wird. Meine Klara spielte Alles wie eine Meisterin und in erhöhter Stimmung, daß alle Welt entzückt war. Auch in meinem Künstlerleben ist der Tag einer der wichtigsten" (Happy evening, which we will never forget. My Clara played everything like a master and in an elevated mood, so that everybody was delighted. This day is also one of the most important ones in my artistic career).[27] The joint concert, with the Schumanns as both celebrated composer and celebrated performer, represents a significant achievement in the intertwinement of their careers.

At home, the couple often studied music together, including fugue technique and the works of Bach. Moreover, there exists a published collaborative composition by the Schumanns. In 1841, they jointly produced a collection of lieder based on poems from Friedrich Rückert's *Liebesfrühling* (Springtime of Love) collection.[28] As Robert notes in early January, "Die Idee, mit Klara ein Liederheft herauszugeben, hat mich zur Arbeit begeistert ... Kl[ara] soll nun auch a. d. Liebesfrühling einige componiren. O thu' es Klärchen!" (The idea, to bring out [a book] of lieder with Clara has given me enthusiasm for work ... Now Clara should also compose a few from the Liebesfrühling. Oh, do it, Klärchen!)[29] Like the marriage diary itself, the song cycle was structured as a kind of dialogue, and in its final form, three of the twelve songs were composed by Clara.[30]

The *Liebesfrühling* cycle provides perhaps the best model for the Schumanns' style of collaboration, both what one finds in the marriage diaries as well as in the rest of their lives. Although the finished product is a joint composition penned by both Robert and Clara, it reflects once

---

27 Schumann, *Tagebücher*, II, 157; Schumann and Schumann, *Marriage Diaries*, 71–2.
28 On the genesis of the *Liebesfrühling* cycle, see Geck, *Robert Schumann*, 135.
29 Schumann, *Tagebücher*, II, 139; Schumann and Schumann, *Marriage Diaries*, 50.
30 On the ambiguity of gender identity in Rückert's poems and the Schumanns' composition, see Melinda Boyd, "Gendered Voices: The *Liebesfrühling* Lieder of Robert and Clara Schumann," *Nineteenth-Century Music* 23, no. 2 (1999): 145–62.

again a turn-taking sort of collaboration, in which each song (like each diary entry) belongs to either Robert or Clara, one of whom composed it in isolation.[31] The Schumanns' marriage diary is thus a joint composition in the same way the book of lieder is: in both cases, the authors compile a set of individual compositions and bring them together in the form of a dialogue. In other words, the structure of the marriage diary might look unusual from a narrative or life writing perspective, but it makes perfect sense as the format of choice for a married pair of musicians. The marriage diary is organized like a song cycle with pieces written by two composers. Lejeune writes, "The diary itself may well be a narrative, but first and foremost it is a piece of music, meaning an art of repetition and variation."[32] The analogy of diary and music is apt, not just in the intended sense of theme and variation but also in terms of the marriage diary's structuring principle, which parallels that of their careers.

If the diary's format does not exactly determine how the Schumanns balance their careers, it at least prefigures the sort of arrangements and compromises that they would strike in their marriage. The problem of not being able to work simultaneously formed an overarching tension in the Schumanns' attempts to pursue two musical careers alongside family life. It begins early on. Already in the second week of their marriage, Clara complains to the diary (and thus to Robert, too), "Es ist schlimm, daß mich Robert in seinem Zimmer hört wenn ich spiele, daher ich auch die Morgenstunden, die schönsten zu einem ernsten Studium, nicht benutzen kann" (It's annoying that when I am playing Robert can hear me from his room, for thus I cannot use the morning hours, the best ones for serious study).[33] Robert's room is the space where he spends his time composing. Thus Clara cannot practice the piano, because the sound of her playing interrupts the music Robert hears in his head. Eighteen weeks later, Clara expresses her frustration in starker terms: "Zum Spielen komme ich jetzt gar nicht; theils hält mich mein Unwohlseyn, theils Robert's Componieren ab. Wäre

---

31 Rufus Hallmark observes that nothing in the available sources suggests that they composed the songs collaboratively: "The extent of Robert's and Clara's collaboration appears to have been their agreement in principle on a joint publication of songs and Clara's amenability to Robert's request to set some poems by Rückert." Rufus Hallmark, "The Rückert Lieder of Robert and Clara Schumann," *Nineteenth-Century Music* 14, no. 1 (1990): 3–30 (12). Hallmark also points out that the original published version of the *Liebesfrühling* cycle gave no indication of who had contributed which songs; it was simply issued as a joint composition.
32 Lejeune, *On Diary*, 180.
33 Schumann, *Tagebücher*, II, 103; Schumann and Schumann, *Marriage Diaries*, 9.

es doch nur möglich dem Uebel mit den leichten Wänden abzuhelfen, ich verlerne Alles, und werde noch ganz melancholisch darüber" (I don't get to play at all nowadays; partly my being unwell prevents it, partly Robert's composing. If only it were possible to resolve the [trouble] of the thin walls; I unlearn everything and because of that might become very melancholic).[34] Clara's entry speaks to two conflicts: first, between her role as expectant mother (referenced obliquely through her "Unwohlseyn," or feeling unwell) and her role as professional musician, and second, in the marriage, between two artists who both want to pursue their ambitions. Robert wants to be a great composer, while Clara wants to be a great pianist. But their decision to share the same living space forces a trade-off: she cannot practice while he composes, and vice versa. It is impossible for both of them to work simultaneously. She finds it hard to practice, both because she is pregnant with her first child and because Robert is engrossed in his first symphony. The only solution to the dilemma of practice interfering with composition was to take turns; only one of them could pursue music at a time. Unfortunately for Clara, this tension was typically resolved in Robert's favor. She did not play the piano while he composed, and one gets the sense from the diaries that Robert devoted himself completely to his work when he was inspired to produce a new piece of music. Clara, dependent on his work schedule, could therefore go days without practicing. While the Schumanns' relationship has sometimes been described as an "ideal marriage between two artists," it is also clear that Clara's role as wife to Robert and mother to seven children held her back artistically.[35]

The marriage diaries afford us the opportunity to view this tension from both perspectives, not only through the lens of Clara's complaints, but also through Robert's attempts to countenance her concerns and respond to them. Robert, for his part, is well aware that his composing interferes with Clara's playing and that neglecting her art exposes Clara to intense feelings of anxiety and regret. In September 1842, for example, he admits, "Sorge macht mir oft, daß ich Kl[ara] in ihren Studien oft hindere, da sie mich nicht im Componieren stören will" (It often worries me that I frequently [hinder] Clara in her practicing, since she does not [want] to disturb me while composing).[36] As

---

34 Schumann, Tagebücher, II, 144; Schumann and Schumann, Marriage Diaries, 56.
35 Geck, Robert Schumann, 134–5. Geck concedes that Clara "played second fiddle" to Robert, whereas Beci writes more pointedly that Clara's professional ambitions were a "point of contention" in the relationship, and that marriage forced her largely to set her dreams aside. Beci, Die andere Clara Schumann, 73–4.
36 Schumann, Tagebücher, II, 249–50; Schumann and Schumann, Marriage Diaries, 178.

considerate as Robert may seem in expressing concern for his wife's piano playing, his awareness of the problem does not inspire him to change. Indeed, his entries on this point more often try to justify the prioritization of his career over hers and encourage resignation to an imbalance that he believes cannot be remedied.

He continues in the same entry about Clara's lack of practice time, "daran bin ich Schuld und kann es doch nicht ändern. Kl[ara] sieht doch auch ein, daß ich ein Talent zu pflegen habe ... Nur so geht es in Künstlerehen; es kann nicht Alles beieinander sein, und die Hauptsache ist doch immer das übrige Glück" (I am [to blame] and yet I cannot change it. But Clara does recognize that I have to nurture a talent ... [That's the only way it works in artists' marriages]; everything cannot go on simultaneously, and the main thing of course is the happiness that remains).[37] Robert accepts responsibility for the predicament and then essentially shrugs it off. Simultaneous work is impossible, so his diary entry stresses the necessity of non-synchronous work habits. In terms of audience, it is interesting that Robert describes Clara's understanding and acquiescence ("Clara does recognize ... ") in an entry that is meant for her to read. His passage seems to function like an implicit command or speech act, an ostensibly denotative statement that is actually meant to bring about the very agreement it asserts. He leans here on life writing's interdependency of life and writing, as he works rhetorically to construct acquiescence to a state of affairs in which his productivity is the couple's primary concern. Moreover, by asserting that her other happiness, outside of work, is the main thing, or *Hauptsache*, he relegates Clara's concerns about practice and performance to the margins.

In February of 1843, Robert hits essentially the same note. Remarking again that Clara does not have sufficient time to practice music, he justifies the situation by noting that her children and her duties to her husband simply do not accord with a musician's life. Once again, Robert recognizes that family life interferes with the pursuit of her musical career, and again, he expresses a tinge of regret. But just as before, no sooner does he countenance a hindrance to his wife's career than he sets out to minimize the issue and explain it away. "Klara kennt aber selbst ihren Hauptberuf als Mutter, daß ich glaube, sie ist glücklich in den Verhältnissen, wie sie sich nun einmal nicht ändern lassen" (Clara herself knows her primary occupation [*Hauptberuf*, which echoes the *Hauptsache* from his previous entry] to be a mother, however, so that I believe she is happy under these conditions, which just simply cannot be changed).[38] It is telling that Robert refers to motherhood as Clara's

---

37 Schumann, *Tagebücher*, II, 250; Schumann and Schumann, *Marriage Diaries*, 178.
38 Schumann, *Tagebücher*, II, 255; Schumann and Schumann, *Marriage Diaries*, 185.

primary *Beruf*, her main occupation, career, or even calling. Of course, this simply reflects the typical mentality about gender roles at the time and would be unremarkable, except for the fact that Clara also happens to be an internationally famous virtuoso pianist.

It is furthermore baffling that Robert asserts Clara is happy with the current state of affairs. In Clara's most recent entry, the one immediately preceding Robert's, she writes of an "unbeschreiblicher Trübsinn" (indescribable sadness) and of "trübe Gedanken für die Zukunft, die mich oft Tage lang nicht verlassen, die ich durchaus nicht verbannen kann" (sad thoughts about the future, which often don't leave me for days on end, which I cannot dispel at all).[39] She connects her sadness directly to her desire to work more and perform more, and thereby earn income for the family. Given that this is the entry to which Robert's words respond, it can only be an act of willful ignorance on his part to imagine that Clara is perfectly content in her role as mother. In fact, on a rhetorical level, he would not be asserting her happiness at all were it not for her repeated expressions of discontent and the fact that she constitutes the entry's main audience. With assertions such as "Clara herself knows," he projects onto her feelings that he wants her to have. He aims to maneuver Clara, through such insinuations, into a position that favors his own artistic endeavors.

There thus exists a tension in this marriage of artists, since the two of them cannot both work at the same time. They need to take turns. In essence, the diary, which has the same constraints—they cannot both write in it at the same time—represents an attempt to construct a solution. It reflects, or fashions in advance, the same kind of sharing and turn-taking that the Schumanns negotiated in their home life. Unfortunately for Clara, the balancing of responsibilities and opportunities is more in evidence in the diary than in the pursuit of their respective artistic careers. In fact, as their musical endeavors become more unbalanced, with Robert's composing taking priority over Clara's playing, the marriage diary reflects that imbalance in a different way. It becomes the inverse or negative image of their musical pursuits. The more Robert works at his music, the less Clara can work at her music. At the same time, the more he works at his music, the less he contributes to the diary.

Robert is very clear when establishing the terms of the diary that each weekly entry must be at least a page long, and he stipulates that the couple should devise an appropriate punishment for meager entries. He goes on to write, "Sollte sich je ein Mitglied unsres Eheordens einfallen

---

39 Schumann, *Tagebücher*, II, 251; Schumann and Schumann, *Marriage Diaries*, 179–80.

laßen, eine Woche lang gar nichts einzuzeichnen, so wird die Strafe sehr verschärft" (Should it occur to [a] member of our marital team not to turn anything in for a whole week, then the penalty will be made very much harsher).[40] Despite the stringency of these initial terms, the couple manages to adhere to the diary's stipulated schedule only for about eighteen weeks, or nine entries apiece. When Robert immerses himself in composing his first large-scale symphony, weeks go by without an entry in his hand. After recording the eighteenth week's entry according to schedule, in mid-January, Clara goes on to take responsibility for the diary for the next four weeks. She acknowledges that her repeated entries week after week run counter to the initial stipulations, but she does not insist on a penalty or punishment. Instead, she supports Robert's single-minded focus on composing. When Robert resurfaces from his work on the symphony, five weeks have gone by, and he first returns to the diary in late February. He resumes his diary writing with the words, "Nun nach fünf Wochen Schweigen zu dir, meine liebe Leserin. Wär' ich nur ganz wohl um Alles recht schön darzustellen, was sich immer begeben" (Now, after five weeks of being silent, back to you, my dear reader. Were I only well enough to describe really beautifully [what] has happened).[41] He casts his resumption of writing duties as a return not just to the diary, but also to its reader, to Clara herself. By renewing his diary writing, he also appears to renew his relationship with his wife.

The point is that when Robert becomes engrossed in his work, his commitment to the diary wanes. Its weekly structure begins to loosen over time, and towards the end of 1841, entries occur less frequently, every two weeks or once a month. After two years, the monthly entries become ingrained, and Clara increasingly takes on the duties of diary writing. Here, the turn-taking in the diary reflects in a mirror image the turn-taking in their musical endeavors. As Robert's composing career flourishes, he consumes more of the available time for music, while devoting less time to the marriage diary. Clara, by contrast, has far less time for music, but she takes over for Robert when he neglects the diary.

The tensions in the Schumanns' marriage and the difficulties of balancing their dual careers are never more apparent than when they discuss Clara's desire to travel more often to give concerts. As a virtuoso pianist, Clara needed to perform regularly, and to widespread audiences, just to maintain her professional image and her prominent place in the world of contemporary European music. Laura Deiulio, in an article on the nineteenth-century actress Auguste Brede, discusses

---

40 Schumann, *Tagebücher*, II, 100; Schumann and Schumann, *Marriage Diaries*, 4.
41 Schumann, *Tagebücher*, II, 148; Schumann and Schumann, *Marriage Diaries*, 61.

what a woman in the arts at this time had to do "in order to maintain a viable career," strategies that included "the careful use of travel to keep her reputation fresh."[42] Like other performing artists of the nineteenth century, Clara feels acutely the pressure to travel, to perform, and to preserve her reputation. In October 1840, for instance, she pleads with Robert via the diary to consent to accompany her on a concert tour of Holland and Belgium. She writes, "laß uns *nur ein paar* Winter noch benutzen—ich bin es ja auch meinem Rufe schuldig, daß ich mich jetzt noch nicht ganz zurückziehe. Es ist ein Pflichtgefühl gegen Dich und mich, das in mir spricht" (let us use *only a few more* winters—I really owe it to my reputation not yet to withdraw completely at this time. It is a feeling of [duty] toward you and myself that speaks within me).[43] Clara recognizes, first, that she needs to capitalize on her reputation now, while she still enjoys wide critical acclaim as a performer, and second, that her professional image will suffer if she does not perform regularly to maintain it. Note further that Clara tempers her request with an offer of compromise: she wants to book concerts, but not every year for the rest of their lives. In other words, she implies to Robert that this would be a temporary arrangement. At some point in the future, she will be willing to give up her musical career and withdraw from the public eye, but she wants to press on for the next few years, while she still can.

All these sentiments are echoed in a similar entry just a month later. The Schumanns had been considering a tour to Petersburg, but that opportunity was looking less viable for the coming winter.[44] Clara reacts to the dashed plans with distress: "Soll ich nun den ganzen Winter still sitzen, Nichts verdienen, was ich doch so leicht könnte? Jeder fragt, ob ich nicht reise—ich komme ganz in Vergessenheit" (Should I now sit [idly] for the entire winter, not earning money, which I could do so easily? Everyone keeps asking why I don't travel—I will fall into total oblivion).[45] Clara emphasizes here the transience of the stature she enjoys, and she confirms Deiulio's point that performers at the time had to use travel strategically to keep themselves in the public eye. If Clara does not perform regularly and maintain her reputation, the window of opportunity for concert tours, and indeed for her career as a pianist,

---

42 Laura Deiulio, "Performing German Women's Professional Identity: The Correspondence of Rahel Levin Varnhagen and Auguste Brede," *German Studies Review* 38, no. 3 (2015): 509–29 (514).
43 Schumann, *Tagebücher*, II, 110; Schumann and Schumann, *Marriage Diaries*, 16.
44 The Schumanns would eventually travel to Russia in early 1844, after a delay of three years. Their record of the trip through Russia constitutes the final section of their jointly written marriage diaries.
45 Schumann, *Tagebücher*, II, 121; Schumann and Schumann, *Marriage Diaries*, 29.

will close. To put it plainly: the less she performs now, the harder it will be to continue performing in the future.[46]

As we know, Clara does travel to Copenhagen in support of a concert tour in late winter, 1842. And Robert, now back in Leipzig and missing his wife's company, reflects in the diary on the challenges they face in balancing their professional ambitions. He writes, "Soll ich denn mein Talent vernachlässigen, um dir als Begleiter auf der Reise zu dienen? Und du, sollst du deshalb dein Talent ungenutzt lassen, weil ich nun einmal an Zeitung und Clavier gefesselt bin? Jetzt wo Du jung u. frisch bei Kräften bist?" (Shall I neglect my talent in order to serve as your companion on trips? And you, should you therefore leave your talent unused, [just because] I am chained to my journal [the *Neue Zeitschrift für Musik*] and the piano? Now, when you are young and fresh with energy?)[47] What Robert laments in this passage is the turn-taking that their musical endeavors necessitate. Just as he cannot compose while she practices, and vice versa, so he cannot compose if they are traveling and she cannot travel if he's composing. He recognizes that they each have a talent to nurture, and it appears—tragically, one supposes—that one or the other of them will have to sacrifice the full use of that talent if they want to be together.

The tour to Copenhagen, however, gives Robert reason for optimism. It points towards a possible solution to the dilemma of how to support two musical talents and not let them get in the way of each other's ambitions. As he describes it, "Wir haben den Ausweg getroffen. Du nahmst dir eine Begleiterin, ich kehrte zum Kind zurück u. zu meiner Arbeit. Aber was wird *die Welt* sagen? ... Ja es ist durchaus nöthig, daß wir Mittel finden, unsere beiden Talente nebeneinander zu nützen u. zu bilden" (We have hit on a way out. You took a female companion for yourself, I returned to the child and to my work. But what will *the world* say? ... Yes, it is absolutely necessary that we find the means to use and develop both of our talents side by side).[48] When Robert celebrates having found a way out, he means that they have found a way out of the either/or, turn-taking arrangement in which only one of them can work at a time. Finally, they can both pursue music simultaneously: she can travel and perform (with a chaperone, of course), and he can stay home and write. There are unfortunately two obstacles that prevent this

---

46 On these tensions, see Veronika Beci, *Robert und Clara Schumann: Musik und Leidenschaft* (Düsseldorf: Patmos, 2006), especially 139–48.
47 Schumann, *Tagebücher*, II, 206; Schumann and Schumann, *Marriage Diaries*, 126–7.
48 Schumann, *Tagebücher*, II, 206; Schumann and Schumann, *Marriage Diaries*, 127.

arrangement from becoming a long-term solution, and Robert refers to one of them in the above passage. Even though Clara is accompanied on her trip, he worries that the image of a married woman traveling without her husband will come into conflict with popular notions of feminine virtue.[49] If Clara were to travel regularly without Robert, it would likely lead to gossip and other unpleasantness.

The second obstacle is Robert's own fragile and perhaps deteriorating emotional and mental health. Clara exerts a stabilizing force in the life of their family, and her presence helps to maintain in particular Robert's emotional wellbeing. In short, when she is away, he is neither especially happy nor especially productive. The entry he writes in her absence opens with the lines, "Vielleicht daß ich mir meine Melancholia durch die Erinnerung an die letzten Wochen, die ich mit Clara verlebte, etwas verscheuche. Es war doch einer meiner dümmsten Streiche, Dich von mir gelassen zu haben. Ich fühle es immer mehr" (That I may perhaps drive my melancholia away somewhat by remembering the last weeks I have spent with Clara. It was really one of the most stupid things for me to let you leave me. I feel it [more and more]).[50] The solution to their conflicting careers was supposed to be letting Clara travel alone, but this turns out not to be a solution at all. Robert quickly regrets deciding to be apart from Clara, mainly because the separation sends him into a deep depression, what he refers to as "melancholia." His depressed state furthermore interferes with his ability to compose, which was the point of his staying behind in the first place. It is thus a poignant moment when, alongside Clara's account of her time in Copenhagen, Robert jots the note, "'Trübsinnzeit' steht in m[einen] Notizen unter diesem Tag. An Componieren war nicht zu denken" ("melancholy times" it says in my notes for this day. Composing was out of the question).[51] He believed they had found, in the joint venture of their musicians' marriage, a way to allow for simultaneous work. But, with Robert's composing at a standstill whenever Clara performs, they remain stuck taking turns pursuing their musical careers. It is precisely the necessity of turn-taking, this inability to work simultaneously, that one finds reflected in the unusual structure of their marriage diaries.

---

49 On the need for female performers "to negotiate overlapping discourses of promiscuity and virtue," see again Deiulio, "Performing German Women's Professional Identity," 509.
50 Schumann, *Tagebücher*, II, 206; Schumann and Schumann, *Marriage Diaries*, 126.
51 Schumann, *Tagebücher*, II, 219; Schumann and Schumann, *Marriage Diaries*, 347 n. 41. Ostwald's monograph is helpful in understanding Robert's depression during this period. It includes passages from Robert's private household book, in which he writes somewhat more frankly about his mood, his excessive drinking, and his inability to compose. Ostwald, *Schumann*, 176–81.

Over time, even the turn-taking format of the marriage diaries begins to come undone. And after the Schumanns return from their long trip to Russia in May 1844, they abandon without comment the conjointly written diary. Nevertheless, neither gives up on diary writing. Clara, who would outlive Robert by forty years, kept a diary through most of her life, and Robert continued to record in notebooks his day-to-day life as well as his travel impressions. Life writing thus remains an ongoing practice for both the Schumanns, but from May 1844 onward, they go about it individually, with an audience and authorship that more closely resemble conventional forms of diary writing. Why do they give up the project of the joint diary? Why does it end at this point in their lives, after the Russian trip and before their fourth anniversary?

Gerd Nauhaus speculates that the marriage diaries end once their purpose "has been achieved, inasmuch as the partners are now so intimately fused with one another that they no longer need the written medium and can quietly discard the 'statute' of 1840."[52] Nauhaus believes, in other words, that in 1844 the Schumanns' marriage has reached the point where the mutual friend of the shared diary is no longer necessary, so intertwined are these two people. The record provides little evidence, however, to support so rosy an interpretation. It is more likely that the Schumanns abandon the diary because they are moving in different directions, and that the shared aspects of their lives are becoming less important relative to their individual pursuits.

Perhaps the project of the conjointly written diary dies out, not because it has fulfilled its purpose and thereby rendered itself obsolete, but rather because the Schumanns' sense of being each other's best audience no longer holds. Robert's mental and emotional deterioration, which accelerated in 1844 and culminated in his attempted suicide in 1854, has been well documented.[53] On the other hand, the tour of Russia looks in retrospect like a prelude to Clara's later performance career, which continued for decades, well into the late nineteenth century. As a concert pianist, Clara directs her creative energies not just towards Robert but outwards, to a public audience, whereas Robert seems to be increasingly trapped in his own mind. In this sense, the marriage diary's particular form of authorship depends on its particular form of audience. Once that audience changes, once the Schumanns no longer

---

52 Gerd Nauhaus, "Foreword to the German Edition," in Schumann and Schumann, *Marriage Diaries*, xxiv.
53 O'Shea indicates that Schumann experienced repeated, debilitating bouts of depression from September 1844 onwards, which suggests a more immediate possible reason for the diary's abandonment in mid-1844. O'Shea, *Music and Medicine*, 129.

believe that their experiences are best addressed to each other, then the impetus for the joint diary, with its split author function, disappears. Robert inaugurates the marriage diary with the vision that it would include "Alles, was uns gemeinsam berührt in unserem Haus- und Ehestand" (everything that touches us mutually in our household and marriage).[54] It could be, however, that after several years, there was less in life that touched them mutually, and that their wishes and hopes were increasingly divergent. In other words, what is being invented through diary writing after 1844 is less the shared aspect of their married life and more the personal attributes that are better envisioned—enacted even—in their individual diaries. Over time, the structure of the conjointly written diary proved to be more fragile, more volatile, than the Schumanns had imagined. It depended on a degree of emotional collaboration that turned out to be unsustainable, and as a result, the shared endeavor split back into two individual diaries.

Bibliography

Beci, Veronika. *Die andere Clara Schumann*. Düsseldorf: Droste, 1997.

Beci, Veronika. *Robert und Clara Schumann: Musik und Leidenschaft*. Düsseldorf: Patmos, 2006.

Boyd, Melinda. "Gendered Voices: The *Liebesfrühling* Lieder of Robert and Clara Schumann." *Nineteenth-Century Music* 23, no. 2 (1999): 145–62.

Culley, Margo. "Introduction to *A Day at a Time: Diary Literature of American Women, from 1764 to 1985*." In *Women, Autobiography, Theory: A Reader*, ed. Sidonie Smith and Julia Watson, 217–21. Madison: University of Wisconsin Press, 1998.

Currie, Norman. "Another Perspective on Robert Schumann's Personality." *Journal of Musicological Research* 30 (2011): 131–63.

de Man, Paul. *The Rhetoric of Romanticism*. New York: Columbia University Press, 1984.

Deiulio, Laura. "Performing German Women's Professional Identity: The Correspondence of Rahel Levin Varnhagen and Auguste Brede." *German Studies Review* 38, no. 3 (2015): 509–29.

Eakin, Paul. *Fictions in Autobiography: Studies in the Art of Self-Invention*. Princeton: Princeton University Press, 1985.

Ferris, David. "The Fictional Lives of the Schumanns." In *Rethinking Schumann*, ed. Roe-Min Kok and Laura Tunbridge, 357–94. Oxford: Oxford University Press, 2011.

Foucault, Michel. "What Is an Author?" In *Aesthetics, Method, and Epistemology*, ed. James D. Faubion, trans. Robert Hurley *et al.*, 205–22. New York: New Press, 1998.

Geck, Martin. *Robert Schumann: The Life and Work of a Romantic Composer*. Trans. Stewart Spencer. Chicago: University of Chicago Press, 2012.

Hallmark, Rufus. "The Rückert Lieder of Robert and Clara Schumann." *Nineteenth-Century Music* 14, no. 1 (1990): 3–30.

---

54 Schumann, *Tagebücher*, II, 99; Schumann and Schumann, *Marriage Diaries*, 3.

Heehs, Peter. *Writing the Self: Diaries, Memoirs, and the History of the Self*. New York: Bloomsbury, 2013.
Lejeune, Philippe. *On Diary*. Ed. Jeremy Popkin and Julie Rak. Trans. Katherine Durnin. Manoa: University of Hawai'i Press, 2009.
O'Shea, John. *Music and Medicine: Medical Profiles of Great Composers*. London: J. M. Dent, 1990.
Ostwald, Peter. *Schumann: The Inner Voices of a Musical Genius*. Boston, MA: Northeastern University Press, 1985.
Plato. *Euthyphro, Apology, Crito, Phaedo, Phaedrus*. Ed. Jeffrey Henderson. Trans. Harold North Fowler. Cambridge, MA: Harvard University Press, 1914.
Reich, Nancy. *Clara Schumann: The Artist and the Woman*. Ithaca, NY: Cornell University Press, 2001.
Schumann, Clara and Robert Schumann. *The Marriage Diaries of Robert and Clara Schumann*. Ed. Gerd Nauhaus. Trans. Peter Ostwald. Boston, MA: Northeastern University Press, 1993.
Schumann, Robert. *Tagebücher*. Vol. II, *1836–1854*. Ed. Gerd Nauhaus. Leipzig: Deutscher Verlag für Musik, 1987.
Smith, Sidonie and Julia Watson. *Reading Autobiography: A Guide for Interpreting Life Narratives*. Minneapolis: University of Minnesota Press, 2001.

Twelve Therese Robinson's *Die Auswanderer* (1852) as Goethe's Future Novel of America

Judith E. Martin

The German-American philologist and novelist Therese Robinson (1797–1870; née von Jakob), who published under the pseudonym Talvj (from the initials of her full name), has been remembered primarily for her founding role in Slavic studies as the translator of Vuk Stefanović Karadžić's collection of Serbian *Volkslieder* (folksongs) into German in 1825.[1] Johann Wolfgang von Goethe encouraged her in this project because she knew Russian, having spent ten years in Russia as a child during the Napoleonic Wars. She and Goethe corresponded about her role as translator, and they met in person several times between 1824 and 1828.[2] In 1828 Therese married the American theologian Edward Robinson and spent three decades in the United States, where she continued her ethnographic research, publishing works on early American colonial history and Native American languages.[3] Her mid-century

---

1 See, for example, the contributions to Gabriella Schubert and Friedhilde Krause, eds., *TALVJ: Therese Albertine Luise von Jakob-Robinson. Aus Liebe zu Goethe: Mittlerin der Balkanslawen* (Weimar: VDG and Datenbank für Geisteswissenschaften, 2001).
2 See Gisela Licht, "Ökonomien des Begehrens. Die Strategien der deutsch-amerikanischen Schriftstellerin Therese Albertine Luise von Jakob Robinson (1797–1870) auf dem Weg zur Berufsschriftstellerin," in *Ökonomien des Lebens: Zum Wirtschaften der Geschlechter in Geschichte und Gegenwart*, ed. Eva Labouvie and Katharina Bunzmann (Münster: Literatur, 2004), 241–63 (241–4, 249–53). See also their correspondence: Johann Wolfgang von Goethe and Therese Robinson, "Briefwechsel zwischen Goethe und Therese von Jakob," ed. Reinhold Steig, *Goethe-Jahrbuch* 12 (1891): 33–77.
3 Edward Robinson ranks among a group of New England scholars credited with introducing German historical biblical scholarship to American religious studies. On Edward Robinson's influence on religious studies in America, see

novels, *Heloise* (1850) and *Die Auswanderer* (1852; *The Exiles*, 1853), were largely forgotten until Martha Kaarsberg Wallach reintroduced their transcultural relevance for addressing the plight of colonized peoples in the Caucasus and North America.

Although Robinson had already published several works, it was her collaboration with Goethe on the *Volkslieder der Serben* (1825–6) that launched her to lasting literary fame.[4] The tone of her letters to Goethe expresses the deep veneration of a young writer for a mentor, whose authority she needs to support her endeavor.[5] Her little-known American novel *Die Auswanderer* can also be understood as a virtual collaboration with Goethe, because its complex content and form adapt suggestions he made in an 1827 book review for combining information and plot in a new form of American narrative.[6] In *Die Auswanderer*, Robinson presents extensive cultural commentary on the United States, framed within a multigenerational plot of German emigration to America. Her blend of informative travelogue with conventions of the historical novel, domestic novel, and religious novel incorporates each of Goethe's structural and thematic elements—American colonial history, romance plot, and religion—but she rescripts them to grapple with issues of gender and authority. Although she draws on Goethe's proposals, Robinson's relationship to her influential predecessor is far from imitative; instead an independent and even distanced response becomes evident. In the intervening twenty-five years, her relationship to Goethe had shifted from that of an admirer to that of a self-confident

---

Jerry Wayne Brown, *The Rise of Biblical Criticism in America, 1800–1870: The New England Scholars* (Middletown, CT: Wesleyan University Press, 1969), 6–8, 40–1, 122–3. For an account of Therese Robinson's life and writings that includes passages from unpublished letters, see Licht, "Ökonomien." After her father lost his professorship at Halle in 1806 because of the Napoleonic occupation, the family moved to Russia for nearly a decade. As an adult, Robinson corresponded with Goethe and Jacob Grimm, and frequented literary salons in Dresden and Berlin. She was in contact with many cultural figures such as Bettina Brentano-von Arnim, K. A. Varnhagen, and Caroline Bardua. In New York she hosted her own salon, whose visitors included Washington Irving and Margaret Fuller (Licht, "Ökonomien," 257–8).

4 Licht, "Ökonomien," 249–51.
5 Licht emphasizes that she needed his masculine authority for success; "Ökonomien," 251. See also Goethe and Robinson, *Briefwechsel*, 35, in which she addresses him as "Hochverehrtester" (most venerated).
6 Johann Wolfgang von Goethe, "Stoff und Gehalt zur Bearbeitung vorgeschlagen," in *Johann Wolfgang Goethe: Sämtliche Werke. Briefe, Tagebücher und Gespräche*, Vol. I.22, *Ästhetische Schriften 1824–1832: Über Kunst und Altertum V–VI*, ed. Anne Bohnenkamp (Frankfurt am Main: Deutscher Klassiker Verlag, 1999), 392–5.

scholar and author. The hybridity and polyvocality of her generic mixture in *Die Auswanderer* enabled her to critique Goethe in an indirect manner by placing critical viewpoints of his writings in the mouths of satirized characters. Yet even at a distance of twenty years since her interlocutor's death, Robinson risks moral criticism of his ideas only under the veil of satire. Recognizing Goethe's suggestions as a structuring principle clarifies how the disparate strands and multiple purposes of this text fit together. Attention to the dialogic dimension also elucidates Robinson's subtly oppositional discourse on gender and its interconnections with her socio-historical and theological interests.

Doubled Plots: History and Romance

Robinson integrates her research on American history into *Die Auswanderer* by situating North American geography within a transatlantic frame of imperial conflicts and the resulting cultural encounters between nations and ethnicities. Her representative figures dramatize the struggle between north and south in the pre-Civil War era, with a focus on tensions between Spain and the United States over Florida during its recent colonial period. Robinson's privileged access to knowledge of American religion also figures prominently in this intergeneric text. The generic hybridity, which reflects Robinson's assimilation of influences that range from antiquity and the Bible to James Fenimore Cooper, Walter Scott, and Charlotte Brontë, has hampered critical reception of the novel. It has attracted limited interest among scholars of the *Amerikaroman* (novel of America), but far less than prolific popular authors in this genre, such as Charles Sealsfield, Friedrich Strubberg, Friedrich Gerstäcker, and Karl May.[7] It differs from the typical frontier settings for masculine adventure tales by focusing on a female protagonist who remains in the east. Although an English translation,

---

7 For an overview of the history and development of the *Amerikaroman*, see Wynfrid Kriegleder, "Sealsfield—Strubberg—Karl May; oder, Der deutsche Amerikaroman wird zum Ego-Trip," *Yearbook of German-American Studies* 46 (2011): 5–19. Kriegleder outlines a mid-century shift, from didactic Enlightenment novels that often posited the United States as an alternative political model for Germany, to a bifurcation into adventure novels and more realistic images of the United States for emigrants (9, 16). For more extensive accounts, see Wynfrid Kriegleder, *Vorwärts in die Vergangenheit: Das Bild der USA im deutschsprachigen Roman von 1776 bis 1855* (Tübingen: Stauffenburg, 1999); Jeffrey L. Sammons, *Ideology, Mimesis, Fantasy: Charles Sealsfield, Friedrich Gerstäcker, Karl May, and Other German Novelists of America* (Chapel Hill: University of North Carolina Press, 1998); and Jerry Schuchalter, *Narratives of America and the Frontier in Nineteenth-Century German Literature* (New York: Peter Lang, 2000).

The Exiles, appeared nearly simultaneously with the German version, *Die Auswanderer* has also suffered undeserved neglect on this side of the Atlantic, and therefore requires introduction.[8]

The story follows the orphan Klotilde Osten, who leaves Germany for America with her fiancé, Franz Hubert, a political prisoner who is released on the condition that he leaves the country. A shipwreck off the mid-Atlantic coast separates the two, and each believes the other dead. Klotilde is saved by a Spanish creole plantation owner in Florida, while Franz is rescued by a ship en route to Maine. When Franz later travels to Charleston as an abolitionist, the couple are reunited, marry, and settle in New England. But their rural refuge is destroyed when Klotilde's Florida rescuer, Alonzo, arrives and kills Franz in a duel, thereby unwittingly murdering his half-brother. Klotilde, traumatized by Franz's death, also soon dies, after giving birth to their stillborn child.

The reader accompanies Klotilde from Alonzo's Florida plantation to his relatives' household in Charleston, where she teaches German and music to the two daughters, the southern belle Virginia, and her half-sister Sarah, a devout Methodist. In addition to developing her religious ethos through these multiple female characters, Robinson also addresses gender relations in their marriage plots.

Midway through the narrative, the subplot of hidden kinship is revealed: Franz Hubert's German father had conceived Alonzo in his seduction of the young Spanish Creole woman Josepha Losado while serving as a colonial mercenary soldier in Florida. He had fought with British forces in Europe during the Napoleonic Wars, and later in the Far East and then in Florida, where he eventually transferred to service with the United States Army. After having two illegitimate children with Josepha in a sham marriage, Franz's father abandons her several years later to return to his German wife, and Josepha spends the rest of her life attempting to atone through obsessive Catholic ritual penitence.

This plot of a fictional Spanish-German-American family that is destroyed by historical forces put into play a generation earlier dramatizes antebellum sectional hostilities. Shirley Samuels's remark that a "relation between the familial and the socio-political" is common in Civil War fiction illuminates Robinson's composition, in which the narrative resolution of a fratricide involving northern and southern

---

8   Therese Robinson, *Die Auswanderer: Eine Erzählung von Talvj. Therese von Jakob-Robinsons Amerikaroman (1852)*, ed. with an afterword by Mark-Georg Dehrmann (Hanover: Wehrhahn, 2010); Therese Robinson, *The Exiles: A Tale. By Talvi, Author of "Heloise," "The Literature of the Sclavic* [sic] *Nations," etc.* (New York: G. P. Putnam, 1853). The translation was by Robinson's daughter, Marie Robinson (Licht, "Ökonomien," 259). Further references to this novel and this translation will be made parenthetically within the text.

half-brothers presents an allegory of the looming American Civil War.⁹ The allegorical mode, by encompassing cultural, religious, economic, and ethnic tensions that resulted from the cultural encounters in (post-)colonial America, allowed Robinson to unite her concerns with colonial history, religion, and gender.

Goethe's New American Narrative

Besides reflecting Robinson's personal interests in colonial history and theology, *Die Auswanderer* is apparently inspired by Goethe's ideas for a future novel of America. Goethe's famous line, "Amerika, du hast es besser als unser Kontinent, das alte" (America, you are better off than our old continent),¹⁰ has immortalized his optimistic view of the New World as a land of the future.¹¹ But in a less well-known essay, also from 1827, Goethe emphasizes America's colonial history. In this piece, a book review from *Über Kunst und Altertum* (On Art and Antiquity) entitled "Stoff und Gehalt zur Bearbeitung vorgeschlagen" (Material and Content Recommended for Revision), Goethe discusses three non-fiction books, which he describes as "sehr lesenswürdig aber nicht lesbar" (very worth reading but unreadable).¹² Their content deserves to be reworked by a talented writer: "Sie sind alle drei von gehaltreichem Stoff, ganz ohne Form, und bieten sich der geschicktesten Behandlung dar" (They are all of substantial content, completely lacking in form, and lend themselves to skillful adaptation).¹³ One of these works, Ludwig Gall's *Auswanderung nach den Vereinigten Staaten* (Emigration

---

9 Shirley Samuels, "Women at War," in *The Cambridge Companion to Nineteenth-Century American Women's Writing*, ed. Dale M. Bauer and Philip Gould (Cambridge: Cambridge University Press, 2001), 143–56 (145).
10 Quoted in Kriegleder, *Vorwärts in die Vergangenheit*, 184.
11 Kriegleder interprets the ironic coda of Goethe's poem "Den Vereinigten Staaten" (1827) as undermining its optimistic opening by suggesting that "die europäische Vergangenheit [hat] Amerika schon eingeholt" (*Vorwärts in die Vergangenheit*, 185).
12 Goethe, "Stoff und Gehalt," 392. All translations from this essay are my own.
13 Goethe, "Stoff und Gehalt," 392. Goethe wrote both the famous satiric verse "Den Vereinigten Staaten" and "Stoff und Gehalt" during a period of his intense interest in the United States. In 1826 and 1827, Goethe was involved in the publication of Duke Bernhard of Sachsen-Weimar's travelogue, *Reise Sr. Hoheit des Herzogs Bernhard zu Sachsen-Weimar-Eisenach durch Nord-Amerika in den Jahren 1825 und 1826* (1828). This inspired him to read Cooper's novels, as well as several histories of America. See Ernst Beutler, "Von der Ilm zum Susquehanna: Goethe und Amerika in ihren Wechselbeziehungen," *Essays um Goethe*, Sammlung Dieterich 101 (Bremen: Carl Schünemann, 1957), 580–629 (600–1). As Peter J. Brenner points out, Duke Bernhard's travel report was not intended for emigrants, but rather reflected his own interests, particularly in military matters. Peter J. Brenner, *Reisen in die Neue Welt: Die Erfahrung Nordamerikas in deutschen Reise- und Auswandererberichten des 19. Jahrhunderts* (Tübingen: Max Niemeyer, 1991), 73–4.

to the United States, 1822), is a rambling account of the difficulties encountered by a group of emigrants.[14] Goethe suggests that this emigrant advice handbook would be better as a novel (Brenner, *Reisen*, 79). Gall's travel report is one of the earliest intended to inform would-be emigrants, and it was followed by others throughout the 1830s and 1840s, including Gottfried Duden's influential but overly optimistic *Bericht über eine Reise nach den westlichen Staaten Nordamerika's* (Report on a Trip to the Western States of North America, 1829).[15] In summarizing Goethe's generic proposals, *Amerikaroman* scholar Wynfrid Kriegleder posits the importance of Goethe's comments for the development of the Amerikaroman: "America as a setting with a deep historical dimension, a modern style of narration based on Cooper, as well as a subject that encompasses the Old and New World; these elements constitute the promise of a future novel."[16]

Robinson's novel can be viewed as a response to Goethe not only because of striking structural and thematic parallels between her text and his review; it is also safe to assume that Robinson knew Goethe's essay, since the same volume of *Über Kunst und Altertum* contains his favorable review of her translation of the *Volkslieder der Serben*.[17] In *Die Auswanderer* she adopts Goethe's recommendation of combining information with narrative by framing her commentary on the United States with a family plot that encompasses Europe and America over several centuries. In addition, Goethe suggests a Protestant cleric as protagonist who leads a group of emigrants, which Robinson rescripts in a metadiscourse of feminine spiritual authority connected to her heroine, Klotilde. Robinson apparently found in Goethe's generic prescription a method for integrating her historical and religious interests within the popular form of a domestic novel.

Despite the novel's unusual form, it has much to offer a careful reader. In *The Sentimental Education of the Novel*, Margaret Cohen contends that "noncanonical texts are fragments of lost solutions or answers to questions we no longer hear."[18] The "unresolved questions" addressed by

---

14 The title of Robinson's novel, *Die Auswanderer*, echoes that of Gall's poorly written travelogue.
15 Brenner, *Reisen*, 75. On this tradition of "Ratgeberliteratur," see Brenner, *Reisen*, 72–9.
16 Kriegleder, *Vorwärts in die Vergangenheit*, 192. Kriegleder suggests Sealsfield's writings as a partial fulfillment of Goethe's future novel (*Vorwärts in die Vergangenheit*, 192).
17 Robinson is mentioned on pp. 383 and 389.
18 Margaret Cohen, *The Sentimental Education of the Novel* (Princeton: Princeton University Press, 1999), 25. Cohen traces the generic shift from sentimentalism to realism in the nineteenth-century French novel as a gendered struggle over market share in the literary field. She argues persuasively for reconsidering non-canonical texts as rejoinders in a dialogue within the process through which realism assumed the dominant position in genre aesthetics.

underread genres "can have to do with the state of the literary field and they can have to do with the ideological and social contradictions shaping society as a whole."[19] Robinson grapples with both: she experiments with genre in a novel/travelogue blend in which she confronts pressing social issues of her day, such as global migration, slavery and ethnic relations (including Germans' position within them), and women's social and religious authority. Robinson's authorial investments in theology and colonial history are uniquely her own, yet the idiosyncrasies and contradictions of the text fit into a comprehensible whole when we perceive Goethe's vision for the novel of America underlying her compositional strategy. *Die Auswanderer* has been criticized for its disjointed form and especially for its implausible and melodramatic conclusion, which has been a source of irritation for critics.[20]

Goethe's lost solutions to the "problem" of the American travelogue help to make sense of Robinson's global colonial frame for a generational family narrative structured by theological tropes of fratricide and exile, but also of her unique generic and thematic choices that address religious practices by Catholic and Protestant women. Robinson's privileging of the domestic and religious novel rather than the frontier adventure novel positions women at the center of her critique of religion in America.[21] This nexus of women and religion, because it negotiates issues of gender and spiritual authority, permits insights into Robinson's metafictional reflections on the state of the literary field, in which she obliquely addresses social contradictions between gender ideology and female authorship. Through successively delineating these interconnected layers of meaning we can recognize a model of conservative, yet socially engaged female authorship, underpinned by the unified historical vision of a scholar of history, religion, and culture.

Rescripting Goethe's Proposals

In his review Goethe proposes the following specific elements: a historical setting that encompasses America's earliest colonization, characters selected from the "dissatisfied" of both continents, and a narrative style that would compete with Cooper. Robinson's setting and plot fulfill Goethe's proposals by spanning several centuries and continents,

---

19 Margaret Cohen, "Traveling Genres," *New Literary History* 34, no. 3 (2003): 481–99 (482).
20 See Kriegleder, *Vorwärts in die Vergangenheit*, 307; and Sammons, *Ideology*, 203.
21 An early review asserts that Robinson's informative treatment of religious life is unique in the contemporary novel of America. Anon., "Romane von Talvj," review of Therese Robinson, *Die Auswanderer*, *Blätter für literarische Unterhaltung* 47 (November 20, 1852): 1230–5 (1231).

and her characters' dissatisfaction runs so deep that it results in a triple death that "thin[s] out the future."[22] Goethe embedded his suggestions in his call for a historically informed author, who also possesses narrative talent, to write a more readable text. Goethe's criteria would have both applied and appealed to Robinson as the author of *Geschichte der Colonisation von Neu-England* (History of the Colonization of New England, 1847), and the translator of *Über die indianischen Sprachen Amerikas* (On the Indian Languages of America, 1834):

> Um dieses dritte Werk [Gall's *Auswanderung*] gehörig zu benutzen, würde das vorzüglichste Talent verlangt, das zu vielen Vorarbeiten sich entschlösse, sodann aber eine freye Umsicht zu erwerben fähig und glücklich genug wäre. Der Bearbeitende müßte den Stolz haben mit Cooper zu wetteifern und deßhalb die klarste Einsicht in jene überseeischen Gegenstände zu gewinnen suchen. Von der frühsten Colonisation an, von der Zeit des Kampfes an, den die Europäer erst mit den Urbewohnern, dann unter sich selbst führten ... bis zu dem Freyheitskriege, dessen Resultat und Folgen: diese Zustände sämmtlich müßten ihm überhaupt gegenwärtig und im Besonderen klar seyn.[23]
>
> (To make proper use of this third work [Gall's *Emigration*] would require a person of the most exceptional talent, who would commit to many preliminary studies, and would then be sufficiently competent and fortunate to acquire an independent perspective. The adapter would need the pride to vie with Cooper, and therefore would seek to gain the clearest insight into overseas matters. From the earliest colonization, from the time of the struggle of the Europeans, first with the indigenous, and then against each other ... up until the War of Independence and its outcome and consequences: this state of things in its entirety would have to be particularly clear and absolutely present to him.)

Although the Europeans' early struggle against the indigenous Americans receives only brief mention, Robinson certainly fulfills Goethe's suggestions through her in-depth knowledge of American history. Robinson's main historical interest lies in the colonial history of Florida that led to the ongoing struggle in the 1830s between the Seminoles and the US army, which Klotilde witnesses.

---

22 Philip Fisher, *Hard Facts: Setting and Form in the American Novel* (New York: Oxford University Press, 1985), 58.
23 Goethe, "Stoff und Gehalt," 394.

Robinson devotes an entire chapter to the region's history, beginning in 1565 with Spanish colonists driving out French Huguenot settlers (56–61). Religious conflict following the Reformation figures centrally from the beginning, with Melendez's declaration after his victory, "Nicht den Franzosen, den Lutheranern geschah dieses" (56) (this was not done to the French, but to the Lutherans [57]).[24] The genealogy of the Spanish American Losado-Castleton family parallels Spanish colonial history in Florida since the mid-sixteenth century. The Losado family loyalty is aligned with the Spanish monarchy and the colonies. For 200 years their sons are educated either in Spain or in colonial capitals, and hold official positions in Spanish Florida (56). The elder Hubert encounters Josepha in 1815, when her mother Lucia supports South American irregular troops who plant the flag of "Neu-Granada und Venezuela" (59) (New Grenada and Venezuela [61]), a last stand of Spanish imperial aspirations. This detailed history of Florida told through a family that belongs to the "Eroberern dieses Landes" (53) (conquerors of this land [53]) forms a fictional counterpart to Robinson's history of the colonization of New England.

With regard to genre, *Die Auswanderer* combines Cooper's Pathfinder model, in which a hero travels through unknown territory, encountering adventures and challenges reminiscent of heroes of antiquity, with Walter Scott's pattern of a broad social panorama set against a period of social upheaval.[25] Robinson knew the genre of the historical novel well, having translated two of Scott's novels into German early in her publishing career.[26] Her novel also corresponds to Alexander Honold's category of the ethnographic travel and adventure novel, and could additionally be designated as an anti-Catholic novel, but the richness of the text exceeds any single label.[27]

Goethe's suggestions for characters are as interesting for Robinson's divergence from them as for their correspondences:

Was den Personenbestand betrifft, so hat weder ein epischer noch dramatischer Dichter je zur Auswahl einen solchen Reichthum vor sich gesehen. Die Unzufriedenen beyder Welttheile stehn ihm

---

24 All translations are from the 1853 English version unless otherwise indicated.
25 Alexander Honold's discussion of Scott and Cooper emphasizes these two distinct types of narrative constellations. Alexander Honold, "Der Landvermesser: Balduin Möllhausen in Amerika," in *Amerika und die deutschsprachige Literatur nach 1848: Migration—kultureller Austausch—frühe Globalisierung*, ed. Christof Hamann, Ute Gerhard, and Walter Grünzweig (Bielefeld: transcript, 2009), 39–57 (39–43).
26 Licht, "Ökonomien," 246.
27 Honold, "Der Landvermesser," 42.

zu Gebot, er kann sie zum Theil nach und nach zu Grunde gehen, endlich aber, wenn er seine Favoriten günstig untergebracht hat, die übrigen stufenweise mit sehr mäßigen Zuständen sich begnügen lassen.[28]

(Concerning the characters, no epic or dramatic poet has ever had such richness to choose from. The dissatisfied of both continents are at his disposal; he can have them perish one by one, but in the end, when he has situated his favorites advantageously, gradually have the others be satisfied with very modest circumstances.)

Dissatisfaction with political oppression drives the two generations of male protagonists to leave Germany: the elder to escape conscription into Napoleon's Russian campaign, and his son for democratic freedoms. Klotilde's admission that she is "auf meine Weise Europamüde" (11) (in my way, "weary of Europe" [4])—a reference to Ernst Willkomm's novel *Die Europamüden* (*The Europe-Weary*, 1838)— also suggests dissatisfaction. But Robinson cannot save her favorites, since in her catastrophic conclusion historical forces overpower the immigrants' attempt at satisfaction with modest circumstances.

In spite of these parallels in historical setting, genre, and character, Robinson does not wholly affirm Goethe's model of authorship. Analyzing the role of Goethe's writings in the narrative indicates that Robinson resisted his poetry as too individualistic and therefore detrimental to religious and filial piety. She inscribes a veiled rejection of Goethe in her egotistical character Virginia, whose romanticizing of Goethe's writings renders her unfit for social integration within domesticity. After Virginia's encounter with Franz Hubert, which leaves her infatuated with him and his German poetry, she is impatient to learn German in order to read love poetry. She exclaims, "O, wie ungeduldig bin ich, Goethe zu lesen, und Schiller" (90) (Oh, how impatient I am to read Goethe, and Schiller [97]); "Geben Sie mir nichts Anderes zu lesen als Lieder der Liebe, Klotilde! ... Goethe's, Chamisso's und wie Ihre großen Dichter alle heißen. Und besonders—Heine's" (106) (Give me nothing to read ... but the poetry of love, Clotilde! Goethe's, Chamisso's, and whatever else your great poets are called. And particularly, Heine's [114]). Although Goethe is not singled out, but instead is one among the Romantic poets Virginia admires, her puritanical sister Sarah specifically indicts Goethe in a letter to Klotilde. Sarah blames Goethe for

---

28 Goethe, "Stoff und Gehalt," 394.

Virginia's unrepentant jealousy and anger after she learns of Franz and Klotilde's marriage, which so affected her emotionally that she became ill and refused to eat:

> "sie war von uns geflohen, um nicht in ihrem unchristlichen Plane, an einer unglücklichen Liebe zu sterben, gestört zu werden. Das war die Frucht ihrer vertrauten Bekanntschaft mit Ihren deutschen Dichtern, Klotilde, gegen deren falsche, verführerische Lehren kein Christenthum sie stählte. Noch deutlich erinnere ich es mich, daß sie Goethe, der den Selbstmord und den Ehebruch vertheidigt, den größten Dichter nannte ... [and that she claimed that] 'Man lebe nur, so lange man liebe' ... Und was dergleichen Unsinn mehr war." (247)
>
> ("she had fled from us so as not to be frustrated in her unchristian plan of dying of disappointed love. This was the fruit of her intimate acquaintance with your German poets, Clotilde, against whose false, delusive doctrines she had no Christianity to steel her. I remember distinctly that she called Goethe, who defends suicide and adultery, the greatest of poets ... that we only lived as long as we loved ... And more of the like nonsense." [283])

This is undoubtedly meant ironically, as Sarah is a satirical figure. Yet although both women voice American misreadings of Goethe, the fact that Robinson associates Goethe with Virginia, one of her most negative characters, indicates her distance from some of his ideas and writings. Robinson's own relationship to Goethe transcends the simplistic poles of Virginia's naïve infatuation and Sarah's rigid, moralistic rejection. The contours of Robinson's authorial profile as literary and cultural critic who understands the limitations of Americans' grasp of German letters become visible here. We see the informed author Goethe calls for, regarding not only history, but also literary culture.

In contrast to this satirical distance from Goethe, we see a productive reception of his suggestions regarding genre, subject matter, and religion. Interpreting seemingly disjointed elements as an expansion and transformation of Goethe's proposals discloses the extent to which Robinson intervenes in contemporary discourses of religion, colonialism, and gender. Examining each element and their interconnections sheds light on her construction of female authorship, particularly issues of authority and voice. The following section delves into Robinson's dense discourse of religion, through which she establishes female social and moral authority. Although this aspect is only obliquely related to Goethe's ideas, it allows insights into the gender implications of her generic choice of failed marriage plots, and their connection to the larger tropes of religion and colonialism. This political and gender analysis of Robinson's theological allegory as it relates to colonialism renders visible the writing subject manifested through Robinson's network of discourses. What emerges is an authorial profile that authorizes female scholarship and authorship, albeit an ambivalent one.

Rescripting Religion

While the historical elements are easily recognizable as responses to Goethe's outline for the *Amerikaroman*, more intriguing is Robinson's multifaceted reconfiguration of Goethe's recommendations that pertain to religion. This is evident in plot structure, symbolic language, social commentary, and on the level of metanarrative. Goethe proposes a Protestant minister as protagonist, who, like Moses, would lead a group of German immigrants into the Promised Land: "Die Hauptfigur, der protestantische Geistliche, der, selbst auswanderungslustig, die Auswandernden an's Meer und dann hinüberführt, und oft an Moses in den Wüsten erinnern würde" (The main character, the Protestant minister, himself desiring to emigrate, leads the emigrants to the sea and then across it, and would often recall Moses in the wilderness).[29] The reference to Moses in the wilderness invokes the biblical concepts of exile and the Promised Land, which are structuring elements of *Die Auswanderer*.

As Wallach notes, the English title of the novel, *The Exiles*, better captures Robinson's protagonists' experiences by denoting an involuntary absence from home rather than a search for new opportunity.[30] Klotilde and Franz experience a double exile from Germany and from their New England home, where they attempt and fail to create a German Idealist Promised Land filled with music, philosophy, and literature, a refuge of German *Geist* (spirit; Schuchalter, *Narratives*, x). After their deaths, their gravestones memorialize this aborted attempt to establish a German-American republican utopia. Further, the narrative ends with the renewed exile of both Alonzo and Virginia. Alonzo's self-imposed banishment is flight from his unatonable sin: "das Kainszeichen sitzt mir auf der Stirn, ich kann die Heimat nicht wieder sehen ... von Land zu Land will ich streifen" (343) (the mark of Cain is upon my brow; I can see my home no more ... I will roam from land to land [397]). Virginia's high-society life in the capitals of Europe masks the emptiness of

---

29 Goethe, "Stoff und Gehalt," 394.
30 Martha Kaarsberg Wallach, "Die Erfahrung der Fremde in Talvjs Leben und Werk," in *Exotische Welt in populären Lektüren*, ed. Anselm Maler (Tübingen: Niemeyer, 1990), 81–92 (86). See also Dorothea Diver Stuecher, *Twice Removed: The Experience of German-American Women Writers in the Nineteenth Century* (New York: Peter Lang, 1990), 54.

her "darbendes, liebedürstendes Herz" (345) (heart thirsting, famishing for love [399]). In terms of Robinson's biblical framework, the Losado-Castleton relatives are exiled from domesticity and community, just as Klotilde and Franz are, with no opportunity for redemption. Although Franz is the only political martyr—a martyr to his idealism and activism against tyranny in Europe and against slavery in the United States—Klotilde is also martyred, and all three of the southern relatives fail in their quest for love and home, even the devout Sarah.

Much of the ethnographic content also thematizes religion.[31] Aside from extensive commentary on the American denominational landscape (including satirical sketches of Puritan and Unitarian views), two secondary characters function to critique both Catholic and Protestant dogmatism: the Spanish American Josepha—Alonzo's penitent mother—and the Anglo-American Sarah, who was raised in New England by her mother. Sarah represents American religious extremism in her strict devotional schedule of prayer and Bible reading and indefatigable churchgoing. Robinson juxtaposes German femininity, which she associates with domestic and spiritual values in Klotilde, with false dogmatism in these Catholic and Protestant variants. Sarah's "methodische[], nüchterne[] Frömmigkeit" (84) (methodical, unimpassioned piety [90]) both contrasts with and yet resembles the "schwärmerischen Erhebung, der ascetischen Inbrunst Donna Josepha's" (84) (enthusiastic exaltation, the ascetic fervor of Donna Josepha [90]). The anti-Catholic content thereby serves to critique a certain strain of Protestantism.[32]

Yet Robinson's emphasis on religion goes beyond explicit polemics against fanaticism to infuse the symbolic patterns of the text, which is structured around themes of exile and fratricide, and thus religion unites its multiple facets of the colonial and the familial. The clash between Spanish and German immigrants contains two elements from the Cain-and-Abel archetype that date back to the Reformation: religious tensions between Catholic and Protestant, and class distinctions.[33] Robinson's imagery reinforces these cultural and socio-economic

---

31 Jeffrey Sammons observes that religion is the most prevalent aspect of identity in *Die Auswanderer; Ideology*, 204.
32 Interestingly, the accounts of religious beliefs and activities recall the classical travel text (and the earliest by a woman) *Pilgrimage of Egeria* (c. 381–84 CE), with its focus "on the devotional practices of the people she encounters"; Carl Thompson, *Travel Writing* (London: Routledge, 2011), 37. There is no evidence that Robinson knew this text, although she reported that she read numerous travelogues in her youth. See Therese Robinson, "Einleitung," in *Gesammelte Novellen von Talvj*, ed. M[arie] R[obinson], Vol. I (Leipzig: Brockhaus, 1874), vii–xxix (xi).
33 Elisabeth Frenzel, *Stoffe der Weltliteratur*, 10th edn. (Stuttgart: Kröner, 2005), 480.

conflicts between Catholic and Protestant and between southern landowner and northern small farmer by associating Alonzo with emblems of aristocracy in the dueling pistols and an heirloom statue of the Virgin Mary, which was engraved in Spain with the Losado coat of arms.[34] *Die Auswanderer* is a "German-American tragedy" of failed assimilation, but it is equally a colonial tragedy with global political, economic, and religious implications.[35] The sexual conquest of the colonial adventurer in Florida a generation earlier causes the fratricide, and the New World Paradise that the exiles attempt to establish is destroyed by colonial dynamics long since set in place.

More importantly, religion justifies Robinson's positing of female authority. She transposes Goethe's figure of a spiritual leader onto her heroine Klotilde, who models the natural, childlike piety of true religion in contrast to the orthodoxies of Puritanism and Catholicism. In this subtle rescripting of Goethe's idea, Robinson constructs a self-authorizing metadiscourse that addresses gender and religious authority, and thereby aligns her text with nineteenth-century transatlantic feminist discourse that drew on women's purported religiosity and domesticity as a source of female authority. Susan Griffin's designation of religion as a site of female power in nineteenth-century American women's anti-Catholic fiction is relevant to Robinson's theological discourse, which resembles that of Harriet Beecher Stowe and other American women writers who were "major purveyors of theologies through the medium of polemical fiction."[36] Although Robinson shares the sentimental and homiletic tone of writers such as Stowe, her theology takes aim at female self-denial, and instead she propounds a concept of women's psychosexual fulfillment in a love marriage.

Interpreting Klotilde as an avatar of Goethe's spiritual protagonist illuminates Robinson's composition, in which Klotilde functions as the nexus that links the disparate thematic strands. The family plot intersects with the religious and the political in Klotilde's feminine quest for

---

34 See Philip Fisher's discussion of dueling pistols as "symbols of a feudal world" in Cooper's *The Deerslayer*; Fisher, *Hard Facts*, 64.

35 Diver Stuecher, *Twice Removed*, 110. Wallach ascribes the tragic ending to the impossibility of either assimilation or return to a German home ("Erfahrung," 87).

36 Susan Griffin, "Women, Anti-Catholicism, and Narrative in Nineteenth-Century America," in *The Cambridge Companion to Nineteenth-Century American Women's Writing*, ed. Dale M. Bauer and Philip Gould (Cambridge: Cambridge University Press, 2001), 157–75 (157, 172). Robinson would have been familiar with earlier ideas of feminine religious virtue from German Pietism and sentimentalism, as well as with feminist ideas of the 1840s. She spent 1840–1 in Berlin, where she had contact with the liberal writer Bettina Brentano-von Arnim, and in 1840s New York the feminist Margaret Fuller visited Robinson's salon (Licht, "Ökonomien," 257–8).

domestic happiness. The narrative begins with the sentimental device of the heroine's departure from childhood dependence on parents and her entrance into the adult task of selecting an appropriate husband. Onto this structure Robinson grafts her own interests in the sociopolitical contexts of her era, addressing German immigrants' positions within the sectional conflicts of antebellum American society by juxtaposing the colonial seducer with his antislavery (anticolonial) son, Franz. As Griffin asserts, religious fiction cannot be separated "from the political, theological, economic, and racial tensions of the period."[37] Robinson deploys religiosity, domesticity, and sentiment to establish a carefully feminine-gendered form of authoritative commentary on these issues. She draws on this authority not only to address domestic relations in the marriage plots, but simultaneously to negotiate gender and national identity, which are inextricably intertwined with religion and colonialism.

Although she does not lead a group of immigrants into the Promised Land as Goethe suggests, Klotilde is destined to lead the impractical dreamer Franz. In fact, Robinson fashions her into the model immigrant, more adept than Franz at integrating into America's culture and economy. It is she who communicates effectively with the taciturn farmers in Vermont, which she accomplishes by attending their church and winning their trust. While they consider Franz "ein Träumer, ein deutscher Bücherwurm" (298) (a dreamer, a German bookworm [343]), Klotilde makes "den günstigsten Eindruck" (300) (the most favorable impression [346]). In the metalanguage of gender, it is the female immigrant who evinces the moral seriousness befitting republican virtue, she who is capable of mediating between learning and feeling, theological orthodoxy and piety, and between American regional ideologies and German humanitarian philosophy. Franz, by contrast, unites Enlightenment skepticism and deism with a Romantic poetic nature. On the level of plot, Klotilde is capable of shrewd and daring action: she arranges Franz's early release from prison in Germany by maneuvering her social connections, and in Charleston she enables his escape from prison by smuggling tools past the guard. Twice she must rescue him from the consequences of his incautious political activities before she can marry him, thereby exhibiting female social authority and agency. This indicates Robinson's independence from Goethe's intellectual influence. She selectively adapts his narratological ideas, while contesting his famous pronouncement on gender and literary characters (from his 1823 review of Johanna Schopenhauer's novel *Gabriele* [1819–20]), which reinforced an active/passive dichotomy: "Epische, halbepische

---

37 Griffin, "Women, Anti-Catholicism, and Narrative," 158.

Dichtung verlangt eine Hauptfigur, die bei vorwaltender Tätigkeit durch den Mann, bei überwiegendem Leiden durch die Frau vorgestellt wird"[38] (Epic poetry and fiction require a protagonist who has to be a man if activity is central, and a woman, if suffering … is at the core).[39]

(Anti-) Sentimental Marriage Plots

The politics of gender, religion, and colonialism all intersect within the generic structure of the romance plot. In the only comment on Robinson by an Americanist, Nina Baym observed that Klotilde's death deviates from the formulaic feminine plot. Baym maintains that, "No other heroine of American woman's fiction fails to recover from a romantic tragedy."[40] In spite of my reading of the conclusion as political allegory, Baym's interpretation of the novel as a female romantic tragedy highlights the fact that three young women (and two young men) fail to achieve a happy ending in the domestic harmony of a suitable marriage. These characters' negotiation of love and sexuality plays out not only within the internecine conflict between the American north and south, but also within trans-oceanic colonial conflicts. Klotilde's marriage to Franz, which is based on a youthful infatuation, ends disastrously. Virginia enters an unfulfilling marriage of convenience, while the puritanical Sarah forgoes a love match with a missionary to India. The unhappy marriages of both southern sisters convey Robinson's critique of an unfeminine denial of true emotion.

The subplot of Sarah's marriage is striking for its echoes of Charlotte Brontë's radical novel *Jane Eyre* (1848), in which Jane turns down the marriage proposal of her cousin, St. John, because it is based on a missionary partnership, rather than passionate love. In Robinson's novel, Sarah's decision to accept a similar missionary marriage of convenience reverses Jane's defiant refusal. Despite Sarah's requited love for

---

38 Johann Wolfgang Goethe, "*Gabriele*, von Johanna Schopenhauer [Über Kunst und Altertum: Vierten Bandes erstes Heft. 1823]," in *Johann Wolfgang Goethe: Gedenkausgabe der Werke, Briefe und Gespräche*, ed. Ernst Beutler, Vol. XIV, *Schriften zur Literatur* (Zürich: Artemis, 1950), 319–22 (319).
39 Translated by Barbara Becker-Cantarino in "Goethe as a Critic of Literary Women," in *Goethe as a Critic of Literature*, ed. Karl J. Fink and Max L. Baeumer (Lanham, MD: University Press of America, 1984), 160–81 (169). Becker-Cantarino discusses other famous quotes on gender and women writers from Goethe's publications and letters, including Goethe's and Schiller's writings on the "Dilettantism der Weiber" (162–4). Christa Bürger also demonstrates a clear link between their concept of dilettantism and women's writing; *Leben Schreiben: Die Klassik, die Romantik und der Ort der Frauen* (Stuttgart: Metzler, 1990), 25.
40 Nina Baym, *Woman's Fiction: A Guide to Novels by and about Women in America, 1820–1870* (Ithaca, NY: Cornell University Press, 1978), 249.

Fleming, a missionary to India, she obeys her church's plan for her to marry a missionary to Africa, even though it is based merely on financial considerations of dividing up Sarah's and Fleming's personal fortunes among the mission fields. Sarah chooses religious obedience over emotional and sexual fulfillment because she views life as "eine Erziehungsanstalt ... für jenseits" (249) (a school for the next [life] [285]). This allusion to Jane's overt rejection of patriarchal religious authority over individual female sexual and emotional fulfillment contrasts with the essential social conservatism of Robinson's novel. Robinson clearly deplores Sarah's acquiescence to an arranged marriage out of a misplaced notion of religious self-denial. Moreover, Sarah's marriage reinforces the tragedy inherent in the colonial project, in that her civilizing mission appears equally detrimental to domestic harmony as the German mercenary's participation in the colonizing process a generation earlier. This subplot, in which Sarah goes to Liberia as a missionary, extends the text's colonial coordinates eastwards, back across the Atlantic, to encompass the world-wide framework of the civilizing mission associated with colonialism.

The generational repetition of arranged marriages discloses the extent to which this narrative rests on inheritance and dynastic ambition. Josepha's mother Lucia was forced into an arranged marriage with the Anglo-Protestant Castleton, whom she regarded as a "Ketzer" (57) (heretic [59]), in order to increase the Losado wealth. Two generations later, the arranged match between Alonzo and Virginia is intended to reunite the Losado-Castleton landholdings in Florida and South Carolina. Mary Paniccia Carden's observation that romance plots "channel multiple currents of desire" illuminates these intercultural alliances driven by erotic or material desire.[41] In what initially appears to be a secondary plot, Franz Hubert's temporary attraction to Virginia unwittingly repeats his father's colonial desire. It eventually becomes clear that this subplot is indispensable for setting in place the duel, which is motivated as much by Alonzo's misplaced sense of Virginia's injured honor as by resentment of the foreign abolitionist. After Franz discovers that Klotilde is still living and they marry, Virginia is embittered by her feelings of abandonment, and makes marrying Alonzo dependent on his "Bestrafung des Verräters" (323) (punishment of the traitor [my translation]). Virginia is caught up in the fratricidal conflict between

---

41 Mary Paniccia Carden, "Making Love, Making History: (Anti) Romance in Alice McDermott's *At Weddings and Wakes* and *Charming Billy,*" in *Doubled Plots: Romance and History*, ed. Susan Strehle and Mary Paniccia Carden (Jackson: University Press of Mississippi, 2003), 3–23 (3).

north and south to an equal extent with her cousin Alonzo. On the level of the romance plot, Virginia functions as the feminine seductress—Alonzo calls her "die glänzende Schlange" (343) (the glittering serpent [396])—who destroys both Franz and Alonzo by inciting the latter to jealous revenge. But her attraction to Franz's foreign German culture—she takes lessons from him in German language and poetry—contains the seed of destruction, and parallels the deadly attraction between north and south, representing the irreconcilable conflict of colonial legacy and anticolonial sentiment enacted on the North American continent. No domestic happiness is attainable—no home, no happy ending, no escape from the dichotomies of colonial contact: Protestant/Catholic, Spanish/Northern European, free immigrant/enslaved African. Robinson has her characters "nach und nach zu Grunde gehen" (perish one by one), because she traces their history "[v]on der frühsten Colonisation an" (from the earliest colonization).[42] Klotilde's death is determined by the author's doubled historical and theological vision of the sins of the father. In this multifaceted tragedy of desire and revenge, brotherhood and fratricide, domesticity and exile, the effects of colonial desire and the dread of contact drive the narrative movement.

Gendered Colonial Theology

The colonial context serves as a vehicle for Robinson to redefine the alignments of German masculinity and femininity. Masculine sexuality is connected with the colonial in the seduction narrative, while femininity is linked to religion and philosophy through Klotilde. Franz and Alonzo's bigamous father, who turns out to be the first "emigrant," aligns German masculinity with colonial conquest and seduction. Within the logic of the text, colonialism figures as the Fall, the original sin that results in loss of innocence and renders the tragedy inevitable. The Cain-and-Abel allusion functions as an extended metaphor for geopolitical tensions, and is thus grounded in materiality. Rather than a productive impetus, Robinson construes the inheritance of colonial sexual and cultural mixing as death, destruction, and permanent exile. Just as original sin is inherited, the generation not responsible for colonial relations suffers their effects. The dead bodies of Franz, Klotilde, and their stillborn child bear the material effects of male sexual adventuring in the colonies.[43] Their deaths convey the novel's political implications by suggesting the demise of German culture in the irreconcilable conflict between north and south. In this way, Robinson's configuration

---

42 Goethe, "Stoff und Gehalt," 394.
43 Diver Stuecher, in contrast, reads Klotilde's attitude as one of resignation; *Twice Removed*, 61.

of biblical and colonial dynamics brings into relief the contradictions between the text's positing of German cultural superiority—it purportedly represents a high level of civilization, aesthetics, and enlightened social and religious sensibility—and German implication in colonial processes.

Within the complex interrelations between romance genre, colonial history, and allegory Robinson envisions no redemptive role for German cultural identity in the United States. Instead her vision "leave[s] readers with indelible impressions of their mobility and of the sense of displacement."[44] Werner Sollor's dichotomous concepts of descent (or ancestry), and consent (or choice) that operate in American national identity apply to Robinson's narrative of failed immigration. The language of descent overpowers the language of consent—the ability to "choose our spouses, our destinies, and our political systems"[45]—and Klotilde and Franz's "lost love reflects the loss of certainty in the cataclysms of modern history."[46] As Baym noted, the text departs from the conventional resolution of the bourgeois romance novel. Rather than lasting social relations in marriage and family, Robinson confronts the reader with the complexities of unresolved conflict in a mobile, unstable world. Her characters are caught up in the "composite momentum" of post-colonial processes unfolding across North American regions.[47] These are the conclusions Robinson draws at mid-century from the "klarste Einsicht in jene überseeischen Gegenstände" (clearest insight into overseas matters) that Goethe demanded of the author who would fulfill his proposals.[48] Over two decades after he wrote his review, the "Resultat und Folgen" (outcome and consequences) of colonial conflicts in North America were heading to a fratricidal military confrontation.[49] Robinson's historical discourse on America on the one hand echoes Goethe's optimistic poem, but on the other hand responds to his statements on colonial history in the book review. An optimistic passage

---

44 Karen A. Weyler, "Race, Redemption, and Captivity in the Narratives of Briton Hammon and John Marrant," in *Genius in Bondage: Literature of the Early Black Atlantic*, ed. Vincent Carretta and Philip Gould (Lexington: University Press of Kentucky, 2001), 39–53 (49).
45 Werner Sollors, *Beyond Ethnicity: Consent and Descent in American Culture* (New York: Oxford University Press, 1986), 6 (quoted by Carden, "Making Love, Making History," 6).
46 Susan Strehle and Mary Paniccia Carden, "Introduction: Reading Romance, Reading History," in *Doubled Plots: Romance and History*, ed. Susan Strehle and Mary Paniccia Carden (Jackson: University Press of Mississippi, 2003), xi–2 (xxvii).
47 Fisher, *Hard Facts*, 70.
48 Goethe, "Stoff und Gehalt," 394.
49 Goethe, "Stoff und Gehalt," 394.

near the end of *Die Auswanderer* that describes the United States as "ein Land, das statt einer Vorzeit eine Zukunft hatte" (341) (a country which, instead of a Past, had only a Future [394]), is juxtaposed with the denouement, which demonstrates how deeply it is determined by past transatlantic colonial relations.

Gender and Literary Voice

Robinson's reconfiguration of Goethe's recommendations pertaining to colonial history and religion brings into focus her theological allegory and her metanarrative of feminine religious and social authority. This in turn uncovers features of an authorial persona that is produced in part by the woman writer's dialogic exchange with her male interlocutor. Cheryl Walker defines the female author's persona as an organizing feature or structuring device, a mask or construct that is broader than the narrator or a character who functions as authorial mouthpiece.[50] By focusing on "patterns of ideation, voice, and sensibility linked together by a connection to the author,"[51] Walker's persona criticism relates texts to wider intellectual and literary contexts that are "broader than the personal."[52] These insights illuminate Robinson's authorial profile as historical scholar, cultural ethnographer, and conservative purveyor of homiletic lessons regarding domesticity and discipline, and bring into relief the metafictional narrative of female authority. Robinson's persona is characterized by the intellectual independence and confidence to transpose Goethe's ideas in accordance with her first-hand experience and research in America. Beyond the structural aspects that build on his suggestions, a departure from Goethe is evident in her negotiations of religion and gender, which manifest a subtle defiance of masculinist notions of feminine gender.

Walker's concept of a female literary persona based on textual representation also alerts us to certain features of style and voice in *Die Auswanderer* that address gendered dimensions of authorship and reading. For example, Klotilde is aligned with the author's persona, both as the representative of religious moderation, and by virtue of several autobiographical characteristics. Yet in a key chapter devoted to cultural commentary, it is Klotilde's husband, Franz Hubert, rather than Klotilde, who articulates the female author's knowledge as

---

50 Cheryl Walker, "Persona Criticism and the Death of the Author," in *Contesting the Subject: Essays in the Postmodern Theory and Practice of Biography and Biographical Criticism*, ed. William Epstein (West Lafayette, IN: Purdue University Press, 1991), 109–21 (114–15).
51 Walker, "Persona Criticism and the Death of the Author," 109.
52 Walker, "Persona Criticism and the Death of the Author," 116.

cultural critic. In this and other passages, Robinson thereby expresses her own authoritative knowledge in a masculine voice. The disparate philosophical preoccupations of the couple correspond to distinct narrative modes that reflect conventional gender alignments. Klotilde's direct interactions and perceptions in Florida and Charleston are related by the third-person narrator, in contrast to Franz's informative reports to Klotilde on his experiences of New England society and culture. While Klotilde observes and participates, his words read like lectures or articles, marking a stylistic break and a narrative digression while the couple rest and get married after fleeing from Charleston. Nina Baym underscores this transition: "By this point in the story, *The Exiles* has become a kind of commentary on America as perceived by the educated foreigner; it is more intellectual and abstract than the typical woman's fiction."[53] This shift in style prompts a rare authorial intrusion that alerts the reader to Hubert's tendency to "philosophisch-dilatorischen Erklärungen" (207) (dilatory philosophical explanations [236]), and explains that each of these sections should be read not as a single verbatim conversation, but as a summary of several. The fact that Robinson places her own observations on American literature, philosophy, and art into the mouth of her male protagonist seems an accommodating gesture towards normative gendered domains of *Bildung*. The reader is apparently to imagine a male scholar sitting at his desk, rather than a woman. The self-authorizing effect of this masculine ventriloquism reaches its epitome in Franz's defense of American women's higher social status, an attitude that was rare in this literature, and therefore perhaps best not propounded by a woman's voice (Robinson, *Die Auswanderer*, 204–7). According to Juliane Mikoletsky, this is the longest passage approving of respect for women in the American novel.[54] Furthermore, through shifting authorial voices and perspectives, Robinson addresses readers of both conventional gender identities, with material to appeal to supposedly masculine interests in history, geography, and society, and feminine interests in domesticity, religious ethics, and romance.

In another passage Robinson thematizes gender and learning through Klotilde's refusal to engage in a discussion about German theological scholars because it exceeds her knowledge (129). This demonstrative denial of scholarly learning echoes Robinson's constructed autobiography, which also emphasizes feminine modesty and valorizes care for

---

53 Baym, *Women's Fiction*, 249.
54 Juliane Mikoletsky, *Die deutsche Amerika-Auswanderung des 19. Jahrhunderts in der zeitgenössischen fiktionalen Literatur* (Tübingen: Max Niemeyer, 1988), 307.

family and home before research and writing.⁵⁵ Robinson's authorial profile emerges from the juxtaposition of knowledge of American history, religion, and literature with such modest disclaimers. The gender polarities that Robinson simultaneously reinforces and challenges are encapsulated in Goethe's famous description of the young Therese von Jakob as having "the heart of a woman, but the brain of a man."⁵⁶ Her autobiographical self-representation and textual authorial mask apparently coincide.

However, her oblique discourse of feminine spiritual authority undercuts these accommodating gestures. In a form of sentiment that privileges women's desire, female subjectivity is authorized by Klotilde's conception of religion as childlike piety and acceptance of God's will, and by her corollary privileging of individual feeling as God-given, and thus not to be denied (118). In challenging the discourse of female selflessness, these elements amount to a metadiscourse of female individuation grounded in the domains to which women were relegated in conventional gender discourse, and align Robinson's writing with that of many nineteenth-century women writers in America and Europe.⁵⁷ The heroine's effectiveness at integration into her adopted home and the disparaging references to Goethe constitute further elements of Robinson's authorial persona as intellectually independent but socially conservative.

The hybridity that, as I have argued, is based on Goethe's generic proposal of travelogue framed by a narrative, creates on the one hand generic instability and lack of cohesiveness, but simultaneously permits a multiplicity of voices and perspectives. Robinson found in Goethe's future novel a structure for connecting her multifaceted articulation of love plots, colonial history, and theological allegory with her commentary on the United States. Although her engagement with religion expands beyond Goethe's single comment on this topic, the religious dimension underpinning the seemingly disparate strands of discourse is best understood when we read the novel alongside Goethe's review. Within a highly idiosyncratic form Robinson also indirectly reflected on

---

55 See, for example, the introduction to *Gesammelte Novellen von Talvj*, where her daughter asserts that she did not wish to be known as a "gelehrte Frau," and that she was proud of attending to her domestic duties before her research and writing (Robinson, *Gesammelte Novellen*, xxvii–xxviii).
56 Quoted in Irma Elizabeth Voigt, *The Life and Works of Mrs. Therese Robinson (Talvj)* (Chicago: Deutsch-Amerikanische Historische Gesellschaft von Illinois, 1914), 42.
57 See Monica Anderson, *Women and the Politics of Travel 1870–1914* (Madison, NJ: Fairleigh Dickinson University Press, 2006), 26.

women's social role and authority to write on a wide variety of subjects. Reading *Die Auswanderer* as a rejoinder in Goethe's dialogue on the *Amerikaroman* inaugurates a deeper understanding of this underread text, especially with regard to the metafictional discourse on gender and the authorial profile that emerges from it. And it clarifies Robinson's response to more recent texts, most notably for a conservative author the explicitly feminist *Jane Eyre*. As a fragment of a lost solution to Goethe's posing of the problem of the *Amerikaroman* genre, we can see that Robinson drew on his suggestions regarding form and content, but used them to transform contemporary discourse on religion and colonialism in precisely gendered ways that establish feminine religious authority and diminish masculine moral authority. The generic experiments through which she accomplishes this should be examined in relation to other texts by women and men.

Bibliography

Anderson, Monica. *Women and the Politics of Travel 1870–1914*. Madison, NJ: Fairleigh Dickinson University Press, 2006.

Anon. "Romane von Talvj." Review of Therese Robinson, *Die Auswanderer*. *Blätter für literarische Unterhaltung* 47 (November 20, 1852): 1230–5.

Baym, Nina. *Woman's Fiction: A Guide to Novels by and about Women in America, 1820–1870*. Ithaca, NY: Cornell University Press, 1978.

Becker-Cantarino, Barbara. "Goethe as a Critic of Literary Women." In *Goethe as a Critic of Literature*, ed. Karl J. Fink and Max L. Baeumer, 160–81. Lanham, MD: University Press of America, 1984.

Beutler, Ernst. "Von der Ilm zum Susquehanna: Goethe und Amerika in ihren Wechselbeziehungen." In *Essays um Goethe*, 580–629. Sammlung Dieterich 101. Bremen: Carl Schünemann, 1957.

Brenner, Peter J. *Reisen in die Neue Welt: Die Erfahrung Nordamerikas in deutschen Reise- und Auswandererberichten des 19. Jahrhunderts*. Tübingen: Max Niemeyer, 1991.

Brown, Jerry Wayne. *The Rise of Biblical Criticism in America, 1800–1870: The New England Scholars*. Middletown, CT: Wesleyan University Press, 1969.

Bürger, Christa. *Leben Schreiben: Die Klassik, die Romantik und der Ort der Frauen*. Stuttgart: Metzler, 1990.

Carden, Mary Paniccia. "Making Love, Making History: (Anti) Romance in Alice McDermott's *At Weddings and Wakes* and *Charming Billy*." In *Doubled Plots: Romance and History*, ed. Susan Strehle and Mary Paniccia Carden, 3–23. Jackson: University Press of Mississippi, 2003.

Cohen, Margaret. *The Sentimental Education of the Novel*. Princeton: Princeton University Press, 1999.

Cohen, Margaret. "Traveling Genres." *New Literary History* 34, no. 3 (2003): 481–99.

Diver Stuecher, Dorothea. *Twice Removed: The Experience of German-American Women Writers in the Nineteenth Century*. New York: Peter Lang, 1990.

Fisher, Philip. *Hard Facts: Setting and Form in the American Novel*. New York: Oxford University Press, 1985.

Foster, Shirley. *Across New Worlds: Nineteenth-Century Women Travellers and Their Writings*. New York: Harvester Wheatsheaf, 1990.

Frenzel, Elisabeth. *Stoffe der Weltliteratur.* 10th edn. Stuttgart: Kröner, 2005.
Goethe, Johann Wolfgang von. "*Gabriele*, von Johanna Schopenhauer [Über Kunst und Altertum: Vierten Bandes erstes Heft. 1823]." In *Johann Wolfgang Goethe: Gedenkausgabe der Werke, Briefe und Gespräche*, ed. Ernst Beutler. Vol. XIV, *Schriften zur Literatur*, 319–22. Zürich: Artemis, 1950.
Goethe, Johann Wolfgang von. "Stoff und Gehalt zur Bearbeitung vorgeschlagen." In *Johann Wolfgang Goethe: Sämtliche Werke. Briefe, Tagebücher und Gespräche.* Vol. I.22, *Ästhetische Schriften 1824–1832: Über Kunst und Altertum V–VI*, ed. Anne Bohnenkamp, 392–5. Frankfurt am Main: Deutscher Klassiker Verlag, 1999.
Goethe, Johann Wolfgang von and Therese Robinson. "Briefwechsel zwischen Goethe und Therese von Jakob." Ed. Reinhold Steig. *Goethe-Jahrbuch* 12 (1891): 33–77.
Griffin, Susan. "Women, Anti-Catholicism, and Narrative in Nineteenth-Century America." In *The Cambridge Companion to Nineteenth-Century American Women's Writing*, ed. Dale M. Bauer and Philip Gould, 157–75. Cambridge: Cambridge University Press, 2001.
Honold, Alexander. "Der Landvermesser: Balduin Möllhausen in Amerika." In *Amerika und die deutschsprachige Literatur nach 1848: Migration—kultureller Austausch—frühe Globalisierung*, ed. Christof Hamann, Ute Gerhard, and Walter Grünzweig, 39–57. Bielefeld: transcript, 2009.
Kriegleder, Wynfrid. "Sealsfield—Strubberg—Karl May; oder, Der deutsche Amerikaroman wird zum Ego-Trip." *Yearbook of German-American Studies* 46 (2011): 5–19.
Kriegleder, Wynfrid. *Vorwärts in die Vergangenheit: Das Bild der USA im deutschsprachigen Roman von 1776 bis 1855.* Tübingen: Stauffenburg, 1999.
Licht, Gisela. "Ökonomien des Begehrens: Die Strategien der deutschamerikanischen Schriftstellerin Therese Albertine Luise von Jakob Robinson (1797–1870) auf dem Weg zur Berufsschriftstellerin." In *Ökonomien des Lebens: Zum Wirtschaften der Geschlechter in Geschichte und Gegenwart*, ed. Eva Labouvie and Katharina Bunzmann, 241–63. Münster: Literatur, 2004.
Mikoletsky, Juliane. *Die deutsche Amerika-Auswanderung des 19. Jahrhunderts in der zeitgenössischen fiktionalen Literatur.* Tübingen: Max Niemeyer, 1988.
Robinson, Therese. *Die Auswanderer: Eine Erzählung von Talvj. Therese von Jakob-Robinsons Amerikaroman (1852).* Ed. with an afterword by Mark-Georg Dehrmann. Hanover: Wehrhahn, 2010 [1852].
Robinson, Therese. "Einleitung." In *Gesammelte Novellen von Talvj*, ed. M[arie] R[obinson]. Vol. I, vii–xxix. Leipzig: Brockhaus, 1874.
Robinson, Therese. *The Exiles: A Tale. By Talvi, Author of "Heloise," "The Literature of the Sclavic [sic] Nations,"* etc. Trans. Marie Robinson. New York: G. P. Putnam, 1853.
Sammons, Jeffrey L. *Ideology, Mimesis, Fantasy: Charles Sealsfield, Friedrich Gerstäcker, Karl May, and Other German Novelists of America.* Chapel Hill: University of North Carolina Press, 1998.
Samuels, Shirley. "Women at War." In *The Cambridge Companion to Nineteenth-Century American Women's Writing*, ed. Dale M. Bauer and Philip Gould, 143–56. Cambridge: Cambridge University Press, 2001.
Schubert, Gabriella and Friedhilde Krause, eds. *TALVJ: Therese Albertine Luise von Jakob-Robinson. Aus Liebe zu Goethe: Mittlerin der Balkanslawen.* Weimar: VDG and Datenbank für Geisteswissenschaften, 2001.

Schuchalter, Jerry. *Narratives of America and the Frontier in Nineteenth-Century German Literature*. New York: Peter Lang, 2000.
Sollors, Werner. *Beyond Ethnicity: Consent and Descent in American Culture*. New York: Oxford University Press, 1986.
Strehle, Susan and Mary Paniccia Carden, eds. *Doubled Plots: Romance and History*. Jackson: University Press of Mississippi, 2003.
Thompson, Carl. *Travel Writing*. London: Routledge, 2011.
Voigt, Irma Elizabeth. *The Life and Works of Mrs. Therese Robinson (Talvj)*. Chicago: Deutsch-Amerikanische Historische Gesellschaft von Illinois, 1914.
Walker, Cheryl. "Persona Criticism and the Death of the Author." In *Contesting the Subject: Essays in the Postmodern Theory and Practice of Biography and Biographical Criticism*, ed. William Epstein, 109–21. West Lafayette, IN: Purdue University Press, 1991.
Wallach Kaarsberg, Martha. "Die Erfahrung der Fremde in Talvjs Leben und Werk." In *Exotische Welt in populären Lektüren*, ed. Anselm Maler, 81–92. Tübingen: Niemeyer, 1990.
Wallach Kaarsberg, Martha."Exile and Nation, Body and Gender in the Works of Talvj (1797–1870)." In *Writing against Boundaries: Nationality, Ethnicity and Gender in the German-Speaking Context*, ed. Barbara Kosta and Helga Kraft, 29–38. Amsterdam: Rodopi, 2003.
Wallach Kaarsberg, Martha. "Talvj: Therese Albertine Luise von Jakob-Robinson." In *Dictionary of Literary Biography*. Vol. CXXXIII, *Nineteenth Century German Writers to 1840*, ed. James Hardin and Siegfried Mews, 280–8. Detroit: Gale Research, 1993.
Weyler, Karen A. "Race, Redemption, and Captivity in the Narratives of Briton Hammon and John Marrant." In *Genius in Bondage: Literature of the Early Black Atlantic*, ed. Vincent Carretta and Philip Gould, 39–53. Lexington: University Press of Kentucky, 2001.

Index

Addison, Joseph 27
aesthetics 2
Albertson, Leif Ludwig 54
allegory 299, 306
Altman, Janet G. 258
American Civil War 298, 299
   antebellum conflict 297, 309
American colonial history 295, 296, 299, 301, 307, 312–14
   history of Florida 297, 298, 302, 303, 308, 315
Amerikaroman genre/German novel of America 297, 299, 300, 306, 317
androgyny 11
anonymity 30, 41, 136–8, 227, 235–6
apprenticeship 28–9
Aristophanes 130, 131
Arndt, Johann 48
Arnim, Bettina von. *See* Brentano-von Arnim, Bettina
Arnim, Ludwig Achim von 125, 187, 192, 193, 194, 195, 205
artist 42
author: definition 23–5
author-couple 22
author function 2, 24
authorship
   co-authorship 23–7
   collaboration and 6–13
      Romantic models 5, 16, 125, 126, 127, 156, 227, 229, 241, 250

   gender and 1–6, 182, 183
   genius and (*see* genius model)
   heterotextual 8
   pathways to 46
      La Roche and Wieland 51–63
   reflexive authorship 16, 255, 257, 260, 267, 271
autobiographical writing 274, 275
autonomy 219
Autor 14, 182, 183, 184, 187, 188, 190, 202, 203, 204, 205
Autor-Funktion/Autorinnen-Funktion 2
Autorin 184–5, 187, 188

Bach, Johann Sebastian 32
Bakhtin, Mikhail 8
Ball, Gabriele 26, 40
Balsamo, Giuseppe. *See* Cagliostro
baptism 247–8
Barthes, Roland 7–8, 23–4, 25, 41
Basedow, Johann Jacob 65
Basile, Giambattista 182
Battersby, Christine 2
Bayle, Pierre 22, 29, 35, 36, 50
Baym, Nina 310, 313, 315
Becker-Cantarino, Barbara 127, 136
Beethoven, Ludwig van 79
Berger, John 219
Berlin 5, 125, 227, 232, 241, 242, 244, 245, 256
Bettig, Ronald 236, 249
Bianconi, Giovanni 46

Bildung/intellectual development 15, 105, 107
  female *Bildung* 106 (*see also* women's education)
  Amanda und Eduard 119–24
  antisocial narratives 107–9, 113, 115–16, 125
  erotic love 109–13, 115–16
  "Marie" 113–19
  self-contained wholeness 116–19, 121–4
  sexual anthropology 108–9, 115–19, 123
Bildungsroman 97
binarism 10–11, 31, 32, 182
  Geschlechtscharaktere 184–8
  vs. hermaphroditic concepts 14, 157, 159–62, 164–6, 169, 173, 174
  male-female/active-passive 213
  Märchenoma and 184, 186, 187, 188, 205
  replacement 199–205
  resistance 195–9
  subversion 192–5
biographical details 23
Blackwell, Jeannine 196
Bloom, Harold 9
Bodmer, Johann Jakob 54, 55, 56
Boisserée, Sulpiz 210
Bonnet, Charles 83
book market 3
Borowski, L. E. 80
Bosse, Heinrich 1, 2, 236
Bottigheimer, Ruth 190
Boyle, Nicholas 65
Brede, Auguste 288
Brentano, Clemens 125, 187, 192, 254, 259
Brentano-von Arnim, Bettina 4, 13, 15–16, 125–6, 138, 205
  Clemens Brentanos Frühlingskranz/Clemens Brentano's Spring Wreath (1844) 254
  collaboration with Grimm brothers 184, 185, 192–5, 199
  defiance of boundaries 253–5
  Die Günderode/Günderode (1840) 254, 256–66
    affinity between Hölderlin and Günderrode 266–70
    construction 257–60
    Ephraim 269
    intellectual reciprocity 258, 263–6
    multiplicity of voices 260, 261–3
    productive disunity 256–7, 258, 262, 265, 270–1
    rhythm 263
    schwebende Religion/hovering religion 265–6
    subjunctive of indirect discourse 260
    "thorns" 268, 269, 270
    Tian (pseudonym of Günderrode) 256, 268
    Zäsur/caesura 270
    zusammen denken 264–5, 270
  Dies Buch gehört dem König/The King's Book (1843) 255
  Gespräche mit Dämonen/Conversations with Daemons (1852) 255
  Goethes Briefwechsel mit einem Kinde/Goethe's Correspondence with a Child (1835) 254, 268–9
  Ilius Pamphilius und die Ambrosia/Ilius Pamphilius and Ambrosia (1848) 254
Brentano-von Guaita, Magdalena (Melina) 259
Brentano-von Savigny, Kunigunda (Gunda) 259
Brinckmann, Karl Gustav von 229

Brontë, Charlotte 297
  Jane Eyre 310, 311, 317
Brown, Hilary 34, 35
Buchmärchen 183

Cagliostro (Giuseppe Balsamo) 14–15, 75
  charlatanism 77, 87
  collaboration with Elisa von der Recke 76–8, 83–7
  exposé by Elisa von der Recke 79–81, 87–93, 96–101
canonical authors 13, 77, 199
canonical genres 3
Carden, Mary Paniccia 311
Carolsfeld, Ludwig Ferdinand Schnorr von 151, 152
Casanova, Giacomo 79
Catherine the Great 77, 79, 84, 98–9
Catholicism 301, 303, 307, 308
Chamisso, Adelbert von 155
Chodowiecki, Daniel 99
classical languages/literature 49–50
  Greek tragedies 163
co-authorship 23–7, 41, 42
Cohen, Margaret 300
collaboration 3, 5–6
  authorship and 6–13
  conjugal (*see* conjugal co-authorship)
  cross-gender 125, 151–3, 213
    Symphilosophie/Symphilosophieren 5, 16, 127–39, 151, 227, 241, 249, 267
  female-female 9, 10
  folklore projects 187–8
    (*see also Märchenoma*)
    Brothers Grimm: collaboration as extraction 188–91
  hermaphroditic collaboration 14, 157, 158, 171, 178
  influence and 9
  power differentials 10, 12
  pronouncements versus practice 28–33
  Romantic models of authorship 5, 16, 125, 126, 127, 156, 227, 229, 241, 250
  translation as collaborative authorship 29–30, 33–5, 36–7
colonialism 295, 296, 297, 298, 299, 301, 302–3, 307, 308, 312–14
conjugal co-authorship
  Gottscheds 13, 21–2, 23, 41, 42
  Schumanns' marriage diary 275, 276
    audience 278, 279
    dialogic element 277, 279, 280
    family life 285–7
    polyphony 282
    ruptures 281–2, 292–3
    stipulations 287–8
    tensions 284–7, 288, 290
consumer society 45
cooperation 46
Cooper, James Fenimore 297, 300, 301, 302
copyright 1, 25, 236, 250
correspondence/letter writing. *See* letters
Cotta, Johann Friedrich 232, 234
Courland 75, 78, 81, 82, 84
(Le) Courrier français 236
Cox, Carrie 78–9
creativity 4
  genius and 187
  hermaphroditism and 158–9, 162, 163, 178
cross-gender collaboration 125, 151–3, 213
  Symphilosophie 5, 127–39, 151

Dämon des Socrates/daemon of Socrates 261, 262, 263
Darmstadt circle 65

d'Aulnoy, Marie-Catherine 197, 199
Deibel, Franz 145
Deiulio, Laura 288–9
de Man, Paul 276
dialectic 27, 38, 137, 151
diaries 274, 275, 276–7
   solipsism 277
Dietrick, Linda 4
Dion 262, 264
Dischner, Gisela 255
divinity 159, 161, 167, 169, 172, 174, 177
Dohm, Hedwig 185
Donnert, Erich 80
drama 2, 4
Drewitz, Ingeborg 255
Droste-Hülshoff, Annette von 183, 184, 195–9, 202, 205
Dualism. *See* binarism
Duden, Gottfried 300
Dumas, Alexandre 100
Duval, Alexandre: *Le Tasse* 236

Eakin, Paul 276
Ebeling, Elisabeth 187
Eco, Umberto 100
economic and social conditions 1, 2
Ede, Lisa 9
editor/editor-as-author 16, 21, 26, 27, 34, 35, 36, 38, 39, 57, 61, 126, 128, 134, 135, 136, 139, 141, 145, 157, 184, 204, 229, 238
education 46, 48–50, 69–70. *See also* Bildung; women's education
Ehnenn, Jill R. 77
Ehrmann, Mariane 27
Eichendorff, Joseph von 155
eighteenth century 76
elements, theory of 161–2, 164, 166, 170

emigration 299–300, 301
   German immigration to the US 296, 298, 306, 309, 313
Empfindsamkeit 47
Enlightenment 1, 3, 11, 15, 47, 48, 76, 78, 80, 87–9
   Haskalah 242
   ideal of reason 93, 95, 98, 101
   Was ist Aufklärung? (Kant) 95–6
epics 2
epistolarity 258
epistolary novels 45, 62, 63, 71, 119, 158
   Brentano-von Arnim 254, 255, 258
erotic love 109–13, 115–16, 133
   Symphilosophie 130–1
essays 4

fables 52–3
fairy tales 181, 182, 190–1, 198, 203
Feen-Mährchen 181, 182, 199
Feilchenfeldt, Konrad 233, 237
female authorship 301, 306, 308, 314
female–female collaborations 9, 10
female protagonists 106, 107
   Amanda und Eduard 119–24
   "Marie" 113–19
feminine genres 2–3
feminine ideal 47–8, 133, 136–7, 173
femininity 157, 159, 167, 172, 174, 177
feminist scholarship 5, 186
Ferris, David 278
Fichte, Johann Gottlieb 15, 17, 105, 106, 131, 245–6
   Reden an die deutsche Nation 244–5
Fleig, Anne 4
folktales/folklore 183, 187–8, 198
   Brothers Grimm: Collaboration as Extraction 188–91
Foucault, Michel 8, 24, 41

Fouqué, Caroline de la Motte 14, 155–6
  Briefe über die griechische Mythologie für Frauen 156, 158–63, 167, 170–1, 173, 174, 177, 178
  Magie der Natur: Eine Revolutions-Geschichte 157, 158, 163, 171–7, 178
Fouqué, Friedrich de la Motte 14, 155–6, 199, 228
  Berlinische Blätter für deutsche Frauen 229
  Undine 155, 157, 158, 163, 164–71, 172, 174, 178
Francke, August Hermann 48
Frankfurt am Main 125, 210, 224, 226, 256
Frederick II of Prussia 89
Freemasonry 83, 85
French Revolution 158, 171, 172
Freud, Sigmund 100
Frevert, Ute 185
Friedan, Betty 22
Friedrich Wilhelm IV of Prussia 253
friendship 53–7, 65, 72, 106, 112
Fronius, Helen 4

Gall, Ludwig: *Auswanderung nach den Vereinigten Staaten* 299, 302
Garland, Henry and Mary 22
gender
  authorship and 1–6, 182
  genius and 2, 5, 77, 183, 187, 205, 227
  literary voice and 299, 314–17
gender binaries/dualism 10–11, 31, 32, 182
  feminine ideal 47–8, 133, 136–7, 173
  Geschlechtscharaktere 184–8
  vs. hermaphroditic concepts 14, 157, 159–62, 164–6, 169, 173, 174
  male-female/active-passive 213
  Märchenoma and 184, 186, 187, 188, 205
  replacement 199–205
  resistance 195–9
  subversion 192–5
Geniekult/cult of the genius 1, 6, 13, 236
genius model
  alternatives to (*see* collaboration)
  gender and 2, 5, 77, 183, 187, 205, 227
Gentz, Friedrich von 229
German-Jewish identity 229, 231, 242–9. *See also* Judaism
German nationalism 244–5
Gerstäcker, Friedrich 297
Geschlechtscharaktere 182, 184–8
(Der) Gesellschafter; oder, Blätter für Geist und Herz 238
ghostwriting 233
Giesler, Birte 4
Gleim, Johann Wilhelm Ludwig 79, 125
Goethe, Johann Wolfgang von 13, 15, 16, 17, 41, 45, 46, 77, 79, 99, 106, 202, 203, 242–4
  Die Leiden des jungen Werthers/ The Sufferings of Young Werther 258
  Faust 224
    Gretchen 213
  influence on Therese Robinson 9, 16, 295, 297, 299, 300–6, 309, 313, 316–17
    "Stoff und Gehalt zur Bearbeitung vorgeschlagen" 296, 299, 302, 304, 312, 313

Sophie von La Roche and 63–5
   correspondence/letters 46,
      66–9
   journal *Iris* as group project
      69–72
   Torquato Tasso 236–7
   Über Kunst und Altertum 243,
      299, 300
   West-östlicher Divan 9, 14, 142,
      209–26
      dialogue 209
      exchange 219
      Hafiz 9, 14, 209, 210, 215, 219
      Islam 209, 223
      Marianne von Willemer 14,
         209–12, 214, 218, 220, 226
      Orientalism 209, 213
   Wilhelm Meisters Lehrjahre 105,
      107, 117
   Wilhelm Meisters Wanderjahre
      237–8, 243
   Xenien, 41
Goethe, Ottilie von 202, 237
Goodman, Katherine 25, 32, 34, 35
Göschen, Georg Joachim 4
Gottsched, Johann Christoph 13,
   17, 21, 22, 24, 26, 49, 52, 125
   collaboration 28–33
   correspondence/letter-writing
      36, 37, 38–9
   Die Vernünftigen Tadlerinnen 26
   income 25
   translation as collaborative
      authorship 29–30, 33–5, 36–7
Gottsched, Luise Adelgunde Victorie
   13, 17, 21, 23, 24, 26, 125
   anonymous pieces 41
   collaboration 28–33
   correspondence/letter-writing
      34–5, 36, 37, 38–9
   Die Vernünftigen Tadlerinnen 26
   essayistic pieces 26
   musical compositions 40
   poetry 40
   translation as collaborative
      authorship 29–30, 33–5, 36–7
   views on women and marriage
      31–2, 34–5
'great author' 2
Greek tragedies 163
Griffin, Susan 308, 309
Grimm, Herman 211
Grimm, Jakob and Wilhelm 13, 14,
   181, 182, 186, 187, 199, 200
   Brentano-von Arnim and 184,
      185, 192–5, 199
   collaboration as extraction
      188–91
   Droste-Hülshoff and 195–9
   Frau Lehnhardt and 192–5, 205
   interaction with female sources
      183
   Kinder- und Häusmärchen 181,
      182, 190, 191, 194, 195
   Viehmann and 183, 189–90, 196,
      197, 205
Günderrode, Karoline von 13, 15,
   16, 125, 138, 176, 256, 259,
   261, 266–70
   Gedichte und Phantasien/Poems
      and Fantasies 259, 260
   "Die Manen"/The Spirits
      259, 263
   "Wandel und Treue"/
      Change and Loyalty 259
   Melete 268
   Poetische Fragmente/Poetic
      Fragments 260
   Tian (pseudonym) 256, 268
Gutermann, Georg Friedrich 48
Gutermann, Sophie. *See* La Roche,
   Sophie von

Habermas, Jürgen 24–5, 27, 36
Hafiz 9, 14, 209, 210, 215, 219
Hahn, Barbara 227
Haller, Albrecht von 50
Hamburger, Käte 243

Index

Hammer, Joseph 210
Hammerstein, Katharina von 107
Hart, Gail K. 213, 224
Haskalah 242
Hausen, Karin 2, 185
Hauser, Arnold 249
Haxthausen, Ludowine von 196
Hegel, Georg Wilhelm Friedrich 25, 27, 186
Heipke, Corinne 2
Heitmann, Annegret 12
Hep-Hep riots 247
hermaphroditic collaboration 14, 157, 158, 171, 178
hermaphroditism 157, 159–66, 173, 174
heterotextual authorship 8
Heuser, Magda 39
historical novel 296
Hock, Lisbeth 185
Hoffmann, E. T. A. 77, 99, 100, 155, 199
Hölderlin, Friedrich 13, 15, 16, 125, 256, 259, 266–70
   Hyperion 107, 108, 258, 261, 267
   Ödipus der Tyrann 261, 267, 269
Homburg 261
homosexuality 10
Honold, Alexander 303
Humperdinck, Engelbert 187

Idealism 108, 125, 150
influence 9
intellectual partnership 209, 213, 221
intellectual reciprocity 258, 263–6, 271
Islam 209, 223
Isselstein, Ursula 249
Iverson, John R. 78

Jacobi, Friedrich Heinrich 64, 65, 69, 70, 150
Jacobi, Johann Georg 64, 65, 69, 70

Jakob, Therese von. *See* Robinson, Therese
Jarvis, Shawn, C. 199
Jaszi, Peter 236
Jewish writers 17
Joeres, Ruth-Ellen Boetcher 185
journeyman 28–9
Judaism 241. *See also* German-Jewish identity

Kahn, Lothar 246
Kaibel, Karl Ludwig 240
Kant, Immanuel 77, 95–6, 105, 150
Karadžić, Vuk Stefanović 295
Karsch, Anna Louisa 125
Keiner, Astrid 151, 152
Kinder- und Hausmärchen (KHM)/ Children's and Household Tales 181, 182, 190, 191, 194, 195
Kleist, Heinrich von 176, 199
Klopstock, Friedrich Gottlieb 50, 56
Koestenbaum, Wayne 10, 12
Kontje, Todd 213
Kord, Susanne 2–3, 35, 235
Kording, Inka 32
Korff, Nicolaus von 81
Korneeva, Tatiana 200
Kriegleder, Wynfrid 300
Kunstmärchen 182, 183, 186, 187, 203

Lacoue-Labarthe, Philippe 133
Laqueur, Thomas 2
La Roche, Georg Michael Frank von 57, 59
La Roche, Sophie von 16, 27, 45, 46, 259
   educational background 48–9
   Geschichte des Fräuleins von Sternheim/History of Lady Sophia Sternheim 16, 60–3
   Goethe and 63–5
      correspondence/letters 46, 66–9

journal *Iris* as group project 69–72
pathway into the literary scene 57–63
Wieland and 46–8
  correspondence/letters 46, 47, 57–8, 60–1, 64
  La Roche as friend and muse 53–7
  Wieland as mentor 51–3, 58, 60, 61, 63
Lavater, Johann Kaspar 77, 79, 82, 83, 87
Leberecht, Peter. *See* Tieck, Ludwig
Lehnhardt, Frau 192–5, 205
Lejeune, Philippe 274, 276–7, 284
Lesniowska, Countess 151–3
Lessing, Gotthold Ephraim 105, 176
  Nathan der Weise/Nathan the Wise 93–5
letters 2, 4, 34–5, 36, 38–9
  Gottscheds 34–5, 36, 37, 38–9
  La Roche 46, 47, 49, 57–8, 60–1, 64, 66–9
  Varnhagen, Rahel Levin 230, 231, 234, 249
  Wieland 46, 47, 49, 57–8, 60–1
Leuchsenring, Franz Michael 64, 65
Liebertz-Grün, Ursula 255
life writing 274, 275
Liszt, Franz 277
literacy 62
literary fairy tale 182. *See also Kunstmärchen*
literary genres 2–3, 45, 62
literary networks 46, 64
literary public sphere 45, 46
literary salons/*salonnières* 4–5, 65, 78, 242, 253
London, Bette 7, 12
love 33, 106, 109–13
Lowenstein, Steven M. 242

Ludwig, Robert
  baptism 247–8
  German-Jewish identity 242, 246–9
  journalistic career 232–8
Lunsford, Andrea 9
Lutheranism 32, 34, 88, 89

MacLeod, Catriona 11
Märchen 184
Märchen-Jungfrau 201–5
Märchenoma/fairytale grandma 14, 181–2, 183
  Brothers Grimm: collaboration as extraction 188–91
  Dorothea Viehmann 183, 189–90
  Frau Lehnhardt 192–5
  gendered dualisms and 184, 186, 187, 188, 205
  replacement 199–205
  resistance 195–9
  subversion 192–5
  terra nullius 186, 189, 193, 205
March Revolution of 1848 13
Marie Antoinette 77
marriage 25, 30, 31, 34–5, 41, 42, 127, 134, 298, 310–12. *See also* conjugal co-authorship
masculinity 157, 159
May, Karl 297
McCarthy, John A. 80
McFarlane, Todd 100
Medem, Friedrich (Fritz) 82, 83, 90
Méliès, Georges 100
Mendelssohn, Fanny 138
Mendelssohn, Felix and Cécile 280
Mendelssohn, Moses 89
mentors 5, 14, 32, 49, 50, 51–3, 56–8, 60, 61, 68, 71, 77–9, 84, 93, 97, 106, 184, 185, 192, 198, 200, 201, 205, 261, 269, 296
Mereau, Friedrich Ernst Carl 106

Mereau-Brentano, Sophie 15, 105, 138
   Blüthenalter der Empfindung 106
   female *Bildung* 106
      Amanda und Eduard 119–24
      antisocial narratives 107–9, 113, 115–16, 123
      erotic love 109–13, 115–16
      "Marie" 106, 113–19
      sexual anthropology 108–9, 115–16, 123
      self-contained wholeness 116–19, 121–4
Mertens-Schaafhausen, Sibylle 202
Mikoletsky, Juliane 315
misogyny 223
models of authorship. *See* authorship
Mommsen, Katharina 223, 224
Morgenblatt für gebildete Stände 230, 232, 233, 234, 235, 237, 243, 249, 250
motherhood 285, 286–7
Müller, Adam 232
Müller-Seidel, Walter 80
Mündigkeit/legal autonomy 3, 96, 101, 105. *See also Unmündigkeit*
muse 42, 53–7, 72
mysticism 82, 83, 84, 121–3
mythology 156–7, 158–9, 161, 162, 164, 166, 167, 174, 177

Nancy, Jean-Luc 133
narrative identity 257
nationalism 244–5
nature
   Romantic *Naturphilosophie* 144, 145–6
   theory of the elements 161–2, 164, 166, 170
   women and 161, 187, 202
Naubert, Benedikte 199–201, 205
   "Der kurze Mantel" 184

Nauhaus, Gerd 292
Nees von Esenbeck, Elisabetha 259
Nenon, Monika 16
networks 46, 64
Neuber, Caroline 17
New Critics 7
Nicolai, Friedrich 4, 79, 87
Nieberle, Sigrid 12
Nitzsche, Gunter 233
Norberg, Jacob 236
Novalis, Georg Phillipp Friedrich von Hardenberg 127, 158
novels 2, 4, 45, 62, 63, 71, 119

Oedipus 267–8
Order of the Black Eagle 243
Orientalism 209, 213
originality 1–2

pantheism 145, 147
Paracelsus 164
   Liber de nymphis, sylphis, pygmaeis et salamandris et de caeteris spiritibus 164
patriarchy 12, 46
Paul, Jean 132
periodical publication 26–7, 39
Perrault, Charles 182, 198
Pietism 107, 123
plagiarism 233
Plato 261, 262, 264
Platonic *eros* 130, 131
Plumwood, Val 186, 188, 189
poetics 49–50
poetry 49
   Sympoesie 129, 130, 151
post-structuralism 24, 275
power differentials 10, 12
privacy 129, 138, 142
pseudonymity 3
Purdy, Daniel 117
Purgstall-Hammer, Joseph von 209

Quéval, Marie-Hélène 33

Raich, Johann Michael 145
reason 93, 95, 98, 101, 129
   faith and 149–50
reciprocity 258, 263–6, 271
Recke, Elisa von der 11–12, 14–15, 75
   battle for agency 76
   collaboration with Cagliostro 76–8, 83–7
   Enlightenment ideals 76, 78, 80, 87–9, 93
   exposé of Cagliostro 79–81, 87–93, 96–101
   lack of formal education 81–2
   obsession with spiritualism 75, 81, 82–3
   social prominence 78–9, 81, 84
Recke, Georg Magnus von der 82
Reed, T. J. 211
reflexive authorship 16, 255, 257, 260, 267, 271
Reich, Nancy 278
religion in literature 299, 300, 301, 306–10
   women and religion 300, 308, 311
religious faith 139, 142, 145–8
religious literature 48
religious mysticism 82, 84, 121–3
Richardson, Samuel 62
Ricoeur, Paul: *Temps et Récit*/Time and Narrative 256–7
Robert, Ludwig 16, 227, 229–31
   Die Macht der Verhältnisse 232, 238–9
   Kassius und Phantasus; oder der Paradiesvogel 239–41
   "Promenaden eines Berliners in seiner Vaterstadt" 237
Robert-Tornow family 250
Robert-Tornow, Marcus Theodor (Ohme) 229, 239
Robert-Tornow, Moritz 230
Robinson, Edward 295

Robinson, Therese (née von Jakob) 9, 16
   Die Auswanderer (1852) 9, 16, 296, 297–9, 300, 303, 314
   abolitionism 298
   allegory 299, 306
   American colonial history 295–9, 301–3, 307, 308, 312–14
   antebellum conflict 297, 309
   Cain and Abel archetype 307, 312
   Civil War 298, 299
   critique of Catholicism 301, 303, 307, 308
   emigration 299–300, 301
   exile 312
   The Exiles (English translation, 1853) 9, 16, 296, 298, 306
   female authorship 301, 306, 308, 314
   fratricide 298, 301, 307, 311
   gender and literary voice 299, 314–17
   German immigration to the US 296, 298, 306, 309, 313
   historical novel 296
   history of Florida 297, 298, 302, 303, 308, 315
   marriage plots 298, 310–12
   mercenary soldiers 298, 311
   race and ethnic relations 297, 302
   religious themes 299, 300, 301, 306–10
   slavery 301, 307
   Spanish Americans 297, 298
   travelogue 296, 301, 303, 316
   women and religion 300, 308, 311
   influence of Goethe 9, 16, 295, 296, 297, 299, 300–6, 309, 313, 316–17

"Stoff und Gehalt
  zur Bearbeitung
  vorgeschlagen" 296, 299,
  302, 304, 312, 313
Talvj (pseudonym for Therese
  Albertine Luise von Jakob)
  295
  translation of *Volkslieder der
  Serben*/Folksongs of the
  Serbs 16, 295, 296, 300
Rohrwasser, Michael 99
Rölleke, Heinz 195
Romanticism 1, 2, 22, 134, 139, 155,
  176, 236, 254, 275, 283
  Black Romanticism 147
  collaborative models of
    authorship 5, 16, 125, 126,
    127, 156, 227, 229, 241, 250
  creativity and spirituality 158
  natural world 144, 145–6, 167
romantic love 109–13, 115–16
Rossini, Gioachino Antonio:
  L'italiana in Algeri 235
Rousseau, Jean-Jacques 15, 62, 65,
  106, 107, 131
Rückert, Friedrich: *Liebesfrühling*
  283–4
Runckel, Dorothea von 34, 39

Salm, Peter 22
salons/*salonnières* 4–5, 65, 78, 242,
  253
Sambursky, Miriam 232
Samuels, Shirley 298
Sand, Georges 100
Savigny, Friedrich Carl von 192,
  259
Schabert, Ina 2
Schaff, Barbara 2, 12
Scherer, Wilhelm 22
Schiller, Friedrich 13, 15, 17, 41, 77,
  79, 99, 105, 106, 199
  Die Horen/The Horae 17, 106
  Kabale und Liebe 234

Schlegel, August Wilhelm 126,
  127, 139, 148, 155
Schlegel, Dorothea Veit 15, 126–7,
  129
  "Anti-*Florentin*" 139–48
  Florentin 5, 128, 134, 135, 136,
    138–9
  religious preoccupations 139,
    142, 145–8
  self-effacement and privacy
    135–9, 142, 143
Schlegel, Friedrich 5, 13, 15, 126–7,
  144, 158, 267
  final years 147–8, 151–3
  Lesniowska and 151–3
  Lucinde 128, 129, 131, 133,
    134–5, 139, 140, 141, 149, 152
  Philosophie des Lebens 148–53
  Poetisches Taschenbuch 140, 145
  Symphilosophie 5, 127–39, 151
  "Wechselgesang" 140–1
Schlegel-Schelling, Caroline 17
Schleiermacher, Friedrich 126, 127,
  133, 151, 155
Schlichtmann, Silke 243
Schlosser, J. G. 80
Schlözer, Ludwig August 80
Schmidt, Arno 155, 156
Schmidt, Jochen 1, 187
Schneider, Susanne 31
Schopenhauer, Adele 184
  "Waldmärchen" 201–5
Schopenhauer, Arthur 186–7, 202,
  205
Schopenhauer, Johanna 309
Schulte-Kemminghausen, Karl
  196, 197
Schülting, Sabine 12
Schumann, Clara and Robert 10,
  17
  marriage diary
    audience 278, 279
    collaboration/male-female
      co-authorship 275, 276

dialogic element 277, 279, 280
family life 285–7
first entry 273–4
polyphony 282
ruptures 281–2, 292–3
stipulations 287–8
tensions 284–7, 288, 290
professional careers and collaboration 283–4, 288–91, 292
Robert's emotional and mental deterioration 274–5, 291, 292
Schwander, S. G. 85, 93, 95
Schwärmerei 88, 93, 94
Scott, Walter 297, 303
Sealsfield, Charles 297
Selbstvertrauen 116, 119
self-development 116–19, 121–4. *See also Bildung*
self-invention 276
self-realization 22
sensibility 47, 70, 107
sexual anthropology
antisocial narratives 108–9, 113, 115–16, 123
erotic love 109–13, 115–16
self-contained wholeness 116–19, 121–4
Shakespeare, William 60, 243
Sinclair, Isaak von 125, 259
Sinclair, John (Freiherr) 135
slavery 301, 307
abolitionism 298
Smith, Sidonie 274
social and economic conditions 1, 2
Socrates 261, 262, 263, 264
solipsism 277
Sollor, Werner 313
Sophocles 267–8
Spalding, J. J. 105
Spanish Americans 297, 298
spiritualism 75–8

spirituality 158, 161, 174
Spontini, Gaspare Luigi Pacifico 232, 233
Stahl, Karoline 183, 187, 190–1, 199, 205
Stark, J. A. 80, 98
Steele, Richard 26
Steig, Reinhold 195
Steiner, Rahel E. 233, 236
Steinwehr, W. B. A. von 35
Stone, Marjorie 8
storytelling 182
Stowe, Harriet Beecher 308
Strauss, Johann 100
Strubberg, Friedrich 297
structuralism 27
Sturm und Drang/Storm and Stress 1
suicide 176, 268–9
Swedenborg, Emanuel 82, 83
Swift, Jonathan 27
Symphilosophie/Symphilosophieren 5, 16, 127–39, 151, 227, 241, 249, 267
Sympoesie 129, 130, 151

Talvj (pseudonym for Theresa Albertine Luise von Jakob) 295
Ter-Nedden, Gisbert 62
Teutonic knights 81
Tewarson, Heidi Thomann 246
theory of the elements 161–2, 164, 166
Thiel, Anne 201
Thompson, Judith 8
Thorvaldsen, Bertel 79
Tian (pseudonym of Karoline von Günderrode) 256, 268
Tieck, Amalie 241
Tieck, Ludwig 125, 132, 199
Der Aufruhr in den Cevennen: Eine Novelle in vier Abschitten 241–2

332 Index

tragic drama 163
translation/translator-as-author
    29–30, 33–5, 36–7
transmission of correspondence
    258
travel literature 296, 301, 303, 316

Unmündigkeit 76, 94, 95, 96, 97, 101
utopianism 107

Varnhagen, Karl August 155, 157,
    228
Varnhagen, Rahel Levin 4, 16, 155
    baptism 247–8
    collaborative ideals 227–9,
        249–50
    contribution to Robert
        Ludwig's journalistic career
        232–8
    as critical reader 238–42
    German-Jewish identity 229,
        231, 242–9
    letters/personal
        correspondence 230, 231,
        234, 249
Veit, Philipp 142
Veit, Simon 143, 144, 147
Vellusig, Robert 62
Vernünftige Tadlerinnen 26
Viehmann, Dorothea 183, 189–90,
    196, 197, 205
Vigliero, Consolina 230, 243, 246
Volkslieder der Serben/Folksongs of
    the Serbs 16, 295, 296, 300
Volksmärchen 183, 194

Wackenroder, Wilhelm Heinrich
    125
Wahlen, Constanzia von der 81
Waldstein, Edith 255

Wallach, Martha Kaarsberg 306
Wallenborn, Markus 210, 212
Warner, Marina 182
Watson, Julia 274
Weber, Carl Maria von 230
Weckel, Ulrike 65
Weigel, Sigrid 119
Weissberg, Liliane 246
Wellbery, David 22
Wieland, Christoph Martin 16, 45,
    46, 64, 82, 182, 186
    correspondence/letters 47, 51,
        57–8, 60–1
    educational background 49–50
    La Roche and 46–8
        La Roche as friend and
            muse 53–7
        Wieland as mentor 51–3, 58,
            60, 61, 63
Wilde, Jean 155, 157
Willemer, Marianne von 14,
    209–12, 214, 218, 220, 226
Willkomm, Ernst 304
Winckelmann, Johann Joachim 11
Wolf, Christa 255, 267
women authors 3–5, 14, 46, 51, 71,
    101
    anonymity 30, 41, 136–8, 227,
        235–6
    concept of the *Autorin* 184–8
women's education 46, 48–9, 50,
    69–70, 81–2
Woodmansee, Martha 2
Württemberg, Prince Eugen of 98

York, Lorraine 12
Young, Edward 82
Young Germany 254

Ziegler, Mariana von 32, 41

www.ingramcontent.com/pod-product-compliance
Lightning Source LLC
Chambersburg PA
CBHW070012010526
44117CB00011B/1534